MEETING CHRIST IN HIS MYSTERIES

In the liturgy of the church, it is principally his own paschal mystery that Christ signifies and makes present ... His paschal mystery is a real event that occurred in our history, but it is unique: all other historical events happen once, and then they pass away, swallowed up in the past. The paschal mystery of Christ, by contrast, cannot remain only in the past, because by his death he destroyed death, and all that Christ is – all that he did and suffered for all – participates in the divine eternity, and so transcends all times while being made present in them all. The event of the cross and resurrection abides and draws everything toward life.

Catechism of the Catholic Church

Gregory Collins OSB

Meeting Christ in his Mysteries

A BENEDICTINE VISION OF THE SPIRITUAL LIFE

the columba press

First published in 2010 by
the columba press
55A Spruce Avenue, Stillorgan Industrial Park,
Blackrock, Co Dublin

Cover by Br Emmaus O'Herlihy OSB
The cover image is the Slain Lamb from the Book of Revelation
surrounded by the symbols of the Evangelists, by Benedict
Tutty OSB. (Copper, Glenstal Abbey Church)
Origination by The Columba Press
Printed in Ireland by ColourBooks Ltd, Dublin

ISBN 978-1-85607-682-1

Contents

INTRODUCTION

In the Beginning was the Trinity ...

Christ's whole earthly life – his words and deeds, his silences and sufferings, indeed his manner of being and speaking – is revelation of the Father ... Christ's whole life is a mystery of redemption. Redemption comes to us above all through the blood of his cross, but this mystery is at work throughout Christ's entire life ...

Catechism of the Catholic Church

What was visible in our Redeemer has passed over into the sacramental mysteries.

Pope St Leo the Great

The mysteries of Christ are our mysteries.

Blessed Columba Marmion OSB

These quotations introduce the guiding idea of this book: the mystery of Christ through which we are called into union with God and its presence in the sacramental mysteries of the church's worship, thanks to which that union becomes effective.[1] Revealed in Christ and the Holy Spirit, God's call enters our lives through the celebration of the mysteries of the liturgy. In the spiritual traditions of Benedictine monasticism, monks have always tried to contemplate the mystery of Christ as a whole, as it unfolds itself in the celebration of the liturgy throughout the year, in meditation on the word of God and in personal prayer.[2]

In the nineteen-fifties the great Benedictine scholar Jean Leclercq developed the idea of 'monastic theology' to describe the attempt to put this experience into words and order it in a more systematic way.[3] This book aims to be an exercise in such 'monastic theology' as that has traditionally been undertaken in the Benedictine world. It is written for non-specialists who do not always have easy access to the riches of the monastic tradition.

The goal of such theology is the vision of the living God revealed in the face of Jesus Christ and disclosed to us in the light of the Holy Spirit. Monastic theology aims not just at theoretical or abstract knowledge but at the knowledge born of love as it emerges in spiritual experience. In the early monastic tradition this was known as vision or contemplation (*theoria* and *speculatio*). The 'method' put forward for attaining this kind of vision was firmly rooted in the Bible and the Jewish origins of Christianity. It entailed a ruminative reading of holy scripture and the texts of the church's traditional wisdom (*lectio divina* and *meditatio*), in the context of the regular and solemn celebration of the liturgy, the church's public, communal prayer.[4]

Such a liturgically inspired, contemplative vision informs this book. In speaking of the liturgy I shall be referring primarily to that of the Ordinary Form of the Roman Rite, excellently restored, reformed and renewed before and after the Second Vatican Council.[5] The renewed liturgy's emphasis on the role of the Holy Spirit in worship, its biblical richness, formal simplicity, variety of ancient and modern texts and traditional dignified ritual, as it is carried out in its monastic form here in Glenstal day after day, is the context in which my spiritual life has been nurtured for the last twenty years.[6] Liturgical prayer, as I shall constantly reiterate throughout this book, is a privileged disclosure-zone through which God, revealed historically in Christ, manifests his presence in the Holy Spirit and comes to meet us here and now.

Hearing God's word proclaimed, chanting the psalms throughout the church's year – the year of the mysteries of Christ – and meditating on them in the silence before and after celebration (*meditatio*) gives birth to heartfelt prayer (*oratio*), the cry of a soul overwhelmed by the excess of God's love poured out for us in Christ and the Holy Spirit. Liturgical celebration, meditation and prayer, together generate a theology grounded in the opening of the heart to the light of God's glory (*doxa*) as it has appeared to us in revelation and is celebrated still in the church's liturgy. That liturgy consists primarily in doxology: praise and glorification of the Father, through the Son in the Holy Spirit.[7]

In the monastic world such theology, being essentially a matter of the vision of the heart, is unimaginable apart from spirituality. Benedictines – but also Orthodox Christians – love the story recounted by Pope St Gregory the Great (called *Gregorios Dialogos* by the Orthodox) in the *Dialogues* attributed to him of how our Holy Father Saint Benedict, rapt in prayer, saw the whole world gathered into one by the light of Christ.[8]

In Orthodox monastic spirituality, Benedict's luminous vision is considered one of the most important testimonies to the transfiguration of the human person by the uncreated light of grace, given in baptism, intensified in the Eucharist and contemplated in prayer.[9] Monastic spirituality in both east and west has always aimed to see everyone and everything in and through the light of the resurrection, imagining a world penetrated and permeated by the transforming energies of God's Spirit.[10] It aims to develop the spiritual senses of the heart which lie dormant in the depths of the soul until they are awakened by the warm and fragrant breath of the kiss of the Holy Spirit.[11]

In the Benedictine tradition in the twentieth century, the two writers who most exemplified this approach to theology and liturgical prayer were Blessed Columba Marmion (1858-1923), the Irish Abbot of Maredsous in Belgium and inspiration for the foundation of Glenstal Abbey[12] and Dom Odo Casel (1886-1948), monk of Maria Laach, theologian of the mysteries and one of the greatest Christian thinkers of all time.[13] They were very different people. Marmion was a pastor and popular preacher whose reintegration of spirituality and theology, reconnected through a living vision of the liturgy, influenced a whole generation of clergy in the Catholic Church. In addition to being a holy man and lover of the liturgy, he was deeply and warmly human, with an ample girth and a jovial sense of humour. The title of this book evokes the memory of his most inspiring work although its form and content are obviously very different.

Casel, a solitary scholar, liturgical mystic and chaplain to Benedictine nuns, almost single-handedly changed the direction of the theology of the liturgy (though not without controversy) and considerably influenced the reforming work of the Second Vatican Council.[14] His fundamental intuition was based on a mystical illumination received during Solemn Mass at his abbey. It was that the founding event and core of Christian faith – Christ's passing over in the holy night of Easter from death to life – is rendered present and operative through the church's sacramental worship.

That intuition restored to the liturgy its primacy in the Christian life after centuries of displacement and put the paschal mystery of death and resurrection right at the heart of the faith. It also had a major influence beyond the frontiers of Casel's own church. The nuns whom he served as chaplain for most of his life testified to his gentle simplicity and humility, notwithstanding his outstanding intellectual gifts and embroilment in the polemics generated by his theology. Both men were typical Benedictines in believing that the Bible read, meditated and prayed in the context of the church's liturgy provides the most nourishing spiritual food and opens the door to contemplation.

Marmion was a liturgist through and through in the sense that he loved the solemn celebration of the mysteries of Christ in his great abbey at Maredsous; Casel was a mystic in the sense recognised in the early church, i.e. one who reflected deeply on the meaning of the mysteries set forth in worship. He was, appropriately enough, called home to God on Easter Sunday 1948, having intoned the threefold *Lumen Christi* ('The light of Christ') on the morning of Holy Saturday, in the (as yet unreformed) paschal vigil. I hope their influence will be evident, however modestly, throughout this book.

Evident also I hope will be the influence of the Rule of St Benedict itself. Although I may not cite or quote it frequently, its basic structures and fundamental ethos – the following of Christ in humility through obedience, stability and conversion of life, constant recourse to scripture in *lectio divina* as the source of wisdom, the need for prayer of the heart and the centrality of liturgical prayer – are the fundamental ideals which inform Benedictine life and I hope, this book as well.[15] The Rule is a like a base camp for trekking in the mountains – it is a place from which one starts and to which one returns, a secure reference point for whatever adventures lie on the way in one's spiritual journey.

At the end of his Rule, Benedict advised his readers to journey east if they wished to find the original, authentic sources of monastic spirituality. In this book I will heed his advice, for in the Christian East, in the traditions of the Orthodox, Oriental Orthodox and East Syrian and Indian churches, the contemplation of God's uncreated beauty in prayer and worship remains the central activity of Christians and the unfailing source of the church's life.[16] I will draw liberally on those traditions, especially that of the Orthodox which has been my main source of theological and spiritual inspiration for years.

Yet, at the same time, this book contains many influences from the Anglican and Protestant traditions as well, especially those of the Lutheran and Reformed churches. With the Second Vatican Council and the late Pope John Paul II, I believe that one cannot be authentically Catholic today without also being a committed ecumenist.[17]

The primary theme of this book is that through the celebration of the mysteries of Christ in the liturgy and their experience in prayer, the one great paschal mystery of his transforming death and resurrection is made present for us so that we can participate in it. Of Christ's living presence in the worship and sacramental mysteries of the church, and of how that marks the whole of life with a 'paschal' character I have never had any serious doubt. There are three reasons why the paschal Christ of the liturgy has always been central for me.

The first goes back to my childhood in Belfast, to my own Confirmation at the age of 11 in 1971. Two or three minutes after the bishop had applied the oil of chrism and I had returned to my seat, without any trumpet fanfares or loud announcements, I was literally wakened up. A presence moved gently into my life and has resolutely refused to go away ever since, notwithstanding my many infidelities, frequent wrong turnings and the numerous obstacles with which I have too often blocked its light. Paul reminds us that we always hold the treasures of grace in clay jars (2 Cor 4:

7a), but the Psalms also observe that God knows of what we are made: God remembers we are but dust (Ps 102(103): 14). Indeed Paul comforts himself that his own weakness serves only to indicate to others that everything comes from God (2 Cor 4: 7b). Confirmation gave me the fundamental assurance that in the church's sacramental liturgy God really does communicate himself.

As a youth I would drop into dark churches in West Belfast, then caught up in its terrible sectarian convulsions, and become aware once more of that presence, this time radiating from the tabernacle or hovering around a statue or an icon. Years later, while pursuing research in Orthodox theology I discovered St Gregory of Nyssa's account of his own spiritual experience which he described as a kind of inner sensation of a presence.[18] I could not have described it that way myself of course as a youngster. I knew only that a hole had been punched in the wall of the world and from the other side, a light gentle and benevolent was shining through. At the age of sixteen, no doubt rather precociously, I began to read voraciously in theology – the Bible (especially St John's gospel), St Augustine, Newman, Luther – in an attempt to understand who or what had punctured the veil between my tiny self and the vast expanse of mystery I knew was lying beyond it. Newman made me aware of an unknown spiritual continent waiting to be explored that he called 'the Fathers'.[19]

The second reason for believing in the Christ of the liturgy was an experience of two different kinds of worship, both of which came to me at the end of the seventies by courtesy of the BBC. The first was a documentary showing the Paschal Vigil at the Russian Orthodox cathedral in London. So far my experience of worship had been limited to uninspiring celebrations in various parishes in Belfast where much was constrained by the difficult social and political situation. The first Easter Vigil I had experienced, far from being an explosion of paschal joy, was something of a damp squib.

The Russian liturgy broke upon me like a spiritual tidal wave. The emotional harmonised chanting, the vigorous and prolonged incensing, the icons and golden vestments and above all the repeated shouts of 'Christ is Risen!' had an effect on my soul that in retrospect I have come to recognise as pure grace. Orthodoxy taught me that God is the source of all that is beautiful. The paschal mystery and its celebration moved into centre stage in my spiritual life and has occupied that position ever since. I fell in love with the Christian East. Although the idealism of that initial youthful attraction has since been considerably tempered through contact with its not always so inspiring reality, I have never fallen out of love with it.

Around the same time the BBC also televised Mass from Downside Abbey near Bath in England. It was the first time I had ever heard the word 'Benedictine'. The style was gentler than the Russian service, but I was just as captivated by the dignified cere-monial, musical accomplishment and sense of the numinous sur-rounding it. I registered to myself that the way of Benedictine prayer, like that of Orthodoxy, was centred on the liturgy.

The third reason is Glenstal. In 1980, the fifteen-hundredth an-niversary of the birth of St Benedict, no less than three monks from that abbey came to speak at Lenten retreats in the Catholic Chaplaincy at Queen's University, Belfast. I am not aware of any-one ever having gone before for that purpose and apart from going back to do the same myself a few years ago, no one else from here has ever repeated the performance. As a result I journeyed down to Glenstal for Easter and experienced three things.

- First was the magnificence of the Paschal Vigil with its Gregorian music, bonfire and solemn chanting of the Easter proclamation (the *Exsultet*). I realised that if one couldn't be Byzantine then becoming a Benedictine monk might not be so bad an alternative.
- Second was a conversation with one of the monks, Br Patrick Hederman. For the first time in twenty years I met someone who understood what I was saying about my relationship with God – or more accurately the relationship I realised God had begun with me. In the intervening years he has been to me guide, friend, brother and, most recently as Abbot, Father in Christ.
- Third was Patrick's showing me an icon then in his care. It is a Russian icon of Christ, so beautiful and spiritually penetrating

that it can only have been painted from a vision based on prayer.[20] It is the Christ of Chapter 2 of St Paul's Letter to the Philippians, the non-grasping God who emptied himself and assumed the form of a slave, becoming obedient unto death even death on a cross, for which God exalted him and enthroned him as the Lord. I recognised in the eyes of that icon the same gentle, benevolent light that had begun to shine on me as a child. It is the light of the Holy Spirit who rests eternally on the Son of God, overshadowed Mary at his incarnation, filled his humanity at his baptism in the Jordan and was finally given to him in fullness at his resurrection and poured out on us through him as God's present, or rather presence – grace.

That presence cannot be earned but only acknowledged, proclaimed, loved, praised and continuously returned to in prayers of gratitude and repentance. It is pure gift. This book is my way of acknowledging and celebrating the presence of that gift, in the firm belief that in liturgical prayer and sacramental worship God does indeed open a door, step into our world and manifest his real presence.

Biblical citations are from the NRSV unless otherwise indicated, with the numbering of the Psalms according to Catholic/Orthodox usage (followed by the Hebrew/Protestant numeration in brackets). Extensive endnotes are included, the purpose of which is to clarify matters discussed in the body of the text, indicate authorities who have influenced me and encourage others to undertake further detective work in exploring the themes presented here. I have limited my references to works in English and have generally given details only of the English translations of works published in a foreign language: those who wish to have access to the originals can do that easily enough. Since the book is aimed at a general readership, however, those who do not wish to delve too deeply into specifically theological matters should feel free to ignore the endnotes.

In the case of quotations from liturgical texts, all translations from the original are my own and aim at comprehensibility rather than elegance. It is not advisable to use the present edition of the Roman Sacramentary (called the Missal by most Latin Rite Catholics) for scholarly purposes as its translations are too loose:

since the new translations are still only on the horizon no other option than a do-it-yourself job was available.[21]

My purpose in this book is to show how contemplation of the revealed mysteries, recorded in scripture and celebrated in worship, is capable of generating a mystical spirituality rooted in the church's liturgy, experienced in the depths of the soul and flowing out into everyday life. In an authentic vision of Christian mysticism there ought to be no dichotomy between a supposedly 'institutional church' (as if the community born of Pentecost could ever be just an institution) and an esoteric 'mysticism' (in danger of degenerating into spiritual luxury and self-indulgence) practised by atomised individuals; nor between communal liturgical celebration and so-called 'private' solitary contemplation.

We need to recover in our era what was understood so well in the early centuries of the church's life and is today still generally the case in the Christian East: that the celebration of the liturgy, grounded in Christ's historical acts, manifesting his gracious presence and filled with the Holy Spirit's power, is the objective point of entry into a genuine Christian mysticism.[22]

Yet nowadays, at least in a post-modern Europe becoming ever more post-Christian as well, it is not sufficient simply to present Christ's mysteries as 'objective' truths or external realities set up over against us. Something more is needed, something which the monastic tradition has always stressed if the gospel is to be proclaimed authentically: spiritual experience of what has been revealed. Today more than ever Christ's mysteries need not only to be proclaimed by the church and 'actualised' in liturgical celebration but also 'realised' in a personal, spiritually fruitful way in the inner temple of the heart.

An integrated understanding of the liturgy and of sacramental experience as the source of the truly mystical, is the greatest gift the ancient (but still vibrant) traditions of Eastern Christianity can offer the worldwide Christian family today. That is certainly the lesson I have learnt after many years of contact with them. Liturgy and the mystical life are – or at least ought to be – always one. In the Orthodox Church, after having received Holy Communion in the Divine Liturgy, Byzantine Christians sing this chant:

We have seen the true light
we have received the heavenly Spirit,
we have found the true faith,
worshipping the Undivided Trinity:
this has been our salvation.

Unlike its modern meaning which generally involves ecstasies and esoteric illuminations, 'mystical experience' as the early church understood it was a secret and hidden thing, an illumination of the heart by grace through communion with God in prayer. It is the goal toward which liturgical celebration ought to lead us. But that becomes actual only if in the light of the Holy Spirit we contemplate the mysteries we celebrate. Then our consciousness, focused on the mysteries of Christ, expands and is led through them into the one great mystery of salvation, into the depths of God's infinite inner life.

By sharing some of the riches of monastic tradition east and west, I hope that this book might help in a small way to foster a Christian vision of reality irradiated by the light of Christ who reveals God's universal love in his death and resurrection (2 Cor 6: 19). It is God's desire to communicate that love to us through the Holy Spirit who has been poured into our hearts (Rom 5: 5). The Holy Trinity has disclosed itself; it has drawn aside the veil and manifested itself to us; but its purpose will not be fulfilled until the Spirit becomes the breath that animates our every breath, the heart hidden deep within our hearts, beating with love for God and for creation (Ps 150: 6; Rom 8:18-28).

God's love for us is a dizzying mystery of divine descent (Phil 2:6-8; Jn 6:38), a voluntarily accepted self-limitation (*kenosis* or emptying) so that he could create us, relate to us and raise us up when we had fallen.[23] The Son of God through whom the world was made descended to our side, embraced the cross and, descending even further, went down into the realm of the dead (1 Pet 3:19-20). Exalted by the Father in his resurrection he ascended on high (Eph 4:8-10), lifted us up and enthroned us with him in glory at his Father's side (Col 3:1-4). Although we do not yet see it openly, the whole earth is vibrant with the presence of the Lord whose glory fills all heaven and earth (Heb 2:8-9).

That glory is given to us in a personal way in the church's sacramental mysteries through the gift of the Holy Spirit. The Spirit too carries out his/her own *kenosis*, descending at Pentecost, and again and again in every liturgy.[24] The Spirit awakens us to who God is and makes us understand God's all-encompassing love. Yet in addition to the *kenosis* of the Spirit and of Christ there is also the *kenosis* of God the Father who gives himself away in love to the Son and Spirit in the Trinity and to us in creation.[25] At one stage after meditating in a Good-Friday-mood on Philippians Chapter 2, I considered calling this book, 'Down and out with God in Christ'; but in the light of Easter it might equally well be called 'Up and in with Christ in the Holy Spirit'. All God's descents are aimed at our ascent. They are *pro nobis*, for us, they have as their goal that we might be raised up and transformed for ever: 'The mysteries of Christ are our mysteries.'

Our liturgical celebrations are the symbolic media through which this one great mystery, the love of the Holy Trinity for humankind and all creation, manifests itself. They are privileged, grace-filled disclosure-zones of divine love which offers itself there, in a special way, to us. There the light of the Father's creative mercy, the Son's redemptive love and the Spirit's transforming grace filters down to us; there the mystery breaks through; there we draw life and light to proclaim to the world the gospel of God's saving grace. There we meet Christ in his mysteries.

Finally some words of thanks are due. Much of this material has been shaped and reshaped over the years in the context of retreats given to various groups, all of whom have helped me understand better the mystery of Christ. I wish to mention a few: the monks of Latrobe, Douai, Ampleforth and Downside; the Benedictine Sisters of St Scholastica's (Duluth), and St Benedict's (Minnesota) as well as many other American Benedictine women I was privileged to meet in Rome. A special word must go to the Benedictine Sisters of St Lioba (Freiburg and Wald in Germany) and the monks of Dormition Abbey (Jerusalem and Tabgha in Israel): they taught me a great deal about the transforming power of beautiful liturgical prayer.

In addition thanks are due to many past colleagues, students and present friends at the Benedictine Pontifical University of Sant' Anselmo (Rome), especially Sr Aquinata Böckmann OSB, Frs Mark Sheridan OSB, Henry O'Shea OSB, Abraham Sanchez OSB, Jeremy Driscoll OSB and Paul Gunter OSB along with Abbot Daniel Hombergen OCSO, and Fr Keith Pecklers SJ, one of today's foremost English-language liturgical specialists. The clergy of the Elphin and Clogher dioceses – dedicated stewards of the mysteries of Christ during a difficult period in Irish Catholic history – should be mentioned. Thanks are also due to all my Anglican and Lutheran friends whose love of God's word and the liturgy has always been an example and inspiration.

I must mention some of Wisdom's children who have helped me glimpse the face of God: first my own extended family; then Dr Margaret Mullett, a truly splendid 'Doctor-Mother' who first sailed me to Byzantium; Professor George Huxley who showed me what Christian Humanism really means; Dr Deirdre Carabine who taught me what we can't say about God; thanks also to Fr Paul Nash OSB, Diarmuid Rooney and Patrick Huser; Patricia, Paul and John whose friendship is one of my most cherished icons of the Trinity; two spiritual mothers, Sr Eoliba Greinemann OSB, and Dr Ruth Ammann, each unique doctors of the soul, and my spiritual sister and theosonic sounding-chamber Dr Nóirín Ní Riain. Thanks are due above all to my brethren here at Glenstal, especially Br Cyprian Love OSB, for a characteristically penetrating theological observation which spurred me into finishing it and for taking time to read the first draft; to Fr James McMahon OSB, for invaluable technical assistance and to Br Martin Browne OSB, Fr Senan Furlong OSB and Fr Brendan Coffey OSB, for help in proof-reading. A special word of thanks is due to Br Emmaus O'Herlihy OSB Cam. for his splendid cover design.

Finally, this book is dedicated to my sister Barbara and her husband Eddie, who have always been there.

PART ONE

The Self-Manifestation of God

CHAPTER ONE

The Mystery of Christ Unveiled

The man Jesus has risen up to a name above all names ... he was crushed in the flesh of sin, bore the form of a servant, was obedient to death; he became *Kyrios* (Lord), *pneuma* (Spirit). He is, then, the same Lord who walked unnoticed and persecuted through the fields of Palestine and at last ended his life like a criminal on the cross; now he rules the world as king and the church is his bride. All his life, beginning in the Virgin's womb, is the great mystery of salvation, hidden from eternity in God and now revealed in the *ecclesia* (church). The deeds of his lowliness in that life on earth, his miserable death on Calvary appear now in a different light: God's own light; they are his acts, revealed, streaming with his light.

Odo Casel

If one were asked to define what is meant by 'Christianity' today, a variety of different responses might be forthcoming. Evangelicals might describe it as a personal encounter with Jesus: being born again, an experience of spiritual breakthrough after a long period of searching or suffering. Roman Catholics, Orthodox and many Anglicans might speak about belonging to the church and emphasise things like authority, continuity with the past and participation in complex communal worship. Other Christians, more liberally inclined, might describe it as a moral code, seeing in the teaching of Jesus a God-given means to transform society and humanise the world. Charismatics or Pentecostals would tend to stress conscious spiritual experience, particularly of the Holy Spirit.

Yet in the letters of St Paul (and those traditionally ascribed to him) Christianity is consistently described as a mystery, *mysterion* in Greek (1 Cor 2:1; Eph 1:8-10; 3:9; Col 1:25-27; 1 Tim 3:16).[1] For Paul and the tradition he generated, this mystery concealed eternally in God has been revealed to us in time, for our salvation. God made it known through the life, death and resurrection of Jesus of Nazareth, whose followers had acclaimed him as the Lord's anointed, the Christ or Messiah longed for by many in Israel (Acts 2:36). According to Paul and the other writers of the New Testament, his death and resurrection brought us new and wonderful knowledge about who God is, along with an invitation to enter through faith into an intimate relationship with him in the community of Christ's followers, his body the church.

Although this understanding of Christianity as the revelation of a hidden mystery was developed mainly in two letters nowadays generally attributed to Paul's followers (the Letters to the Ephesians and Colossians), it is also present in those which were certainly written by the apostle himself.[2] For example, at the end of his longest and most influential work, the Letter to the Romans, Paul says, in a concluding doxology or prayer glorifying God:

> Now to God who is able to strengthen you according to my gospel and the proclamation of Jesus Christ, according to the revelation of the mystery that was kept secret for long ages but is now disclosed, and through the prophetic writings is made known to all the Gentiles, according to the command of the eternal God, to bring about the obedience of faith – to the only wise God, through Jesus Christ, to whom be glory forever! Amen. (Rom 16:25-27)

Paul was writing in Greek against the background of both his own Jewish faith and the complex religious situation of the Greco-Roman world. This dense passage would have touched major chords in the understanding of those who heard and read him. Yet the text is neither a theological treatise nor a statement of belief but a prayer at the end of a letter, praising God for what he had done for the world. What, in Paul's view, had God actually done?

For Paul, echoing the early Christian proclamation, God's action was no less than his self-manifestation and the disclosure of his will to save the world. It did not come completely out of the blue. It was rather the culmination of an ancient dialogue God had begun with the people of Israel to whose prophets he had first revealed his will. That dialogue had been destined to have immense consequences for the rest of the human race. God had established his covenant with Israel, aiming to create a perfect partner to carry out his will in the world but fallen human beings were unable to accomplish that. In Jesus the Jewish Messiah, God himself stepped into the human scene and became that partner himself. He brought his covenant-plan to completion and revealed it for our enlightenment.[3] God's will to save became manifest in sending his Son into the world (Gal 4:4-5), a son whom he appointed as its Saviour (Acts 1:22-35).

By perfect obedience to God's will, shown in his acceptance of an unjust death imposed by human wickedness, Jesus took away sin, healing our rebellion and restoring friendship again between the world and God (2 Cor 5:14-15). In raising Jesus from the dead by his own glory, the Father completed the reconciliation process ratified in his death and opened up a glorious future again for human beings (Rom 6:4-11). Jesus is humanity's liberator from sin and death who reconciled the world to its creator.[4]

Paul never taught that God had to be reconciled to us: on the contrary it was *we* who had to be reconciled to *him*. God is faithful, human beings so often unfaithful (2 Tim 2:12-13). Jesus the Son of God, rejected by his own and crucified by the Gentiles, was revealed through his resurrection as the Christ, the mystery hidden from endless ages but revealed by God in history at the appointed time. The mystery of Christ is the event through which God emerged from silence, unveiled himself and made himself known to us. The mystery is God-becoming-present in the flesh, blood, life, death and resurrection of his only Son, Jesus the Christ, *Emmanuel*, God-with-us (Mt 1:23).

According to Paul this mystery made known to us in Christ was a secret kept from eternity hidden deep within the heart of God's silence. This hidden secret, nursed eternally in the divine heart, is the very thing God has chosen to reveal. But now that it has been revealed it is meant to be proclaimed to the whole world as good news, a salvation reaching far beyond (though always including) the people of Israel (Eph 3:7-13). Despite so much Christian misunderstanding of Judaism – and with such hideous consequences in history – there can be no question of God ever having broken his covenant with the Jews. They remain his first chosen people, the elder brothers and sisters of Christ and of Christians (Rom 9).[5]

Yet the revelation of the mystery is God's invitation to the whole human race, Gentiles included, to enter into this covenant relationship, which before had been offered uniquely to the people of Israel. Previously the Gentiles had not known God in this privileged way but in Christ, who gave up his life out of love for all, the covenant God first made with Israel was broken wide open, renewed and confirmed eternally, so that the blessings of God first conferred on Abraham might be extended to all peoples everywhere (Gal 3:13-14). That is the core of the message proclaimed by Paul: in the person of his Son, God was reconciling the world to himself, not holding our offences against us (2 Cor 5:18-21).

God has commanded this liberating message of reconciliation to be proclaimed so that his saving love might reach to the ends of the earth (Rom 15:7-12). All nations and peoples, the entire human race, are invited to accept this good news and enter into the obedience of faith which will reconnect them with God.[6] The Lord has made known his salvation, has unveiled himself and become present to us (Ps 97(98):2-3). He invites us in turn to turn to him, believe in him and open ourselves to his light (Is 45:22-23). We are asked to respond by becoming present to God who renders himself present to us. We are invited to end the hostilities, sue for peace and surrender to God, recognising that his will is not a ruthless or relentless power but one of limitless love, which we should allow to shape our lives and guide us as he wishes.

The essence of the mystery is that of mutual self-presencing: our becoming present to God who first makes himself present to us in Christ. In St Luke's gospel, Zachariah the father of John the Baptist declared that such would be the blessing conferred by the coming Messiah on those who would put their trust in him:

> Thus he has shown the mercy promised to our ancestors,
> and has remembered his holy covenant,

the oath that he swore to our ancestor Abraham,
to grant us that we,
being rescued from the hands of our enemies,
might serve him without fear, in holiness and righteousness
before him all our days. (Lk 1:72-75)

Letting go of fear and giving way to God, learning to walk before him in faith is entirely reasonable for, as Paul says, God is the
only wise one (*sophos*), the overflowing fountain of wisdom
(*sophia*) who calls the whole world into communion with himself
through the revelation of his mystery.

For Paul, therefore, Christianity is a deeply 'objective' thing. It
is not first and foremost a subjective personal experience; neither
is it simple adherence to a set of moral regulations nor even sharing in a sacred tradition. None of those answers is false in itself.
There is indeed a subjective spiritual experience of God that can
be had in prayer. There is a Christian ethics that has to be lived
out. There is also participation in ancient traditions of worship
and adherence to bodies of doctrine. But they are the consequences of Christianity rather than its essence as such. Christianity as a living religious reality does not emerge in us by our
own strength nor does it bubble up out of the depths of one's own
spirit. It cannot be fixed in rigid formulae or definitions. It is above
all the gift of new, indestructible, divine life,[7] life that comes to us
from beyond ourselves as a pure gift from God in Christ (Jn 10:
10): 'I have come that they may have life, and have it abundantly.'

God's revelation of the mystery concealed eternally in him
and revealed in time to us is like an explosion of light out of the
dark depths of the infinitely mysterious God who far transcends
all human imagining. In the words of the second-century martyr
bishop, Ignatius of Antioch, it is a word coming forth from the
silence of God, an echo of the inner recesses of the Father's heavenly heart.[8] It is God's Word which took flesh as Jesus of Nazareth
and was acclaimed after his resurrection as the Christ, the Lord's
anointed and the Saviour of humankind.

CHAPTER TWO

God's Presence to the World: the Mystery's Many Modes

It is important be aware of the difference between the word *mystery* as it is used in the New Testament, the liturgy and theology, and the meaning it tends to have in contemporary culture. When, for example, we speak of reading a 'murder mystery', our natural assumption is that at the end of the book the complexities of the plot will be resolved and we will discover who committed the murder and why they did it. All obscurity will be ended and the mystery will disappear in the clear light of knowledge. Nothing could be less true of mystery as that word is used in the Bible and in Christian worship. A text from Christmas which we sing in our monastery liturgy illustrates this well: 'The mystery, which was hidden from earlier ages, is now made clear.'

This does not mean, 'Now there is no longer any mystery.' It means rather that what has been made clear is the mystery itself, the fact that there *is* one. It is the mystery *itself* that has been revealed. Growing in knowledge of the mystery does not, therefore, make it less mysterious. On the contrary, it becomes even more so for the mystery is God revealing himself as the Trinity in his saving love for the world.[1] Yet the forms God adopts in his self-revelation certainly do manifest him, otherwise they would be pointless. There is here a tremendous and spiritually important paradox because while the transcendent, invisible God has to use words and visible forms to appear – yet because he remains always transcendent, even in the act of disclosing himself – those media simultaneously hide him in the very moment in which they reveal him. That is inevitable. God in his inscrutable, infinite mystery is always radically 'other' and can never be fully represented by any symbolic medium he chooses to employ.

The mystery of God's own being and life will never be fully penetrated by human understanding, either in this world or in the next. Even at the end, in the light of the Beatific Vision in heaven, when God's glory will shine on us as light (1 Tim 6:14-16; Rev 22: 3-5), he will remain infinitely unknown in his innermost being. God is absolutely unfathomable to all created understanding, whether human or angelic: we will know him but not exhaustively.[2] He does really give himself, does really radiate out towards us, but his innermost centre remains a secret known only to his own tri-personal self.

That is why there will never be any boredom or satiety in heaven.[3] Since God is infinite and eternal, he is infinitely attractive and eternally fascinating. God's self-revelation comes to us like rays of light flowing out from an inexhaustible Sun. God is an unstoppable source pouring himself out in manifestations of goodness, truth and beauty, yet the source itself is so limitless that it can never be fathomed or drained dry. God descends to us in energies of love but his innermost essence and the ultimate secret of his heart lie always beyond our comprehension.[4]

We must now clarify what is meant by God's 'becoming present' in revealing the mystery of Christ. He does not do this as if for the first time, as if he were not already at all times and in all places present to the universe as its endlessly creative source (Acts 17:24-29). God the transcendent one is also the immanent ground of all that is, present in all things. God is the soil in which all beings are rooted and the source which gives them life. The universe in all its magnificent variety is already the manifestation and expression of his creative will, a kind of sacrament of divine presence. According to the traditional wisdom of all the ancient cultures of the world, reaching from the plains of North America to the deserts of Australia, present also in South America, Africa and ancient Ireland, the secret of life was to recognise the divine, present in the cosmos and the rhythms of nature. Nature was a temple filled with divinity, of which the temples made by human hands were only images.[5]

Ancient paganism was at heart deeply spiritual, attuned to the divine reality underpinning the world even if, bearing the inevitable scars of sin, it often contained within it elements of vice and brutality such as human sacrifice; and in the developed religious philosophies the sense that God's mighty presence is running through everything, yet not contained by anything, reached levels of astonishing profundity. The greatest of the Greek philosophers such as Plotinus (c. 204-270) saw nature as the fringe of a mighty depth of being cascading endlessly from its hidden divine source.

Indian and Chinese Sages broke through the veil of appearances to discover the secret, silent invisible divine presence lying at the heart of everything. An Indian religious text, to select only one from the countless possibilities available, gives splendid expression to that intuition, seeing in nature a kind of sacrament of the invisible divine presence which embodies and images God's creative self-manifestation:

> In the beginning all was Brahman, ONE and infinite. He is beyond north and south, and east and west, and beyond what is above and below. His infinity is everywhere. In him, there is neither above, nor across, nor below; and in him there is neither east nor west.

> The Spirit supreme is immeasurable, inapprehensible, beyond conception, never-born, beyond reasoning, beyond thought. His vastness is the vastness of space.

> At the end of the world, all things sleep; he alone is awake in eternity. Then from his infinite space new worlds arise, a universe which is the vastness of thought. In the consciousness of Brahman the universe is, and into him it returns.

> He is seen in the radiance of the sun in the sky, in the brightness of fire on earth, and in the fire of life ... Therefore it has been said:

> 'He who is in the sun, and in the fire and in the heart of man is ONE. He who knows this is one with the ONE.'[6]

But this was neither mere speculation nor arid intellectualism. On the contrary, it was opening up a spiritual path, a way of return to God from whose presence we, and the whole of nature, have issued forth. Indian spirituality was and still is intensely practical. Its greatest representatives were not content simply to contemplate the world as God's self-manifestation: they sought return to him through the sacramental world of nature he has given us. An essential prerequisite for that return was inner purification, the rectification of desire and the stilling of the tumult of thoughts. Therefore the same text goes on to teach:

> When a wise man has withdrawn his mind from all things without, and when his spirit of life has peacefully left inner sensations, let him rest in peace, free from the movements of will and desire ... For it has been said:

> 'There is something beyond our mind which abides in silence within our mind. It is the supreme mystery beyond thought. Let one's mind and one's subtle body rest upon that and not rest on anything else.'

Eventually Indian religious tradition developed the idea that God periodically takes on human form, appearing on earth when the human race is in dire need of support and redemption. Thus India knows many 'incarnations' of the divine.[7]

The Jews too experienced that heaven and earth are filled with the glory of the Lord (Is 6:3; Ps 18(19):1-6). But they held that God had uniquely spoken to them and established a covenant with them, choosing them to be his special people. In the later prophets, that originally rather limited and exclusive conception opened out into a more universal perspective: they were to be bearers of the light to the whole world (Is 49:6-7). God, it was believed, had indeed set up his tent in Zion and established his special dwelling place in the temple at Jerusalem (Ps 131(132):13-18; Ps 98(99):1-5). He would appear there in a numinous cloud filling the Holy of Holies (1 Kgs 8:10-13). Yet they always acknowledged that the Lord who transcended all things could never be captured or held in one place. Jewish spirituality, reflected in the traditions of the temple and especially in the psalms, knew of God's presence in the whole cosmos and praised him with the three young men in the fiery furnace of Babylon as the source of all being (Deutero-canonical insertions between Dan 3:23 and 3:24).[8]

However, in making himself known through Christ's death and resurrection, Christians believe that God intensified his presence to a degree previously unimaginable to us. God's eternal Son became human and offered his life for the salvation of the entire cosmos. The life of the incarnate Son of God was thus a new mode of presence assumed by God in relation to his creation when the Word became flesh and lived among us (Jn 1:14). Still more, through his resurrection from the dead and ascension into heaven, the risen Christ filled the entire universe with his glorified presence (Eph 4:7-11). That is the deepest meaning of the statement in the Christian *Credo* that he is 'seated at the right hand of the Father'. It is a metaphorical way of saying that since God the Father is present everywhere so the risen Christ is present everywhere as well.

Yet there is a further extension of presence no less remarkable than that. Thanks to the sending of the Holy Spirit by the Father and Son after Christ's resurrection from the dead (Acts 2:33), God the Holy Spirit, the Lord and Giver of life, takes up a new way of dwelling in human beings. The Spirit comes to live in human hearts as in a temple (1 Cor 6:19-20). God, who is the source of being for all creation and dwells in it from the beginning, becomes the source of a new and indestructible eternal life for his creatures which begins here through faith and grace but is brought to perfection in the vision of God's glory in eternity.

All these modes of God's presence to us, in creation as discovered by traditional wisdom and philosophy, in the Jerusalem temple as revealed to the Jews and finally and most effectively in Christ the incarnate Word, come to completion in the presence of the Holy Spirit in the hearts of believers. Yet the revealed mystery is neither vague nor amorphous. It has name and form and definite content. It is a human being whom Christians recognise as the incarnate God – Jesus of Nazareth, the prophetic wandering Jewish teacher of wisdom who proclaimed the in-breaking of God's kingdom and died rejected by the Jewish religious establishment and the Roman authorities.

Jesus is the human embodiment of God's saving mystery: in him the manifold modes of divine self-presencing come to perfection. As the one whom God raised from death and exalted to his own right hand in glory, making him the source of the Holy Spirit,

Jesus is the perfect place of manifestation, the final temple through which God becomes present in the world (Jn 2:21).[9] He has become *par excellence* the place of divine epiphany. He is God's eschatological Word – literally the 'last' and final word spoken by God. Both Meister Eckhart and St John of the Cross asserted that in truth God only ever speaks one word but in that single word all things are contained and all things revealed to us: it is Jesus, the Word incarnate.[10]

It is wrong to imagine Christian faith as some timeless 'system' of thought or as an edifying mythology embodying eternal ideas divorced from space and time. A sentimental song popular in Ireland a few years ago contained the lines, 'God is watching us, God is watching us, God is watching us – from a distance.' Yet nothing could be less true about the God revealed in Jesus Christ. God is *not* watching us from a distance, hovering like some benign but ultimately uninvolved fairy godmother above our heads.

In Christ, God bridged the distance, came down to us and shared our human situation. Jesus is the living embodiment of God, his decision to share the lot of creatures. He is not a Hindu avatar, one of the divine manifestations or incarnations which are not ultimately real incarnations in the fullest sense but merely temporary appearances. Nor is he a kind of cosmic security blanket projected out of our deepest needs, a Jesus who appears at times to make us feel good, dropping down from the sky like a divine Mary Poppins to fix things when they are broken.

Jesus is the revelation of the true God in the flesh, blood, tears, suffering and sweat of a real human being who can be dated historically and located easily on a map (1 Jn 1:1-7). Christianity is not just spirituality, 'chicken soup for the soul', or a nice message about a well-disposed ultimate source of being that smiles occasionally on us. Nor is it about human beings bettering themselves so much that they become quasi-angelic by realising their deepest inner potential. That kind of bourgeois spirituality hardly does justice either to the harsh reality of life for the majority of people on this planet, or to the mind-blowing wickedness of which human beings are so capable and which reveals just how un-angelic and badly in need of redemption we really are. Nor indeed does it cor-

respond to the covenant-faithfulness of the God displayed in the
history of Israel who cannot be so easily controlled or manipulated.

The New Testament witness keeps before our eyes the hard
fact of suffering. The very one whom the apostles acclaimed after
his resurrection as God's Son and anointed Messiah was not some
demi-god or mythological being. He was truly human and really
suffered under Pontius Pilate, a real Roman Governor in real time.
He died the most shameful death imaginable among Jews and
Gentiles in the ancient world – condemned as a criminal by
Roman law and cursed by Jewish law because he had been hanged
on a tree (Gal 3:10, echoing Deut 27:26). He did not proclaim a
'spirituality', or *gnosis*, one of the enlightening systems of doctrine
so readily available from many other religious teachers in the
ancient world. He did not proclaim *himself* primarily, but God's
kingdom and himself as its harbinger.

Above all, as the First Letter of St John puts it, he came with 'water
and with blood', (1 Jn 5:6) his own blood shed on the hard wood of
the cross. Christ was not an enlightened guru basking blissfully in
the light of contemplation, nor a teacher of meditation breaking
through to enlightenment, nor a military conqueror. He was a
saviour who gave his life, dying rejected and in agony for his flock
and for the whole world (Mt 27:46; Jn 11:50; 12:32). The gospel of the
revelation of God's mystery proclaimed by Paul and the other apostles is anything but an ethereal and nebulous 'spirituality'. There
was and will always be an element of scandal in him, an irreducible
and immovable stumbling block (1 Pet 2:8). It is called the cross.

It is hardly surprising that in speaking about the revealed mystery, in his First Letter to the Corinthians, Paul wrote starkly of
Christ as God's crucified wisdom, declaring that God's making
his will known through the cross was a scandal in which wisdom
seems more like folly and strength more like weakness (1 Cor 1:17-
31). Yet in the powerlessness and apparent futility of the cross the
most remarkable truth of all has been revealed: the astonishing
depths of foolishness to which the all-wise God was prepared to
descend so as to subvert our human 'wisdom' and break down
our self-erected barriers, revealing in his apparent 'foolishness',
the depth of divine love for us.

No wonder that the Jews, with their long developed awareness of God's power and majesty as the King of Israel and their hope of a glorious Saviour, would find it scandalous; or that the Greeks with their fatalistic and deterministic philosophical worldviews and hyper-transcendent (or Stoically immanent) ideas about God would find it foolish. The scandal of the cross deconstructs all our carefully erected and edifying spiritualities, reminding us that, as Rowan Williams once put it, '… Christ remains a question to all human answers and to all attempts at metaphysical or theological closure.'[11] A Lutheran writer, Carl E. Braaten, highlights the scandalous nature of how the mystery has been revealed and the challenge it directs at all our deepest religious assumptions:

> We do not by nature – our fallen nature – wish to accept God in the humble place where he graciously has chosen to disclose himself. We expect to find God in a sacred temple or royal castle, not in a barn or on a cross. Our religious expectations are frustrated and reversed by the gospel.[12]

The cross of Christ has been raised up before us by God as the authentic litmus test for what is 'spiritual', the objectively revealed benchmark against which all lovers of 'wisdom' ought to assess their 'spirituality'. Only in the light of the crucified, incarnate God, are we enabled to assess the world objectively; only in the power-renouncing Messiah hanging on the cross are we given true power to unlock the agonising mystery of human sin and suffering; only in the transfiguring light of infinite love revealed at Calvary can we be transformed into people who really love, not in self-seeking – however refined or subtle that may be – but in the genuine giving of self for others. As Luther loved to say, '*crux probat omnia*', the cross tests everything.[13]

CHAPTER THREE

Deepening Insights
into the Mystery of Divine Persons

Still greater depths are contained in the revealed mystery of Christ but to sound them one must turn to later New Testament letters such as Ephesians, Colossians, 1 and 2 Timothy and Titus. Although as we have seen, they are probably not directly from Paul's hand they do represent the expansion and consolidation of his teaching within the wider circle of his disciples and have always been recognised by the churches as authentically 'Pauline' in the sense that their authors deepened and developed his ideas. Since we are not concerned with the process by which the New Testament reached its final form but with how the finished product operates in the church, I shall follow the convention of referring to their author in the traditional manner as 'Paul'. The same will be true of other New Testament writers cited here, such as 'John'.[1]

At the beginning of Ephesians, Paul set out a magnificent hymn celebrating how God chose us in Christ before time began so that his freely-given grace might be praised, declaring that God's purpose was to gather all things together into one through Christ (Eph 1:3-14). He went on to sound the same note as we heard at the end of the Letter to the Romans, though it plays a much greater role in the theology of this letter. The Christian gospel is the message of the revelation of God's glory made known for our enlightenment:

> I pray that the God of our Lord Jesus Christ, the Father of glory, may give you a spirit of wisdom and revelation as you come to know him, so that, with the eyes of your heart enlightened, you may know what is the hope to which he has called you ... (Eph 1:16-18a)

As in Romans, Paul insists that it is all exclusively God's work, to which we can initially contribute nothing but the obedience of faith. As the revelation of salvation it is pure grace: God's stooping down in love and mercy to rescue the human race which had wandered far from him (Eph 2:8-10). In Chapter 3 Paul makes the content of this proclamation much more precise. It is the mystery of Christ, made known to the apostle by grace and revelation, which he proclaims everywhere (Eph 3:1-3). Previously it was God's own jealously guarded secret, hidden within his inscrutable depths, unknown even to the angels. But now it has been unveiled for our faith to accept and gradually to penetrate with comprehension:

> In former generations, this mystery was not made known to humankind, as it has now been revealed to his holy apostles and prophets by the Spirit ... (Eph 3:5)

The apostles whom Jesus chose and to whom he appeared after his resurrection were constituted by the Holy Spirit as privileged eye-witnesses to his triumph over death. Christ's community is, therefore, always apostolic since it was founded on these witnesses to the activity of Jesus. But the 'prophets' too, most likely inspired Christian teachers who declared God's truth and interpreted his will in their communities, were also recipients of revelation. Christianity was more than just a past event. It was a living, present reality. Speaking and acting in and through them all was the Holy Spirit, God's *pneuma* or breath, his power released into the world through Jesus after his return to the Father in his ascension. The early church gradually came to differentiate this Holy Spirit from Christ himself (the first 'paraclete', meaning consoler, comforter, counsellor and advocate for the defence). Hence in John's gospel Jesus calls him/her 'another paraclete' (Jn 14:15-17).[2] In the coming of the Spirit they experienced the return of Jesus (Jn 14:18).

As the Christian community grew in its understanding of what God had done, it became more and more aware that this Holy Spirit is also divine, just as Jesus also had to be recognised as somehow one with God. Only God can testify to God in an absolute sense and sanctify believers, just as only God can save and redeem. Yet like Christ, the Holy Spirit normally chooses not to operate without the mediating action of others. God takes up and uses created things, filling them with the breath of his Spirit. He used the witness of the apostles and prophets, proclaiming the word of the gospel through them and, by means of the church's proclamation, he continues to make his wisdom known to the world (Mt 28:19-20).[3]

Paul goes on to repeat what was said in the conclusion to Romans. The mystery consists in the fact that through the revelation brought by Jesus, God opened a way for all people to enter into living contact with him, extending the covenant he had made with the Jewish people to the whole of humanity. He has flung his arms open to everyone in the world in an inclusive gesture that kindles the light of saving hope for all people. The message proclaimed to the Shepherds on Christmas night triumphantly summarised this all-embracing revelation: 'Today a saviour has been born to you: he is Christ the Lord!' (Lk 2:10-11). In the light of Christ's coming no human being can ever be imagined as excluded from God's loving plan. All are called to the banquet of life in the kingdom of the Father's love:

> ... the Gentiles have become fellow heirs, members of the same body, and sharers in the promise in Christ Jesus through the gospel. (Eph 3:6)

Paul's commission as an apostle was to bring others to know the plan of this mystery:

> ... this grace was given to me to bring to the Gentiles the news of the boundless riches of Christ, and to make everyone see what is the plan of the mystery hidden for ages in God who created all things; so that through the church the wisdom of God in its rich variety might now be made known to the rulers and authorities in the heavenly places. (Eph 3:8b-11)

This was so that God's will to unite all people in love might be accomplished. Destroying the enmity between Israel and the nations through the death of his only Son, God tore down the wall that divided them (Eph 2:14) – most likely a reference to the banning of non-Jews from entering into the heart of the Jerusalem temple. In so doing God united Jews and Gentiles in one body.

Once again the Holy Spirit is mentioned (Eph 3:5) for it is by the Spirit that we are brought together through Christ into a living relationship with God the Father. The Spirit is God's personal breath and the one who fully discloses the divine presence to us. The church, the community of all who through baptism are incorporated into Christ, becomes through the Spirit's action the true temple in which God can dwell, a temple not made out of stones but built from living people united with one another and with God (Eph 3:16-18, cf 1 Pet 2:4-6).[4] Proclaiming this mystery of the gospel is so urgent that Paul cries out in words possibly sung in early Christian worship:

> Sleeper, awake!
> Rise from the dead,
> and Christ will shine on you. (Eph 5:14)

The bringing about of peace – between God and the human race as a whole and between the chosen people and the rest of humanity whose election is revealed through Christ – lies at the very heart of the mystery. The God of Jesus Christ is a bridge builder whose secret plan revealed in Christ is to save all people by uniting everyone and all things in him. This is the revealed truth of the Christian gospel, God's gift offered to the world. Reconciliation, peacemaking and the creation of harmony lie at its heart.

Drawing on ideas about God's creative word and wisdom in Jewish tradition, the Letter to the Colossians helps us to understand this reconciling work of Christ in its cosmic dimensions by describing him as God's icon or image, the original template according to which all things have been made:

> He is the image (*eikon*) of the invisible God, the first born of all creation; for in him all things in heaven and on earth were created, things visible and invisible ... all things have been created through him and for him. He himself is before all things and in him all things hold together. He is the beginning, the firstborn from the dead, so that he might come to have first place in everything. For in him all the fullness of God was pleased to dwell, and through him God was

pleased to reconcile to himself all things, whether on earth or in heaven, by making peace through the blood of his cross. (Col 1: 15-20)

For Paul and the early church, as they reflected on the person of Jesus as God's anointed messenger whom he had raised from death and exalted into glory, and as they worshipped him as the Saviour of the world, it became ever more clear that such a remarkable divine intervention in human history could not have begun only with Jesus' birth in time. Guided by the light of the Holy Spirit whom Jesus had promised, and pondering God's plan as revealed in the Jewish scriptures, the church came to understand that Christ's origin goes back much further – or, to be more precise, that he had always existed beyond the spatial and temporal boundaries of this world.[5]

Gradually it became evident that Jesus is eternally one with the Father as the perfect image, idea and instrument by means of which God imagines, thinks and carries out all things (1 Cor 8:6). Christians found a useful means to express this notion ready at hand for Jewish thinkers had already speculated much on the presence within God of various creative emanations, such as his word or wisdom, by means of which God connects with creation. Rigorously faithful, however, to their monotheist inheritance, they did not imagine them as distinct persons within the Godhead but included them in the worship of the one God whose attributes they were. Paul and other New Testament writers took up such ideas and pressed them into service in their attempts to expound the mystery of Christ.[6]

As pre-existent, Christ was understood to be God's wisdom (*Sophia*) (1 Cor 1:24; Col 2:3) and Word (the *Logos* of the fourth gospel), his image (*eikon*) which had been revealed in human form (Col 1:15). This 'cosmic Christ' is simultaneously the means by which God calls everything into union with himself (Eph 1:10) and God's original blueprint for the created world (Col 1:16). The Book of Revelation accordingly has the glorified Jesus refer to himself as the beginning (*protos*) and the end (*eschatos*) (Rev 1:8). He is the heavenly Lamb, destined to be slain from before the foundation of the world and duly revealed in time (1 Pet 1:19-21).

In Genesis it had already been taught that God created human beings according to his own image and likeness but for Christians God's primordial image was the Son in whom he reveals his true face.

Christian tradition in the following centuries drew the obvious conclusions from this understanding of pre-existence, about the divinity of Jesus and his equality with the Father – with far-reaching consequences for both theology and anthropology: not only does Jesus reveal what God is like but also what human beings are called to become by grace. He is the image both of God and of perfect humanity, for as the pre-existent Son and *Logos*, he is the pattern according to which we have been made. Human beings are images of the one great Image. No wonder Paul in the First Letter to Timothy could exclaim:

> Without any doubt, the mystery of our religion is great:
> God (*following the variant reading*) was revealed in flesh,
> vindicated in spirit,
> seen by angels,
> proclaimed among Gentiles,
> believed in throughout the world,
> taken up in glory. (1 Tim 3: 16)

Jesus was recognised to have been more than just another divinely guided messenger or inspired prophet: he was God's very presence made manifest among us. As Paul put it in the Second Letter to the Corinthians:

> … God was in Christ (*variant reading*) reconciling the world to himself, not counting their trespasses against them, and entrusting the message of reconciliation to us. So we are ambassadors for Christ, since God is making his appeal through us; we entreat you on behalf of Christ, be reconciled to God. (2 Cor 5:19-20)

Through the manifestation of Christ and the drama of his death and resurrection the God who is perpetually present to the world as its creator, showed his ability to enter and embrace it in a new way. Many other New Testament texts indicate the church's growing understanding of Jesus' deepest identity as being one with God.

The second chapter of Paul's Letter to the Philippians (Phil 2:6-11) contains a text about Christ, possibly a hymn (the famous *carmen Christi*) either written by Paul himself or borrowed from the church's worship, which tells how Jesus was in the form (*morphe*) of God yet, 'emptied himself' to assume the form of a slave, becoming obedient not just to death but to the most ignominious form of it imaginable in that culture. For that very reason God exalted him to his own right hand, conferring on him the supreme name of Lord (*Kyrios*), the name of God himself. That text has given us the word *kenosis* which has become a technical term in theology to describe the self-emptying, the voluntary self-limitation Jesus accepted in coming to redeem us. I will use the word often in this book. By means of it, God has opened a door for us through the revelation of the mystery of Christ and given us access to the heart of what later tradition called 'the Holy Trinity'. *Kenosis* is one of the most valuable ideas available for articulating a Christian vision of reality.[7]

In its turn the anonymous Letter to the Hebrews, one of the New Testament's most polished and sophisticated theological treatises, calls Christ God's appointed heir to all things, through whom the universe has been created:

> He is reflection of God's glory and the exact imprint of God's very being, and he sustains all things by his powerful word. (Heb 1:1-4)

Hebrews insists that Jesus is higher than the angels, even though for a short while during his life on earth, he consented to be made lower than them (Heb 1:5-14; 2:5-18).[8]

But it is certainly in the fourth gospel, (stemming from the circle around the mysterious 'beloved disciple') and in the First Letter of St John, that we find the culmination of this exalted understanding of Christ. The prologue to the gospel describes him as the Word (*Logos*) – a complex Greek term with connotations of word, reason, discourse, thought, speech and intelligence – through whom all things were made. The Word is with (or more precisely *pros*, i.e., 'towards') God the Father and is itself God (Jn 1:1-2). This *Logos* is the life of all people, the true light that enlightens everyone coming into the world (Jn 1:9).[9]

Yet, as St Augustine later observed, this idea which was present both in Greek philosophy and Jewish speculation, was taken to an unexpectedly new stage of development as John announced the astounding message:

> ... the Word became flesh and lived among us, and we have seen his glory, the glory as of a father's only son, full of grace and truth. (Jn 1:14)

The Greek word used (*skenao*, to encamp or dwell) speaks literally of the Word pitching his tent or tabernacle among us, a reference to God's presence among the chosen people in the Ark of the Covenant during their wandering in the wilderness and to his presence in the Holy of Holies in the temple at Jerusalem (Ex 40: 34-38). The prologue concludes with a massive paradox: 'No one has ever seen God' but goes on to say about the Word made flesh, 'It is God the only Son, who is close to the Father's heart, who has made him known' (Jn 1:18). As Augustine pointed out, Greek philosophers had broken through to the idea of an eternal *Logos* but no one had ever ventured to say that that exalted being had become 'flesh', still less that it had been crucified.[10]

The same gospel concludes with the apostle Thomas adoring the risen Christ with the words, 'My Lord and my God', the most explicit confession of Christ's divinity in the entire New Testament (Jn 20:28). In the light of all this it should be evident that the Christian understanding of God as a Trinity of persons, a doctrine thrashed out during long centuries of bitter and divisive disputes in the church, was more than just a luxurious speculation indulged in by scholars or advanced by ecclesiastical politicians.[11]

The development of the doctrine of the Trinity was forced on the church if it wished to make sense of the records bequeathed to it by the original witnesses and of its own experience of Jesus and the Holy Spirit in prayer and worship. Some coherent account had to be developed if the church were to witness to the radical nature of God's self-opening to the world and his becoming present in it in a new and unprecedented way through Jesus Christ and the Holy Spirit.[12]

John's First Letter poetically captures the paradoxical character of the apostles' experience of Jesus:

> We declare to you what was from the beginning, what we have heard, what we have seen with our eyes, what we have looked at and touched with our hands, concerning the word of life – this life was revealed, and we have seen it and testified to it, and declare to you the eternal life which was with the Father and was revealed to us … (1 Jn 1:1-3)

Although, as Louis Bouyer observed, the word mystery is not actually used in the works traditionally attributed to 'John', the basic sense of the idea is present everywhere.[13] Jesus is described as the Word (*Logos*), in terms which suggest that he comes forth eternally from the Father as God's perfect self-expression and is the medium through which he created all things.[14] The 'flesh' (*sarx*) assumed by the *Logos* in the incarnation expresses both natural fragility and humanity's estrangement from God. Yet in the incarnation it becomes the very medium which manifests God and through which the Father makes his will known to us. By his death and resurrection this en-fleshed Word revealed God's glory in the world and after his exaltation and return to the Father's side sent the Holy Spirit to continue his work on earth (Jn 16:4-15).

For John, Jesus the Word-made-flesh is like a kind of sacrament manifesting and actualising the invisible God and rendering him present to us. Not only is there no contradiction between Paul and John on this crucial point but, notwithstanding the differences in language, a striking agreement is evident. That correspondence is made even clearer when John speaks of the wonders wrought by Jesus as 'signs'.[15]

Through such signs as healing (Jn 4:46-54), feeding a hungry crowd (Jn 6:1-15), giving sight to a man born blind (Jn 9) and raising the dead (Jn 11:1-44) the glory (*doxa*) of God was manifested, calling those who witnessed it to believe. As the fourth gospel says about the transformation of water into wine at the wedding banquet at Cana:

> Jesus did this, the first of his signs, in Cana of Galilee, and re-
> vealed his glory; and his disciples believed in him. (Jn 2:11)

As the mystery in person, Christ's 'flesh' (meaning his entire existence culminating in death and resurrection) manifests God's presence to us. He is the great sign raised up by God (Jn 12:32; 19: 37; cf Lk 2:12; 34) which fulfils the hopes and yearnings of all peoples of all times and places. Jesus is the perfect gift given us by God to enable us to share his life. Christ the en-fleshed Word, has made known an essential truth.

God shows himself and reveals his will through created agencies, first of all his own humanity, but also his 'signs': the glory of the presence is always a mediated one. God is the absolute, the wholly other who is high above all beings in this world or the next, invisible, intangible, impenetrable and immeasurable, 'a consuming fire' (Heb 12:29). The unveiled vision of his face would simply burn up the one admitted directly to his presence.

If, therefore, God is to draw near to us, he has to employ some kind of medium as the filter of his presence and the means to manifest his glory. In the Old Testament he did that both through the medium of angels and through manifestations such as the hovering luminous cloud of presence with which he filled the temple and which even today, according to Orthodox Jews, is believed to hover over the heads of worshippers in the synagogue.[16]

According to John, the en-fleshed Word – the embodied mystery – is the perfect sign of God's glory, the tabernacle and the revelation of his nature.[17] Liturgically, this has found magnificent expression in the Roman tradition in the first Preface of the Mass for Christmas, a text traditionally attributed to Pope St Leo the Great. This majestic poem, sung to introduce the recital of God's saving deeds in the Eucharistic Prayer, summarises the Johannine vision of how God chose to emerge from his transcendent invisibility and become both visible and tangible in the body of Christ:

> In the mystery of the Word incarnate,
> there appeared to the eyes of our mind
> the new light of your splendour.
> For knowing God visibly,

by means of him,
we are caught up
to the love of invisible realities ...

The revelation of the mystery through the incarnation of the
Word is the fundamental Christian truth. Yet it in turn establishes
what John Henry Newman called the sacramental principle. The
fact that the absolute transcendent God comes to dwell with us in
Christ enlightens us to see that God always deals with his creatures by way of sacramental mediation.[18] Created by the Father in
and though Christ, the eternally pre-existent Word, the universe
is already potentially 'flesh and blood' for Christ. All its beauty is a
proleptic prefiguration of the radiance to be revealed in his
incarnation. There is, as St Maximus the Confessor taught, a kind
of partial and provisional incarnation of God always taking place
in the created world since it manifests God's plan and embodies
his creative ideas. It is a beautiful and ordered world because it is
the product of divine words (*logoi*), ideas and images grounded in
Christ the *Logos*.[19]

The light of the incarnate Word reveals not only who God is
but also, in the words of the poet Gerard Manley Hopkins, that
'the world is charged with the grandeur of God.'[20] Because of the
flesh assumed by Christ, we know that God's presence to the
world is always a mediated one. Seeing his full and final revelation in the incarnate Word, we know that wherever we encounter
beauty, goodness and truth, we encounter rays from the splendour of God's glory. Christ is the beacon which gives light to the
whole universe. Because of that, Christians can acknowledge the
on-going manifestation of God in the created world and in the
great religions and philosophies as well as in the inner sanctum of
the conscience: wherever truth is found it consists in sparks and
rays exploding out of the burning furnace of the incarnate Word.
Yet as Christians we are also committed to the uniqueness and
specificity of Christ, God's most full and final revelation, the incarnate *Logos* who gathers to himself and redeems the *logoi*
(words) of God scattered throughout the world.

St John Chrysostom (quoted by the Second Vatican Council)
spoke of this humble self-limitation as God's accommodation of

himself to our human limitations so as to communicate with us, his coming near to us by using created media in such a way that we are not destroyed by his overwhelming magnificence.[21] Russian theologians of the 20th century even daringly suggested that the world itself is actually the creative fruit of an original kenotic choice made by the Holy Trinity. The Absolute voluntarily limits itself, accomodating itself thereby to our limitations, so that relative being – the world – may emerge and stand before its maker.[22] It is a magnificent vision of God as one who withdraws his boundless self in divine humility so as to grant his creatures time and space to be.

Yet we know this not just from human intuition alone, for our eyes are blinded by sin, but because the rays of light disclosed in the incarnation of Christ and ever flowing from their source can pierce our darkness – even where the name of Christ has never been heard. He is already there as the pre-existent *Logos*, the divine creative ground of the world. Jesus, whether acknowledged or not as having received the 'name above all names', is the anonymous light enlightening all who gaze upon the world and who discern within it and discover through it the mystery of divine presence, giving rise to the million and one names people have used to call on God in very age and culture.

Even if unknown to themselves, guided by this light, all people are illumined by the undying Sun of justice and Shepherd of beings, God's all embracing cosmic *Logos*, who holds all things in being and gathers them to himself. By means of his anonymous hidden presence, through the secret effulgence of his gracious light, he has always enlightened and saved all who are born into this world (Jn 1:9) – whenever and wherever they respond to the mystery sensed within the world and open their hearts to truth and love.[23]

Yet, thanks to the fall of humankind, the world has to a great extent lost its transparency to divine light. It has become opaque through sin and evil so that many not only fail to recognise the light but actively deny its very existence (Rom 1:18-32).[24] Unfortunately the world is not simply peopled by well-meaning spiritual seekers but by us: fallen human beings prone to egoism and the desire to dominate and even consume our fellow human beings. For that reason, incarnation alone did not suffice to gather all things back to God. The Son of God took flesh and died in order to punch a hole in the hard wall surrounding the heart and call us to conversion. He came to lift us up and redirect us to the transcendent goal God has set for us: undying life together, in the communion of the Holy Trinity. But for that to come about, Christ had to embrace the mystery of the cross.[25]

CHAPTER FOUR

Gazing into the Mystery of Christ's Saving Work

> Yet it is not to be understood
> that the Father was ever angry toward him.
> For how could he be angry toward his beloved Son,
> 'in whom he was well pleased'?
>
> *John Calvin*

Christ brought the idea of God's humility to its ultimate limit: God, entering into the world, casts off the image of his glory and puts on the image of his creation (see Phil 2:6-8). He subordinates himself to the laws of creaturely life. He does not violate the world order. Nor does he strike the world with lightning or deafen it with thunder, as pagans thought (recall the myth of Zeus and Semele). He only burns like a meek light before the world, drawing to himself his sinful and weary creation, not punishing it but calling it to wisdom. God loves his creation and is tormented for its sake, is tormented by its sin. God extends his arms towards his creation, implores it, calls it, awaits his prodigal son …

Of course, the dogmatic idea is expressed imprecisely here. But this is done intentionally, in order to represent experience in a rougher and therefore more clear-cut form.

> *Paul Florensky*

The mystery of the cross of Christ – but also knowledge of history and honest reflection on the human situation as it confronts us in the world at any time – sets before us a very bleak picture of reality, one so bleak that only God could save us. Christ's suffering does indeed declare God's loving-kindness. It is the manifestation of divine goodness and *philanthropia*, ('love for humanity') revealing the Father to be a 'human-loving God' (Tit 3:4).

Yet we should not sentimentalise the mystery of Christ nor reduce it merely to the level of a lesson in human ethical re-education on God's part. The deepest solidarity demonstrated by the incarnate God was not just his compassionate identification with our weakness and suffering. It was much more radical than that: it was identification with us in the alienated state into which sin and evil had plunged the human race.[1] In and through that identification Jesus Christ performed the greatest miracle and mystery of all time: no less than the taking away of the sins of the whole world (Jn 1:29) and the reconciliation of humankind with its creator. Paul's words are very stark:

> For our sake he (God) made him (Christ) to be sin who knew no sin, so that in him we might become the righteousness of God. (2 Cor 5:21)

At the heart of the mystery of Jesus is the story of a God who not only descended to be with us through the incarnation but who also voluntarily stepped into the objective space of estrangement we human beings had opened up between ourselves and God. We have been speaking of various 'disclosure-zones' in which God breaks through to us, but human beings had created a fundamental *closure-zone* by saying 'no' to God. Jesus stepped across the gaping chasm between the All-Holy Trinity and sinful humanity and in our self-created closure-zone disclosed the loving kindness of the Father for us (Tit 2:11-14). For the first and only time in history since the fall, a human being lived, who by his own free will existed in perfect harmony and obedience with the will of God. He closed the gaping abyss opened by us in our desire to be as gods (Gen 3: 5).[2]

His obedience both judged and cancelled our disobedience, his humility conquered our overweening pride, his forgiveness replaced our stubborn refusal to forgive; and he did it all as the incarnate God, being at one and the same time both the perfect manifestation of the Trinity and the perfect representative of the human race – both united in one person. But in discussing this mystery we should aim to avoid all rash speculation, observe reverent silence before his suffering and death and try to remain faithful to what has been revealed and its (total) recording in the scriptures. The church here can show us the way, for throughout her long history, almost no final and binding dogmas have been issued about precisely how Christ redeemed us.[3]

Two errors above all may mar the proclamation of the mystery of Christ's redemptive sufferings. The first is the idea that any form of punishment was deliberately inflicted on Jesus by the Father in the mystery of his suffering and death, so that his death somehow had the character of a penal substitution. Some Christians (including at times some Roman Catholics) actually hold that Christ's atonement, the reconciliation process brought about by God between himself and sinful human beings, consisted in an angry Father striking a Son who took a punishment which ought really to have fallen on us. According to that view, all the retributive justice of God against the human race for breaking his law descended instead on the innocent head of Jesus who stepped into our place so that his condemnation might secure our acquittal.[4]

Such a theological opinion is often mistakenly attributed to St Anselm, a 12th century Benedictine monk and Archbishop of Canterbury, but he was not really responsible for it – at least not in that form. Living in the feudal system of medieval Europe, Anselm wanted to vindicate the goodness of God. He insisted that God, being infinitely just, had established a moral universe but that mankind had offended his honour by rebelling against him in disobedience.

Jesus Christ, the incarnate Son of God, atoned for our disobedience with his perfect obedience (which being that of a divine-human being had infinite value) and in that way restored the correct balance of the universe: but in Anselm's understanding that did not entail Jesus appeasing an angry Father. Rather both persons of the Trinity acted together in restoring cosmic justice. In a medieval world often wracked by capricious injustice, Anselm emphasised divine fidelity to good order, an order God had himself established as a moral God. The main point was to establish that, since God is good by nature, he is never simply capricious or arbitrary in his decisions.[5]

To deny penal substitution is not to minimise the seriousness of sin but one must try to understand correctly what constitutes sin and what conditions it creates. Some words on this subject by the theologian Paul S. Fiddes offer a helpful clarification. After mentioning various modern theories which stress Christ's solidarity with us as social beings, Fiddes speaks of the objective situation of estrangement and alienation sin has generated between us and God:

> ... but with other theologians, we may go further to see the cross as the occasion for Jesus to endure the experience of estrangement from God as well. By entering a situation where he dies as an outcast, under human judgement, Jesus is in a position to undergo a death of total estrangement from both human companionship and from God. This makes it possible for Christ to endure the same penalty against sin that human beings experience, dying under the 'no' that God speaks against a human life which is characterised by rebellion against the divine purpose. Such a view does not envisage God as directly inflicting a penalty on Christ; rather Christ participates in the human situation of being under divine judgement, which might be called 'exposure' to the divine 'wrath' against sin, or the personal opposition of God to sin.[6]

One arrives at the notion of Jesus as a victim of penal substitution by misinterpreting biblical texts and plucking them out of context. But above all one gets there by forgetting the fundamental context in which any theology of Christ's redeeming work has to be located: the universal loving will of God expressly declared in the New Testament to save the whole human race by sending his own Son in the likeness of sinners.[7]

The second erroneous idea that mars the proclamation of the good news is equally unacceptable. It is that of limited atonement, in other words that Jesus died to save only a chosen section of the human race and not all people everywhere.[8] It is therefore worth noting some places in the New Testament where the universal nature of God's saving work – Christ having offered himself for all people – is clearly affirmed:

For while we were still weak, at the right time Christ died

for the ungodly. Indeed, rarely will anyone die for a righteous person – though perhaps for a good person someone
might actually dare to die. But God proves his love for us in
that, while we were still sinners, Christ died for us.

For God has done what the law, weakened by the flesh,
could not do: by sending his own Son in the likeness of sinful flesh, and to deal with sin, he condemned sin in the
flesh, so that the just requirement of the law might be fulfilled in us, who walk not according to the flesh but according to the Spirit. (Rom 5:6-8; 8:1-4)

Later New Testament writers (in two texts attributed to Paul)
also clearly teach the doctrine of Christ's redemptive death for all:

First of all, then, I urge that supplications, prayers, intercessions and thanksgivings be made for everyone, for kings
and all who are in high positions, so that we might lead a
quiet and peaceable life in all godliness and dignity. This is
right and is acceptable in the sight of God our Saviour, who
desires everyone to be saved and to come to the knowledge
of the truth. For there is one God; there is also one mediator
between God and humankind, Christ Jesus, himself
human, who gave himself a ransom for all – this was attested
at the right time. For this I was appointed a herald and an
apostle (I am telling the truth, I am not lying), a teacher of
the Gentiles in faith and truth.

For the grace of God has appeared, bringing salvation to
all ... (1 Tim 2:1-6; Tit 2:11)

Finally there is a strong text in the First Letter of St John:

My little children, I am writing these things to you so that
you may not sin. But if anyone does sin, we have an advocate with the Father, Jesus Christ the righteous; and he is the
atoning sacrifice for our sins, and not for ours only but for
the sins of the whole world. (1 Jn 2: 1-2)

Only by ignoring or misinterpreting such texts could such an
erroneous misunderstanding as that of limited atonement have
arisen, for their meaning is plain.

In approaching the mystery of the redemption it is important to recognise that it can only be expounded in metaphors and images which set the mystery of Christ's redeeming work before us for our contemplation. But it is a serious error to privilege any particular metaphor or image over others, to project into them more than they actually say or to pluck them out of the greater context of the mystery of Christ as a whole, forcing them to act as systematic definitions rather than metaphors. A definition aims to capture life and fix it in a formula. A metaphor, like a symbol or a parable, opens out on to a reality to which it gives privileged access but which yet far transcends its limitations.

'Redemption' is a good example. In human terms, that usually entails someone buying back something (or some*one* in the days of official slavery). Yet when used of God it is erroneous to ask to whom God 'pays' the ransom money.[9] It is a metaphor which works by analogy. The part of the analogy that is similar to our experience is that of rescuing and restoring something or someone. The part that is not relevant may be discarded. Nothing better kills a metaphor, symbol or parable than literalism.

In considering the issue of Christ's redeeming death, two questions are often raised regarding the atonement: 'Did Jesus have to die?' and, 'Was an angry God appeased by the death of his Son?' The second question is usually part and parcel of the doctrine of penal substitution. In answer to the first question it ought to be admitted that there was a chilling inevitably about the death of Jesus. But that was not God's doing, but ours. Given who he was, what he said and what he did, it was inevitable that Jesus would come into conflict with the religious and political establishment of his era – or any era. Once he became a threat, as with most prophetic figures, there was only one way that they could deal with him. His death had the kind of necessity that accompanies the final choice of a particular path of action. Once you take the decision to follow a certain route and initiate a certain course of action, a certain end becomes inevitable. You cannot make an omelette without breaking eggs: you cannot pursue the course of action Jesus did without setting yourself up for suffering and death at the hands of threatened authorities (Jn 11:45-53). The violent deaths suffered by other prophetic figures throughout history are further illustrations of that inevitable law.

The second question is more complex and therefore calls for more careful consideration. Calvin insisted that there is no evidence anywhere in the New Testament to suggest that the Father was ever angry with Jesus in any way, even if he did hold that God had punished him instead of us.[10] Yet it is a fact: there is talk in both Testaments of God's righteous indignation and even at times of his burning anger (Is 9:13-21; 10:1-4). Here again we need to respect one of the basic rules of all theological language: in every analogy we employ to speak about God – analogies which are always based on human experience – the *difference* is always *infinitely* greater than the similarity we posit.

In scripture, God's 'anger' is a metaphor and is a very different thing from ours, even if analogical points of contact can be established. In our case anger is almost inevitably tied up with egoism and pride. It often stems from an exaggerated sense of our own importance (which as psychologists remind us may actually betoken a deep sense of inferiority) and our having perceived that that has been somehow slighted; and it is usually laced with jealousy, hatred and a host of other vices. That is usually even more the case when it involves so-called righteous indignation, the worst examples of which are surely to be found in fanatical religious zeal. St James warned against such anger (Jas 1:19-20). Early monastic writers such as Evagrius insisted that anger is one of the worst human passions inhibiting spiritual growth.[11] Zeal is frequently the other side of insecurity.

It is wholly other in the case of God's 'anger'. When scripture speaks of his wrath it is a way of describing his absolute holiness which is love. While the New Testament expressly declares that God is love, it speaks of divine anger in an impersonal way as 'the wrath'. Yet such anthropomorphic language can be a helpful corrective to a tendency to project too easily on to God our own sentimentalised notions of 'love'. As the cross reveals, divine love is anything but sentimental: it is God's holy love. Yet in responding to all the evil and injustice with which human beings have oppressed each other throughout history, God's righteous holy love can only appear to us as wrath.

If we are tempted to drop completely the metaphor of 'anger' in relation to God, then we may need to ask ourselves if we are still speaking about the Lord who revealed himself to Israel as a personal God of righteousness with a special interest in the poor, the weak and the oppressed – and of the Father of Jesus Christ in whose crucified light our human darkness stands ever more exposed and condemned for what it is.

When we survey history – peppered liberally with atrocity after atrocity – the burning of women as witches, the Armenian massacres, the shovelling of the ashes of the Jews out of gas ovens, the African slave trade, child abuse, drug pushing, domestic violence, human sex-trafficking, torture, the nightmare of Rwanda and most recently the potential destruction of our very planet – it would be naïve to subscribe to facile myths of inevitable human progress. We might even find ourselves ready to agree with Paul: 'The human race has nothing to boast about to God!' (1 Cor 1:29, *Jerusalem Bible* version).

The 20th century, with its two world wars and extermination camps, ought to have put paid forever to the myth of inevitable human progress toward the good. Having grown up in Belfast in the 1970s, with its institutional injustice, political duplicity, religious bigotry, racial hatred, sectarian and political murders and the creeping brutality that accompanied it all, and without denying the human capacity for greatness, I for one have never been inclined to downplay the reality of evil. Sts Paul and Augustine, along with Luther and Freud, were surely not so wide of the mark at times in diagnosing what afflicts our human nature.

But that is not to say that in the face of such negativity, God's 'anger' at our wickedness is simply like our own when we are faced with negative situations. In every analogy the difference between God and us is always infinitely greater.[12] What we call the anger of God is the manifestation of love confronted by injustice. It is God's love, burning to eradicate wickedness so that human beings might really live and attain their happiness in union with him, and it is directed against evil as such – never against 'evil people'. All have been made in his Son's image and likeness.

As scripture says, all have sinned and fallen short of God's glory (Rom 3:23) so that all of us are at some time in our lives potentially (and unfortunately all too actually) capable of real evil. Yet no matter how depraved people may become, they remain always images of Christ the true Image of God. That image-quality may be soiled, tarnished, obscured and disfigured, but is never wholly lost, never totally destroyed.

Here Catholics, Orthodox and most Anglicans often part company with many other Christians in asserting that no matter how far we fall we are incapable of entirely obliterating that quality of our being, for it is rooted in God. His 'anger' is how we, warped by our evil tendencies, force him to appear. It is but the dark side of his eternal holiness, goodness and love which always want the best for creatures no matter how flawed we are. The more we commit sin the more we weave a web around ourselves, voluntarily blocking out his light. That is why in the incarnation God punched a hole in our self-woven cocoon and thrust in a hand to drag us out: that is why Christ descended into our hell of God-forsakenness – so that we could not go on pretending to ourselves – and in that way justifying our own ghastliness to ourselves and others – either that there is no God or that an angry God does not love us.

Some of the wisest words on this subject have come not from the pulpit or the university but from the silence, solitude and contemplation of a woman's monastic cell. What was 'shewn' to the gentle mystic Julian of Norwich may offer us the last word on this mystery. There is ultimately no anger in God because the apparent dichotomy between his justice and his mercy pertains only to how we experience him through the filter of ourselves. The mystery is precisely this: that in God all is one in love. To be finally at one ('oned') with him will be to share in that resolution:

> For, this which was continually shown in all, was a high marvel to the soul which beheld with great diligence: that our Lord God, concerning himself, may not forgive, for he may not be wrathful – it were impossible. For this was shown: that life is all grounded and rooted in love, and without love we may not live; and therefore to the soul that by his special grace sees so much of the high, marvellous,

goodness of God, and that we are endlessly oned to him in love, it is the most impossible that it may be that God should be wrathful, for wrath and friendship are two opposites; for he that destroys and dispels our wrath and makes us meek and mild for him it must be that he is ever one in love, meek and mild which is the contrary of wrath; for I saw very surely that where our Lord appears peace is taken and wrath has no place; for I saw no manner of wrath in God, neither for a short time nor for a long, for truly, as I see it, if God might be even a touch wrathful we should never have life nor place nor being ...[13]

The cross of the only begotten Son is God's 'disclosure-zone' in showing us how serious our situation is when such a drastic intervention in history was required: God's becoming in his turn the victim of human injustice. But in the forgiveness he expressed in dying and in the universal scope of his death, Jesus revealed the all-embracing nature of God's love: 'Father, forgive them; for they do not know what they are doing' (Lk 23:34). Most noteworthy of all is the fact that after his resurrection, unlike other victorious conquering kings, he did not settle scores nor display any anger against his friends who had betrayed him. On the contrary his recorded appearances are distinguished by their gentleness (Jn 21), even if he still had to rebuke some of them for their unbelief (Lk 24:25; 38).

Yet accepting that the death of Christ involved no penal substitution, there is still a genuine substitution to be proclaimed in the Christian gospel of redemption. According to that gospel, the Holy Trinity is the reconciling subject who acted to bring about peace with human beings. The human race, through no fault of God's, had wandered far from him. To accomplish reconciliation, God the Son (Jn 1:10), the Word who is the perfect expression of the Father and the ground of creation through whom all things were made (Col 1:15-16; Heb 1:1-4), voluntarily descended into the world (Jn 3:31-34; 6:38) to bridge the gap between God's holy being and that of a world not only fragile and limited but actively hostile to God (Rom 5:10).

For that to happen – indeed the only way it could happen –

God had to choose freely to limit himself, accommodating himself to human weakness (Phil 2:7-8), abandoning his power, if he were to draw near to us in our extremity (Mt 26:53-54). In fact, it was not such an alien thing for God to do at all. In willing the existence of the created world in the first place, the Absolute had voluntarily accepted some degree of self-limitation, otherwise nothing else could ever have come into being. But there was no necessity in any of that, unless one wants to say that love itself imposes a kind of necessity.

The Son, therefore, having assumed the human condition through his kenotic self-emptying, consented in perfect solidarity with us to step into the place of estrangement we inhabit (2 Cor 5: 21). That brought him finally to death through an unjust and particularly cruel form of execution. Having abandoned himself completely, he experienced the ultimate abandonment in solidarity with rebellious humanity: the apparent disappearance of the Father from his life, before as the gospels of Mark and Matthew tell us he breathed his last, crying, 'My God, my God, why have you forsaken me?' (Mk 15:34; Mt 27:46).

Jesus the representative human being, the sinless one, became totally at one with lost humanity: he became one with our God-forsakenness. Self-surrendered, he accomplished the salvation of the human race. Like an enormous sponge he absorbed into his own person all the evil carried out by every human being since the world began until, utterly wrung out, he carried us in union with his own humanity into the furnace of love burning eternally in the heart of the Holy Trinity.

In his resurrection from the dead the Father and the Holy Spirit responded to him in redeeming love (Acts 2:22-32). Easter Sunday was his justification, the divine confirmation of his mission and ministry (Rom 1:3-5). They reached down and saved him, lifted him up and brought him back from death – and with him us as well, whom he contained within his own humanity (Col 2:1).[14]

Exalted and glorified in God's presence, his crucified humanity was transformed by the light and fire of the Holy Spirit which he poured out on his disciples at Pentecost (Lk 24:49; Acts 2:2-13). He appointed them apostles and heralds, empowering them to pro-

claim to the world the good news that humankind has been definitively, objectively and finally reconciled to God (Gal 1:1; 2 Cor 5:
20). The Holy Spirit in turn voluntarily descended – and descends –
to extend the saving grace of Christ through the church's preaching to the uttermost ends of the earth.[15]

At every point the initiative for reconciliation and atonement
rested with God who stepped freely into the breach we had
opened up between ourselves and him. As St Paul wrote:

> All this is from God, who reconciled us to himself through
> Christ, and has given us the ministry of reconciliation; that
> is, in Christ God was reconciling the world to himself, not
> counting human trespasses against them, and entrusting
> the message of reconciliation to us. So we are ambassadors
> of Christ since God is making his appeal through us; we en-
> treat you on behalf of Christ, be reconciled to God. (2 Cor
> 5:18-20)

It was not God who needed to be reconciled to us, but we who
had to be brought back to God; not God who had made himself an
enemy to us but we who had made him an enemy. God remains
the same for ever, a faithful God of love and mercy, but we are
those who stray. It was and always is all God's work:

- What proves the Father's love for us is that he sent his Son to
  die for us even while we were still his enemies (Rom 5:6; Jn 3:
  16-17).
- What proves that the Son loves us is that, through his voluntary
  death, the love with which the Father loved him from all eternity
  (the Holy Spirit) is now able to be in us as well (Jn 17:26).
- What proves that the Spirit loves us is that s/he comes to help
  us in our weakness (Rom 8:26) interceding for us with the
  Father even when we do not know how to pray as we ought.

This is the mystery of redemption, the saving work of Christ:
the Father's loving gift of Christ, the Son's gracious self-offering
and the communion of the Holy Spirit who is their mutual gift to
us (2 Cor 13:13).

CHAPTER FIVE

Divine Presents: the Sacramental Mysteries

In this sacramental dispensation of Christ's mystery, the Holy Spirit acts in the same way as at other times in the economy of salvation: he prepares the church to encounter her Lord; he recalls and makes Christ manifest to the faith of the assembly. By his transforming power he makes the mystery of Christ present here and now ... Christian liturgy not only recalls the events that saved us but actualises them, makes them present. The paschal mystery of Christ is celebrated, not repeated. It is the celebrations that are repeated, and in each celebration there is an outpouring of the Holy Spirit that makes the unique mystery present.

Odo Casel

According to the clear testimony of scripture and the unanimous witness of the early church, Christ through incarnation and redemption established a number of ritual acts either during his time with the apostles before and after Easter, or through his body the church under the influence of the Holy Spirit.[1] The two principal ones, baptism and the Eucharist, are explicitly attested to in the New Testament but the Orthodox, Oriental Orthodox and Roman Catholic Churches hold that there are at least five others – laying on of hands with oil to 'complete' baptism and confer the Holy Spirit ('chrismation' in the East, 'confirmation' in the West); confession of sins with absolution; anointing of the sick with oil; marriage and ordination to the church's ministry.[2] Tradition in the East calls these actions mysteries and in the West sacraments, but increasingly both sides use each other's terminology. Protestants and most Anglicans generally acknowledge only baptism and the Eucharist as full and complete sacraments of the gospel but some at least are often willing to call the other five 'sacramental ministrations'.[3]

Yet these mysteries are only manifestations of one great mystery-sacrament: Jesus Christ himself, the Son of God incarnate and glorified. What he accomplished in his death, resurrection and the sending of the Holy Spirit remains for ever the primordial sacramental mystery, the foundational saving event and the overflowing source of grace for his people.[4] Rooted and grounded in Christ, his body the church – the assembled Christian community – celebrates the sacramental mysteries bequeathed to her by him, the two principal ones being the sacraments of baptism and the Eucharist. In and through these two ritual actions the one mystery of Christ is manifested through the power of the Holy Spirit so that we can share in it.[5] Christ the incarnate and crucified God, exalted into glory and seated at the right hand of the Father, continues to act in the world today, effectively mediating the divine presence as he did during his earthly ministry: only his mode of working is different.

In addition, the holy scriptures, the inspired written record of those who witnessed the saving actions of Christ, were viewed in the early church as a kind of great sacrament through which Christ spoke.[6] Indeed it is a basic principle of the renewed liturgy in every church today that there can be no effective celebration of any of the sacramental mysteries without the reading and preaching of the word of God as well: no celebration without proclamation.[7]

The mystery – the saving life, death and resurrection of the incarnate Word – is given to us by the Spirit, therefore, principally in the great sacraments of scripture, baptism and the Eucharist. But the mystery also gives rise to a profusion of lesser mysteries or 'sacraments' which in turn mediate his one single mystery. Radiating out from Christ's sacramental act, they form a vast field of spiritual energy which comes to us through secondary mediations called sacramentals in the Roman Catholic Church and lesser mysteries in the eastern traditions. This rich sacramental economy is a sign of God's gracious self-accomodation to our created condition for we are not simply spiritual beings. We are creatures of flesh and blood who need a flesh and blood God.[8]

There is an obvious analogy between the sacramental rites the church carries out in worship and the one great mystery of the

death and resurrection of the incarnate Word. Just as the incarnation mediates God through flesh and blood, through the sheer
facticity and historicity of the incarnate Christ, so in Christian
worship, visible, tangible elements such as water, oil, bread and
wine, along with human activities such as ritual actions are taken
up by God and used to communicate his gracious presence.
Through these physical media, endowed with new energies (and
in the case of the Eucharist with new being), contemporary believers experience again the coming of Christ. Present in heaven, he
becomes manifest again among us so that we can participate in
the gift of his salvation.

Through the power of the Holy Spirit, Christ renders present
his original redeeming act in all its power for us, today, here and
now. The concrete actions through which Christ redeemed us
(supremely his death on the cross) are of course, being past
events, entirely unrepeatable. Yet through the church's worship
their saving presence and power is manifested and made vibrantly alive through the action of the living Lord Jesus who descends
in the Holy Spirit from his place in glory at the right hand of the
Father in response to the praise and petitions of his people.[9]

Even though as historical happenings the events themselves
belong to the past, the fire at their heart, the redeeming love
(agape) which brought Christ the incarnate God to his birth,
epiphany, ministry and transfiguration and culminated in his
passion, death and resurrection is actualised, realised and made
operative for us through the worship we celebrate in the power of
the Spirit.[10]

The Letter to the Hebrews teaches that Christ has become the
true high priest by being exalted to God's right hand in heaven
and that his perfect self-offering, made once and for all in time is
the final act by means of which God has purified the world from
sin. It is the end of all other sacrifices (Heb 9:11-28; 10:1-14). Christ,
priest and victim, the Lamb sacrificed in love standing before the
face of the Father, is himself the living centre of the liturgy of heaven,
the very embodiment of praise and glorification (Rev 5:1-14; 7:9-
17; 8:1-5). He is the perfect worshipper, offering adoration to his
Father in our name in the power of the Holy Spirit.[11] The same

Holy Spirit, given to him in perfect abundance in his resurrection, descends on the church through this heavenly liturgy, being sent by him when Christians celebrate their worship and implore his/ her coming (Acts 10:44-48).

Christ the high priest of heaven is the real celebrant who presides invisibly in every earthly service for, as a text in the Byzantine liturgy says, he is both the one who offers and is offered.[12] His presence is invisible yet real: acting through the symbolic mediation of the church and her ministers in the sacramental liturgical rites, he unites us as members of his body with the perfect worship he offers to the Father. In the various traditions of the early church (reflecting the Jewish mystical tradition of ascent to God's throne) the liturgy was understood as an act of ascension, a going up in the Spirit to the ascended Lord in heaven: 'Let us lift up our hearts! We have them to the Lord,' as one sings (in various different ways) in all the classical liturgies of the church.[13]

In Reformed Protestantism as well, under the influence of John Calvin, special emphasis is laid on the fact that in worship the ascended Christ lifts up the assembly of his people to the throne of glory. He offers the members of his earthly body to the Father in the liturgy of heaven where, accompanied by saints and angels, he celebrates God's glory in unending song. But it is all the work of grace. We do not ascend by our own power: rather we are carried up on high by Christ who first descends to us so that he may lift us God-ward on the wings of the Holy Spirit.[14]

Yet God does not wish us to be merely passive before him. The divine gifts offered to us have to be consciously received by us. We certainly cannot just reach out and grasp at God's presence for we are not capable of that. Yet through the grace granted us in worship God empowers us to respond to his summons, enabling us to take hold of him as he reaches down to become present to us. Assembled for our liturgical celebrations, we make ourselves present to God who makes himself present to us. In the words of the third Eucharistic Prayer of the Roman Mass, the aim of the liturgy is that we become ourselves an everlasting gift to the giver of all good things.

How can we actually do that? How can we, receiving the

breath of life, the earth and above all the gifts of Christ and the Holy Spirit, become ourselves a gift to God in return?

Traditional sacramental churches have always recognised the vital importance of liturgical prayer in accomplishing this. In his loving kindness, God's gift of himself in Christ to the apostles and disciples does not pertain only to past times. He has also made provision for that self-gift to go on being given throughout the ages to come until the end, so that all human beings and eventually the whole world might come to share his divine life. Hence the one saving mystery is manifested through the centuries in the mysteries of the church, in her sacramental worship in the Holy Spirit.

It is given to us today through the mediating forms of Christian worship which extend the original redeeming act of the incarnate Word into ever-widening circles of grace and divine presence. How can that be understood? It is helpful, as we have seen, to distinguish between primary and secondary mediations. By primary acts of mediation I mean the three principal 'sacramental mysteries' given us by God to enable us to receive this gift of new life: the mysteries of holy scripture, baptism and the Eucharist; by 'secondary mediations' those actions through which Christ extends his grace-giving presence into the world. We shall therefore consider first the three primary mediations before looking at some lesser ones. Since there are many lesser acts of sacramental mediation, I shall focus consideration on three only: the celebration of Christ's mysteries in the church's year, the mystery of the icon and the mystery of personal prayer.

A. THE SACRAMENTAL MYSTERY OF HOLY SCRIPTURE

The fathers, with the light of faith to guide them, saw everywhere – in the law, the prophets, the acts of Old Testament
kings and saints, here more clearly, there less – the figure of
Jesus, glowing in the half-darkness, until it emerges in the
gospel's brightness. What the ancients gradually and
wearily came to was as clear as noonday when the world's
own light shone: the keys to all mysteries were in Christ;
when this unfailing instrument, the Key of David, is put to
the explaining of scripture, the whole beauty, depth and
clarity of Christian allegory is seen for what it really is in the
liturgy. Its heart is the redeeming work of Christ and everything we read and pray in these texts points to that.

Odo Casel

The Bible, with its Old and New Testaments, is much more
than merely a collection of sacred texts or holy books. It is inspired
holy scripture, 'God-breathed writings' to borrow an expression
from the early church (2 Tim 3:16).[15] Scripture is one of the fundamental *loci* where we encounter the revealed mystery of Christ. It
is a tabernacle of his presence and a place of encounter. Through
the mediating words of holy scripture we come into direct contact
with God's living Word, Jesus Christ.

Notwithstanding the differences, there is an evident analogy
between how God's Word took flesh in Jesus Christ and is still
communicated to us in the sacramental mysteries, and the way in
which the Bible mediates the word of God to us today. In the
incarnation of the eternal Son, God's living Word assumed the
condition of our human existence with all its limitations including
the fragility and vulnerability of life in the world. This act of divine
generosity was only possible through an act of *kenosis* on Christ's
part, a freely chosen decision undertaken by God the Son in harmony with the will of the Father and the Holy Spirit to temporarily
lay down his glory and divine privileges so as to become capable
of sharing our human lot.[16]

In a not dissimilar way, God's communication of his word
through the written texts of holy scripture also requires a kind of

divine accommodation, a *kenosis*. Just as the Word-made-flesh shared all the temporal and spatial limitations of human life, so the word of God in the Bible comes to us with, in and under all the limitations of time and space entailed by human speech and writing. The human nature of Christ was like our own – inseparable from the social and political contexts in which he lived and died. It both bounded and limited the infinity of God's Word while yet revealing it through the prism of human words and actions: it manifested God even as it concealed him.

God's Son and Word did not just hover above us or sail around us like a ghost. He took flesh in real time, in a real place within a real context. Karl Barth spoke powerfully of the fact that the Word did not just 'become flesh' – rather he became Jewish flesh, thus rooting himself in a real people and a particular context. Similarly, Barth spoke of how God appropriates and takes human language to himself, transforming it, liberating it from its intrinsic limitations and elevating it to become a suitable vehicle for his Word.[17]

God's word became 'flesh' as holy scripture at specific times and in specific places throughout history in a marvellous co-operation between the Holy Spirit (the 'original' author in the sense of the deepest inspirer of the texts), and the human writers whom God called, set apart and sanctified to communicate his truth. The limitations of place, time and individual literary style typical of each of the biblical authors (as well as the historical process, the formation of the authorised 'canon' through which the church recognised which books are truly inspired and therefore normative for faith), became the human instrument for conveying God's word. Those limitations were not just bypassed but taken up, used and transfigured so that the writers could become bearers of the Word.[18]

Indeed those very limitations, far from being simply a negative obstacle to the communication of God's truth, are in fact powerful sacramental vehicles by means of which the word is wonderfully conveyed. Each writer's personality and literary ability (often very considerable) was placed in service of the Word of God so that, as the Greek Fathers taught, the sacred pages of the Bible may be justly called a kind of flesh and blood of the Word.[19]

The Bible is like an extension of the incarnation. It is a further ex-emplification of the sacramental principle revealed in Christ: the invisible and intangible God communicates with his creation by raising visible things to the level of symbols. Analogous to the sacramental appearances of bread and wine in the Eucharist, they are bearers of a mystery far surpassing them.

Because Christianity is an historical religion based on the real incarnation of God in time and space, the Catholic and Orthodox churches do not accept a fundamentalist reading of the Bible. Scripture mediates God's word in the most privileged way. It is the written record of God's living voice and a constant source for the church not only of life and consolation but also of challenge and rebuke. But the written text cannot simply be identified in a simplistic way with the Word as such, any more than the flesh of Christ may be simplistically described as 'God' in an absolute sense: by analogy with Christ's humanity, human words are joined to the Word and become transparent to the divine.[20]

Christ's 'flesh' (his humanity) is of course truly and perman-ently united to the Second Person of the Trinity, so much so that one can point to Jesus and say 'there is God'; but it would be theo-logically more accurate to say that Jesus is 'God incarnate'. The reality of his humanity is never swallowed up by his divinity, other-wise the very humanity he came to save would be endangered. Instead, taken up and united to God and elevated far above its limitations, it is permeated with divine energies. The humanity of Jesus, rooted and grounded in his divine person, is like a glorious stained glass window suffused and permeated with the light of his divine nature, which shines through it but is never confused with it or simply absorbed into it.

The Hebrew scriptures say that when God looked on the world he had created he pronounced it to be very good (Gen 1:31). Christianity repeats that positive affirmation when it insists that notwithstanding the fall and the world's sinfulness, God gave up his only Son that it might have life in his name. The created world for which Christ gave his life is not doomed simply to be absorbed into God like a drop of water falling into an ocean. The saving work of Jesus is so marvellous precisely because he not only saves us from sin but because he also saves us from being overwhelmed by God.[21]

In the flesh-and-blood-humanity which Christ assumed, saved, transfigured and brought into heaven in his ascension, God assures us that the created order's existence is eternally affirmed. It will never be destroyed or negated by the divine. That is one of the major differences between a Christian and a Hindu or a Buddhist worldview: created nature is saved, not absorbed or abolished.

In a similar way the texts of holy scripture, connected as a medium to God's Word, serve as its filter. Scripture is the sacrament in which the revealed mystery of Christ has been recorded and is transmitted to the church throughout the ages. It is one of the fundamental disclosure zones where God reveals his will and our constant reference point for entry into the mystery of Christ. It is never an end in itself, but a created medium utilised by God for contact with himself. Fundamentalist approaches to scripture tend to deny the nitty-gritty facticity of the incarnation by undermining the reality of historical processes and created limitations.

They are akin to the ancient heresies of Docetism and Monophysitism which denied that the Son of God had assumed a real humanity, thereby making everything in him divine and interpreting the divine itself as something essentially abstract and static; or with the heresy of Nestorianism which distinguished Christ's divine person and nature from his human nature so much that it risked making the latter substantially independent, thus sundering the unity of his being altogether.[22] Both heresies tend to undermine the real and abiding union of the divine and human in Christ.

With a firm sense, therefore, of how scripture mirrors the incarnate Word (one divine person and nature who has assumed a human nature) one should not fear to affirm the human reality of the biblical texts, locating them in their historical, social and political contexts. That can be an invaluable help towards investigating their content, illuminating their forms and elucidating their meaning: anything else amounts to a denial of the incarnation.

Yet we receive these scriptures as the Book of the Church. The

Bible is made up not just of separate books, independent fragments (or even fragments of fragments) gathered together by various editors throughout the centuries. While they certainly began
their life that way, the Christian community (as the Jews also did
for the Hebrew scriptures), gathered the fragments and combined
them into a unified whole in which each individual part illuminates all the others. It is the whole Bible that is the definitive witness
to God's plan. For the Catholic and Orthodox churches, the one
great mystery of Christ, announced, prefigured and prophesied
in the Hebrew and Greek scriptures of the Old Testament where it
lies latent, concealed within a host of mysteries and symbols in
narratives, poems and laments, is made clear in the New
Testament.[23]

Having seen the face of God in Christ and received the illumination of the Holy Spirit after Pentecost, the apostles and evangelists saw that the unveiling of revelation lifted the mystery of
Christ out of the shadows and images of the earlier covenant. It
now stands open, bathed in the fullness of light revealed by the
events of Easter (2 Cor 3:7-18; Lk 24:27; Jn 5:39-40). Every one of the
inspired writers of the New Testament, especially the four evangelists, St Paul, the writer of Hebrews and St Peter, reflecting on
the older scriptures found therein some aspect of the resplendent
fullness of revelation as they saw the light of Christ shining retro-
spectively on them.

Yet since the Bible is the 'Book of the Church', consensus about
which writings really are inspired was reached largely on the
basis of which were chosen for proclamation in the church's worship assemblies. The common prayer of the liturgy has always
been and still is today the natural environment in which the reading of the Bible has flourished.[24] Because the books compose a collection, gathered together in the canon, no single book ought to be
interpreted apart from the witness of the others, nor should one
book or author (Paul for example) be taken as the final word in explaining the contents of the whole, even allowing for the fact that
not all books have the same importance.[25]

In addition to the theological criteria required for discerning
that, a certain Christian common sense is also necessary. One does

not have to be a theological genius to recognise pretty quickly that
the Letter of Jude is rather less significant than the Letter to the
Hebrews or the third letter of John than the gospel ascribed to
him. Yet that does not deny them their own, limited importance
and their legitimate place in the canon. In practice, that means no
Paul without James, no Luke without John, no Matthew without
Galatians and, above all, none of them without the constant backdrop of the Jewish scriptures.

Consequently, three things need to be stressed in considering
the unified nature of the collection of sacred books recognised and
cherished by the church. The first is that the Bible is the written,
codified and 'canonised' sacramental mediation of the mystery of
Christ. In addition to analysing it critically, a much deeper and
more important task has to be performed. It has to be read 'contemplatively' in faith, with prayer, reverence and love, if it is to
manifest the mystery to which it bears witness.

Like the sacramental liturgy in general, the sacrament of the
word is meant to be celebrated, proclaimed, spoken, sung and
broken open by preaching so that its hidden depths may flare out
and its inexhaustible springs of life flow forth in every generation.
Both Luther and Karl Barth rightly asserted that it becomes existentially and effectively God's word – gospel or good news –
above all as it is proclaimed in worship, preaching and teaching.
The Second Vatican Council likewise taught that when scripture
is read in the worship assembly Christ truly speaks to us today.[26]

Next, in reading contemplatively one needs to make use of a
synthetic methodology. In medieval monasticism that type of
reading was bound up with the spiritual practice of *lectio divina*. It
meant developing a sense of how each individual book and every
part of each one interacts with and casts light on all the others. In
Catholic theology, a key principle for growing in knowledge of
the revealed mystery is this: to allow the individual mysteries of
Christ recorded in scripture to lead us together into his one great
mystery. Each one is related to the others and to the whole, in such
a way that deeper knowledge of one entails further comprehension of the others. There is no better place to do this than the
church's liturgy, the supreme school for hearing and learning

God's word. The liturgy, with its connection-making capacities, alerts us to the interconnectedness of the mysteries in the one great mystery of Christ.[27]

To take just one example, that of Christmas Midnight Mass: in that context the liturgy of the word combines the promise of Isaiah (9:1-6) supremely fulfilled at Christmas that a child will be born to us who will be called 'wonder-counsellor' and 'mighty God', with the account of the birth of Jesus recorded in the third gospel (Lk 2: 15-20). It comments on this first reading through the use of Psalm 95(96) whose deepest meaning is disclosed when it is used to announce God's coming to rule the earth in the incarnation. In the second reading (Tit 2:11-14) Paul reminds Titus that the grace of God has been revealed, making salvation possible for all, but that we await its final revelation on the last day. In the meantime we are exhorted to live self-restrained and upright lives in hope. That last great appearance is called significantly in the original Greek text Christ's 'epiphany', thus re-connecting his final coming with his first.

Finally all of this is interwoven with texts such as the *Gloria* of the Mass (first sung at Christ' birth), the very rich ancient prayer texts spoken by the President of the liturgical assembly and the use of a verse from Psalm 2 (7) as the entrance chant (*Introit*): 'The Lord said to me you are my Son: it is I who have begotten you this day!' (*Dominus dixit ad me, Filius meus es tu*), to bring home in the most synthetic, holistic way imaginable that the Old and New Testament readings and the prayers of the liturgy are meant to focus our attention on the birth of the incarnate God as Saviour and Messiah. Thus the liturgy itself is the primary catechesis and the place of theological interpretation. The same can be asserted of every liturgical feast and especially the paschal liturgy, the centre of the church's year. That is where holy scripture is at home.

The theologian's task consists in cultivating the capacity given as a gift from God (but also demanding study and reflection) of recognising the connections between the mysteries, what the First Vatican Council called the *nexus mysteriorum*, the network or inter-connectedness of the mysteries.[28] That is why the task of theological interpretation is pursued as much (indeed much more) by way of intuition and imagination, analogy and sensitivity to symbol and metaphor, as through academic training or professional expertise, important though these are. A theologian who cannot 'do' analogy or recognise connections between the multi-faceted aspects of the mysteries is doomed to certain failure. As in life so in revelation and the theology which comments on it: truth discloses itself above all in the relationships we are able to discern between realities.

This principle is supremely true in reading or rather contemplating the sacrament of holy scripture in the Bible, the church's book. If I want to have as complete a picture as possible of who Christ is and of what he achieved, then I cannot content myself with reading only John or Paul as individual authors. I have to read each one in the light of all the others. I also need to pray the texts, using especially the Psalms, the prayer book of both church and synagogue and the mainstay of the church's worship since at least the 4th century. In those inspired songs, as the church Fathers recognised, one hears the echo of the voice of the living Christ, crying out to the Father both in joy and agony.

Such a method of reading holy scripture is spiritually very demanding. It calls for a kind of *kenosis,* an emptying out of one's own plans, desires and ideas so as to become free and open to God's Word. It demands self-disciplined attentiveness and most importantly repeated prayer. There is a liturgy of private reading that corresponds to the law of the church's public worship. Invocation (*epiclesis*) of the Holy Spirit, appealing to God for light is an indispensable condition for making the memory of Christ (his *anamnesis*) in which he becomes really present. Only such reading is able to enlighten and confer spiritual understanding. The monastic traditions of the west have always known that sacred reading or *lectio divina* is hard work, the work of God (*opus Dei*) and that it makes its own ascetical demands.[29] But it bears great fruit in the joy and delight of communion with God granted by the Holy Spirit through our pondering of the *sacra pagina,* the sacred page. One reads in the prophet Isaiah:

With joy you will draw water from the wells of salvation.
And you will say in that day:

> Give thanks to the Lord,
> call on his name;
> make known his deeds among the nations;
> proclaim that his name is exalted. (Is 12:3-4)

Through contemplating in prayer, praise, faith and a spirit of wonder the marvellous sacrament of the Bible with its many mysteries, the light of God's presence breaks through the text in marvellous ways. It irradiates the word written, read and preached, revealing through it the mystery of Christ, God's primordial Word.

Finally, the scriptural word has to become flesh and blood in us. It has to be realised in life and action so that the written word can become incarnate in an entirely new context far beyond the very different one in which it was originally set down. Only by being existentially appropriated in a living way can the sacred book of the church become a privileged 'disclosure-zone' for God. His presence to us has to shine out with transforming power in us, in both communities and individuals. Only if the text of the Bible, received as the sacrament of God's presence, is like the bread of the Eucharist broken, given, shared and consumed, can there be living and transforming contact with the mystery of Christ, of which the New Testament writers are the primary and permanent witnesses. That is why scripture has been given us by God: so that we may become ourselves the message.[30]

B. THE SACRAMENTAL MYSTERY OF BAPTISM

O useful element and clear!
My sacred wash and cleanser here,
My first consigner unto those
Fountains of life, where the Lamb goes!
What sublime truths and wholesome themes,
Lodge in thy mystical, deep streams!
Such as dull man can never find
Unless that Spirit lead his mind,
Which first upon thy face did move,
And hatched all with his quick'ning love.

Henry Vaughan

In holy scripture this mystery has such an overwhelming significance that a great variety of images and metaphors are used to describe it such as illumination (Eph 5:8), rebirth and renewal (2 Tit 3:5) and clothing with Christ (Gal 3:27). One of the most suggestive images, the one which has most influenced Christian reflection on this sacrament throughout history is contained in the sixth chapter of Paul's Letter to the Romans (Rom 6:1-14), the importance of which is demonstrated by the fact that in the Roman liturgy it has been appointed since ancient times as the New Testament reading in the Mass of the Easter Vigil. Describing how the newly-baptised Christian is called to break definitively with sin, Paul elucidates his vision of baptism as a personal sharing in the one great mystery of Christ's death and resurrection:

How can we who died to sin go on living in it? Do you not know that all of us who have been baptised into Christ Jesus were baptised into his death? Therefore we have been buried with him by baptism into death, so that, just as Christ was raised from the dead by the glory of the Father, so we too might walk in newness of life. For if we have been united with him in a death like his, we will certainly be united with him in a resurrection like his. We know that our old self was crucified with him so that the body of sin might be destroyed, and we might no longer be enslaved to sin. For whoever has died is freed from sin. But if we have died with

Christ, we believe that we will also live with him. We know that Christ being raised from the dead, will never die again; death no longer has dominion over him. The death he died, he died to sin, once for all; but the life he lives, he lives to God. So you also must consider yourselves dead to sin and alive to God in Christ Jesus.

Central to this passage is the awareness that in baptism something is done to us by God. It does not depend on any activity of our own beyond being present and suffering God's action on us: we are the passive recipients of a gift. A similar emphasis on the gratuity of the gift, coupled with the idea of baptism as entry into new life, is found in the later Letter to the Ephesians:

But God, who is rich in mercy, out of the great love with which he loved us even when we were dead through our trespasses, made us alive together with Christ – by grace you have been saved – and raised us up with him and seated us with him in the heavenly places in Christ Jesus, so that in the ages to come he might show the immeasurable riches of his grace in kindness toward us in Christ Jesus. For by grace you have been saved through faith, and this is not your own doing; it is the gift of God – not the result of works so that no one may boast. (Eph 2: 4-9)

For Paul, baptism confers a real participation in the mystery of Christ's death and resurrection. Commenting on the symbolism of total immersion in the baptismal waters, the method of baptism most frequently used in the early church, still the norm among Orthodox Christians, obligatory for Baptists and at least an available option nowadays for Catholics, Paul identifies in the ritual action a likeness (*homoioma*) of the death and resurrection of Christ. Just as after his death Jesus was placed in the tomb and went down among the dead, so the Christian is plunged bodily into the waters of the font; yet as Jesus was raised again by the Father on the third day, so too the Christian emerges from the watery tomb as from a spiritual 'womb', regenerated, a new-born member of Christ's body the church. It is the ritual image of the *kenosis* and exaltation of the Lord in his descent into the tomb, resurrection from the dead and reception of the Holy Spirit.

The Christian is filled with the Holy Spirit, God's eschatological (i.e. final and perfect) gift, his living *pneuma* or breath and receives a new orientation to eternal life in heaven as his or her goal.[31] Paul never loses sight of the eschatological (in this case meaning 'future') orientation of baptism: we are indeed really initiated into Christ and called to newness of life but the resurrection of the body still awaits us in the future: 'We will certainly be united with him in a resurrection like his.' Yet this spiritual birth into new life occurs through a very humble medium: immersion in water accompanied by simple sacramental words invoking the grace of the Father, the Son and the Holy Spirit. It is not magic but sacramental liturgy: as St Augustine famously put it, the word is joined to the water and the sacrament is brought about.[32]

The fact that it is done to us by another and not by ourselves is emphasised.[33] In the gift of baptism Christ empowers the church to communicate to her members, through a ritual act, what he achieved for us through the *kenosis* of his death. That death was anything but a beautiful sacred ritual. It entailed an agony of painful and humiliating suffering. Nor was the resurrection which followed it a ritual performance: Christ was really raised to life by God through the exaltation and transformation of his crucified body. But in baptism we die symbolically by having a ritual enacted upon us which carries out a likeness of Christ's death and resurrection.

The rite of baptism involves sacramental symbolism of the strongest kind. In carrying out the ritual, which is done in the power of the Holy Spirit, the act of Christ's original passage (*pascha*) from death to new life, the redemptive act accomplished by him is enacted on us, and its saving reality imparted and applied to us. We are loosed from sin, cleansed and renewed through the love of God poured into our hearts by the Holy Spirit. The symbolic ritual action opens to us a share in the reality it conveys. Our world today often suffers from a truncated understanding of symbolism. It is important to recover its older, fuller meaning if we wish to understand both the New Testament and the action of the church's liturgy. For ancient authors such as Paul, a symbol was never just a bare or empty sign. Nowadays we often hear it said that something is 'only' a symbol or a 'mere' symbol but such an impoverished understanding misses the point: a true symbol is always anything but 'mere' or 'only'.[34]

For St Paul, closely followed by the Fathers of the church, the great Latin scholastics, Luther, and even to some extent Calvin, as well of course as for the historic liturgies of Christendom, symbols were never just empty signs of absent things. Rather, they in some sense convey the very realities they represent. Indeed they re-present those things in the strongest possible way. In baptism, the symbolic act of plunging symbolises the drowning and eradication of sin through the death of one's old self while the dramatic rising up out of the waters symbolises the regeneration of the self through resurrection into life. It is a real participation in the past act of Christ's salvation and an equally real anticipation of its fulfilment on the last day. Past and future meet in the sacramental present.

In the same act in which it is celebrated and ritually symbolised the reality itself actually occurs. As the church Fathers put it, it is accomplished mystically. 'Mystical' in their understanding (a word coined by them), did not as we have seen, entail the kind of subjective emotional experience it tends to designate today. Rather, coming to us from the Greek word *mystikos* (secret or hidden), via Paul's use of the word mystery, it denoted the secret action of the Holy Spirit, who conveys the reality of Christ's redeeming act to the Christian through interior regeneration and renewal. At the same time as it is effectually symbolised in the ritual, it is also activated in the heart of the newly-baptised, igniting there a spark of grace, inserting a spring of spiritual energy which begins to well up into eternal life. The sacramental mystery of baptism is the gateway to the mystery of Christ.[35]

Emerging reborn from the waters of the font, one is invited by Christ to enter the communion of the church and to follow the path of discipleship mapped out by the Lord, walking consciously in God's presence. Baptismal life is the doorway to ecclesial life, life in Christ's body.[36] It is never sufficient (at least for an adult

though infant baptism raises other issues), merely to have 'suffered' the ritual action of the sacrament in the sense of having had
it 'performed objectively' upon oneself. Paul and the other New
Testament writers insist that the only adequate response to the
revelation of the mystery is living faith which finds expression in
the transformation of one's life. The spiritual death so powerfully
symbolised by the rite is meant to lead through the renunciation
of one's 'old self' with its narrow, limited understanding and egoistic habits, to resurrection into a new mode of existence, becoming a new creature in fact as well as name. To correspond to
Christ's will for his followers, that new life ought to be rich in
faith, hope, love and works of charity undertaken freely for the
good of one's neighbour.

Baptism, although passively received, has to pass over into
action through co-operation with grace since one has been adopted
by God as his beloved child in Christ.[37] The Christian life remains
always radically baptismal since it involves a daily commitment
to an ecstatic way of life, a freely-chosen going out from one's old
self (*ekstasis*) so as to enter into a living relationship with God.
Baptism is an invitation to take the daily path of *kenosis*, the path
traced out by Christ.

The Holy Spirit draws us out of the various prisons, psychological or spiritual, in which we are held captive, strips us of our
prison garb and leads us into the freedom of faith, into a life lived
in openness to God's commanding presence.

Faith, at first flickering and feeble, gradually grows into experience. Through prayer, the gift received and the ability to respond
to the Holy Spirit who lives in the heart through baptismal grace,
ought to take possession of one's life, making one's whole being
an offering of thanks and praise.

C. THE EUCHARIST: THE FULLNESS OF THE SACRAMENTAL MYSTERY

1. Effective Recall of the Mystery of Christ

Baptism leads to the communal celebration of the Eucharist, the bath of regeneration to the table of spiritual nourishment, the mystery of death and resurrection to the gift of imperishable life. In Christian understanding *kenosis*, (self-emptying) always leads to *koinonia* (communion) with the risen Lord and his people. The New Testament writers did not often mention the Eucharist explicitly, yet when they did (in the three so-called synoptic gospels, in Paul's first letter to the Corinthians and more obliquely in the fourth gospel and Book of Revelation) what they said is so significant that it casts enormous light on the mystery of Christ. That is very apparent in what is probably the oldest account of the institution of the Eucharist, contained in Chapter 11 of the first letter to the Corinthians.

The context of the passage is important. Paul scolded some greedy and self-indulgent members of that community for their idiosyncratic practices at the celebration of the Lord's Supper. They had, it seems, been rushing ahead of others and even getting drunk. Paul reminded them of what the supper means and therefore what it ought to entail.

He claimed to have received this teaching 'from the Lord'. Yet, as he almost certainly never met the Lord before Christ's death and resurrection, we may assume that he actually received it from the tradition of the apostolic community as that which was 'handed on'. The Eucharist was handed over to the church by Christ, which in turn handed it on to Paul so that he could pass it on to others. This highlights the crucial role the Christian community plays in communicating Christ. To receive from the church is in effect to receive from Christ himself – for in the mind of Paul, Christ the head and the church his body may never be separated (1 Cor 12: 12-31).

Christian tradition in the best sense is more than just a static collection of fossilised religious remains preserved in a museum of sacred artefacts or a warmly pious nostalgia for the past. It is a dynamic process driven by the Holy Spirit in which the Christian community passes on the revealed mysteries of faith, and the liturgical customs in which they find articulation, from those who have gone before. Yet although it is made up of links with the past, it is too narrow a perspective simply to identify tradition with the past. Tradition is an activity, a living process in which what was transmitted from the Lord to the apostolic community at the beginning, is handed on and developed as the church journeys towards her Lord, who comes to meet her from the future. The Spirit, whom the Lord promised would remind the disciples of all that he had said (Jn 14:26), leads the Christian community into all truth (Jn 16:13). Just as in the individual lives of Christians, here too the Holy Spirit 'comes to help us in our weakness (Rom 8:26).[38]

Paul reminds the Corinthians (1 Cor 11:17-32) that Jesus instituted this supper on the night of his betrayal, when he identified the broken bread with his body that would be given up to death on Golgotha and the cup of wine with his blood that would be poured out there in sacrifice. He declared that the body he was giving to them was broken for them and that the cup was that of the 'new covenant' to be ratified in his blood. Modern scholars have debated intensely what the original context of that first supper celebrated by Jesus actually was: the Passover or another kind of Jewish meal? Are we to hear echoes of Jewish prayers of blessing or thanksgiving – or maybe of both?[39]

In addition, recent research not only pays attention to the (correctly) much-stressed continuity between the Lord's Supper and the Passover but also examines how the supper picks up and evokes themes from Jewish Temple worship. Reading Paul alongside Hebrews and the Book of Revelation it looks as if the church's tradition wove themes associated with the Passover into those typical of the great Jewish Day of Atonement.[40]

Christ's earliest disciples would surely have had little difficulty grasping immediately that the context of this eucharistic meal was heavily redolent of sacrifice, but the last few lines of Paul's account are the most significant.[41] Here he presents one of the first theologies of the Eucharist, showing how in the context of Jesus' thanksgiving to the Father, the eating and drinking is essentially connected with his redeeming death, the heart of the mystery of Christ:

... and when he had given thanks, he broke it and said,

'This is my body that is for you. Do this in remembrance of me … This cup is the New Covenant in my blood. Do this, as often as you drink it, in remembrance of me.' For as often as you eat this bread and drink the cup, you proclaim the Lord's death, until he comes (1 Cor 11:24-26).

It is always important to pay attention to the original text of the New Testament but perhaps never more so than here. What Paul wrote (*touto poieite … eis ten hemen anamnesin*) might be literally translated as 'Do (or make) this as my memorial.' He tells the Corinthians that Jesus commanded them not just to recite a form of words but to perform an action with the bread and cup in a context of thanksgiving. As he says in an earlier chapter it is 'the cup of blessing which we bless.' The Lord's Supper is a ritual act centred on the taking and breaking of bread and the blessing of a cup of wine as God himself is blessed for his gifts to us in creation and redemption, God's own blessing of us. The Jewish context, whatever it may have been precisely, makes that abundantly clear. We are given an action, something to do, not just a form of words, something to say.[42]

The most significant word used is *anamnesis* (*anamnesin* in the accusative form used by Paul). The rediscovery of the original meaning of this word by scholars in the 20th century has finally gone some way toward clarifying what the Catholic and Orthodox churches mean when they describe the Eucharist as a 'sacrifice'. The word reveals a very Jewish way of understanding God's dealings with the world stemming from how they celebrate the Passover and other feasts. *Anamnesis* signifies 'objective memorial' in the sense that as one ritually proclaims God's past act in the present celebration, that past event becomes effective again. Time is conquered because the living God can never be limited by it. God can reactivate the essence of a past event in all its power, in response to the invocation made by his people here and now, an invocation he has himself commanded them to make and which he empowers through the Holy Spirit.[43]

Yet the original, historical event is never repeated. It cannot be for what is past is past. In the Jewish understanding of the world, time was real. It was not just an illusion. Past events, therefore, could literally never be repeated. Yet the inner essence of a saving act carried out by God in the past, its deepest meaning and power, are capable of being rendered present and effective at a later time, so that God can produce the same saving results in a new context as he did in the past event. The classic example in Judaism is the Exodus from Egypt, proclaimed in every Passover with words of compelling power: this is the night when Israel came out of Egypt. Of course the new historical context in which the past event is recalled and proclaimed is entirely different from that in which the original event occurred; but what remains the same is the motivating impulse lying at the heart of God's original deed: his saving, redeeming love (*agape*).

This Jewish understanding was taken over into the Christian vision of Christ saving the world through the sacrificial offering of himself, an offering rooted in God's eternal plan, translated into flesh and blood in the incarnation, effected on the cross, ratified in God's raising Christ from death, and given eternal validity in his enthronement at the Father's right hand. Christ's sacrifice (which included not just his death but his entire life of obedience including his resurrection and ascension) was, according to its historical actuality, unrepeatable. Some wise words of Otto Semmelroth are helpful here:

> It should, however, be noted that a 'continuation' of the historical sacrificial act of Christ ... must always be taken into account – because no one enters eternity without his history. He who enters eternity at death is marked by his whole history. Indeed the whole history which here on earth was spread out over a succession of moments goes with him into eternity, where there is no succession. 'Their works follow them' (Rev 14:13). Hence Christ is eternally with the Father along with his sacrifice – which was the fulfilment of a whole life under the sign of obedience (Phil 2:8). His sacrifice has an eternal mode of being, a supra-historical as well as a historical one, though it is numerically the one sacrifice.[44]

Every time the church celebrates the ritual meal he bequeathed to her, the sacrificial love which animated Jesus' obedience to the

Father and led him to the cross is reactivated by him for us. In the great act of thanksgiving (*eucharistia*) the Christian community, reminding God in prayer and supplication of his own loving remembrance of us and the mercy and compassion with which he created and redeemed us, enumerates with gratitude those mighty acts – in truth the several movements of Christ's one great symphony of redemption – by which he saved the world. One of the most comprehensive 'lists' is probably that contained in the Byzantine liturgy ascribed to St Basil the Great:

> Therefore also, O Master,
> remembering his saving passion,
> his life-giving cross,
> his burial for three days,
> together with his resurrection from the dead
> and his ascension into heaven,
> as well as his being seated at your right hand,
> O God and Father,
> and finally his glorious and awesome second coming ...
> we offer you your own from what is yours
> in all for all![45]

This effective, dynamic power of remembering lies at the heart of the eucharistic celebration. It is the Christian community's Spirit-inspired recalling before God of past grace, confident that in remembering God's deeds in this way, the same saving act can be made operative once again.

If sacrifice had been understood in this way in the Christian Church – in terms of the Jewish and patristic context of effective recall, blessing and thanksgiving – then centuries of sterile debate and painful polemics between Catholics and Protestants might have been avoided. Protestants feared (sometimes with good reason) that the Catholic Church's insistence on the Eucharist as sacrifice risks making the outrageous claim that the death of Jesus on the cross must have been somehow insufficient, so that to their profound distaste, Jesus is imagined somehow to die again in every Mass. They feared thus that his unique sacrifice was actually held by Catholics to be repeatable, in direct contradiction of the

New Testament's explicit affirmation of the once-and-for-all character of Christ's death (Heb 9:25-28; 10:12-14).[46]

In most Protestant traditions since at least the 18th century, the notion of objective remembrance was either completely lost or gradually whittled away until the Eucharist was understood primarily as an act of psychological recall. The Lord's Supper seems to have been seen as a privileged occasion for thinking about the death of Jesus as we reap its spiritual fruits in the present. Danger also lurks in such a viewpoint: the perspective narrows, sacrifice is identified too exclusively with death and the objective aspect of memorial is itself sacrificed to a notion of merely subjective recall.

The relative neglect of the Eucharist in most Protestant churches until the early 20th century (something never intended by either Luther or Calvin), and even still in some quarters today, is a sign that, as its original meaning was lost, it often ceased to have much significance in Protestant spirituality. Today, however, the mainstream Protestant churches are recovering much of the older theology of the Eucharist with great benefit for their spiritual life and Christian witness in the world.[47]

Catholics for their part also largely lost the original meaning of objective memorial lying at the heart of eucharistic celebration, and like their Protestant brothers and sisters became fixated on the idea of sacrifice as death alone. However, the virtual freezing of the Roman Church's liturgical life through the fixing of officially imposed printed books after the upheavals of the 16th century had the advantage that it avoided the hatchet job done on early Christian liturgical tradition by the Protestant Reformers: it did at least preserve many of the treasures of ancient Christian worship intact even if as though preserved in a kind of liturgical fridge.[48]

Against some Protestant Reformers (particularly Zwingli), the Roman Catholic Church argued correctly that the Mass is much more than just a service of remembrance in a narrow, subjective sense, insisting rather that its celebration facilitates the effective realisation among us today of the original event of Christ's sacrifice.[49]

However, despite the generally moderate and traditional presentation of eucharistic doctrine by the Council of Trent, on which

Eastern Christian tradition had considerable influence,[50] later Catholic attempts to explain what occurs at Mass were often clumsy, bordering at times on the bizarre and even on the downright weird. Jesus was actually imagined by some to undergo a new kind of *kenosis* through consenting to the indignity of existing under the form of food!

Catholics also became accustomed to using the word *sacrifice* with little reference to its biblical and early Christian meaning and without clearly delineating the unique, unrepeatable, historical offering of Christ in his cross and resurrection from its sacramental making present in the repeated liturgical celebrations of the church. One-sidedness and a style of debate in which insufficient effort was spent listening to what the other was really trying to say, effectively polarised understanding between Catholics and Protestants on this matter for many centuries. Theological polemics leave little room for subtlety.

In the 20th century, however, thanks to a new ecumenical openness on the part of the churches, increased mutual understanding based on dialogue, scholarly research into early liturgical texts and above all living contact with the Eastern churches, a better understanding of the word *anamnesis* (memorial), has allowed us to resolve many past difficulties. In the Eucharist we do not – in any sense – ever repeat Christ's death. That is simply impossible. As Paul wrote to the Romans:

> We know that Christ being raised from the dead, will never die again; death no longer has dominion over him. The death he died, he died to sin, once for all; but the life he lives, he lives to God ... (Rom 6:9-10)

The celebration of the Eucharist is neither a psychological act, a subjective recalling of Jesus while sharing a sacred meal of bread and wine, nor a new sacrifice with a repeated death. The unanimous tradition of the churches of east and west in the first millennium testifies to that. It is rather an active memorial in the strong Jewish sense: as we perform the rite itself in obedience to Christ's command, the core reality of the original event of salvation, his passing from death to life, is rendered present and operative among us. Christ himself is in truth the real 'performer', the real celebrant of every Eucharist.[51]

We lend our hands and voices to the performance of the rite but it is definitely the Lord's Supper. And of course the actual historical event as such is not made present since that belongs to past time. But through the action of the Holy Spirit, the inner meaning and power of the event, the love Christ revealed in becoming the Father's gift to us and offering himself to God as a sacrifice for the redemption of the world, is truly made present.

Given what the New Testament announces about Jesus after Easter, that is not at all difficult to grasp. The church confesses a living, triumphant Saviour since Christians proclaim that Christ was raised from dead by the Father's power (Easter Sunday) exalted to God's right hand (Ascension) and poured out the Holy Spirit on the church (Pentecost). He continues to send the same Spirit today especially when the church assembles for her worship. In the power of that Spirit, the risen, glorified Jesus is made present and the inner kernel of his sacrifice, accomplished literally and historically in time past and essentially unrepeatable, is made operative again among us today.[52]

No other sacrifice for sins exists than the one Jesus offered historically: but he is himself that sacrifice as both priest and victim, the risen one who stands in the presence of the Father in heaven. He is the Lamb ordained for sacrifice before the foundation of the world but raised after death into the glory of God. As Christians celebrate the Lord's Supper, the Holy Spirit makes Christ present so that he can offer us with himself to the Father. We are caught up into his redeeming, sacrificial action and offered up by him ourselves on high. The celebration of the liturgy is the passage of the Christian assembly from death to life, from time into eternity, from here to there, from the past to the future.

Yet Catholics and Orthodox would wish to stress another aspect too, one which has always found expression in the historic rites of the church. As we are taken up into Christ's offering and in turn offered by him to God, we are also granted the capacity to offer Christ ourselves: his sacrifice is given to us by God to be our own. All human offerings, tainted by sin and self-interest, are unacceptable to God who in their place has given us Christ as the only sacrifice truly pleasing to him.

That is why both traditions place so much emphasis on the transformation of the being or substance (which is deeper than their physical reality) of the gifts of bread and wine we place on the altar during the liturgy. These created things, 'bread to offer which earth has given ... fruit of the vine and work of human hands', are symbols of ourselves and of the world we inhabit. They are fruits of nature formed by human artifice into products destined to nourish our bodies and gladden our hearts (Ps 103(104):14-15). We bring them before God as our presents offered in the name of nature and the world of human work. They are the offerings brought by Christ's faithful people who share in his priesthood by virtue of having been baptised.

When we present them to God at the preparation of the gifts in the liturgy, carrying them forward in procession and placing them on the Lord's Table, they symbolise the offering of our very selves. But they are not *as yet* a true sacrifice: rather they are on the way to becoming one. We do not offer a sacrifice of bread and wine to God in the Mass for our offerings have to be transformed into God's own gift, the sacrifice of Christ which he gives to us.[53]

The Holy Spirit descends and transforms the inner being of our gifts. In this marvellous exchange, Christ becomes sacramentally present in our midst by means of them; Christ who is the one and only sacrifice acceptable to the Father. He allows us to become concelebrants of the heavenly liturgy which he brings down to earth or into which he raises us up, depending on which spatial metaphor we prefer. Both are appropriate but equally limited ways of describing the mystery.

In baptism we were entirely passive before God who did not require any co-operation on our part in saving us and granting us admittance to the mystery. In the Eucharist also, the primary init-iative lies always with God. He saved us through the sacrifice of Christ and puts that sacrifice into our hands at the Lord's Supper by transforming our gifts into his present, the real presence of the risen Jesus whom we receive from him. However, God does not wish to leave us merely passive recipients: he wills to empower us to offer. As the second Eucharistic Prayer of the renewed Roman

Mass puts it, we are called to stand in his presence and serve him. God certainly finds us prostrate on the earth but he never leaves us there. Instead he raises us up, conferring on us as his people the dignity of a royal priesthood which is given to all the baptised.[54]

St Maximus the Confessor emphasised this paradoxical truth that our offering of anything to God depends entirely on God's having given it to us in the first place:

> Scripture exhorts us to offer gifts to God so that we may become conscious of his infinite goodness. For God receives our offerings as if they were entirely our own gifts and he had not already given us anything. In this way God's untold goodness towards us is fully evident, for when we offer him things which in reality are his own he accepts them as if they were ours, and he makes himself our debtor as though they were not already his.[55]

If that is true in general it is even more so within the liturgy, for God, like a mothering fount of infinite love, contrives this means to empower us his beloved children so that we may become capable of returning to him what he has freely given us in the first place: his beloved Son who offered himself for our salvation. God's gift of grace takes shape in us as our responsive gratitude. In becoming the church's sacrifice of praise and thanks – its Eucharist – the gift given at the Lord's Supper perfectly completes the circle of God's loving descent to us in our ascent to him, through, with and in Christ, priest and victim, the perfect sacrifice.

The Romans had a Latin saying *do ut des* which speaks of human self-interest in the giving of gifts. If we are really honest we would surely have to admit that much human gift-giving is in fact prompted by benevolent self-interest. That can lead to unfortunate instances of manipulation such as, for example, parents putting pressure on children to pass examinations by promising them expensive gifts because the parents need their own social or familial affirmation; or when someone tries to 'buy' another's love with gifts and presents. Yet it is not always a bad thing, as the gifts exchanged in diplomatic visits made by heads of state can remind us. It is also an acceptable way of oiling the mechanisms which help society to function smoothly.[56]

Such a notion, deeply rooted in the human psyche, has always found religious expression in every culture. Offerings have always been made, whose primary purpose was to influence or placate the gods by making them gifts. The Jewish-Christian scriptures, however, insist that it is inappropriate – and indeed utterly impossible – to behave that way with the God revealed in the Old Covenant and as the Father of Jesus Christ. The Hebrew prophets and psalms made it abundantly clear that, unlike the false gods of the nations, the true God is never in any way in need of human offerings (Ps 49(50):12-15):

> If I were hungry, I would not tell you,
> For the world and all that is in it is mine.
> Do I eat the flesh of bulls,
> or drink the blood of goats?
> Offer to God a sacrifice of thanksgiving,
> and pay your vows to the Most High.
> Call on me in the day of trouble;
> I will deliver you, and you shall glorify me.[57]

No religion ever had such a relentless sense of self-criticism regarding sacrifice and cultic offerings as ancient Judaism. The prophets repeatedly criticised the official sacrificial system, reminding Israel that the only true sacrifice is a broken and contrite heart (Ps 50(51):17), an admonition echoed in Jesus' criticisms of the restored second temple and his insistence that in God's sight, mercy is better than sacrifice (Mt 9:13). According to God's own revelation there is no room for *do ut des* in our approach to him because he is never beholden to us in any way: the Lord is God and Master of all things.

Yet *do ut des* can actually be pressed into service to illustrate a deeper truth. There is a real meaning to it but it lies not in our giving God something so that we may get something back but in God's giving to us so that he may empower us to give to him: something we are entirely incapable of doing by our own strength or on our own merits. He does it not because he needs anything from us but because, out of pure love, he wishes to empower us to stand in his presence and serve him.

God may be imagined as saying to us: 'I freely give my Son to you, so that you may give him back to me.' In the Eucharist, through the sending of the Holy Spirit, he transforms our gifts (bread and wine) into the glorified body and blood of Christ so that they become his gift to us. As Christ actualises the heart of his self-offering in and through the Eucharist, he gives himself to the Father and to us, but, in the excess of love, empowers us also to offer him to the Father. In that act, all human longing to draw near to God, the deep-seated need to offer sacrifice to God which is built (by him) into the human soul, finds its perfect expression. Carried up by the Holy Spirit – becoming as the Roman Liturgy puts it, 'one body, one Spirit in Christ' – we are carried in, inserted in the endlessly circulating flow of sacrificial self-giving which constitutes the inner life of the Trinity and of which Christ's sacrifice is the perfect expression: hence the importance of the Eucharist, the sacramental sign of that sacrifice, in the life of the church.

In his account of the Lord's Supper, Paul also reminds us how important the future is to our Christian faith. In eating the bread and drinking the cup while proclaiming the death of the risen one, we are given a fresh orientation towards his final coming. Past and future meet in the eternal present of the living Christ who manifests himself at his supper. For the one whose death we proclaim at every Mass is not now dead: rather he lives and reigns in glory at the Father's side as Lord of heaven and earth. Yet at every celebration of the Eucharist we are reminded that, although he has personally triumphed over death, the kingdom he inaugurated on earth is still in the process of coming. As the Letter to the Hebrews says, we do not yet see all things subjected to his rule (Heb 2:8-9): that will come only when the last enemy, death itself has been destroyed (1 Cor 15:26).[58]

For that reason, like everything else in the church, Christian worship is always provisional. Waiting expectantly, we look forward with hope to the return of our glorified Lord, for the church is not yet the kingdom of God but only its messenger and partial embodiment. It is the sacrament of the kingdom. As we carry out in the liturgy the objective memorial (*anamnesis*) Christ has given us, recalling his death and looking forward with hope and expectation to the last day at the end of time when he will manifest his presence (*parousia*), we are given strength to work for the expansion of the kingdom of his love.

Because God is transcendent, standing above and outside time, he is able to enfold its three dimensions of past, present and future in one single embrace. Transcending time, God sees it before him as a single moment: all things are simultaneously present to God. In the Eucharist we articulate this truth ritually. We recall and proclaim what God has already achieved in the past; we affirm that he can make it effective in the present; we direct our hope towards the glorious future which we know will dawn on us on the day of his final coming. Roman Catholics and Anglicans therefore sing at the Eucharist: 'Christ has died, Christ is risen, Christ will come again!', and Orthodox Christians sing in their Easter Vigil:

> O Christ, Wisdom, Word and Power of God;
> grant that we may partake more fully of your banquet
> in the day of your kingdom
> which knows no evening![59]

The Eucharist is the sacramental mystery-rite in which through the Holy Spirit, Christ becomes present to us and makes his redeeming action operative among us once again. Like Christ himself, it is a mystery of incarnation being accomplished by means of signs and symbols which truly convey the fullness they represent. Yet even as the visible sacrament of bread reveals to the eyes of faith the invisible presence of Christ the Bread of Life, so to the uninitiated who do not have eyes to see, it simultaneously conceals his saving presence and his act of redeeming love. In the Eucharist he is a hidden God, as concealed as he was during his life on earth and especially as he hung on the cross. St Thomas Aquinas wrote in the hymn *Adoro Te*:

> Godhead I adore thee fast in hiding; thou
> God in these poor shapes, poor shadows, darkling now:
> See, Lord at thy service low lies here a heart
> Lost, all lost in wonder at the God thou art.

Seeing, touching, tasting are in thee deceived;
How says trusty hearing? That shall be believed:
What God's Son has told me, take for truth I do;
Truth himself speaks truly or there's nothing true.

On the cross thy Godhead made no sign to men,
Here thy very manhood steals from human ken!
Both are my confession, both are my belief:
And I pray the prayer of the dying thief.
Jesu whom I look at veilèd here below,
I beseech thee send me what I thirst for so,
Some day to gaze on thee, face to face in light
And be blessed for ever with thy glory's sight.[60]

And in another of his great Eucharistic hymns he affirmed:

Faith alone the true heart wakens,
to behold the mystery!

That is why in Roman Catholic and many Anglican services, having recounted the narrative of Christ's institution of the sacrament, the President of the liturgical assembly invites the congregation to 'proclaim the mystery of faith'. In the sacramental celebration of the liturgy, the one great mystery of Christ is set before us in symbols and effectively recalled so as to awaken faith in us. Faith alone can pierce the screen of visibility to uncover that which discloses itself to us in and through the symbols of the liturgy, just as only faith could recognise in the crucified humanity of Jesus the Lord's Messiah, the image of the invisible God and the power of triumphant love. Only faith could see in the emptiness of the tomb the witness to the resurrection of life.

2. The Eucharist as the Mystery of Real Presences

Closer attention to the words of Paul in their Jewish context has helped us recover the original sense of the Eucharist as a sacramental mystery, an effective memorial through which God conquers time, making present the core reality of Christ's sacrifice so that we may share in it through worship. But a revitalised awareness of the mystery-character of the Mass can greatly help us to understand better the presence of the risen Christ in the Eucharist as well. It can help to resolve at least some difficulties still remaining between Catholics and Protestants regarding what the former have called for centuries 'the real presence' of Christ in the Eucharist.[61]

Here again St Paul can guide us. Commenting earlier in the first letter to the Corinthians on Christians partaking of food offered to idols, he made a very strong statement:

> The cup of blessing that we bless, is it not a sharing in the blood of Christ? The bread that we break, is it not a sharing in the body of Christ? Because there is one bread, we who are many are one body, for we all partake of the one bread. Consider the people of Israel: are not those who eat the sacrifices partners in the altar? (1 Cor 10:16-18)

What does it mean to say that our eating and drinking at the Lord's Supper are a sharing or participation in Christ's body and blood? Bitter disputes in the past between Protestants and Catholics, and among Protestants themselves, about what this entails have marred relations between the churches. Some Protestants imagine that the Roman Church thinks that Christ's 'real presence' literally entails pieces of bleeding flesh somehow 'contained' behind the filmy surface of the host at Mass, and that the chalice 'contains' the blood of Christ as if it were literally spilt again from his body.[62]

In fairness, Catholics ought to admit that, although such crude literalism forms no part either of the official theology proposed by the church's authorities or of the church's liturgical rites, one does at times encounter it in the literature and devotions of popular Catholicism.[63] Protestants are perfectly right to protest against that sort of vulgar misunderstanding and to remind us that the presence of the risen Christ is definitely not of that kind. Unfortunately too they have often gained the impression that by speaking of his 'real presence' in the Eucharist Catholics forget his presence in numerous other ways, such as in holy scripture and the Christian community as the temple of the Holy Spirit.

Yet Catholics, Orthodox, and most Lutherans and Anglicans continue to insist in their turn that in the Eucharist we really do encounter a special presence of Christ in a privileged way, a way more full and therefore more 'real' than all the other modes of presence listed above. They insist that in the Eucharist we are offered the fullest possible presence available to us this side of eternity. But that does not in any way deny or undervalue the numerous other ways in which the risen Christ comes to meet his people. The Second Vatican Council listed them carefully: God in Christ is present through his Spirit in the word of the readings as they are proclaimed, in the assembled people as the Christian community, in the sacred ministers who represent his presence among them and in the celebration of the other sacraments.[64] We should also add, according to Matthew, chapter 25 and the witness of the saints (including St Benedict), that Christ is present in a privileged way in the poorest of the poor, where he awaits our ministrations.[65]

In all these varied ways, Christ comes to meet us. But in this time of waiting, between the resurrection and the second coming, Christ, in his overwhelming generosity, fulfills the promise he made at the Last Supper (Jn 14:18), 'I will not leave you orphaned; I am coming to you.' In his great love, he gives us a unique mode of presence more intense than all the others: his sacramental mystery-presence brought about by the consecration of our gifts of bread and wine which, by the power of the Holy Spirit, become his glorified body and blood, concealed in sacramental signs. This presence is one of great intensity and fullness.

However, even that is not yet his full and final gift of presence. We should not imagine that this side of heaven any mediated presence – including the eucharistic gifts – can ever be as full, final or real as the face-to-face encounter with God awaiting us in heaven. St Thomas Aquinas calls that final presence 'the Beatific Vision', because it confers perfect, lasting happiness. On earth the sacraments and particularly the Eucharist prepare us for the full vision of heaven where no veiled presence will be required: all veils will be drawn aside forever (1 Cor 13:12; 1 Jn 3:2). In the manifestation of Christ, shining with the light of uncreated glory, the Holy Spirit will grant the revelation of the Father's face shining through that of the Son. God the Holy Trinity will be seen by all the blessed through the direct vision of Christ.[66]

But 'here below' the eucharistic presence is the fullest and most real one available to us. By means of it Christ becomes one flesh with the members of his community, constituting them as his body the church, making them his presence in the world. The eucharistic meal is the foretaste of the wedding banquet of the lamb announced in the Book of Revelation at the end of the Bible (Rev 21:1-2). The nuptial metaphor is a strong reminder that in the eucharistic celebration Christ's glorified body is joined in love with that of the church his bride, already brought to birth through the Holy Spirit in baptism.

So too the assembly of Christians, convoked by the Spirit, comes together for the sacrificial-sacramental meal. Answering God's call and receiving this wonderful sacrament of unity, it is joined to Christ, united together, and admitted to communion with the Holy Trinity. In every celebration of Mass each eucharistic community, by sharing in the one bread and one cup, is mystically joined to all the others who do the same thing throughout the world. In the Eucharist, the Holy Spirit, who has brought the church to birth in the waters of new life, feeds her with the presence of the risen Lord and builds her up into the one body of Christ, the temple of God's presence in the world.[67]

That is why in speaking of this wonderful presence of Christ in the Eucharist we ought to banish from our understanding any crude materialism. The presence of Jesus in the Mass is the supreme mystery-presence of a glorified Lord who manifests himself to us through effective symbols so as to dwell in us and make us one body with himself. It is certainly not just the presence of a dead person from the past to be evoked only in memory; but neither is it to be misunderstood in a merely carnal sense. In his eucharistic discourse in the sixth chapter of John's gospel, after having insisted firmly that we must eat his flesh and drink his blood, Jesus asserted:

Does this offend you? What if you were to see the Son of Man ascending to where he was before? It is the Spirit that gives life; the flesh is useless. The words that I have spoken to you are spirit and life. (Jn 6: 61b-63)

It is worth mentioning two things here: first that Jesus hints at his kenotic descent from where he had been 'before' and of his future ascension into glory; and second that 'spirit' for the Jews did not have the kind of abstract, bloodless, non-material connotations that it possesses today: it was a dynamic attribute of God. In the power of the Spirit of Pentecost, Christ becomes present among us as the living Son of God risen from the dead and seated in glory at the right hand of the Father. The same gospel shows how after his resurrection Jesus was able to enter and leave the upper room where his disciples were hiding, even though the doors were locked for fear of the authorities who were searching for them (Jn 20:19). Although the marks of the passion remained visible in his flesh, causing Thomas to recognise him at last (Jn 20: 27-28), Jesus had been transformed by the light of glory. He remains for ever God-made-human but with his humanity gloriously changed. He is so transformed as to be capable of becoming present simultaneously in a multitude of places.

Just as God is able to transcend and even conquer time, so neither is he bound by the category of space. The transfigured humanity of Jesus, filled with the energies of his divine nature, kenotically concealed in the incarnation but revealed in the resurrection, is gloriously free of all spatial and temporal limitations. So also will they be who after the general resurrection, having received from him the bread of life in communion, shall have cleaved to him in faith and love:

> Very truly I tell you, unless you eat the flesh of the Son of Man and drink his blood you have no life in you. Those who eat my flesh and drink my blood have eternal life, and I will raise them up on the last day; for my flesh is true food and my blood is true drink. Those who eat my flesh and drink my blood abide in me, and I in them. Just as the living Father sent me, and I live because of the Father, so whoever eats me will live because of me. (Jn 6:53-57)

Earlier in the same gospel Jesus says that the Father who is the source of life has made the Son the source of life as well (Jn 5:26). For that reason Orthodox tradition calls the Eucharist 'the medicine of immortality'; while St Thomas Aquinas described it as 'the pledge of future blessings'.[68] Yet the glorified Christ's blood (signifying for Semitic peoples the principle of life) will never again be separated from his body in death. For that reason the Council of Trent taught that the whole Christ – body, blood, soul and divinity – is fully present in and through each particle of eucharistic bread and in and through the consecrated wine in the chalice. It is not that the cup somehow contains *only* blood and the bread *only* 'flesh'. Rather, the transfigured Easter Christ, the most unified and integrated human being imaginable, becomes overwhelmingly present in all his fullness, in and through each of the sacramental media offered to us.[69]

This mystery-presence of the risen Lord cannot be neatly pinned down by logical analysis or captured in a definition. His sacramental presence is the unanticipated gift of a fullness which is not 'local' in the sense of limiting. It is precisely because of this that he is even more present in the Mass than he would be if he were 'locally present' for in truth Christ is not 'contained' in the elements of the sacramental meal: rather he contains them in himself. They are bursting with the presence of the risen one.

Catholics are accustomed to speak of Christ as being 'in' the chalice or 'on' the altar. That is true as far as it goes and is a valid reflection of the language of love and devotion. One does not always need to speak in precise categories nor should the overflowing sentiments of the heart be squeezed into the textbook terms of a manual of theology! But in reflecting more deeply on the Eucharist and above all in explaining to other Christians what it means to us, we ought to remember that the mystery-presence of the glorified Lord cannot be so easily cut down to size. Christ's presence is the gift of his love. It entails an excess of presence. He is there in overwhelming fullness as he communicates himself to believers through eating and drinking the consecrated gifts after they have heard his word and offered thanks and praise to the Father.

In the Eucharist we have the most perfect mode of mystery-presence. It is Christ's 'self-presencing' among us, again and again, through the form of food and drink and the joy of a commu-

nal banquet. That in itself is crucially significant. Although the
Orthodox and Catholic traditions both insist that the inner being
of the elements is changed in the liturgy, that does not mean that
'mere' appearances are left behind. What we call the 'sacramental
species', that is the visible signs of bread and wine through which
the incarnate Word communicates his presence, are anything but
'mere'. The sacramental appearances which remain after the
bread and wine have been made to yield their essential being to
the risen Christ are in fact the fullest and deepest kind of symbols.
As phenomena they simultaneously conceal and reveal their
deepest reality in communicating the mystery-presence of the
Lord. In the sign of bread we see in faith and receive in truth the
real Bread of Life who comes in and through it; in the sign of wine
we see in faith and receive in truth his blood poured out in sacrifice.[70]

Bread is already a wondrous thing, a work of transformation
forged by human hands, made from wheat harvested from the
fields and moulded and baked through human ingenuity in a furnace of fire. The wine is already a marvellous work of transformation, made from grapes crushed together in the press and trans-
muted into a wonderful elixir able to fill the heart with joy.
Human creativity and its products reflect God's own creative activity. They strengthen and gladden the heart.

Jesus, having passed through the baking furnace of suffering
and trodden alone the wine press of his passion (Is 63:3), is among
us as bread come down from heaven to strengthen us in following
him; he gladdens us with the new wine of his inebriating grace,
anointing our heads with the oil of the Holy Spirit's presence. In
the mystical banquet of the Mass the heavenly lamb shares his
wedding cup with his bride the church, pouring out for us the
wine of love. It is an inebriating draught, a mystical drink with
power to draw us ecstatically out of ourselves and into the one
who comes to embrace us and fill us with his love (Ps 22(3):5; Ps
115(116):13). The risen Christ accomplishes this embrace in the
power of the Holy Spirit who streams like light from Christ's
transfigured body as we celebrate the wedding banquet of the
Lamb and eat and drink the holy gifts.[71]

Such an understanding of 'real presence' as the mystery-presence of the glorified Christ in the Lord's Supper should go a long way towards resolving some of the painful historic differences between Catholics and Protestants. Between the dry, barren emptiness of 'mere' signs, (an absent Christ represented by bread and wine, a notion which betrays a reductive, impoverished understanding of symbolism) and the crude literalism of newly slaughtered flesh somehow 'contained' beneath the 'mere' appearances of the elements (a dead Christ trapped in an equally impoverished symbol system) lies the early church's authentic understanding of how Christ is really present in the Lord's Supper.

It is by means of his mystery-presence, thanks to which the glorious conqueror of sin and death can also conquer space as triumphantly as he conquered time (a risen Christ). In the power of the Holy Spirit he communicates himself through the liturgical symbols, re-presenting himself to us, becoming manifest among us again that he may feed and strengthen our faith with the bread and wine of understanding and fill us with delight at the banquet of his love, the banquet of incarnate Wisdom (Proverbs 9:1-6).

Of course after hundreds of years of division not all the difficulties can be easily resolved. Catholics, Orthodox and many Anglicans stress that since Christ re-presents himself through the transformation of the inner being (the substance or essence) of the bread and wine, though that remains a mystery impenetrable to rational analysis, his mystery-presence endures even beyond the celebration of the liturgy in the reserved sacrament, whereas most Lutherans and many Anglicans say that in the sacramental eating and drinking the bread and wine are somehow joined to the presence of the risen Christ but do not outlast the time of celebration. Most Reformed, many Anglicans and the majority of Pentecostals hold that the mystery-presence is not intrinsically 'linked' to the bread and wine but that the risen Jesus is present spiritually at the table and in the meal to nourish and renew the participants.

Yet almost all agree that it is the Holy Spirit who makes the mystery-presence of Jesus possible either by transforming the elements of bread and wine from within or by communicating the

power of Christ's risen body to the one who eats and drinks the
holy gifts. Catholics and Orthodox ought to stress that we do not
speak of 'mere appearances' of bread and wine in the Eucharist
even though we certainly believe that their deepest reality has
been transformed (a strictly non-material metaphysical change,
officially designated 'transubstantiation' by Catholics and usually
'transformation' by Orthodox).

It is not insignificant that the risen Jesus presences himself
among us through the forms of food and drink. Not only are the
symbolic associations of eating and drinking the consecrated
food of vital importance, but in consuming these sacramental
signs we are vividly alerted to how energetically God loves us. He
wishes to be not only 'God-with-us' but also 'God-in-us'. Thanks
to his mystery-presence in the Eucharist, Christ penetrates
through our senses into the deepest recesses of the heart. He enters deep within us as we consume his holy mysteries, the sacramental signs of food and drink. While this presence is certainly
not just crudely carnal, it is also more than merely immaterial or
'spiritual' in the weak sense that word so often carries today. It is a
mystery both profoundly embodied and spiritual, for Eucharist,
incarnation and the Holy Spirit may never be divided.[72]

CHAPTER SIX

The Mystery Expands for Us

Though, of course, the sacraments form the regular channel of communion with God, they are by no means the only channel in such a sense as would exclude all others. We may say that in the present age the church is the body of Christ precisely in being that eucharistic body on which are bestowed the eucharistic gifts of the Holy Spirit, the giver of life in Christ. To the church as a whole the plenitude of the manifestations of divine Wisdom is present ... it is thus impossible to confine the church to the limits of the world of humans alone. We are bound to include in it that nature with which humankind is united ... The blessings provided for such natural and artificial objects as water, fruit, and buildings, considered the first stage in their penetration by Wisdom in the power of the Holy Spirit, yield clear evidence of the activity of the church beyond the limits of the world of humans. This is the preparation of nature for that transfiguration of all things, when 'new heavens and a new earth' shall be revealed, wherein justice may dwell.

Sergius Bulgakov

So far we have considered holy scripture, baptism and the Eucharist, the three great mysteries which are the chief ways through which Christ realises his presence among us. The Torah, the inspired writings of the prophets, the songs of the psalmists and the privileged apostolic witnesses to the death and resurrection of the incarnate Word have been gathered by the church into the canon of scripture which functions permanently as an objective benchmark of truth for the Christian community in its journey through time. In baptism, Christians are plunged into the mystery of Christ's death and resurrection so as to experience the grace conferred on them in his sacrifice. In the Eucharist, that sacrifice is manifested through sacramental signs so that Christ can offer his people and, in turn, be offered by them to the glory of God the Father. Through communion in Christ's Spirit-filled body and blood, his church is built up for its service of witness to the world.

Catholics describe the work of God's grace as happening *ex opere operato*, which means that the gift given through the sacramental mysteries is an objective act guaranteed by God, and not therefore subject to the faults, failings or inadequacies of those responsible for carrying them out; nor in turn is their efficacy prevented by weakness in faith on the part of those who receive them. Protestant tradition, too, generally stresses the objectivity of God's gifts which are grounded on the word of Christ's promise and the grace of his covenant.[1]

Yet in neither case should that be understood mechanically as if simply performing the sacramental rituals alone sufficed for personal transformation. It is merely a negative guarantee of their objective efficacy. Grace is certainly given by God but it has to be consciously received by those to whom it is communicated to achieve the purpose intended by God's will: the sanctification of human beings and the transformation of the world. The seed of grace given in the sacramental mysteries has to find a soil well-prepared if it is to germinate, grow and bear fruit.

Among the secondary, lesser forms of mediation of the mystery of Christ I shall consider three. Calling them lesser is not intended to underestimate the important role they play in connecting us to God. It is simply to assert that they flow out from and circulate around the three primary ones like rays of light or ripples of water. Their deepest meaning lies in the three major mysteries through which the one great mystery of Christ's incarnation, death and resurrection extends beyond itself in an ever-widening field of radiating spiritual energy.

As we have seen, the objective gift of the sacramental mysteries always calls for a subjective response on our part. Scripture has to be opened, read and incarnated in ethical activity. Baptism having been received has to be lived out in a daily dying to sin and rising to new life. The Eucharist has to be celebrated and received if it is to have a transforming effect in one's life and in that of the Christian community. So too, each of the three lesser mediations contains and communicates an objective gift. But for them to bear spiritual fruit in our lives even more depends on our subjective response to and participation in the grace made present through them.

The three lesser mysteries under consideration are the celebration of the church's liturgical year (Christ's year of mysteries through which the one mystery of redemption is manifested in the cycles of time);[2] the mystery of the icon (which extends the transforming power of the incarnation and the Eucharist out into the material world);[3] and the mystery of personal prayer (in which Christ manifests his presence in the temple of the heart through meditation on the word of scripture).[4] Through all these means (as also through the church's ritual blessings), creation is penetrated, permeated and transfigured by the Holy Spirit of wisdom.

A. THE CHURCH'S YEAR OF MYSTERIES

I find you in your mysteries!
St Ambrose

Through the celebration of the mysteries of Christ in the course of the church's year, the one great mystery is manifested anew by the Holy Spirit. The Latin liturgy speaks of it in a Christmas hymn as the *circulus anni* or 'circle of the year', the circle speaking of eternity as having neither beginning nor end but simply returning ceaselessly upon itself. It is a powerful image yet it is only one way of describing that year: in fact the reality is rather more complex. It is now well established that the original celebration of Christ's mystery in liturgical time was that of his exaltation (comprising his passion, death, resurrection, sending of the Spirit and final coming) though most likely the original celebration was Sunday, the existence of which preceded the evolution of the actual feast of Easter.[5]

Yet once Easter had been established, this solemn Feast of Feasts became like a stone dropped into the pool of time. It generated periods of graced time, flowing 'backwards' and 'forwards': backwards in that (at least at Rome) it eventually caused the forty days of preparation called Lent to arise – a season entirely focused on the coming celebration, forwards into the rejoicing of Eastertide – a season wholly concentrated on what had occurred and on its culmination at Pentecost. That last Sunday of Easter is not a separate feast of the Holy Spirit but the conclusion of these fifty great days of paschal rejoicing (*pentecoste* in Greek), during which the church recalls the appearances of the risen Jesus and commemorates the outpouring of the Spirit.[6] It is one great Easter Sunday.

Just as it was his principal work in the history of salvation, so Christ's paschal mystery – his passing from death to new life through the cross and resurrection – is the central event commemorated by Christians in their worship. The Lord Jesus Christ, crucified and risen, is the objective point of origin from which the circling processions of the liturgical year begin, the centre around which they revolve and the endpoint towards which they are always moving.

However, in the 4th century, greater interest began to develop in the humanity of Jesus and the economy of salvation, centred not surprisingly on the church of Jerusalem. It was partly stimulated by the archaeological excavations organised by Helena, mother of the recently 'converted' Emperor Constantine. This resulted in the finding of what was held to be the true cross and the building of the first basilica of the resurrection at the site of the crucifixion and resurrection (known to western Christians as the Holy Sepulchre and to the Orthodox as the *anastasis*, or 'resurrection').

This tendency both represented and further encouraged a growing desire on the part of Christians to celebrate individual events of the mystery of Christ as it had been manifested in time. Thus new feasts commemorating particular aspects of Christ's life appeared in the 4th century, such as Palm Sunday, the Ascension, Christmas (a Roman feast that was exported east though not as far as Armenia) and various events in the life of Mary of Nazareth the Lord's Mother. While the result of this was a great enrichment of the church's liturgical life, it was not without some ambiguity.

There was a certain risk (not always successfully avoided in later Christian history) that Easter might end up being viewed as just another feast of the Lord – one among the others – rather than the foundational event grounding and giving meaning to all other feasts.[7]

Since that time there has been a certain creative tension in Christian liturgical life between an eschatological vision of time focused on Christ's exaltation (his lifting up on the cross, resurrection, ascension and sending of the Spirit) which signifies God's final absolute intervention in history – the in-breaking of the kingdom in the risen Lord – and a chronological-historicising thrust which speaks of a 'liturgical year of mysteries' proceeding one after the other, organised in a historically determined sequence running from the birth of Jesus to his death. Yet the best theologians and spiritual writers of the Christian tradition have never forgotten the first dimension, recognising that in the resurrection of Christ God objectively accomplished the salvation of the world and filled time with his glory.

Nor has the liturgy itself ever forgotten that. Every celebration of a feast is centred on the Eucharist in which the proclamation of the death and resurrection of Christ and the sending of the Spirit are commemorated; and in the texts and liturgical actions of individual feasts there are many reminders that we always celebrate the single, unique paschal mystery. On Palm Sunday, for example, the entrance chant of the Roman Rite proclaims 'the resurrection of life' and even as we venerate the cross on Good Friday we sing of Christ's Easter triumph. Many other examples could be adduced from the Eastern liturgies.

Thus alongside the integral celebration of the mystery of Christ (his death, burial and resurrection) centred on Easter, there developed also a new dimension focused not just on the essential acts of redemption but on their preparatory phases and diverse manifestations in the ministry of Jesus, the life of his Mother and the lives of the saints. Christmas and Epiphany focused attention not only on what Christ had accomplished in the work of salvation but on the deepest mystery of his being, on who he is as the incarnate Son of God. Yet the centrality of the *pascha* of the Lord was never forgotten: each feast is marked with the sign of the cross, bathed in the light of the resurrection and overshadowed by the power of the Holy Spirit.

His birth at Bethlehem, pushed by harsh necessity to the edge of town; his manifestation as the true king to the Wise Men from the East followed by Herod's ruthless massacre of the innocents; his presentation in the Temple where he was acclaimed as the light of the nations and the glory of Israel but also declared to be a sign that would be rejected; his baptism in the Jordan prefiguring his descent into the tomb and resurrection to everlasting life; his transfiguration, the fullest revelation of glory during his earthly ministry but following which he took the Jerusalem road to humiliation and death: in all these individual mysteries of his life and ministry the light of the one great mystery of his death and resurrection is proclaimed, celebrated and opened up for our participation.[8]

This is equally true of the mysteries of his mother's life. Mary's feasts commemorate her participation in the saving work he accomplished, revealing how his passage from death to life was manifested in her – in her freedom from sin brought about through his sacrifice on the cross, her being offered in the Temple, her divine motherhood and the glorification of her body after death, the fruit of his resurrection. Each of these triumphs of grace in her human person was the actualisation of her Son's paschal triumph and his glorious victory over sin.[9]

Finally, as a further manifestation and extension of the grace of Christ, the church celebrates the feasts of the saints. We commemorate them not primarily for their own sake but because of their testimony to Christ. In them his paschal triumph was made real through lives of witness, suffering, and in the case of the martyrs, death. That is why the first category of saints to be commemorated liturgically was that of the martyrs. In their *transitus* (the Latin for *pascha*, or passage) through death to eternal glory, they become icons of Christ who passed from death to life at Easter. The saints are living copies of Christ painted by the Holy Spirit: Christ the eternal Son revealed in time, the unique Image of the invisible God.

Yet they are not merely slavish or external imitations. In each one the grace of the paschal mystery finds a unique and unrepeatable actualisation with all the diversity that marked their particular circumstances of life and death – from the Roman catacombs to the 20th century death camps or from the plague hospitals of Medieval Europe to the leper colonies of Molokai. They are reiterations of Christ's original saving act, realised in the multitude of his members. That was also the original reason for the veneration of relics in the early church, although it was later obscured in the practice of the Latin West and therefore entirely rejected by Protestantism.

The martyred bodies of the saints were seen as temples of the Holy Spirit who had shaped them in the form of Christ's passion. They were held to be 'places' where his glory (*doxa*) dwelt. Relics thus had a liturgical meaning. Embodying the witness of the saint who had been filled with the Spirit, they were an *anamnesis*, an objective memorial of Christ's passion, death and resurrection and of the coming *eschaton*, the Last Day, when the body will be taken up and transfigured into Christ's likeness in God's kingdom (Phil 3:20-21). As Paul wrote:

> We know that God makes all things work together for good for those who love God, who are called according to his purpose. For those whom he foreknew he also predestined to be conformed to the image of his Son, in order that he might be the firstborn within a large family. And those whom he predestined he also called; and those whom he called he also justified; and those whom he justified he also glorified (Rom 8:28-30).[10]

In the Roman Catholic Church the remaining Sundays, not immediately linked to the great events of Easter and Christmas, form their own cycle running throughout the year. Nowadays it is designated 'Ordinary Time'. Yet each Sunday is a little Easter and a little Pentecost, for on each one the great mystery of Christ is celebrated over and over again. The Anglican and Lutheran traditions establish the wholeness of the year and the reference of such 'Ordinary Time' to the two great cycles of Lent-Easter and

Advent-Epiphany, through the tradition of naming those Sundays with reference to the cycle they precede or follow after (e.g. 'Sundays before Advent,' and 'after Epiphany', 'after Trinity,' etc).[11]

It reflects therefore an impoverished understanding of the church's year to imagine it as being merely like the civil or financial years – made up of divisions of time moving in a linear direction from beginning to end (e.g. from January to January for the civil year). Unfortunately, many Catholics have become accustomed to speak of such a 'Church Year' which is supposed to begin at Advent and end in the 34th week of Ordinary Time before beginning afresh again at Advent.

But the church's year does not simply run in a line from beginning to end, punctuated by a series of great feasts. Its movement is circular and it revolves around a centre. Its heartbeat is the paschal mystery of Christ's death and resurrection which manifests its grace everywhere. The liturgical calendar is more like a spiral than a straight line: each circling year as it returns on itself, brings us back to the same point from which we departed, yet leaves us established on a higher plane.

In this wonderful movement of liturgical time as it revolves around the Easter mystery, yet also moves forward through the repeated celebration of the feasts of Christ's life and the Sundays of Ordinary Time, two notions of time are reconciled and harmonised. The primarily Greek and Indian idea of time as circular and repetitive – a moving image of eternity – is reconciled and harmonised with the primarily Jewish idea of time as a sequence of events extending into a future determined by a final goal. The church's year of mysteries is able to synthesise these two different notions because it lives the creative tension generated by the incarnation and resurrection of the eternal Word.[12]

In Christ's taking flesh, eternity entered time and was made manifest on earth. Yet having been raised to glory out of time, thanks to his ascension into heaven, Christ brought the humanity he had assumed and transfigured within time back into eternity. Admitted to God's presence after his glorification, the divine-human Christ was freed from the limitations belonging to earthly time: he became a universal person available to all. Far from withdrawing from us and depriving us of his presence, Christ in being universalised for us is not less but more available and accessible after his entry into heaven.

Living and reigning beyond time, through the power of the Holy Spirit, Christ is able to re-present himself to us again and again in every moment of time, becoming active in the church's liturgy as her great high priest. We can truly say that through the Spirit-inspired gift of faith we become his contemporaries in a way that those who actually met him during his life on earth (e.g. Pontius Pilate) were not. As Paul said, the important thing is not having known Christ according to the flesh but knowing him as he is now (and for ever) – the glorified Lord who comes to us in the Holy Spirit (2 Cor:16).

Being both divine and fully human, Christ is the final end towards which we travel in time. Like a heavenly magnet drawing the church and the world beyond themselves, he pulls us forward through time to our fulfilment in his future kingdom. Yet in the liturgy as the Spirit descends, manifests the risen Lord and lifts the church heavenwards in her worship, we enter already into the kingdom, tasting in the transfigured gifts of the eucharistic banquet the glorious end awaiting us. The Eucharist is the foretaste of heaven; in the celebration of the church's feasts Christ's gifts are given once again, though in an undercover way, under the veils of the sacramental signs: but the reality remains the same.[13]

It is therefore erroneous to think of the church's year as a mere historical commemoration, such as Remembrance Sunday in the United Kingdom or one of those interminable days of remembrance that so afflict Northern Ireland with the memory of past atrocities, neither forgiven or forgotten because perpetually recalled. The Christian Year is much more than a simple catalogue of meaningful dates dedicated to the dead or to the past; nor is it yet another manifestation of the contemporary craze for anniversaries. It is the celebration of the presence here and now of the risen Lord Jesus Christ and his saving acts in the power of the Holy Spirit.

Once again a fuller understanding of *anamnesis* as objective memorial (such as we have seen it operate in eucharistic theology) is helpful for correctly understanding the meaning of a Christian feast. In every feast in the church's year, no matter what we are celebrating, we make essentially one memorial: the objective re-call of the one great mystery of our salvation, the saving passage of Jesus Christ the incarnate Son and Word of God from death to life in his paschal mystery. In the feasts, in a way similar to the Eucharist, we do that not merely by means of subjective recall but as an objective memorial, an *anamnesis* of the single mystery in the individual liturgical mysteries.[14]

When we celebrate any of the mysteries of Jesus (e.g. his trans-figuration), the transfigured Lord, vibrantly alive today, through the power of the Holy Spirit, 'reactivates' among us the original grace of what occurred in the past. Each event in the saving activity of Christ was a manifestation in time of God's eternal love. Each one, but especially his death and resurrection, has been engraved in the being of Jesus who even in his glorified flesh displayed the painful marks of his passion. The power of divine-human love poured out in death and ratified for ever in his resurrection en-dures for ever.

As we celebrate our feasts, the Holy Spirit renders Jesus present in our worship as the sacrificed and glorified Saviour, the High Priest of the new and everlasting covenant. Through the liturgy, the grace and power of the original event is reactivated and shared afresh with us. That is why on great feasts in the Catholic and Orthodox churches we sing texts proclaiming that everything is happening *today* (*hodie* and *semeron* in Latin and Greek). Today Christ is born! Today the Lord is baptised! Today the Holy Spirit came! Yet there is no suggestion that the original event in its hist-orical originality is being repeated for that is simply impossible.[15]

But in celebrating the event (the original meaning of 'to cele-brate' in the early church having been 'to accomplish') the Lord brings about among us once again the inner power of what he did in time past. As the feast recalling the mystery is repeated, the one great mystery of Christ's transforming passage which informed all his actions is activated and made effective. Far from being a simple series of historical commemorations, the liturgical year with its feasts celebrating the mysteries of Christ, is a powerhouse of grace and spiritual energy. It is one of the most privileged of the Lord's zones of self-disclosure. In the liturgy, Christ carries out his priestly work among us, making present once again the power of the love by which he saved us, and opening up once more the one great mystery for our participation through the joy and beauty of the feast.

Year after year in the church's sacramental liturgy, Christ represents the mystery of salvation, making it known through the individual mysteries we ritually celebrate. St Augustine and later Luther both described Christ as *sacramentum et exemplum* (sacrament and example) meaning that he is both the real, effective sacramental sign of God's love and an example to us; both a gift of grace and a summons to imitate the virtues he exemplified in the mystery being celebrated.[16]

A feast is a Spirit-filled celebration made up of various sacramental signs by means of which the incarnate Word renews again among us the objective acts by which God redeemed us in the past; but it is also a pattern we are called to reproduce in our own lives. One need only think of the humility of the sinless Christ in submitting to baptism in the Jordan: in the liturgical celebration of the baptism that is vividly set before our eyes and ears. We are invited as we celebrate the feast to enter into and participate in its reality and to receive through the Holy Spirit's power a share in Christ's humility which led to his final glorification.[17]

From the crib to the cross, from *Pascha* to Pentecost, the liturgical year with all its feasts is a repeated invitation issued by God to draw life from the springs of Christ's mysteries and to let each one lead us into the infinite reservoir of love spilling out of the heart of the Holy Trinity. The Holy Spirit, sent by the Father in answer to Christ's prayer (Jn 14:16-17), is the divine person who manifests the mystery of salvation in our worship. S/he it is who brings about the grace of the sacraments and indeed all grace. The same Spirit directs us in forming our lives according to the pattern of the mysteries we celebrate, reproducing in our lives the archetypal patterns revealed in Christ. The Spirit is the one who spurs us on to follow Christ's example.

Christian existence takes its shape from the paschal mystery which consists in entering into new life through death. So too Christian ethical activity ought to flow from the liturgical life of the church where that transforming grace is given to us under the form of symbols to enable us to follow Christ's example. Liturgy and life are always meant to be at one.

A prayer in the Roman liturgy for the ordination of presbyters (priests) expresses this well. As the bishop hands the newly ordained the paten and cup containing the elements required for the celebration of the Eucharist, he admonishes them to imitate the mystery they celebrate by modelling their lives on the mystery of the Lord's cross. The same might well be said to every Christian as year by year we progress through the celebration of the church's feasts.

In the mystery of worship the Holy Spirit acts like a Mother, a role often attributed to the third divine person in the Syrian tradition. S/he is a maternal Spirit bringing us rebirth in Christ and in turn bringing Christ to birth in us. The Spirit's maternal care enables us to realise the truth of Columba Marmion's saying: 'The mysteries of Christ are our mysteries'; and through the Spirit's nurturing we are enabled to make our own the words of St Ambrose, saying with him to Christ: 'I find you in your mysteries.'

In the power of the Holy Spirit, we celebrate at Christmas the love which brought Christ into the world and we experience his birth spiritually within ourselves. At Epiphany we celebrate the manifestation of his light as once he manifested it to the wise men, and are ourselves illumined. As we celebrate his baptism in the Jordan and the transformation of water into wine at Cana, Christ once more lets his glory be seen, so that we, like his original disciples, might believe in him. On Good Friday we die spiritually with him and on Holy Saturday are buried with him, interring him spiritually in our hearts.

On Easter Sunday we celebrate his rising and we rise with him as well, experiencing the explosion of an indestructible new life and an inexpressible joy within ourselves. In celebrating his ascension into glory, we experience our being carried up by him on high and enthroned with him in the heavenly places (Col 3:1-4;

Eph 2:4-7) – for where our treasure is, there our hearts will also be found (Mt 6:21). And every year in Advent we remember his future final coming when he will appear in all his glory in the company of the saints (Mt 25:31-46; Phil 3:21-21; Lk 21:25-28). Through the Holy Spirit all the treasures of Christ's grace are opened to us in our worship when we celebrate the mysteries of the Christian liturgy with faith and hope, love and eager expectation.[18]

B. THE MYSTERY OF THE ICON: IMAGING THE PRESENCE

As the tabernacle of the covenant
held the presence of God,
so the icons manifest the presence
of the one we worship and revere!
It is our glory to kneel
and adore the incarnate Christ.
Come O faithful, let us embrace the icons
and cry out:
O God save your people
and bless your heritage!
Hymn from the Byzantine Rite, Fifth Sunday of Great Lent

In recent years there has been something of an explosion of interest in icons among western Christians. They are now used ever more frequently in prayer and worship even in many churches which had in the past traditionally been wary about employing figurative art. Nowadays one can even find icons displayed in some Swiss Reformed churches and in one of the Anglican Cathedrals in Dublin.[19] In the Roman Catholic Church their growing use is indicative of dissatisfaction with the poverty of much ecclesiastical art of the 19th and 20th centuries, an 'art' which often veered between the tasteless products of the repository and the barren minimalism of the nineteen-sixties. Nor in assessing this phenomenon should one exclude the fascination for all things 'eastern' so often operative in the west: yet 'Orientalism' alone is hardly sufficient to explain the phenomenon.

One of the main reasons why the icon has today acquired such popularity is surely because many sense what the Orthodox

Church has always understood: the remarkable capacity of the icon to function as an opening on to the mysteries of Christ. It is another filter, through which the one great mystery can manifest itself and reveal its power. In Orthodoxy the art of 'writing' an icon involves much more than just painting. It is never simply art for art's sake. It is rather a priestly act, a form of sacramental activity meant to take place in the context of prayer and worship. Its purpose has always been to allow Christ to mediate his presence and his work of salvation.[20]

The icon is thus much more than merely an adjunct to worship or a book painted for the illiterate. On the contrary, it is a powerful witness to the sacramental principle. The Spirit-bearing capacity of matter taken up by God in the incarnation of Christ and continued in the Eucharist is given artistic expression in the icon which thereby becomes a privileged disclosure-zone of grace. Divine and uncreated beauty, revealing itself through the beauty of the icon, offers us access to and experience of the presence of God in a particularly intensive way. It calls us to contemplation.[21]

Michael Paul Gallagher, a Jesuit and therefore familiar with the use of the imagination in prayer, comments on Hans Urs Von Balthasar's explorations of imagination which, according to him:

> … he puts at the centre of both anthropology and spirituality. In line with the medieval tradition, he insists that every kind of expression of spiritual vision relies on imagination. Images, in his view, can create inner space and point beyond themselves towards mysteries that they both reveal and conceal. An authentically human intuition is possible only through the mediation of the imagination.[22]

Among the three great Semitic religions, (Judaism, Christianity and Islam), Christianity is unique in recognising this primacy of the image and imagination and encouraging the use of figurative art (although many communities stemming from the Protestant Reformation still ban such art from their churches). For Judaism and Islam, God is so radically transcendent and infinitely other that any figurative depiction of the divine or human is generally held to be idolatrous and a betrayal of God's radical otherness.

This has not in practice led either religion to place an absolute ban on the use of art but only to prohibit the portrayal of God – and in general the human and angelic forms (with some exceptions in both traditions).[23]

It is also worth remembering that ancient Hebrew spirituality, (some of which is preserved in the older psalms) centred on the first temple in Jerusalem, greatly emphasised God's 'appearing' and assuming shape in public worship, probably represented by light or the smoke of incense. The mother religion of Christianity has always had a strong belief that God's light and glory can become visible in the world.[24]

As the Christian church gradually disengaged itself from its Jewish matrix (a birth probably still not fully accomplished everywhere until around the end of the 4th century AD), Christians began to produce forms of symbolic art focused on images from the Bible but drawing on the fund of images offered by contemporary culture as well. The birthplace of the icon was most likely Egypt although it was influenced more by popular artistic production than the art of the Pharaohs. In its formal elements, it is a fusion of popular Egyptian funerary portraiture with the Greco-Roman Imperial artistic heritage of the art of Late Antiquity – yet all raised to a level of artistic refinement that represents a divine assumption of created being into the service of God.[25]

Eventually in both East and West (though not without great internal upheavals in the 8th and 9th century Byzantine church) a sophisticated and complex Christian art evolved providing detailed narrative programmes for decorating churches with scenes from the Christian faith – festal cycles of images based on the liturgical celebrations or wider ones drawing on the whole life of Christ. For Orthodox Christians this has fostered an intense awareness that the church building itself is an extended icon. Filled with the presence of the saints and the mysteries of Christ, it is an image of communion between the Holy Trinity and redeemed humanity.[26]

This sense of presence indicates that there was much more to the development of the icon than a mere fusion of styles or the provision of Christian teaching aids or propaganda, the latter aspect of iconography being that which generally dominated Christian art in the west. As the Byzantine Fathers reflected on the revealed mystery of Christ, and as ever richer and more symbolic forms of liturgical worship developed, art itself became a witness to the wonders God has done in Christ for the salvation of the world. The icon was seen to testify to the mystery of Christ, the reality of God's incarnation, in a number of significant ways. It was a shining silent witness to the Word-made-flesh, a 'visible word' that re-presents the content of the preached and written word of the Bible: the glorified Lord Jesus. Painted from vision, it awakens vision.[27]

According to Christian understanding, God's incarnation was real: the divine did not simply make fleeting appearances in human form to assist the world in its needs, as in Greek or Hindu mythology, but truly became flesh to save and sanctify creation and to re-establish communion between God and humanity. Christianity is not simply mythology (even if like all great human phenomena, in the course of its long history it subsequently generated its own mythology). Byzantine Christians realised that according to the logic of the incarnation it must be possible to make a depiction of a truly incarnate God. St John's gospel asserts that no one has ever seen God but goes on at once to insist that God the only Son has made him known (Jn 1:18).

The icon is a standing reminder of what the doctrine of the incarnation proclaims: Christ is *Emmanuel,* i.e. God who enters into communion with us. He is not a phantom or ghost after his resurrection (Lk 24:39-40). Christ was, is and remains for ever, real flesh, real humanity. The icon testifies that God has sanctified creation through the flesh of Christ. In not disdaining to become a human being, God uttered a resounding 'yes!' to the reality of creation while at the same time revealing its transcendent dignity, future destiny and high vocation: to become a transfigured bearer of divine light.

Christ the incarnate Word in his individual person and in his saving mysteries is the fundamental basis and exemplar for the icon, while the possibility of depicting the Mother of God, saints and angels flows from this. Angels are also depicted even though they are not, strictly speaking, incarnate beings. The angels cross the intermediary zone between heaven and earth as visible heavenly messengers. Yet being creatures they stand firmly on the created side of the infinite gulf that divides the uncreated God from the world. They are therefore also in need of redemption by the divine-human Christ and are relegated in the Letter to the Hebrews to a subordinate role in comparison with him (Heb 1:5-14). Usually depicted in their role as servants and bearers of the divine will to humankind, they are also often shown in Orthodox churches as heavenly deacons serving at the celestial altar where Christ the high priest offers his completed liturgy.[28]

However, as every Orthodox Christian knows, the icon can never simply be identified with the reality it depicts. In Orthodox understanding icons are highly complex entities. They are sacramental objects that operate as effective symbols, mediating invisible realities to us and in turn allowing us access to what lies 'beyond', 'behind' or even (in a carefully qualified sense) 'within' them: thanks to the union of divine grace with artistic skill purified by prayer, a certain kind of presence dwells in them and is mediated and manifested through them. For that reason the true icon can only be born out of prayerful contemplation of the mysteries of Christ, in an ambience faithful to the tradition of the church and its liturgical vision of reality.

The icon exists by analogy with the incarnation of Christ, God's fundamental disclosure-zone through which he manifests his presence among us. It is a secondary but also privileged disclosure-zone where Christ continues to appear, radiating the grace of his mysteries or through the figures of his Mother and the saints calling us to communion with God and the church. In these sacramental objects (which are not only painted but may also be carved, woven or mosaic) divine transfiguring power works in and through the art of the icon writers and their physical materials.

The painters, opening hearts purified by prayer and fasting to the radiance of Christ's glory and invoking the descent of the Holy Spirit, are expected to eschew all egoistic urges to self-expression. This is the art of communion and cannot come into being unless there is a real personal *kenosis*. Faithfully adhering to the rules of the iconic tradition (once again demonstrating communion with the church) the icon writers become a medium through which the mysteries of salvation find a fresh dwelling place once again in the sacred images which emerge under their brush. Heaven opens its doors and the epiphany of the sacred occurs. The process is analogous in some ways to the celebration of the Eucharist, in that it provides a Spirit-filled space, a 'place' for the invisible to manifest itself through the visible.[29]

Yet the Orthodox Church insists sharply on the essential qualitative difference between the icon and the eucharistic liturgy. In the Eucharist, the holiest of sacraments, the fullness of Christ's presence is intrinsically linked to the sacramental forms of bread and wine after their consecration: they yield their deepest inner being to God's transforming touch, so as to give place to him. Through the power of the Holy Spirit they are transfigured into the glorified body and blood of the risen Lord. Making himself present through the sacramental appearances of food and drink allows Christ to penetrate into the deepest recesses of the bodies and souls of those who receive him.

In the production of the icon, no such yielding of being or absolute identification occurs between the being employed and the one depicted. The carved, woven or painted image retains its essential being, becoming a dwelling place and vehicle for the disclosure of a presence rather than being so transformed that it is intrinsically identified with that presence. It is a medium used by Christ and his saints through which they disclose themselves.

The icon is also both like and unlike the feasts of the liturgical calendar. Like them it re-presents the mysteries of Christ so that the risen Lord can act through it; yet unlike the liturgy, whose ritual acts consist of a series of moving images, it is a kind of static snapshot, a small piece of created reality so wonderfully transformed by the co-operation (synergy) of human artistic skill and God's creative grace that material elements are empowered to become transparent, translucent filters for invisible realities.

Ultimately the icon's deepest meaning, like that of the church's liturgical feasts, is both ecclesiological and eschatological. It is a manifestation in our midst of that communion with the

Holy Trinity in the company of all the redeemed which awaits us in its fullness in heaven but is given to us here below in the communal worship of the liturgy. Its still, calm, poised and beautiful presence points to the final vocation of all created beings which are called by God to become bearers of divine light in his glorious kingdom.[30] Written from a vision of faith, it can only be understood within the climate of faith and in contemplative prayer. To quote Michael Paul Gallagher again:

> … prayer requires that the eyes of the imagination enter into a zone of response that becomes contemplative receptivity.[31]

The icon with its material elements transfigured by grace and human artistry is a vivid reminder that the Creator of all things chose to become part of his own creation in order to elevate it and lead it to the transcendent goal established for it from the beginning. It is a supremely liturgical art, fashioned like all the sacraments by the power of the Holy Spirit who brings it out of the darkness of contemplative prayer and into the light through a marvellous co-operation (synergy) between the painter's skill and divine grace. Through that harmonious activity the divine energies lying concealed and latent in the material world are given symbolic expression in the faces of the Lord, his Mother and the saints.

It is a pointer towards Christ's fullest presence on earth, his mystery-presence in the Eucharist and a reminder to Christians of their vocation: recognising God's presence in other human beings – the definitive icons of God – we are to venerate Christ in them and become one with them in communion. Realising that we are, each one of us, his icon, is a call to ascetical *kenosis*: to pray and work that, purified from illusion, fantasy and sin and transformed by grace, we may be made into Christ's living likenesses through communion with him in prayer. The fundamental iconic disclosure-zone is the human face. The beautiful faces of the icons, created images of Christ, his Mother and the saints mediate the uncreated beauty of God, the source of all beauty. They point to the goal of the entire mystery of salvation: the final transfiguration of the world through grace when the risen Christ, the cosmic Shepherd, will return in glory at the end of time to gather all his scattered sheep, visible and invisible, into communion in the kingdom of the Father's love.

C. PERSONAL PRAYER: INTERIORISING THE MYSTERIES

The purpose for which Christians are already called
here and now in their life histories
within universal history
is that in the self giving of Jesus Christ to them,
and theirs to him,
they should enter into their union with him,
their union with Christ.

Karl Barth

Like everything that comes to man
through God's self-revelation in Christ …
prayer is ultimately rooted in God himself
and in his triune exchange of life.
Beyond all purely creaturely motives and needs,
Christian prayer is a participation
  in the inner life of the divinity,
which is revealed, prepared and accomplished
in the world by Jesus Christ our Lord
and by him made available for us to take part in.

Hans Urs von Balthasar

For the mystery of Christ to become active in our lives, it is not enough that it should remain only an 'objective' divine revelation, a manifestation and action of God standing over against us as an external truth. In the death and resurrection of Christ and the coming of the Holy Spirit, God has disclosed his tri-personal nature to us in involving himself with us – for he is *Emmanuel*, God with us (Mt 1:23). The Father grants us freedom in the Holy Spirit (2 Cor 3: 17) inviting us to share the life of the Holy Trinity as responsible moral agents set free from sin by Christ. God asks each one of us to surrender to his action in our lives and to reproduce in our own small way the great mysteries of salvation accomplished for us by Christ. This is the third dimension of the mystery – its taking root in our personal experience through faith, hope and love that find expression in prayer (1 Cor 13:13).

Without this dimension, which like that of the liturgy involves the descent of the Holy Spirit and the objective recalling of Christ, the mystery of salvation tends to become merely a series of 'objective' revealed truths to which we give only nominal assent, or a religious event that we celebrate in liturgies. It may remain simply an ideology and an ethics, rather than becoming the transforming force God intends it to be for all of us.

This irreducibly personal third dimension of the mystery becomes real only through our response (itself awakened and sustained by grace) to God's invitation to take possession consciously of his transforming power in our daily life and conduct. It is the mystery of Christian vocation and discipleship, of our graced yet free response to Christ's call to follow him (Mt 4:19-20). God's cosmic plan for us comes to fulfilment as we enter into the intimate relationship with him that he wills for us through his beloved Son. In this dimension of the mystery of Christ – the mystery lived and experienced – Christians develop through grace a new way of being. Living by faith, we learn to give way increasingly to Christ who dwells within us (Gal 2:20). We learn to acquire the mind of Christ (Phil 2:5; 1 Cor 2:16), who as he prayed on the cross, commended his whole life into the hands of the Father (Lk 23:46).

As a stimulus to acquiring the mind of Christ much help is available to us in the ancient spiritual disciplines known in monastic tradition as sacred reading (*lectio divina*), meditation (*meditatio*) and prayer (*oratio*). To read and meditate according to the classical monastic traditions means cultivating a spiritual practice consisting in repetitive rumination of short passages from holy scripture – passages one reads over and over again until one has 'got them off by heart'. Through such repeated reading, the message of the sacred texts becomes like a second nature. The word read and meditated has to be turned regularly into prayer. That is why the Psalms are such a tremendous resource for this kind of meditative reading.[32]

Ruminating in this way on the inspired word of scripture opens our eyes to recognise the whole of nature and history as a book that speaks to us of God's providential plan and encourages us to look for that plan in our own lives. The word becomes truly a lamp to our feet and a light to our path (Ps 118(119):105), a symbol shining with the light of God's presence. As we gently repeat the word with our lips, letting it echo and re-echo in the sounding chamber of the heart, it enkindles in us a spirit of prayer: the word itself becomes prayer in us.

Gradually a fund of sacred scripture comes to be stored within the heart. Growing familiarity with the word leads to greater knowledge of the story of salvation, its progressive unfolding throughout history as recorded in the Bible and its regular re-presentation in the church's liturgy. Ever deeper insights into God's will are obtained in the light of the Holy Spirit by this mulling over the revealed word. It is God's medium through which he speaks to us and by means of which he asks us to respond in faith and love. The Swiss mystic Adrienne von Speyr has written profoundly about this dialogical union of reading and prayer and how it expands Christian understanding:

> No word of the Lord's is isolated; each is related to all. It is precisely in prayer that these connections become visible. Each word of the Lord (and his actions too are lessons and words) has the power to reveal further connections to the person at prayer and to initiate him into the mysteries of the Son's earthly life and of his eternal life in the Father … in both prayer and reading, his approach will become more markedly contemplative.

Speyr shows how this progressive growth in prayer and understanding helps the soul to grow also in abandonment to God's will and to put on the mind of Christ:

> The self, which had already retired into the background at an earlier stage of prayer, is now even more stripped and abandoned; now the only important thing is the word of God, its truth and its realisation. This word grows in the soul until it takes charge entirely, until the meaning of God

has become the meaning of life, until the soul has been re-fashioned totally into the handmaid of the Lord.[33]

Reading and meditating the Bible in this way demands both self-restraint and self-discipline. It requires a focused unhurried attention to the text so that it is contemplated rather than simply analysed or assessed, in order that the light of revelation might break through its words. Tradition calls the first stage of this process *lectio divina* because as a 'method' it developed around reading the Bible as the privileged place of God's word. But without denying the priority of holy scripture, monastic tradition also encourages a similar style of reading when engaging with other texts as well. Everything in God's providential working may function as a vehicle for the Spirit to communicate Christ's transforming word.

God's word recorded and contained in scripture thus nourishes our faith through meditative reading. As the symbolism of baptism and the receptive nature of faith demonstrate, we are saved by God without any activity at all on our part (Eph 2:8-9). Christ accomplished his work alone (Is 63:3), without any help from us, and in the same way the initial movements of his grace in us are entirely unmerited. But having received that initiating grace, we are not then left merely passive. We are invited to enter into relationship with God and collaborate with the Holy Spirit in the spreading of the gospel message.

Spiritual abandonment, learning to yield oneself to God's will, is the required attitude but it is never mere passivity in a superficial sense. One has to consent to become malleable material in God's hands, clay flexible enough to assume the shape of the mission he entrusts. One has to acquire freedom and learn resignation to God's will. Eastern Christian monastic tradition calls this growing attitude of inner freedom *apatheia*, or freedom from passions. It entails a radical letting go of all one's negative thoughts, desires, obsessions and fixations so as to deliver oneself fully into God's hands. It ought never to be confused with mere apathy or inertia.[34]

In the Catholic Church the Jesuits, following St Ignatius Loyola's teaching, recommend *indiferencia*, a total abandonment of one's own ideas, thoughts and plans so as to be of service to God in the salvation of the world;[35] while the Dominicans, faithful to the insights of the great German mystics of the Middle-Ages, teach the need for *Abgescheidenheit* and *Gelassenheit* (detachment and letting-be), so that God may have the freedom to speak and act through the self.[36] Protestant spiritual tradition, heir in many ways to that of the medieval German mystics, asserts something similar with its central doctrine of justification by grace alone, so profoundly articulated by Martin Luther in his early work, 'The Freedom of a Christian.'[37]

Luther preached a spirituality of 'letting-God-be-God' so that he may act through his faith-filled follower without let or hindrance. The followers of Calvin for their part aim to refer everything to God's greater glory, offering all their actions for the furtherance of the gospel of grace.[38] Like monastic *apatheia*, such surrender of the will, far from being opposed to freedom, is actually its most authentic manifestation: rooted and grounded in God's love, the will is liberated from its blind attachments and set free to embrace God's will which initiates us into the deepest acceptance of reality. Learning to say, 'Your will be done on earth as it is in heaven' (Mt 6:10; Mk 14:36-40) does not crush our freedom but instead liberates it into the only secure harbour of lasting peace and happiness: God's will which underpins everything.

The prayer which corresponds to this attitude is essentially simple. Like the request of the blind man in the gospels, it consists in crying out to God in short phrases or even single words that flow straight from the heart (cf Mt 9:27). As St John Climacus, a Byzantine monastic writer put it:

> Pray in all simplicity. The publican and the prodigal son were reconciled to God by a single utterance.[39]

Many examples from scripture (particularly the Psalms, but also the teaching and example of Jesus) could be adduced in which such simple, fervent but effective prayer is encouraged (Mk 14:36; Mt 6:9-13; Lk 18:13).

Orthodox monastic writers (and St John Cassian in the west) taught the use of such forms of prayer and St Benedict codified the tradition in his *Rule* when he taught that prayer should be short,

fervent, pure, reverent and offered with tears.[40] In the Orthodox
Church, (systematically from the 12th century on, but certainly
much earlier), it gradually crystallised into the varied forms of the
famous 'Jesus Prayer' in which one calls repeatedly on the Lord
Jesus for mercy for oneself and others, with the certainty that
prayer made in his name is always heard (Acts 2:21). Orthodoxy
places great faith in the sacramental power of the holy name of the
Lord Jesus Christ who is 'Yahweh's salvation' and the anointed
Messiah of the Lord (Mt 1:21). Yet even here the name must be an
icon, not an idol.[41]

Through this acquired passivity, this letting-God-be-God that
finds expression in the prayer of the heart, the mystery of Christ
recorded in scripture and celebrated in the liturgy flows out into
life. Prayer awakens compassion to the needs of one's neighbour
as the inevitable consequence of having been seized by the 'logic'
of Christ's law of love. The mystery of Christ embodies God's
mercy, his compassion towards the world and his active love for
human beings and for all creatures everywhere. To allow the healing grace of this mystery to penetrate one's heart is to take seriously
Christ's command which he issued at the conclusion to his parable of the Good Samaritan: 'Go and do likewise!' (Lk 10:37).

There is nothing selfish about such sustained personal prayer
for it is really a kind of evangelisation of the self. One gives thanks
repeatedly for mercy received and experienced through the continuous invocation of the Saviour's holy name. God's mercy in
turn expands the heart, empowering it to have mercy on others
just as it has received mercy from the Lord. One learns to sing with
the Psalmist (Ps 48(49):9, from the Latin Vulgate):

We have received your mercy O Lord,
in the midst of your holy temple!

Human experience reaches conscious articulation only through
reflection, however rudimentary that may be. Like the spendthrift
younger boy in the parable of the Prodigal Son, we have to 'come
to ourselves' to gain any serious understanding of our real situation before God (Lk 15:17). The often chaotic raw material of our
existence – supplied by what happens to us – has to be shaped into

intelligible patterns so that we can begin to understand it. That is why personal tragedies which saturate the self with an unanticipated excess of reality are so capable of overwhelming us.

In reaching such a level of conscious articulation in the Christian life, it is impossible to exaggerate the character-forming power of prayer and meditation as one applies it to the events of God's revealed mystery. Through such spiritual disciplines one learns consciously to appropriate the grace that has been granted and configure one's life to God's plan. Without the sustained effort of prayer and meditation it is very difficult to expand one's Christian consciousness and develop a real relationship with God. Prayer, like every other relationship, withers without contact.

In baptism and faith we are plunged objectively by Christ into the mystery of his saving work and granted access to a relationship with God in the Holy Spirit. But in prayer we are invited to embrace the paschal mystery through personal participation. The inner 'logic' of Christ's mystery is this: risen life comes only through suffering and death (Lk 24:26). That 'logic' is already inscribed at the heart of human existence. It is recognised in one form or another by all great religions and philosophies of the world and in the common experience of ordinary people everywhere as they live, love and die together.

Yet it has been given a new and unimaginable depth of meaning through the manifestation of Christ and the redeeming acts by which God saved the world. *Per crucem ad lucem* (through the cross to the light) is the fundamental law of Christ's gospel: we enter the light of glory only by taking the way of the cross; we do not first ascend to heaven without descending into humility. In all of this Christ is the archetype, pattern and model we are called to follow. In the light of the new and radiant vision given us in his paschal mystery, Christ allows us to read our own experience through the message of his cross and resurrection.

Thus we learn in prayer that each encounter with the darkness of life and its more bitter aspects offers us a share in the passion of the Master. The darkness may be one's own, such as the painful experience of personal limitations, vulnerability, inadequacy, lost or wasted opportunities or physical or mental suffering. It may be that of others' suffering, or the impact on oneself of their dark and negative energies experienced as betrayal, anger, infidelity or jealousy.

It may be a crippling burden of guilt which is not just a groundless psychological complex but the unbearable fact that my conscience witnesses to having really damaged someone else. Continual conversion and repentance, saying and truly meaning the penitential part of the Jesus Prayer, with its 'have mercy on me a sinner,' (or as the Greek formula puts it, 'me the sinner' as though I were the only one!) entails bringing these dark forces into the judging, forgiving and healing light of Christ's death and resurrection. We have to learn to expose our wounds to Christ, our wounded God, so that through the gentle laser surgery of love he might transfigure them.[42]

The path to resurrection consists in following Christ's descent into the dark and, in union with him, embracing whatever comes in abandonment to God's will. Entering the dark cavern of the heart we find that we are not in fact alone for Christ has gone before us. He awaits us there: through his entry into the heart in baptism he is already enthroned within us. He issues an invitation from that place to come and join him; or to borrow the imagery of the gospels, to leave our boats and walk to him across the dark and stormy waters (Mt 14:22-33).

Many images and metaphors are needed to describe the spiritual adventure of going deeper in prayer. It is like journeying towards an abandoned temple which is hidden in a jungle. The deepest recesses of the heart are only reached by making the most demanding efforts. But there Christ sits enthroned in the sanctuary, awaiting our coming if we are ready to set out on the journey; or it is like a diver seeking a treasure lying at the bottom of the sea. One has to become a spiritual deep-sea diver, ready to descend into the depths. Staying on the surface and refusing to make the descent, or turning away in fear at the entrance to the jungle, can lead to inner atrophy and paralysis of soul. In the spiritual life, superficiality is the death of the self. Nothing important in life will ever happen if we never have the courage to descend into the depths. It is a way that cannot be avoided if we wish to be identified as disciples of the one who took the way of descent to come to us (Phil 2:7-8).[43]

Having conquered death and hell and ascended into heaven, Christ has descended and entered our souls through baptism. He dwells within, concealed at the centre of the heart, calling us to look towards him and receive the light (Ps 33(34):5). The revelation of the Christian mystery passes between two impenetrably deep abysses. One is the abyss of the divine darkness from where it issues forth as a summons from the heart of the Holy Trinity, taking form in the life, death and resurrection of Christ. The other is the abyss of the human person, grounded in God, constituted through freedom, intelligence and love, but with the frightful capacity to reject the creator.

Through the Holy Spirit Christ has entered into the darkness of this abyss through the senses of the body, by means of his Word and sacramental mysteries. God pours out his presence there, the light of his grace, in the dark womb of the heart where it is received by faith. In that inner sanctum he becomes a burning, shining lamp. Drawn inward by that light, one experiences a heart-to-heart encounter with God, a mutual self-presencing of lovers, one to the other (Song of Sol 2:14; Ezek 16:1-14) which is the fulfilment of all desire.[44]

Of course the relationship will remain for ever utterly unequal for it is grounded in grace alone. It is always God who chooses, initiates, sustains and perfects it – even in the face of infidelity. We shall never understand or explain why God should love us in this way, doing everything possible to accommodate himself to us, standing knocking like a beggar at the door of the heart, waiting to elicit our free response (Rev 3:20).

Our need for love – the deepest of all our drives – can be satisfied only by the infinite love of God; for only in the luminous radiance of divine beauty shall we be filled with everlasting joy. Faith's groping in prayer through darkness, and our innumerable failures to respond cannot stop the torrent of God's love:

> Deep calls to deep
>   at the thunder of your cataracts;

all your waves and your billows
   have gone over me. (Ps 41(42):7)

The anonymous author of the Song of Songs, the Jewish and Christian mystical book of the Bible *par excellence,* wrote (Song 8: 7a) of love:

Many waters cannot quench love,
neither can floods drown it.

Through the work of prayer and spiritual descent we are led and guided by the Spirit into the presence of the One who dwells within us. There God uncovers his very self to us in his Son and Holy Spirit. He embraces us, penetrates us with transforming light and establishes the soul as his beloved bride whom he loves (Song 4:9), the one in whom he takes his rest for ever (Jn 14:23). Mystical prayer in the hidden sanctuary of the self makes of the heart a spiritual bridal chamber where God's disclosure of self becomes complete. He strips us of all our sins and unites us to himself:

I will betroth you to myself for ever,
betroth you with integrity and justice,
with tenderness and love;
I will betroth you to myself with faithfulness,
and you will come to know the Lord. (Hos 2:21-22, *JB*)

In the vision of the Christian East this mystical marriage is also a mystical liturgy, an inner act of worship celebrated on the altar of the heart. The Holy Spirit, descending in response to prayer, unites Christ with the soul, his beloved bride, and carries them both to heaven, to the Father's glorious throne. Thus the mystery of Christ recorded in scripture and celebrated in signs and symbols in the church's sacramental liturgy attains its end: the mystical marriage between God and the self in the bridal chamber of the heart.[45]

PART TWO

Meditating on the Mysteries in the Liturgical Year

Transition

Having considered how the one great mystery of salvation revealed in Christ is disclosed to us in holy scripture, baptism, the Eucharist, the icon, the church's year and personal prayer, it is time to contemplate its individual mysteries in more detail. Through the varied feasts of the liturgy, the Holy Spirit unveils it for us in the course of the year, enabling us to share in the mysteries through celebration, prayer and spiritual experience so as to enter through Christ into a deeper relationship with the living God.

The goal of such participation is an attentive, contemplative focusing of the mind on Christ's mysteries, the cultivation of a loving gaze that enables his light to flood and transform the heart. To assist in doing that that I shall consider various scenes from an icon cherished here in the monastery at Glenstal, a large panel probably from western Russia and most likely written in the early part of the 19th century (Fig 1). It depicts the mysteries of the liturgical year as it is celebrated in the Byzantine tradition, followed by Orthodox and many Eastern Catholics alike. However, given what we have noted about how eastern Christians view their icons, these images should not be seen simply as illustrations to the text or beautiful adornments which might equally well not appear at all.

As we have seen, the icon is always more than merely an embellishment of worship or prayer. It is a locus of presence and a focus for vision, an in-breaking of the one great mystery of Christ through the depiction of an event from the history of salvation, or from the lives of his Mother and his holy ones, the saints. It impels us to break through the veil of appearances and open ourselves to the contemplation of the light which shines on us. The scenes in this icon depict the main mysteries of Christ celebrated in the liturgy. Like the feasts they accompany, and of which indeed they form an integral part, such images are a privileged disclosure-zone in which God manifests the presence of the mystery of Christ.

In contemplating the mystery revealed in each of these small images I shall focus attention on some of the scriptural and liturgical texts used in the celebration of the feasts. Since, however, liturgical celebration entails much more than words I shall not deal with texts alone. Worship, especially in the Byzantine and Benedictine traditions, is made up of a multitude of liturgical gestures and actions. Therefore in unfolding the meaning of the mysteries I shall at times also mention some of the symbolic gestures used in the church's rites of worship. Liturgy is a complex human activity and as such can never be identified only with words.

It is about action, movement and symbolic gestures which engage the five senses in communal prayer and, by calming the mind and focusing attention, lure the heart into contemplation. In the Christian East and in Benedictine tradition, liturgical worship is seen as a kind of vision. By contemplating the sacred choreography of the solemn ritual we are meant to detect in the worship of the earthly church an icon of the liturgy of heaven.

I shall therefore refer a great deal to the liturgical rites of the Orthodox and sometimes other Eastern churches as well. This is not only because we shall be contemplating a Russian icon but above all because Orthodoxy's rich liturgical life is particularly well supplied with symbolic resources for re-presenting the mysteries of Christ: yet as a treasure gathered largely in the first millennium of the church's life, before the lamentable division of the Greek and Latin churches, Orthodox worship contains a patrimony common to all Christians.

As a Benedictine monk belonging to the Latin part of the Roman Catholic Church, I shall follow St Benedict's advice to look to the east for light. Theology and spirituality today ought to be done with ecumenical sensitivity since the overwhelming fullness of the mystery of Christ cannot be confined in any one system. It will always break the banks we make for it. Tradition is a polyphonic motet.

In accordance with what has been said about the nature of the liturgical year, I will not follow a straight line in describing the mysteries, i.e. one following the sequence of Christ's life from birth to death and resurrection. Instead I will do as the icon writer did, placing the resurrection right at the centre, with the mysteries of the passion, death and burial circulating around it.

The feasts of the Lord and his Mother are in turn placed around them on the outer part of the panel. Thus our iconographer, well-grounded in the ethos of the Byzantine liturgy and the paschal-centred spiritual vision of the Orthodox Church, admirably demonstrated how the liturgical year like the whole work of salvation spirals around its true centre – the light of Christ rising from the dead.

We begin our meditations on the mysteries of Christ therefore where the Christian community itself began two millennia ago, and at the point where the liturgy and the church's year take their origin and find their end: Christ's paschal triumph. Everything that preceded it and everything that flows from it will be viewed as the apostles and evangelists saw them – bathed in the warm light of Christ's Easter joy. For a Christian there can be no other perspective.

CHAPTER SEVEN

The Mysteries of Exaltation

A. Easter Triumph (Fig 2)

> This is the night when Jesus Christ broke the chains of death
> and rose as Victor from hell!
>
> *Roman Liturgy, Paschal Vigil*

The paschal victory of Christ, his triumph over death, is like a spiritual bonfire lit at the first Easter and blazing ever since at the centre of the church's life. Through its daily, weekly and yearly celebration in the liturgy, the Holy Spirit sends out sparks of light and grace: these in turn kindle the feasts which emanate from Easter and revolve around it.[1] There is nothing in Christian life, theology, worship, spirituality or ethics which does not have the resurrection of Christ as its source, support and goal. Easter is literally everything, the core content of the gospel message we are called to proclaim. 'Christ is risen! He is risen indeed!' shout Christians of the Byzantine tradition at every Easter vigil and repeatedly throughout the season of Eastertide.[2]

This icon contains two depictions of the resurrection, two different ways of viewing it (Fig 2). The bottom scene shows the mystery of Holy Saturday and Christ's descent into the Underworld (*Sheol* for the Jews, *Hades* for the Greeks), the unseen region of darkness, the shadowland into which the souls of the departed descended after death. Not surprisingly, the Nordic races imagined it as a cold place. Jesus goes there after his death on the cross and burial. Sometimes this journey, (the *descensus ad inferos* in Latin) is also called 'the descent into hell'.[3]

But it is worth remembering that in the ancient church the terminology for describing the places where the dead were believed to be detained was still quite fluid. It was only in later centuries that it crystallised into the familiar categories of what has been called eschatological geography – heaven, hell and purgatory.[4]

Yet it is erroneous to think of purgatory as some halfway house between heaven and hell: according to a correct understanding of Catholic doctrine, those in purgatory are saved but are undergoing purification by divine love to fit them for the unveiled vision of God's face.[5] According to the traditional doctrine and iconography of this mystery then, Jesus goes down to the land of the dead.

Above the scene of his descent he is shown rising triumphantly from the tomb and appearing in glory to Peter in the presence of an angelic witness. In earlier Orthodox tradition, the scene of his descent to the underworld would have sufficed to depict the resurrection, for tradition had always respected the fact that no one witnessed Christ's actual resurrection from the dead: rather they had a series of encounters with the risen one. The icon of the descent is still normally the image exposed for veneration in Orthodox churches in the Easter season. However this 19th century Russian icon adds the second image as a kind of confirmation of the original event, just as the gospels include his post-resurrection appearances. It is a helpful reminder that the apostolic faith in Christ's resurrection was not primarily created by the sight of an empty tomb but by the experiences the apostles were granted of the risen Jesus.

B. *Descent into the Underworld: the Mystery of the Light's Immersion in Death*

Today Hades sighs with tears:
'O would that I had never received
the one who was born of Mary!
He has come to me and destroyed my power!
He has broken down my bronze gates
and as God has delivered the souls
I had taken prisoner!'
O Lord, glory to your cross and resurrection!

Today Hades groans:
'My power has disappeared.
I received the one who died as mortals die,
but was unable to hold him

and I lost those over whom I had ruled.
I have controlled the dead since the world began,
but behold he raises them all up with him!'
O Lord, glory to your cross and resurrection!

Byzantine Rite, sixth week of Great Lent

The doctrine of Christ's descent to the dead first entered the creeds of the western church used at baptism in the 4th century, but as a belief its roots lie in the east. They reach far back into the history of the church, being found in various popular texts which, though beautiful and profound, were not admitted to the official canon of holy scripture. There are only a couple of places in the New Testament where the mystery is suggested and even then its meaning is obscure and allusive (Acts 2:25-28; 1 Pet 3:18-20). But the belief functions at a much deeper level than that of analytical logic or rational understanding. It is a perfect example of the power of the church's liturgy to draw out hidden depths of meaning in the events of salvation and present them in the language and imagery of symbolism.[6]

The descent into the Underworld is a symbolic way of imagining where Christ was in the period between his death and resurrection while his body lay in the tomb. Elaborating on it in the poetic style appropriate to liturgy, the texts of the Roman and Byzantine rites offer a rich array of symbols and images to stimulate meditation on his redeeming work. He is seen as Christ the victorious one (*Christus Victor*) a hero descending in triumph to the dead, going into Sheol to proclaim the resurrection to the just men and women of the Old Covenant and all who waited for God's saving light to dawn in history.[7] Holy Saturday is particularly rich in liturgical texts celebrating and probing the meaning of this mysterious event. At the early Office of Matins in our monastery liturgy for Holy Saturday, we sing the following ancient chant:

Our shepherd,
the source of living water has departed.
At his passing the sun was darkened,
for he who held us captive
is a captive now himself.

Today our Saviour has shattered the bars
and battered down the barricades of death.
He has torn down the barricades of hell
and overthrown the power of Satan.

Christ the conquering hero enters the realm of the dead. There through his death and rebirth he slays death, personified as a living being. The Byzantine tradition in particular, as our icon indicates, celebrates the announcement of the good news of salvation to Adam and Eve, our proto-parents. Christ reaches out his hand to drag them from the jaws of death, shown as a great devouring fish like the whale that swallowed Jonah. Jesus himself had spoken of his death and burial in precisely those terms (Mt 12:38-41) but the notion of all-devouring death is a perfect example of an archetypal image in the sense in which the psychologist Carl Jung developed that idea.[8] Such images rise up out of the primal matrix of the unconscious, the fecund source of all imaginative symbolism, turning up as common images in all cultures and civilisations wherever reflection is made on the mystery of death.

The emphasis on Christ as a triumphant hero passed over into the medieval west, particularly in Anglo-Saxon England, where it was called 'the harrowing of hell.' In those depictions Christ often carried his cross like a weapon, spearing the fish of death in its throat or dominating the figure of Satan.[9] Some texts from the Byzantine services for Holy Saturday illustrate this note of triumph well. They sing of the astonishment of the hosts of angels when they realised that the mystery of salvation had been kept secret from them through endless ages. As they see the source of life being laid in a tomb they are dumbfounded:

The choirs of angels were dazzled
when they saw the one
who was in the bosom of the Father,
the immortal one,
now lying as dead in the tomb.
The hosts of angels surround him
and glorify him
while he is counted with the dead in Hades:
for he is the Lord!

Embracing death the Lord strangles it, thereby dealing it a deadly blow. His light dispels the shadows of the Underworld with all its dank gloom and depressing misery. The same angels now sing in amazement as they see Christ rising from the dead:

Immortal life,
when you surrendered to death,
you destroyed Hades
by the splendour of your divinity
and raised the dead from under the earth.
All the powers of heaven cried out,
'O Christ our God, the giver of life
glory to you!'

The note of triumph is clearly sounded

Hades was vanquished,
Adam restored to life
and the curse abolished.
Eve was delivered,
death was crushed,
and we were made to live again!

Such imagery and the complex symbolic actions carried out at both the western and eastern paschal liturgies – the night vigil (including in western tradition, the kindling of the new fire and lighting of the paschal candle, 'wounded' yet incandescent symbol of the risen Christ) and the entry into the closed and darkened church in both traditions – is of the very essence of liturgical celebration. The mystery of Christ as new life made known after death is dramatically set before us in symbols stemming from the earliest centuries of the church, but arising also out of the creative matrix of the human imagination as it ponders the wonderful things God has done for us. As the Psalmist sang, centuries before Christ's rising from the dead:

When the Lord restored the fortunes of Sion,
we were like those who dream.
Then our mouth was filled with laughter,
and our tongue with shouts of joy. (Ps 125(126):1-2a)

But what does it mean and what spiritual significance can it possibly have for us today? Is it all just beautiful imagery or even mythology?

It is important to note that Christianity (like Judaism its parent faith) takes history seriously. The core events of the Christian faith are not mythological in any simple or narrow sense. They are events which really happened: Jesus really lived, really died and really rose again, or to speak in the language of the New Testament, was really raised by the power of the Father. The body of Jesus, torn and abused in the horrible death he suffered, is the same body that rose transfigured from the grave. Although the fact of an empty tomb is not enough to convince anyone of the truth of the resurrection (as we see from the unflinching incredulity of Jesus' enemies in the gospels (Mt 27:62-66)) it is much more than a mere literary embellishment to the story. The empty tomb is a silent witness to a fact: the one who had been buried there was no longer to be found in that place, for he had risen.

Yet the resurrection of Christ was a unique event in that it was both historical and trans-historical. It was historical in that it really occurred in time and place; but even as it occurred it passed out of time and out of history, into eternity. Christ's resurrection is like a kind of inverse image of the incarnation itself: there the eternal one kenotically self-contracted into space and time. Here time itself was taken up into eternity.[10]

This much is clear according to the unanimous witness recorded in the New Testament: Christ's resurrection was not just the resuscitation of a corpse, a bringing back to quotidian existence of a man who had been dead and would be dead again in the future, such as had been the case with Lazarus whom Jesus raised from death (Jn 12:9-11). The resurrection of Christ was of a very different order. It was his transformation by the Father's glory, his transfiguration by the power of the Holy Spirit (Rom 6:9-11; 1 Cor 15:1-11; 35-58; 1 Pet 1:21; 3:18). It was a radical, irreversible entry into a new undying life, the indestructible life of the resurrection.

However, to interpret what happened, the sacred authors and the church's liturgical traditions have often had recourse to mythological motifs. It was reasonable for them to have done so in attempting to describe a trans-historical event because the message had to be communicated in the language and culture of their time. That meant pressing into service many different ideas: Jewish mystical and mythological beliefs, Greek philosophy, ideas taken from esoteric systems current in the ancient world and mythological images ready at hand, which occur wherever human beings reflect on the mysteries of life, death and the nature of absolute reality. The gospel message of the mystery had to be inculturated for it to speak effectively to the human condition. But the wide range of images and ideas adopted were not just accepted at face value or swallowed uncritically: they were baptised and purified so as to serve a higher purpose, the proclamation of the saving gospel of Christ.

The imagery of Holy Saturday, with its descent into the Underworld, belongs at that level of reflection. It is not literal 'history' but mythology baptised into the service of Christ. However, that does not make it less true but true in a different way. With its symbols it proclaims the triumph of the crucified Son of God, the victory of divine power over death and the proclamation of Christ's saving message to the uttermost ends of the earth. It asserts that no dimension of human reality or experience has been left untouched by the saving action of God in the death and resurrection of his beloved Son.

It is a remarkable fact that the 20th century witnessed an unprecedented revival of interest in this mystery of Holy Saturday and an attempt as never before to understand what the church is saying to us through its overwhelming imagery. The explanation of it in the Roman Catholic Church will be forever associated (though not without controversy) with one of the greatest theologians of the last century, the Swiss Hans Urs Von Balthasar, although he claimed only to be offering a systematic account of what his friend the mystic Adrienne Von Speyr experienced spiritually every year during the celebration of the Paschal Triduum.[11]

Why this sudden surge of interest in the last century in the descent of Christ into the Underworld? Throughout this book I have used the expression 'disclosure-zone' to describe those events and places through which the mystery of Christ has been manifested to us. But the New Testament mentions another mystery, 'the mystery of iniquity' (2 Thess 2:7, according to the *King James Version*) which is also disclosed on earth. It was to do battle with that power of iniquity that the Son of God descended from heaven, became incarnate and embraced the cross.

Iniquity too has its privileged disclosure zones. They are gaping holes on the face of the earth where evil has erupted from the depths in a horrible 'pseudo-incarnation', places where death and misery have held dominion over all. Such places were in recent years (to name but a few) the European colonial empires of Africa, the Nazi death camps, Stalin's Gulags and the killing fields of Cambodia; such is the 'industry' of abortion; such were the slave and coffin ships that crossed the Atlantic; but such are all the places where human ingenuity, twisted by evil and driven by avarice and anger, places itself at the service of what John Paul II called 'a culture of death'.

Auschwitz may well serve as the perennial symbol for the disclosure-zones of the mystery of iniquity, the symbol of the dreadful synergy of demonic and human energy in the service of chaos and mayhem where man has crowned himself king and functioned as a self-appointed god: in a word, as a symbol of hell. It is hardly surprising in the light of 20th century experience that the theology of the descent of Christ into the Underworld should have made such a striking resurgence in contemporary theology and spirituality.

Since human ingenuity created hell on earth, the Holy Spirit reminds us of the opposite: God's willingness to go to the utmost lengths with human beings in order to rescue what was lost. The Fathers say that Christ came down to seek and save lost Adam and Eve but was unable to find them on the earth. Learning that they had died, he realised that he would have to die himself, descending into the depths, knowing that only thus could he regain the lost sheep and carry them home on his shoulders. It is a mythological image but a beautiful one. In the parable which inspired their reflections (Mt 17:12-14) Jesus asserts that it is never the Father's will that a single one of his little ones should ever be lost. The universal love of God is what the ministry of Jesus showed: his going to the dead demonstrated its limitless extent.

It is important to insist on this universal love. The earliest traditions stressed that Christ's descent involved God honouring his saving promises to the dead of the older covenant (such as David and Solomon) but the more modern interpretations emphasise that, in this mystery, his saving will really is shown to be truly universal. Christ goes to the underworld to shed the light of the gospel of grace on all human beings who have followed the light that was in them and tried to live virtuous lives.

Notwithstanding the pessimistic theology of Augustine which set limits on God's universal saving will, western Christianity before the Protestant Reformation never officially denied that Christ had given his life for every human being who has ever walked – or ever will walk – on earth. In the Christian east that has never been seriously questioned. Despite the theological axiom that there was no salvation outside the church (which was generally less exclusivist than some insist today), the medieval scholastics devised various theological ways around that, making the church's boundaries more elastic so as to extend God's mercy beyond the visible borders of Christendom.[12]

Since, as we have seen, the New Testament teaches it so clearly (Tit 2:11), Orthodox, Roman Catholics, most Anglicans and most Lutherans uphold the same teaching against the belief of some Christians that Christ's death was offered only for the elect, a specially chosen contingent selected for salvation from the condemned mass of sinful humanity. In that perspective Christ goes into the Underworld only to fetch those who have been predestined to salvation. Such an understanding of the mystery distorts the gospel message, making it very bad news indeed. It delivers a picture of God that is not awesome and majestic but truly rather appalling. As with redemption understood as penal substitution, we need to be careful that in 'explaining' God theologically he does not come out looking worse than human beings.

This icon, the traditional liturgical celebrations it accompanies and the magnificent exposition of the mystery of the theology of salvation offered not only by the Roman Catholic Balthasar, the Protestant Barth and the Orthodox Bulgakov, highlights the

Catholic/Orthodox (and authentically Evangelical) view that no human being is ever deliberately excluded by God from his all-embracing, saving love.

However, a universal vision of divine love is not the same as 'universalism'. It does not mean that all must *necessarily* be saved. Balthasar observed that it is really only after Christ's revelation that the frightful possibility of hell begins to unveil its ugly face. For supposing that, even after all God has done for us, people should still be so obtuse, so immured in wickedness as to turn their backs on love, what would happen then? Freedom after all pertains to the very essence of being human and, above all else, love cannot be forced. The offer of salvation has to be freely accepted if is to be truly received even though it is indeed offered free to all. Inevitable or mechanical salvation would destroy the infinitely precious freedom of the human person and reduce us to mere objects in God's sight. God's self-revelation as love teaches us that the one who loves us seeks our free response. Without such freedom – however limited or impaired – there can be no such response.[13]

Those who have carried out truly horrendous deeds cannot imagine that their guilt might be simply wiped away as if those deeds had never happened. The incarnation teaches us that God takes time, history and human responsibility with the utmost seriousness. There can be no simple waving of a divine hand to wipe away the horrors of an event like the Holocaust, no superficial notion that torturers and their victims can simply sit down together in the banquet of God's kingdom as if nothing needed to be explained. Yet even a Nazi criminal was created in the image and likeness of God. In the light of the revelation of God's all-embracing love and forgiveness on the cross and in the depths of the Underworld, one must dare to hope that the spark of life granted to everyone by the Holy Trinity can never be entirely extinguished – no matter how much its bearers have ignored, buried or denied it.

A wise Trappist Abbot once suggested to me that the images of Holy Saturday speak of how God beats continually on the doors of the heart until one day they are – finally – voluntarily opened from within by one who comes to see the truth. But in the case of someone who consigned countless millions to suffering and death, that ought surely to mean that the face of every single being whose life was ended or blighted by his hatred has to come before his eyes until he can finally accept responsibility for the evil inflicted and the sheer enormity of what was done finally dawns on him, forcing him to his knees before God. The modern understanding of the descent into hell offers us a move in that direction, but still the frightful possibility remains that some might go on for ever saying 'no' to God in a self-negating orgy of twisted self-justification. It is indeed a frightful possibility.

Yet the Orthodox Church sings at its Easter Vigil, 'The light of Christ shines on all!' Certainly there must be no minimising of human evil or responsibility; but if for us human beings 'to understand is to forgive', we may surely hope (and ought at least to pray with St Edith Stein, Pope John Paul II and Hans Urs von Balthasar) that it will be still more true for God, who understands everything – even the perverse and twisted byways of the heart. We surely ought to hope and pray that the universal love and grace of God revealed in the paschal mystery might one day really reach to the ends of the earth and open the eyes of all, however depraved and hateful they have been to their fellow human beings in this life. As Fr Sergius Bulagkov suggested, it would be blasphemous to imagine that evil might have the last word and claim as its own any living being loved by God and created in the image of Christ. In the light of God's infinite and eternal compassion – of which we are assured by his sending his Son to redeem the world – it is surely unthinkable that it might be so.[14]

Modern writers on this theme highlight another aspect of the descent of Christ, one more characteristic of classical Protestantism (especially that of Calvin) but with roots going deep into the tradition of the Latin Church. In descending to the Underworld, Christ is seen less as making a triumphant entry into Hades and more as showing God's solidarity with us in consenting to share the lot of sinful humanity, death included – where death is seen as final and total separation from God. He is the Father's peacemaker, his ambassador to our land of disobedience. Having stepped into the place of Adam and Eve, a place of self-imposed isolation, refusal of communion with God and rebellion against God's law, Jesus Christ identified with us to the bitter end. He became 'forsaken among the dead' (Ps 87(88):5) tasting the bitterness of absolute separation between humankind and its Creator which is the fruit of human egoism, a condition in which God can only be experienced as an enemy because one has made him into that.

Of course, the source of all life and love can never be an enemy in reality but we make God so by refusing his love and relating to him in a negative way. Human beings are all too often like angry disaffected adolescents, who cannot see beyond their limited resentments. We project on to God an image of him as an angry, vengeful parent. Jesus the only-begotten Son, the beloved first-born of the Father, elected in kenotic, self-emptying humility to join his brothers and sisters in their self-imposed condition of alienation. By enduring it to the end in unbroken faith, hope and love, but in indescribable bitterness of soul, he transfigured it from within.

In him, the bridge of communion between God and sinful creatures has been repaired for ever. We are enabled to cross over it with him and so to enter into life. Christ so united himself with our fallen nature that in him we were lifted up out of the realm of death and raised on high to the heavenly places. God made the sinless Christ in Paul's startling expression, 'into sin,' through an act of unimaginable divine solidarity with fallen humanity and in him has made us able to become the righteousness of God (2 Cor:21).

The image of the descent into hell shows the absolute nadir of the *kenosis* of the Word, whether with the Reformed tradition we choose to see it as the last and darkest moment of humiliation, or with the Lutherans (and Orthodox) as the first sounding of the note of resurrection.[15] It will be completed only by his ascension into heaven when, leading captivity captive, he carried our humanity, healed and saved in his own person, right up to God's throne to reign for ever in glory at the Father's right hand (Eph 4: 7-10; Acts 3:14-15). It is the culminating moment of that *sacrum et mirabile commercium,* the holy and wonderful exchange between God and humankind, of which we sing in the Christmas liturgy and about which Luther wrote so majestically.

Christ accepts all that is ours – suffering, death, abandonment, isolation from God due to the penalty imposed by his infringed law, a penalty from which we are incapable of freeing ourselves – and gives us what is his in exchange: eternal life, communion with God and adoption as his sons and daughters. He absorbs our darkness so that we might become light in him. As we have seen in discussing the passion, however, the genuine Christian idea of redemptive substitution is never penal. It is rather the freely-chosen, loving substitution of one of the persons of the Trinity (acting always in union with the other two): the divine-human Jesus who laid down his life not only for his friends (Jn 15:13) but also for his enemies (Mt 5:43-48; Lk 23:34).

These aspects of the mystery of Holy Saturday can speak to our experience today. I have found that this image and its message can be a useful therapeutic aid in dealing with people afflicted with depression. In the midst of a spiralling downward movement into the most terrible darkness, it is encouraging to be reminded that God the Son too descended into the darkness of the tomb and was enveloped by the overwhelming obscurity of the Underworld. The message of the gospel is that no situation is ever so dark or deep that God in Christ has not been there before us. He is, therefore, able to empathise with us in our suffering (Heb 2:14-18; 4:14-16)

Yet at least one modern psychologist has criticised the traditional Holy Saturday imagery, claiming that it speaks only of divine violence, of Christ battering down doors and forcing his way into the underworld in an aggressively penetrative, 'phallic' way which proves that he (and Christianity or rather 'Christianism' as he terms it) was incapable of learning the lessons of the dark. There is perhaps some truth in the criticism if the triumphant motif is used to foster a 'macho,' excessively masculine, heroic approach to spirituality.

But it need not be so. The sadness and darkness of Holy Saturday speak loudly of God's merciful, loving-kindness. To do justice to the absolute emptiness of Christ's *kenosis*, we need a corresponding fullness (*plethora*) of counterbalancing images and metaphors, to hold as many aspects of the mystery as possible in sight. Yet we also need to let Christ lead us forth into light, to bring us beyond our desolation.[16]

Balancing Christ's triumphant victory over death with his kenotic passivity, submission to the depths and resting in the tomb as found in modern interpretation, allows room for a healthy use of the descent image in connecting Christ's redemptive work to therapeutic issues in counselling and analysis. This Christ is one who shares our lot and consents to be in our place, even at its most dark. He teaches us the need for acceptance and passivity, for waiting. Yet he does not just leave us alone among the dead but raises us with him in triumph. As he rises, grasping us like Adam by the wrist, he wrenches us out of the maw of the abyss and raises us with him to new life and a living future. I can think of no more positive image of hope and redemption in the whole of Christian tradition.

C. The Risen One Appears

> Hasten and proclaim to the world
> that the Lord has risen
> and has conquered death
> for he is the Son of God
> and Saviour of humankind!
> > *Byzantine Easter hymn*

This scene conflates the actual resurrection of Christ (Mt 28:1-7; Lk 24:1-7) attested to by the angelic witness sitting at his right, with one of the appearances of Jesus found in the 21st chapter of St John's gospel (Jn 21:1-19). It is recorded there that he revealed himself to Peter and the other apostles as they were fishing on the Sea of Galilee. Peter was naked but clothed himself when he realised it was the Lord. All Christ's resurrection appearances are remarkable. They have about them a dreamlike quality, notwithstanding the practical, quotidian details (such Christ's cooking breakfast) on which the evangelists laid so much stress. The mood of Christ's post-resurrection appearances is very different from that of the Paschal Vigil during the night of passage from Holy Saturday to Easter Sunday itself. Then it was a matter of the first triumphant shouts of *Alleluia* and *Gloria* after their long absence from the liturgy of Lent, and the explosion of joy following the darkness of Good Friday and the silence of Holy Saturday. But here the mood is not that of exultation but of reflection and even of reconciliation. It is the quiet time after the drama of the three days.

Similarly, in the Latin liturgy the opening chant (*Introit*) of the Mass of Easter Sunday morning is a long, slow, lingering profoundly meditative reflection on the return of the Lord from Sheol taken from the Latin Vulgate translation of the Bible:

> I have arisen and am still with you, alleluia, alleluia, alleluia. (Ps 138(139):18)

The appearance described in John 21 is the prelude to one of the most moving scenes in the New Testament. Jesus asks Peter three times if he loves him, thereby offering him a chance to make good his threefold denial on Holy Thursday night (Lk 22:54-62). Responding to Peter's repeated protestations of love, he confers on him the charge to feed his lambs and shepherd his flock (Jn 21: 15-19).

This apostolic commissioning occurs, therefore, in a context which is very painful for Peter. Jesus discreetly reminds him of his previous failure. It is utterly lacking in the triumphalist connotations associated with the promises to Peter recorded in Matthew's gospel, that the gates of the Underworld (the very place from which Jesus had returned in his resurrection) would never prevail against the church he would found on Peter the rock (Mt 16:13-20).

The scene reminds us that the risen Christ arrives unrecognised in the midst of our lives with all their preoccupations, anxieties and cares, but that he is especially present when we are oppressed by the sense of our own unworthiness or failure. With infinite tenderness Jesus draws Peter out of his guilty self-obsession, making him focus not on what Peter imagines he wants or needs and not allowing him to sink back into the oblivion of immersion in the mere business of daily existence (Jn 21:3). He asks him instead squarely to confront the harsh reality of his past failures. Given those failures, does he truly love Jesus – the brother, friend and teacher of the past who has now become his Saviour and his Lord?

Jesus reveals a real vulnerability in this story. A short time before, as recorded in the same gospel, we find him offering to show his wounds to doubting Thomas so as to elicit faith and worship from that sceptical apostle. The body of Jesus was traumatised, made vulnerable in his passion. But in these post-resurrection showings he uncovers the deepest wound of all – that of his soul. It was wounded by the denials, rejection and betrayal inflicted on him by Peter and the others (with the exception of the 'Beloved disciple,' his mother and the other women).

No better proof could be given us that after his resurrection, notwithstanding the glorification of his body, Jesus is still authentically human, still the same one with whom they had walked the roads of Palestine before his passion. That it occurs in the very gospel which lays so much stress on his divine origin and nature offers striking confirmation of the reality of the incarnation of the Word.

The possibility for transformation Jesus brings when he appears is like his entire life, deeply incarnate. It does not just hover above us. It is a light that breaks in and suffuses our daily life, a gentle light of love that comes to meet us in our most vulnerable situations. It invites us to move beyond ourselves and our wounds, however painful – and to love. For anyone called to pastoral service of the Lord's flock (not only popes and bishops but certainly them as well) this story should be an encouragement to welcome Christ into the broken, vulnerable, guilty and traumatised areas of one's life. The human situation itself, our daily life with all its trials, failures and frequent falls, is revealed to be a disclosure-zone all its own: but in it the light of resurrection dawns when we welcome Jesus, our wounded but transfigured, incarnate God.

D. Ascending on High (Fig 3)

> I saw that Christ, having in himself
> all of us who shall be saved by him
> graciously presents us to his Father in heaven;
> and this gift his Father receives most thankfully
> and courteously gives it to his Son,
> Jesus Christ.

This gift and action is joy to the Father,
bliss to the Son
and delight to the Holy Spirit.
                                        Julian of Norwich

As we have noted, from the 4th century onwards, following
the chronology established by St Luke's gospel and the Acts of the
Apostles which continues and completes that work, the church
began to develop distinct feasts of Christ's mysteries such as that
of his ascension into heaven. Before that time Christians spoke, as
do most of the New Testament writers but particularly the author
of the fourth gospel, of Christ's exaltation as a single mighty act in
which God glorified his Son by raising him from death and exalting him to his right hand as Lord and Saviour (Phil 2:9-11).

The establishment of a separate feast of the ascension is another
instance of the historicising trend that arose in the church after the
Emperor Constantine granted it the right to exist and lavished his
patronage on it. However, even at the risk of fragmenting the single mystery into its component parts, it must be admitted that the
ascension is one of the most beautiful and spiritually powerful of
Christ's mysteries as they are celebrated in the course of the liturgical year.[17]

The Roman Preface for the Mass of the feast describes the
essence of the mystery:

The Lord Jesus,
the king of glory,
victor over sin and death,
today ascended into heaven
amongst the choirs of celebrating angels.
Mediator between God and humankind,
judge of the world and Lord of the universe,
he has not separated himself from our human condition
but has gone before us
into an eternal dwelling place,
granting us to trust serenely
that where he the head and firstborn has gone,
we also,

his members,
may be united with him
in the same glory ...

Christ's ascension is one with his resurrection in being an essential part of his exaltation. Notwithstanding our celebration of a special feast in its honour, it should never be separated from his Easter triumph. He became 'the firstborn from the dead' (Col 1: 18) in rising from the tomb but in this mystery he was constituted also as head of the church (Col 1:18). The ascension is not just another moment in the life of Christ. It represents rather the fullness of his exaltation and glory. Having glorified the Father on earth by finishing the work he had been sent to do (Jn 17:4) Christ is in turn glorified by the Father in his return to the throne he had voluntarily relinquished in undertaking the kenotic mission of his incarnation (Jn 17:5):

So now, Father, glorify me in your own presence with the glory that I had in your presence before the world existed.

The ascension and the period succeeding it, passing into Pentecost, marks the end of Christ's kenotic self-emptying.[18] It is the sign that God the Father had received his completed sacrifice and fully ratified it (Heb 10:12-14). Having come forth like a bridegroom coming from his tent and rejoiced like a champion to run his course (Ps 18(19):4-6), in this great mystery of the ascension Christ entered fully into glory and took possession of his kingdom. *Kenosis* culminated in *koinonia*, communion, as he re-entered the circle of the Trinity and came home to reign forever with the Father and the Holy Spirit.

The preface of the feast carefully delineates some of the contours of the mystery. Jesus is mediator between God and humanity, not just because he combines the natures of both in his own divine person, but because having gone up on high with his sacrifice completed, he has been constituted as High Priest of the new and eternal covenant established in his own blood. The Letter to the Hebrews offers an extended commentary, as beautiful as it is profound, on this mystery. Christ enters heaven not only bearing his sacrifice: he is himself the sacrifice, being both priest and victim (Heb 9:25-28).

Standing in the Father's presence, Jesus is the unblemished Lamb, predestined from before the foundation of the world whose sacrifice, offered in time, is taken up into heaven to be eternally ratified by the Father (1 Pet 19-21). In his own person he is both *anamnesis* and *epiclesis*: *anamnesis* as the objective memorial, the living memory of his own saving work; and *epiclesis* as the one on whom the Holy Spirit rests perpetually, and through whom the Spirit is sent forth into the world. The ascended Jesus is the ground and basis of all true worship.

He presents himself before the Father, offering him in one eternal 'moment' his priestly acts of praise, thanksgiving, adoration and glorification, doing this in the name of all human beings whose condition he has shared, whose sins he has borne and whose guilt he has carried away (Is 53:4-6; 12; Jn 1:36). Yet he has not abandoned us, but remains for ever fully human. Since the ascension of the Lord into heaven our mortal nature has been given an immortal worth. Our humanity, triumphant over death and transfigured by grace, is enthroned at the heart of all reality, in the bosom of the Holy Trinity. The ascension is God's pledge and promise that the material world he created and loves so much is destined, not for dissolution and disappearance, but for transfiguration. It is the feast that celebrates the divine confirmation of the cosmos, the fulfilment of God's promises of fidelity to us, God's final yes to the world he has created.

As with all his mysteries, Christ accomplished it alone without the help of any other human agency:

The Lord alone guided him;
no foreign God was with him.
He set him atop the heights of the land ... (Deut 32:12-13)

Yet like all his mysteries, he carried it out for us. As the representative human being, Christ carried all of us in himself into the presence of God who has appointed him head of his body the church. Thanks to the ascension we have the serene assurance that our real life is hidden with Christ in God and that we are waiting only for that life to be visibly revealed when he appears again at the end of time (Col 3:1-4). In the midst of a world wracked and torn by suffering, it is a joy and comfort to remember that in Christ we have already passed through the veil dividing this world from the next (Heb 10:19-23) and been given access to the Holy of Holies, the inner shrine of the divine life. The root of our true existence is securely planted in heaven.

Employing as usual a minimum of means, our icon sets these truths before us. At the top of the image is Christ blessing, enthroned in the heavens and enveloped in the mandorla, the luminous full-body halo which indicates the presence of the divine. The radiance of God's energies, his uncreated grace, is pouring out through Christ's transfigured human nature. He has gone up on high into God's glory (*doxa*), into the presence of the Father. Two angels point towards him, indicating that in the epiphany of his ascension we are granted a glimpse of the opening of heaven (Acts 1:10-11).

The halo around the head of the exalted Saviour bears the usual Greek inscription *Ho On* meaning 'being.' It is the great 'I am who I am' and 'I will be who I will be', the divine name made known to Moses at the burning bush at Mt Sinai (Ex 3:13-15). The scene is a theophany, a disclosure of God's presence, a reminder that the presence is now concentrated in Christ as the new temple (Jn 2:21). He is the place of mercy as well as majesty and has become the final 'place' of encounter with God (Jn 20:12).

Below on the mountain top stands the Mother of God (the *Theotokos*), with two apostles, John and Peter. Mary is not mentioned in the accounts of the ascension, but the icon is not pretending to be a merely historical depiction of a past event. It is a liturgical image for the feast, and like it a disclosure-zone revealing the deeper meaning of the mystery. Mary the God-bearer, John the beloved friend of Christ and inspired exegete of the mysteries of the incarnation, and Peter the Rock, represent the church. Mary was the one who listened to God's will and responded with obedience and faith (Lk 1:38); John the one who drew out the mystical depths of meaning in the incarnation by resting in friendship on the heart of the Lord (Jn 13:23); Peter the one who proclaimed to the world the manifestation of God's liberating act in Christ (1 Peter 2:24).

The icon of the ascension is the icon of the church in all its different dimensions: worship and mission, contemplation and proclamation. The two angels ('the men in white' mentioned by St Luke, Acts 1:10) remind us that the church's task is not just accomplished by gazing perpetually into heaven. Prayer, worship and contemplation can become good alibis to excuse inertia. There is a message to be proclaimed, the gospel of God's forgiving grace to be made known to all peoples, and a task to be carried out in the evangelisation of the world. It is the 'great commission':

> And Jesus said to them, 'All authority in heaven and on earth has been given to me. Go therefore and make disciples of all nations, baptising them in the name of the Father and of the Son and of the Holy Spirit and teaching them to obey everything that I have commanded you.' (Mt 28:18-29)

The church will always have two principal dimensions in her life. There is a 'monastic' one, her spiritual separation from 'the world' (Jn 17:14-17) symbolised by her call to worship and contemplate the Lord; but there is also a missionary thrust, a necessity to be in the world even though not 'of' it, going out in the Lord's name to proclaim the good news that through Jesus' death and resurrection, humanity has been objectively reconciled to God.

The deepest meaning of the ascension is that in completing his kenotic work of salvation and entering into his reward, Christ received from the Father the fullness of the Holy Spirit, so as to pour out God's gifts on the church:

> But each one of us was given grace according to the measure of Christ's gift. Therefore it is said,
>> 'When he ascended on high he made
>> captivity itself a captive;
>> he gave gifts to his people.'
> When it says 'He ascended,' what does it mean but that he had also first (*alternative reading*) descended into the lower parts of the earth? He who descended is the same one who ascended far above all the heavens, so that he might fill all things. The gifts he gave were that some would be apostles, some prophets, some evangelists, some pastors and teach-

ers, to equip the saints for the work of ministry, for building up the body of Christ, until all of us come to the unity of the faith and of the knowledge of the Son of God, to maturity, to the measure of the full stature of Christ.

… speaking the truth in love, we must grow up in every way into him who is the head, into Christ, from whom the whole body, joined and knit together by every ligament with which it is equipped, as each part is working properly, promotes the body's growth in building itself up in love. (Eph 4:7-13; 15-16, with reference to Ps 67(68):18, quoting from the Septuagint text)

In one and the same 'moment' the ascended Jesus is both at rest and perpetually at work. Resting in the vision of the Father, his divine-human gaze enraptured by the radiance of beauty, goodness and truth pouring out in the Holy Spirit from the paternal heart of light, Christ becomes the source through which the Spirit is given to us his people. He builds up his body in the world as his witness and co-worker in proclaiming the gospel. The fulfilment into which Jesus entered at his ascension into heaven was therefore anything but a state of spiritual unemployment. He carries out there the most important *opus Dei* (work of and for, God): sending the Holy Spirit to build up the church (Jn 14:15; 25). Jesus in heaven is a living *epiclesis*, a standing invocation of the Spirit. His death and resurrection took place so that the third person of the Holy Trinity, the Creator Spirit, might be revealed and sent into the world and the Christian community, to breathe into them the new life of grace.[19]

E. *Pentecost: the Coming of the Holy Spirit* (Fig 4)

The Holy Spirit is light and life,
a living fount of all spiritual things:
the Spirit is the essence of wisdom,
the Spirit of knowledge,
goodness and understanding who cleanses us from sin!
Divine, the Spirit makes us so!
The Spirit is fire poured out from fire!

Byzantine hymn for the feast of Pentecost

Strictly speaking, there is no separate feast of the Holy Spirit in the church's liturgy. Pentecost, the fiftieth day after the celebration of the resurrection, is the culmination of the Easter season which ends by recalling the descent of the Holy Spirit on Mary and the apostles as they prayed together in the Upper Room in Jerusalem (Acts 1:13-14; 2:1-4). It is the public appearance of the church which had been formed in embryo during Christ's common life with his disciples before Easter.[20]

According to various church Fathers including the Syrian St Ephrem, the Greek St John Chrysostom and the Latin St Augustine, the Christian community was born out of Christ's pierced side on the cross when the two great sacramental mysteries of baptism and the Eucharist (signified by water and blood) poured out in profusion (Jn 19:35-37 with reference to Zech 12:10; 1 Jn 5:6-9;).[21] Yet the church needed to receive the full gift of the promised Holy Spirit in order to be manifested and sent into the world to fulfil its commission to preach the gospel.

In the eastern traditions, the day of Pentecost is also the final manifestation of the mystery of the Holy Trinity which had been initially revealed at the baptism and transfiguration of Jesus. It is the eschatological (i.e. final, perfect and definitive) revelation of who God really is. In the Orthodox Church Pentecost is generally considered to be what we in the west would think of as Trinity Sunday. The eastern churches do not celebrate a separate feast of the Trinity as western Christians have done since the Middle Ages. The manifestation of the Spirit means the complete self-disclosure of God's being as Trinity. The historical descent of the Spirit in Jerusalem is actually commemorated on Pentecost Monday.

The coming of the Holy Spirit, therefore, completes the revelation of God's love by showing us the existence of a third divine person, distinct from the Father and the Son.[22] Both in east and west, theologians and mystics (Latin Catholics in the early and medieval church, and many Russian Orthodox in the modern era) speak of the Spirit as the embrace or kiss in which the circle of divine love reaches completion within God's inner life. Pentecost reveals the mystery of that inner life to us, an area into which human beings cannot pry but which can only be revealed to us in grace.

God makes his life manifest to us as a communion (*koinonia*) of divine persons, so perfectly united that they are but one single nature, a community of eternal and infinite love. This is not something we could ever have discovered for ourselves. For the Byzantine tradition, it is the supremely *apophatic* mystery, in that it speaks of the eternal Godhead, existing beyond all thought, speech and imagining. Yet through the kenotic descent of Christ and the coming of the Holy Spirit at Pentecost, divine love has indeed disclosed it to us: it is therefore also the source of *kataphatic* theology, of all discourse about God.[23]

Two great Orthodox saints, the Byzantine Nicholas Cabasilas (14th century) and the Russian Seraphim of Sarov (19th century) taught that the principal purpose of Christ's 'economy of salvation' (his incarnation, death and resurrection for the salvation of the world) was the sending of the Holy Spirit; yet when we speak of 'sending', it would be wrong to imagine the Spirit as somehow subordinate to Christ. Although Jesus himself promised that he and the Father would send 'another Advocate' after his resurrection (Jn 14:15-17; 25-26; 15:26; 16:7-15), the New Testament shows the reciprocal harmony and co-operation of the Son and Spirit, who work together to carry out the Father's will, a will they have in common with him.

Before the Trinity's manifestation at Pentecost, the nature of the Spirit had been somewhat obscure. However, under the new dispensation, his/her distinct personal identity becomes more evident. The gospels of Matthew (Mt 1:20) and Luke declare that it was by the Spirit's agency that Jesus was conceived (Lk 1:35) just as it was by the Spirit's descent that he was anointed and manifested at the Jordan as the Messiah (Mk 1:10; Mt 3:16; Lk 3:22; 4:1). The Spirit it was who drove him into the wilderness to commune with the Father and do battle with Satan in the desert (Mk 1:12); and it was thanks to the Spirit's appearance as a luminous cloud that he was revealed in glory on the mountain of transfiguration (Mt 17:5). It was through the Holy Spirit, according to the Letter to the Hebrews, that Jesus offered himself as an acceptable sacrifice to the Father (Heb 9:14) and it was in the power of the Holy Spirit that God raised him from the dead (1 Pet 3:18).[24]

The action of the Spirit before Pentecost had been that of forming the humanity of Jesus, revealing him as the Christ and accompanying and empowering him in his work as the one whom the
Father had anointed and sent into the world for its salvation. The
Spirit was the witness of the sufferings of Christ.[25]

Yet even after the dramatic descent on Pentecost Sunday, this
third divine person remains enigmatic and mysterious. Orthodox
theologians love to dwell on this aspect of the Spirit's work, speaking of an appearance which is actually a kind of non-appearance.
The Holy Spirit does not reveal his/her own face: instead the
Spirit is the light that shines on the face of Christ and is reflected in
the faces of those holy people (the saints) who do God's will in
love. The third person remains supremely a mysterious, 'mystical
Person,' the breath of divine life and energy that the Father and the
Son breathe into the church and believers to accomplish their task
of bearing witness to Christ. The Spirit is like the life's blood of the
body of Christ, for after Pentecost every act of the church's life and
worship is accomplished only in the power of the Holy Spirit.[26]

Through the Spirit, hearts are touched and converted by the
message of the gospel; the regenerating waters of baptism become
the womb of new life; the transforming presence of Christ in the
Eucharist is brought about; the liberating word of forgiveness is
pronounced in absolution; the consecration of human love in matrimony makes married couples living icons of God's own life and
creativity; the configuration of fragile human beings to Christ as
his ministers in ordination is made possible for the good of
Christ's people; the healing power of grace is poured out through
consecrated oil in the anointing of the sick; the self-sacrificial love
of the martyrs is perfected; the wisdom of the church's Doctors is
conferred; the folly of her sins corrected; the graces of mystical
prayer and union with God are granted to all God's people if only
they open their hearts to the Spirit's grace.

Notwithstanding all the sins and infidelities of which the
church of Jesus Christ is capable, she is his beloved bride, continually reconstituted and maintained in truth by the Holy Spirit, recovering anew her focus on Christ when it has been lost. All this is
possible only because the Spirit of wisdom and truth, the Lord and

Giver of life, is sent by the Father and the Son from above, after Christ's ascension into heaven. Without the Spirit, there would be no church, no faith, no baptism, no love and ultimately no hope.

Yet one must also affirm much more. The Holy Spirit was not sent into the world to confine God's grace to a holy ghetto called the church. There is a universal cosmic dimension to the work of the Spirit. The revelation of the *Logos* in the flesh of Jesus Christ has made known God's creative presence in nature and the cosmos, revealing the world as a book filled with words (*logoi*) which speak of God. The pre-existent Christ is the Father's Word, reason and thought, in which God grounds and guides creation, giving it its logic and inner intelligibility. Illumined by the light of Christ, we begin to see God's presence everywhere.[27]

So too the Holy Spirit is the breath of wisdom which hovered over the formless mass of matter into which God breathed as he formed the world 'in the beginning' (Gen 1:1-5). Every culture and civilisation on the planet has known, however obscurely, the presence of creative and life-giving divine energy – called *shakti* in India, *chi* in China, *shekinah* in Israel and *neart* in ancient Ireland. All ancient peoples imagined the world as a sacred cosmos filled with divine presence, a living image and temple of the divine.[28] The Russian thinker Sergius Bulgakov spoke of creation as being already a form of 'natural grace'. Nature is God's epiphany, God's self-manifestation, for those who know how to see and listen: our difficulty as human beings is that sin casts a veil over our inner eyes and ears.[29]

The coming of the Holy Spirit opens them afresh to behold a universe animated and vivified, echoing with the sound of the mighty wind of God. On Pentecost morning in the Latin liturgical tradition, we sing an ancient entrance chant at Mass drawn from the Book of Wisdom:

> *Spiritus Domini replevit orbem terrarum, alleluia;*
> *et hoc quod continet omnia scientiam habet vocis,*
> *alleluia, alleluia, alleluia.*
> (Wis 1:7 following the Latin Vulgate version)

In translation this obscure and enigmatic text seems to mean,

'The Spirit of the Lord fills the whole world, and that which contains all things has knowledge of the voice.' God's Spirit of wisdom is the divine *pneuma,* thanks to whose presence the poet Gerard Manley Hopkins ascribed 'the dearest freshness deep down things':

> Because the Holy Ghost over the bent
> World broods with warm breast and with ah! bright wings.[30]

Through the wind of Pentecost we learn that the universe is suffused by the breath of the Creator Spirit, the Lord and Giver of life. All life is an out-flowing manifestation of the divine life which in-breathes everything and everyone from the dawn of the first day of creation. The German Dominican mystic Meister Eckhart spoke of God's inner life as being like a boiling (*bullitio*) cauldron of love: in the Holy Spirit that love 'boils over' (*ebullitio*) on to us.[31]

Therefore in the Latin Church during the liturgies of Pentecost, we even invoke the Holy Spirit directly, singing *Veni Creator Spiritus* ('Come Creator Spirit') at the office of Vespers, and *Veni Sancte Spiritus* ('Come Holy Spirit') at Mass. In addition, since the reform of the liturgy after Vatican II, at every major sacramental moment of the church's life, we call upon the Holy Spirit. In the Orthodox Church almost every act of worship begins with a short hymn from the Office of Pentecost, invoking the Spirit as 'the treasury of all good gifts and giver of blessings, everywhere present and filling all things'.

Modern Orthodox theologians say that the Spirit's work, like that of the Son, also has its own kenotic character.[32] In Christ's case it is easy to understand what *kenosis* entailed by reading Philippians 2 and other New Testament texts: it was his voluntary abandonment of divine glory and the privileges he enjoyed as God in becoming human, embracing the agony of the cross and descending to the dead. Every crucifix keeps Christ's self-emptying before our eyes. But the Holy Spirit's *kenosis* is of a different kind for the third person of the Trinity did not take flesh and die. There was no incarnation of the Holy Spirit any more than there is one of the Father: becoming human (including death) is unique to the Son.

As Bulgakov saw, inspired by the last chapters of St John's

gospel, the Spirit's kenosis lies in a refusal to take centre stage. Instead the Holy Spirit focuses on witnessing to Christ and his work of redemption. Certainly the Spirit is not in any sense subordinate to Jesus but it is equally true that the Spirit does voluntarily give way to him out of love and humility just as Christ himself gave way to the Father's will. Jesus declared that he had come not to do his own will or to testify to himself but to fulfil the will of the one who sent him (Jn 4:34; 5:19; 30; 7:16). The non-grasping nature of Jesus, who defers to the Father, is reiterated and mirrored in the non-grasping nature of the third divine person who, being supremely the Spirit of love and communion, in turn lovingly defers to the Son.

Just as Jesus announced beforehand, the Holy Spirit does not speak about him/herself but bears witness to Christ (Jn 16:13-15), taking the things that are Christ's and revealing them to the disciples: yet as Christ says, all that he has comes from the Father. As the Spirit of truth (Jn 14:17) the Advocate is like a spotlight or ray falling on an object that lets the truth be clearly seen. Such humility entails the Spirit declaring only what s/he hears (Jn 16:13). The Spirit will remind the disciples of all that Jesus has said to them.

Such divine discretion is also apparent in the Spirit's way of relating to human beings. Just as Christ forced or coerced no one into accepting his message, so the Holy Spirit deals gently with humanity's foibles, interrupting people and gently derailing their plans, coaxing, cajoling, encouraging, leading, nudging and gently pushing – at times confronting – but never, ever imposing God's will by force. The Spirit of love and communion calls us to love and communion with God, who never denies, degrades or destroys our grace-given human freedom, flawed, feeble and impaired as it undeniably is.

The Holy Spirit will not do that, for freedom is one of the essential elements constituting human beings as created images of God. In the work of redemption, as Paul insisted, Christ set us free for freedom (Gal 5:13). If therefore God were to overpower us or overrule our freedom it would be the ultimate contradiction in terms. God is a divine lover who in the normal course of things woos the soul, inviting her to become his bride (though some are

Figure 1:
The icon of the Mysteries of Christ in the liturgical cycle
See page 130

Figure 2:
The icon of Easter: Christ's descent into hell
and appearance to Peter
See page 133

Figure 3:
The icon of the Ascension
See page 148

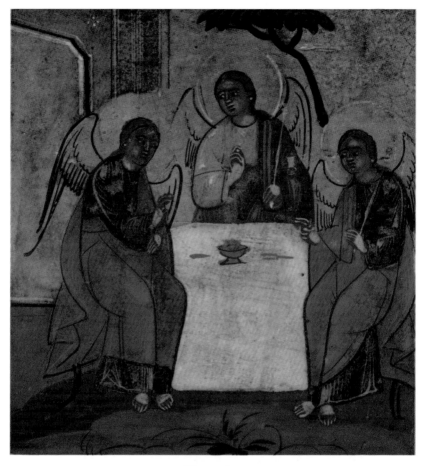

Figure 4:
The icon of the Trinity, revealed at Pentecost
See page 154

Figure 5:
The icon of the Raising of Lazarus
See page 165

Figure 6:
The icon of the Entry into Jerusalem
See page 170

Figure 7:
The icon of the Washing of the Feet. See page 176

Figure 8:
The icon of the Last Supper. See page 178

Figure 9:
The icon of the Agony in the Garden. See page 180

Figure 10:
The icon of the Betrayal. See page 184

Figure 11:
The icon of Jesus before Pilate. See page 186

Figure 12:
The icon of the Crucifixion. See page 187

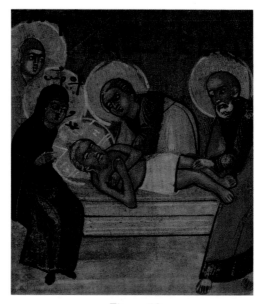

Figure 13:
The icon of the Burial of Jesus. See page 193

Figure 14:
The icon of the Exaltation of the Cross. See page 199

Figure 15:
The icon of the Nativity. See page 207

Figure 16:
The icon of the Presentation of Jesus in the Temple. See page 212

Figure 17:
The icon of the Baptism of Jesus
See page 218

Figure 18:
The icon of the Transfiguration
See page 228

Figure 19:
The icon of the Presentation of Mary in the Temple. See page 249

Figure 20:
The icon of the Annunciation. See page 253

Figure 21:
The icon of Mary's Dormition
See page 260

Figure 22:
The icon of the Trinity
See page 279

so obdurate that, like St Paul, they have to be knocked off their horses).

God never violates us or forces us to associate with him against our will, leaving us broken, bruised and humiliated. One must, of course, accept unreservedly the New Testament's message of the absolute priority and constant necessity of divine grace in the Christian life; but one must also reject the idea of an irresistible grace that would see us as objects to be manipulated in God's hands. God never treats us as though we were merely puppets.

Catholicism and Orthodoxy (contrary to much Protestant thinking on this matter) agree in affirming that despite the fall, human freedom has not been wholly destroyed. An irreducible element of free response is required if the grace offered by God is to take hold of a person's life. God displays the greatest respect in dealing with us, doing everything possible to elicit such a free response from his poor, damaged, sinful creatures which he cherishes with infinite love because he sees us as he means us to be.[33]

Such kenotic discretion and gentle handling is characteristic above all of the Holy Spirit as the one who works behind the scenes in the drama of redemption. The third person is both the prompter and the stage manager who moves the scenery when all the lights go out. S/he pushes the play ever onwards towards its final, glorious denouement.

An early heresy called 'subordinationism' attempted to organise the persons of the Trinity in a descending hierarchy, making the Spirit subordinate to the Son and the Son to the Father.[34] It thereby contradicted both the scriptures and the unanimous tradition of the church's worship since earliest times. Yet like all heresies it contained a grain of truth. Properly understood there is a genuine subordinationism but it is common to all three persons of the Trinity: it is the *freely-chosen, self-subordination* of kenotic love, which always aims to take the humbler part (Jn 14:28; 31), giving way to the other and thereby manifesting its greatness.

Hence like Jesus, the Holy Spirit did not just stay enthroned on high but 'came down' and 'comes down', again and again, in every sacramental mystery.[35] In these descents of the Son and Spirit, in their outward missions to the world which take them in a new way from the bosom of the Trinity right into the heart of created reality, we are shown something intrinsic to God's inner life: we see how these persons are when they are 'at home' in the inner heart of the Trinity. Their missions reveal to us that God is a community of persons united in non-grasping, self-emptying love.

Yet the language of divine *kenosis* must always be handled with care and its metaphors properly appreciated. We are dealing with divine mysteries impenetrable to unaided human intelligence. The Holy Spirit, who is the sovereign God no less than the Father and the Son, *chooses* to pursue this descending path: no more than in the case of the Son is it ever forced upon the third person by God the Father. Kenosis by its very nature must be free and voluntary. In Greek the word *pneuma* means not merely breath but wind, and the Spirit is as unpredictable as is that natural element. S/he brings strong, bright, fresh spontaneous effusions of divine energy wherever s/he blows. Jesus said:

> The wind (pneuma) blows where it chooses, and you hear the sound of it, but you do not know where it comes from or where it goes. So it is with everyone who is born of the Spirit. (Jn 3:8)

God's creative breath cannot be tied down, boxed up or in any way domesticated – not even (or perhaps especially) by the church. Nor can it ever be exhausted by human understanding. Jesus declared that no one knows the Father except the Son just as no one knows the Son except the Father (Mt 11:27). That is equally true of the Spirit for by analogy with the human spirit the Spirit of God alone is, as Paul put it (1 Cor 2:10), capable of searching the depths of God. Yet he added:

> Now we have received not the Spirit of the world, but the Spirit that is from God, so that we may understand the gifts bestowed on us by God. And we speak of these things in words not taught by human wisdom but taught by the Spirit, interpreting spiritual things to those who are spiritual. (1 Cor 2:12-13)

The Spirit of the Lord whom we have received in baptism

shares with us the mind of Christ, cries out in us 'Abba! Father!' and confers on us the status of God's adopted children and heirs (1 Cor 2:16; Gal 4:6-7; Rom 8:14-17). We receive fresh visitations of the same Spirit again and again every time we celebrate the Eucharist, in every act of liturgical worship and in every stirring of prayer that turns our hearts to God, because our very turning is inspired by God's breath: our desire to praise God is itself God's gift, as a prayer in the Roman Mass puts it.

Thanks to the Spirit's creative energy and repeated descent in the eucharistic liturgy, Christ's work of redemption is realised afresh among us day by day. The Spirit pushes the church forwards and upwards to the goal that lies ahead, our final entry into the kingdom of God. S/he does this by indwelling the hearts of all God's children. Through him/her we are enabled to cry out 'Abba, Father!' The Spirit in him/herself (as the one true God) is always 'outside us' (*extra nos*). But, being breathed into us through Christ's sacramental mysteries and in prayer, the Spirit comes to be 'inside us' (*intra nos*) as a spring of water gushing up to eternal life (Jn 4:14). Yet that spring is never just my deepest self, or my own religious subjectivity expanded to infinity.[36] The Spirit is the supreme, sovereign, transcendent God who gives him/herself in absolute freedom, with a gratuitousness that cannot be controlled, commanded or commandeered (but which is never in any sense merely capricious).

I need to invite God the Father in persistent prayer to expand my consciousness, open me more fully to the presence of his Son and make me more and more transparent to the divine guest of the heart – the Holy Spirit of wisdom, the Lord and Giver of life, who is the source of all relationship with God (Rom 8:26-27; Jn 4: 21-23), of the church's communion (2 Cor 13:13) and of all true liberty: for where the Spirit of the Lord is, there is freedom (2 Cor 3: 17).

CHAPTER EIGHT

The Mysteries of the Passion

Joy to you, O life-bearing cross,
bright paradise of the church
and tree of incorruptibility.
You have won for us the joy of everlasting glory.
Through you
the hosts of devils are driven out,
the choirs of angels rejoice
and the whole company of believers assembles
to celebrate the feast!
Unconquerable weapon,
impregnable foundation,
triumph of kings and glory of priests:
make us witnesses
to Christ's passion and resurrection!

Byzantine hymn

Arranged around the central resurrection scenes of this Russian icon are those depicting the mysteries of Christ's passion, death and burial and his gesture of washing the disciples' feet on Holy Thursday evening. The images go on to show the celebration of the Last Supper and his struggle with the will of the Father in the garden of Gethsemane; they also depict his betrayal by Judas, condemnation by Pilate and scourging and crowning with thorns, before culminating in his crucifixion and burial.

Each little image is a like a snapshot showing the depths of kenotic humility to which the incarnate Saviour was prepared to descend out of compassion for the human race he created. The image of Christ's entry into Jerusalem on Palm Sunday is found on the outer cycle of the panel since it is reckoned as one of the great feasts of the Lord. But before contemplating the events of Holy Week (beginning with Palm Sunday) let us follow the example of the Orthodox Church which first remembers the miracle and mystery of Jesus' raising of his friend Lazarus from the dead.

A. *Unbounded Life: the Mystery of Absolution* (Fig 5)

The cords of death encompassed me;
  the torrents of perdition assailed me;
the cords of Sheol entangled me;
  the snares of death confronted me.

...but the Lord was my support.
He brought me out into a broad place;
  he delivered me, because he delighted in me.
(*Psalm 17(18): 4-5; 19*)

The bringing back of Lazarus from the dead is recorded in the 11th chapter of St John's gospel where it is the last and greatest of the signs given by Jesus before his passion. Standing as it does on the threshold of what the Orthodox call 'the Holy and Great Week' it sets the scene for the deadly conflict about to occur between Jesus and the authorities, which will end in his crucifixion. In the Roman Rite it is commemorated on the fifth Sunday of Lent. The story of the raising of Lazarus is a powerful and moving one. Having postponed visiting his friends at Bethany (Jn 11:5-6) – despite having heard of Lazarus' illness – Jesus, when he finally decides to go, encounters Martha and Mary and is moved to tears (Jn 11:35). The scene is a carefully constructed drama in which the incredulity of the bystanders (Jn 11:37) contrasts sharply with Jesus' confidence in the Father as he expresses it publicly in prayer (Jn 11:41) before restoring Lazarus to life from the grave (Jn 11:43).

Personally I have never felt any inclination to doubt that Jesus actually did it.[1] Yet it is important to grasp the essential difference between the raising of Lazarus and the resurrection of Jesus. The first entailed the restoration of a dead man to the conditions of ordinary life. Lazarus would duly die again and indeed the gospel mentions that plots were already afoot to put him to death not long after he had been raised (Jn 12:9-11).

The resurrection of Jesus belongs to an altogether different order. It involved the complete transfiguration of his body and its exaltation to a new kind of existence. It was his entry into a risen life through the power of the Holy Spirit and his lifting up to the right hand of the Father (Rom 6:4). The raising of Lazarus was a sign of what was coming, a prophecy of Christ's future victory over death. Yet that decisive event would be fully accomplished only in his resurrection at Easter. Like the virginal conception, Jesus' parables and other healings, the raising of Lazarus has a primarily eschatological meaning. It is not a 'natural' event at all, at least not according to the conditions of life to which we are accustomed: but it is entirely natural where God's kingdom of light, love and eternal life is breaking through. It was a disclosure-zone in which the life of the world to come shone out.

It can be interesting to compare this mystery to one of the sacramental mysteries recognised by Catholics, Orthodox and many Anglicans and Lutherans: the forgiveness of sins through confession and the declaration of absolution by an ordained minister of the church. It would be anachronistic to imagine that Jesus in his earthly life 'instituted' confession and absolution as a separate sacrament. There is no historical evidence for that at all. He certainly did institute baptism and the remission of sins but the sacrament of reconciliation as we know it developed only gradually under the influence of the Holy Spirit in both the eastern and western parts of the church, mostly thanks to monastic (Irish and Byzantine) influence.

In the monasteries individuals were encouraged to open their hearts to spiritually enlightened elders, laying bare before them all the thoughts and impulses arising in their souls and the temptations assailing them, so that the wise elder (an *Abbas*, *Geron* or in the Russian tradition *Staretz*) could help them to understand what was happening in their spiritual lives and discern what came from God or from darker forces such as demonic influence – or simply from the soul's own unconscious depths. In the western church, where the sacrament developed especially under Celtic monastic influence, its administration was eventually limited solely to priests although that process was not finally codified until the sixteenth century reaction to Protestantism.[2]

In the Orthodox Church, despite the constant attempts of

canon lawyers to limit absolution to ordained priests, the dividing line between ordained confessors and charismatic monks has often been more blurred. Although required to confess their sins in the strict sense to priests alone, most Orthodox will take their 'soul-problems' to whoever is recognised as a wise spiritual elder (male or female) whether ordained or not, thus preserving a strong sense of the charismatic nature of the church.[3]

It is worth observing that in Latin Catholicism the recent reform of the liturgy greatly enhanced the celebration of this sacramental mystery by freeing it from the straitjacket of a certain legalism, highlighting its spiritually medicinal and therapeutic nature and rooting it firmly in the mystery of God's love revealed in Christ and the Holy Spirit. One might say that the liturgical reforms unbound the sacrament and let it go free.

It is too simplistic to assert sweepingly that Protestants 'do not go to confession'. In Luther's case and despite the unfortunate scrupulosity which had afflicted his practice of confession, he valued it very much as a help for troubled souls even if he did not in the end wish to call it a specific sacrament. Some sectors of contemporary Lutheranism (and Anglicanism since the nineteenth century) have witnessed a considerable revival of confession and absolution.

Finally, the psychologist Jung recognised its therapeutic value and recommended it to Christians who could still find meaning in the symbol-system of the church. He acknowledged its similarity, practically speaking, to psychotherapy, although he did not confuse them and always insisted that an analyst and a priest have different roles and functions.

The sacrament of confession is not without ambivalence for many people today but it is still possible for clergy to do immense good through celebrating it sensitively. Confession may consist in superficial encounters with penitents who simply rattle off supposed offences against God's law without engaging in a serious analysis of real sin or its underlying roots: every experienced confessor will have dealt with such persons at some time in his ministry. It can be a place where neurotics engage in punishing self-criticism in the presence of another person. But it can also be a privileged disclosure-zone where the mystery of Christ becomes manifest, a 'place' where God speaks liberating words through the mouth of another human being, a place of transformation where grace is disclosed and suffering relieved.

Above all, as Luther understood so well, it is a privileged opportunity to proclaim and communicate the gospel of grace and mercy: 'Go in peace, your sins are forgiven.' That is the real purpose of the sacramental mysteries. Having saved the world and established the forgiveness of sins, Jesus committed it to his community the church: 'If you forgive the sins of any they are forgiven them …' (Jn 20:21). He did not establish with detailed precision the exact forms in which that liberating event would take place. But the Spirit-guided evolution of this sacrament – to which its long evolution throughout the church's history testifies – is a potent reminder of the power of liturgical symbols in communicating the grace of the mystery.

Here, as in every liturgical action, human words and gestures become transparent. They mediate the loving kindness of the Holy Trinity, the God of grace. Although this happens 'objectively', though the celebration of the rite itself, sustained by the Holy Spirit, it is not simply an automatic process. There are irreplaceable human factors involved. Quite apart from the fact that the penitent must be genuinely sorry and willing at least to attempt to make amends, the personality of the priest is more involved here than in any other sacramental ministration of the church (apart perhaps from the anointing of the sick) and for better or for worse.

For better, in that he can genuinely lend his humanity to the mystery of forgiveness and reconciliation; for worse, in that although he cannot actually block God's grace, he can distort how it will be received by getting in the way through impatience, harshness or indifference. Priestly responsibility for the flock of Christ's little ones is never more evident than at this point of contact with the faithful.

The words of absolution in the renewed Roman form of this sacrament are a concise summary of the mystery of Christ: God the Father of mercies who reconciled the world to himself through Christ's death and resurrection and sent the Holy Spirit for the forgiveness of sins communicates the power of that event through the ministry of the church, admitting the repentant sinner to a new life of pardon and peace with God and his or her fellow human beings.

Through the ministry of the church made manifest in the presence of the priest, God's mercy is concretised and actualised in the present moment. Confession and absolution are among the most striking examples of how liturgical celebration makes the mystery present. Through the objective recalling of what Christ did in the past (*anamnesis*) and the invocation of the Holy Spirit in the present moment (*epiclesis*), communion (*koinonia*) is re-established between and among God and human beings. That is why this sacramental mystery, quite apart from its objective reality, can be such a powerful subjective and even emotional experience.

United by the liturgical wisdom of the church to objective words and gestures of forgiveness, reconciliation and freedom (the laying on of hands and absolution accompanied by the sign of the cross), the life-giving grace of God enters the soul through the senses and performs its transforming work. Sacramental absolution is a mystery of liberation from the powers of sin, darkness and death. 'Unbind him, and let him go' (Jn 11:44). In the story of Lazarus, when the dead man emerges from the tomb, bound in strips of cloth, the original Greek has Jesus saying, *lusate auton* or 'loose him'; in the Latin of the Vulgate it is *solvite eum*. In confession we speak of 'absolution,' an English word coming from the Latin *absolvere* which means 'to loose'. Its German equivalents *Lossprechung* or *Freisprechung* are even more evocative, meaning literally 'speaking someone free.' That is what the priest does in this sacramental mystery, with the authority of Christ and in the power of the Holy Spirit. He speaks words of liberation. From what does confession loose and unbind us and for what are we set free?

The original monastic understanding of confession and absolution came very much to the fore in the renewed rite of penance after Vatican II but it had long been the norm in the eastern churches. They had always tended to view it less in narrowly juridical terms (making reparation for offences committed against divine law) and more 'medicinally' or 'therapeutically'. It is a mystery of personal encounter in which God mediates his grace through one sinful (but forgiven) human being who meets another sinful person in Christ's name. Sin and guilt are destructive of life, our own as well as that of others. They are like tight bands of constricting cloth which confine us, bandages tightly bound around us. Sin is a crippling, limiting, hindering force that stops us from becoming what God wants us to be.

The word of absolution is a pronouncing of divine pardon to someone who turns to God for forgiveness – or to put it more accurately – to someone turned to him by grace. It cuts away those strangulating bands. God's liberating word pierces the darkness and penetrates into the tomb of the heart. It calls us out into light and life. That word enables us to move and act with new freedom. It infuses into us the energy of the Holy Spirit who frees us from the boa-constrictor-like, crippling grip of evil. It is a word from the God of freedom which frees us and sends us out empowered to love again in freedom.

That today is where the focus ought to fall in the celebration of this sacramental mystery: not simply on repenting of individual acts of sin which break God's law but on the renewal of the inner sanctuary of one's personality, the living ground out of which all one's actions – sin included – always flow, the deep zone of interiority which the Jewish tradition, Jesus the Lord, the early church and monastic writers all described as 'the heart' (Mk 7:21; Mt 15:10-20). It is there that God's liberating word of grace must enter if it is to transform people from within, freeing them from sin and guilt, unloosing their bonds, unlocking their prison doors and renewing their communion with God who never breaks his covenant with us (2 Tim 11-13).[4]

B. Palm Sunday: the Mystery of Entry (Fig 6)

Woe to you when all speak well of you, for that is what their ancestors did to the false prophets. *Luke 6:26*

All four gospels record that Jesus made a triumphant entry into Jerusalem, riding as the prophet Zechariah had foretold, on the back of a donkey (Mt 21:1-10; Mk 11:1-11; Lk 19:28-40; Jn 12:12-19). With this highly symbolic gesture, combining humility with the loud proclamation of the advent of God's kingdom, he inaugurated the last days of his ministry and made the final showdown with the Temple and Roman authorities inevitable. Therefore Christian tradition commemorates this event liturgically as the opening of the mysteries of Holy Week. It is a mystery of entry: the true king Christ enters into his own city just as when a child he was brought into the Temple. But it is also the entry of the church, liturgically speaking, into its most important season: the greatest days of the year, devoted to the commemoration of Christ's saving death and resurrection.[5]

The western churches imitate his action ritually with a blessing of palms (or greenery) and a procession and entry into the church building after the proclamation of the relevant gospel passage.[6] Then, in the course of the normal Sunday Eucharist, the long narrative of his passion is proclaimed from one of the three synoptic gospels. The hymn of *kenosis* from Philippians 2 is read as the second reading and (in many monasteries) chanted to a particularly beautiful and moving Gregorian chant melody as an acclamation to greet the reading of the passion narrative.

The Palm Sunday celebration is an excellent example of how the liturgy, like an icon or a medieval painting, conflates many events into one. It is reminiscent of the Overture of a Wagner Opera in which all the main themes of the great work that will be heard are sounded in advance. We are taken right through the mysteries of the coming Paschal *Triduum* from the Lord's Supper, Gethsemane and Golgotha to the taking down of his body from the cross and burial by Joseph of Arimathea. Although the reading of the passion narratives stops there, the resurrection is never forgotten. In addition to being mentioned in the Opening Prayer of the Mass, it is also proclaimed in a responsory sung as the people and ministers make their solemn entry into the church at the conclusion of the procession:

> While Christ was making his entry into the Holy City,
> the children of the Jews,
> proclaiming in advance
> the resurrection of the Lord of life,
> were waving branches of palm

and crying aloud:
'Hosanna in the heights of heaven!'

Liturgy is a bit like dreaming. Just as in sleep many different
times are mixed up and interconnected in the unconscious, bringing together people and places which were originally far apart, so
the imaginative mind of the church, guided by the Spirit, forms
the events of Christ's life and ministry into a whole, yet always
seeing everything through the subsequent light of the resurrection and his victory over death.

The mystery of the triumphant entry is a stark reminder of the
fickleness of the heart and the capacity of a crowd to change its
allegiance: almost certainly most of those shouting 'Hosanna!'
were the same ones shouting 'Crucify him!' only a few days later
when the triumphal procession of a king would be replaced by the
howling frenzy of a lynch mob (Mk 15:13-15). A popular hymn
puts it well:

> Sometime they strew his way
> And his sweet praises sing;
> Resounding all the day
> Hosannas to their King;
> Then 'Crucify!' is all their breath,
> And for his death
> They thirst and cry.

Yet here we must be very careful to avoid all anti-Jewish
prejudice. Unfortunately the past celebration of the church's Holy
Week liturgies cannot be so easily absolved from the guilt of fost-
ering such dreadful tendencies. In the unreformed Roman Rite,
before the Second Vatican Council refashioned the liturgical
books, and in the still untouched Byzantine services for Holy
Week, one finds a substantial number of texts of an anti-Jewish
nature which surely contributed something to the horrors inflicted
on the Jews since the Middle Ages and especially in the 20th
century. There has been a great deal of healthy soul searching and
acknowledgment of guilt by Catholic leaders in recent years but
more is needed.

We must be clear about this: the Jewish Jesus was put to death

by an unholy alliance of Roman power and corrupt religious leaders, the Temple authorities whose authenticity was contested by
many other Jewish groups in Israel at that time.

The mob crying for his crucifixion was – like any other mob in
history – incited by a mixture of astute political manipulation and
elemental lust for blood. 'His blood be on us and on our children'
(Mt 27:25) was an idiomatic Hebrew way of saying they (the mob)
took responsibility for that death: it was not a universally binding
statement of guilt expressing some permanent curse on Jesus'
own beloved people. The mystery of Jesus, called 'the Christ' by
Christians but rejected by the Jews as their Messiah, certainly did
open up a heartrending rift between the two groups that has never
been healed, but the Jews remain the first children of God's
covenant, the plant on to which we Gentiles have been grafted (cf
Rom 9).[7]

They are – and remain forever – the people of the Lord and the
flock that is led by his hand (Ps 99(100):3) just as much as we are.
They are saved by fidelity to his covenant. There ought to be no
'Christian missions to the Jews,' no evangelisation programmes
aimed at them. Instead we should ask them to teach us the faith
that pulsed through the veins of Jesus, Mary, Joseph, John the
Baptist and the first Christian disciples. Jesus told the Samaritan
woman at the well that salvation comes from the Jews (Jn 4:22).
We ought to do two things:

- Firstly we should ask forgiveness from them for the horrors inflicted on Jews by Christians in the name of our faith – faith in
  one we claim to have been the Jewish Messiah!
- Secondly we should exhort them to fidelity to the covenant,
  and in discussions with Jews who have lapsed from the practice of their faith encourage them to attend the Synagogue.
  There should be no proselytising but instead a profound reverence for the one covenant of the one true God.

The Orthodox Church mentions the raising of Lazarus many
times in the course of its Palm Sunday celebration and also combines images drawn from the Lord's glorious presence in the
Temple with the humble appearance of Jesus the Son of David

seated on a donkey, proclaiming in that way the depth of his
kenosis:

> The Word of God the Father,
> the Son who is co-eternal with him,
> who has heaven for his throne
> and earth for his footstool,
> today has humbled himself
> by riding on a donkey …

> O Christ who ride on the Cherubim
> and are praised by the Seraphim,
> the children praised you with hymns
> just as David sang praises to God:
> glory to you O merciful God
> and lover of all humankind!

This feast is the mystery of entry: the entry of the true king to
take possession of his city, the entrance of the Lord into his holy
place – and his solemn entry to accomplish the paschal mystery of
death and resurrection. Hidden within all this is a mystical meaning to his entry which has found expression in a liturgical form. In
many churches of the west in the Middle Ages (and still today in
our monastery) a short but pregnant ceremony occurs between
the end of the procession and the entry of the ministers into the
church. The doors are closed and the Abbot and his assistants
stand before them. Then some verses of Psalm 23(24) are sung in
alternation between the ministers who have been temporarily
closed out of the church and a group of chanters inside (Ps 23(24):
7, 10):

> Lift up your heads, O gates!
> and be lifted up, O ancient doors!
> that the King of glory may come in.

> Who is this king of glory?
> The Lord of hosts,
> he is the king of glory.

At the end, the Abbot knocks on the door with the foot of the processional cross, the doors are opened and the procession surges into the building. Originally this psalm probably referred to the entry of the king into the Temple at Jerusalem; here by extension it recalls both the triumphant entry of Christ into the Holy City and its ritual re-enactment and liturgical realisation in the liturgy of the day. It is a moving icon of the original event, itself rooted deeply in Jewish religious history. But there is yet more. The deepest mystical meaning derives from what Paul wrote to the Corinthians:

> ... do you not know that your body is a temple of the Holy Spirit within you, which you have from God? (1 Cor 6:19)

The heart is the sanctuary Christ wishes to enter so that enthroned within it he may begin to reign. But he does not force his way in. He comes with humility and knocks on the door of the heart, waiting for us to open up and let him in. He calls us to attention by knocking with the instrument of his self-abandoned love, his holy cross through which he redeemed the world.

The Byzantine Rite for Holy week reminds us of the imperative to stay awake, ready to open up when the Lord shall come and knock (1 Thess 5:1-11; Phil 3:20; Mt 25:1-13; 19-30).[8] That refers primarily to his holy and glorious second coming in majesty to judge the living and the dead. But it is also a reminder and a warning to stay awake at all times since he comes at every moment of one's life. The big mistake is not to be at home in oneself when he does come. Liturgical tradition invokes the intercession of the angels, called in the Syrian Christian tradition 'watchers', on account of the endless vigil they maintain before the face of the all-Holy Lord; and the Byzantine Holy Week services highlight this note of vigilance:

> Behold the bridegroom is coming
> in the middle of the night:
> blessed is that servant
> whom he shall find awake!
> But the one found neglectful
> will not be worthy of him.

Therefore beware, O my soul!
Fall not into deep sleep,
lest you be handed over to death
and the door of the kingdom closed upon you.
But rather, watch and cry out:
'Holy, Holy, Holy are you, O God!
Through the intercession of the angelic hosts
have mercy upon us!'

C. Washing the Apostles' Feet: the Mystery of Divine Humility (Fig 7)

Love is the lesson which the Lord us taught.
Edmund Spenser

This incident, recorded in the 13th chapter of St John's gospel,
is a striking illustration of what Jesus taught in many other places
about humility and the service of others (Mk 10:35-45; Mt 25:31-
46). His whole life had exemplified kenotic self-emptying, from
his entry into the world (Heb 10:5-10) through his hidden life at
Nazareth (Lk 2:51), descent into the waters of the Jordan (Mk 1:9-
11) and battle with the devil in the desert (Mt 4:1-11; Lk 4:1-13).
Now as it approaches its climax on Calvary, he goes down on his
knees in front of his friends to perform one of the most menial acts
of service possible in the ancient world. Peter does not understand and attempts to argue with him but Jesus tells him that if he
does not let himself be washed he can have no part in him. Peter,
impulsive as ever, cries out that the Lord should therefore wash
not only his feet but his whole self (Jn 13:6-9).

What is the meaning of this strange scene? Ought we to take it
at face value as a simple lesson about humility, or does it offer
deeper layers of meaning that are waiting to be mined? Some
church Fathers (particularly St Ambrose) saw it as a sign of the
coming sacrament of baptism Jesus would commit to the apostles
after his resurrection and this may well be a factor that ought to be
taken into consideration. The Swiss Protestant biblical scholar
Oscar Cullman once noted that there are many sacramental hints
and resonances in the fourth gospel (though perhaps not quite so
many as he detected) and some in the local church of Milan after
Ambrose's time were open to the idea that foot-washing was a

sacrament.[9] Jesus after all had explicitly commanded his followers to do it, and western theology traditionally defined sacraments as visible rites which confer grace, commanded by the Lord.

Baptismal motifs such as washing and illumination are surely hinted at in this most allusive of all four gospels. But there is a danger that by placing the focus there and concentrating at this point on extracting hidden meanings, one might miss the deepest meaning which in this case is displayed on the surface. It is too easy to water down this washing, with its shocking connotations, by turning it into a beautiful ritual. Such a danger is probably not always avoided by those churches which act it out liturgically as part of their worship on Holy Thursday.

Once, for example, I attended a gorgeously ornate eastern liturgy in the Holy Land where a bishop washed the feet of twelve sumptuously attired colleagues, each of whom was wearing a mitre almost as big as himself. One would hope that the reverend gentlemen were deeply imbued with the kenotic spirit of their Lord but the visual effect tended to work somewhat in the opposite direction. Sometimes too the danger of reducing it to nice meaningful ritual has struck me on Holy Thursday in our monastery church when each carefully invited guest presents a foot previously washed and (sometimes perfumed) so that the Abbot can dab it with some (pre-heated) water from a brass ewer and dry it with a newly laundered towel.

But the original event was not at all ritually uplifting: it was indeed, as the gospel indicates, rather shocking. It seems to me that when Jesus told Peter he could have no part in him (*meros* in Greek, meaning 'portion') if he did not let him wash him, we might expand and paraphrase what he was saying something like this:

> Peter, if you miss the point at this point then you will have missed it completely. You call me 'Teacher' and 'Lord' – and you are right for that is what I am. So if I, your Lord and Teacher, have washed your feet, you also ought to wash one another's feet. For I have set you an example, that you also should do as I have done to you. I am telling you something fundamental about God and about being in charge if you are able to accept it.

Jesus is the great 'I am', the Lord (*Kyrios*) who appeared to Moses at the burning bush (Ex 3:1-14) and gave the Law on Sinai (Ps 98(99):6-7), yet here in the Upper Room he reveals himself to us in the form of a servant. He carried through a religious revolution which deconstructed all previous notions of power and authority from the sphere of the divine to that of human institutions. To misunderstand that is to misunderstand the whole mystery of Christ. It was particularly imperative that Peter, the chosen rock (Mt 16: 18), the foundation stone of the church and the one whom history will dub 'Prince of the Apostles', should not miss the point. Jesus was not so much establishing a sacramental ritual as revealing the one great sacrament of divine humility, mercy and compassion which engenders all sacraments: himself.

D. The Last Supper: the Mystery of Self-Giving (Fig 8)

> Love makes the body.
> > Jean Luc Marion

Our contemporary post-Freudian culture has taught us to be more obsessed with the erotic than we probably need to be. The inevitable 'return of the repressed', so accurately and convincingly prophesied by Freud, means that sex, eroticism and the body's glamour is now everywhere on display – in advertising and in all forms of public media, in the culture of psychoanalysis, in the massive trade in human sex trafficking and in expensive cosmetic reconstructions which aim to correct nature in the direction of an artificially contrived 'beauty'. Everything is appearance, glitter and facade. Yet the elderly, the overweight, the less than obviously physically 'perfect' (i.e. most human beings) and the disabled – not to mention the starving – may well want to ask what 'beauty' really is. Bodies are increasingly defined as desirable things, objects of *eros* programmed by society to 'make love'.

Yet in the Eucharist that perspective, with its overemphasis on appearance, is reversed. By his *kenosis* Christ has turned the world's values upside down. Through the sacramental signs of his self-emptying, which effect what they symbolise, 'love makes the body.' Love makes the body, as the en-fleshed Word of God speaks his word of grace and forgiveness, and in so doing identifies the bread and wine at a Jewish feast with his very self, making them his body and blood. 'Fruit of the vine and work of human hands ... which earth has given,' become the body of the Word. Thomas Aquinas wrote in his hymn *Pange Lingua,* sung on Holy Thursday evening,

> Word made flesh,
> by word he maketh
> very bread his flesh
> to be ...

Christ who is God's present to us, presents us with the fullest possible presence of himself for he is pure gift. In breaking the bread and handing it over he gives us the sign of his own handing over in betrayal, 'betrayed into the hands of sinners' (Mk 14:41). 'Not one of his bones shall be broken' (Ps (33)34:20, *Grail translation*) we read in scripture but what broke on the cross was the dam of Christ's divine-human heart, filled to overflowing with God's love for the world. In the piercing of his side a torrent of new life streamed out over us, coming forth as water and blood so that we might drink our fill and never grow thirsty, eat and never hunger again (Jn 4:13-14; 6:35). Connecting St John's account of the passion to a prophecy of Isaiah, the liturgy speaks of it in the poetry of the Mass:[10]

> From his open side flowed blood and water,
> the fountain of sacramental life in the church.
> To his opened heart
> the Saviour invites all people
> to draw water in joy
> from the wells of salvation!

Denys the Areopagite spoke of Christ as the centre of a radiating circle of goodness, for God the Supreme Good is like the sun – naturally diffusive of itself. Just as the solar disk pours out waves and rays of life-generating energy, so in the sacrament of the Eucharist Jesus emerges from his personal individuality and shines forth as a corporate person in his body the church. He is mystically 'distributed' by the power of the Holy Spirit, taking up his dwelling place in the hearts of individual human beings and making them one in unity and love. Sharing communion together creates the community which is Christ's body the church.[11]

Just as love makes the body on the altar so love makes the body of the church. Only love could have devised such a marvellous method of self-transcendence, allowing Christ to go out from himself, exiting from his single, individual being so as to become present in millions of individuals, making them into 'one body, one Spirit in Christ'. Love makes the body because, as modern theologians remind us, through the sacrament of the Eucharist the Lord Jesus forms and builds his community, binding its many members into one. 'We who are many are one body, for we all partake of the one bread,' Paul wrote to the Corinthians (1 Cor 10:17).[12]

But the gift of such unity was not cheap: St Peter wrote, 'You were bought at a great price' (1 Pet 1:18-19). Paul Celan, a Romanian Jewish poet whose parents were murdered during the Second World War, touched the paradox of this mystery of suffering when he wrote:[13]

> … the Lord broke the bread,
> the bread broke the Lord.

As Jesus broke and poured the sacramental bread and wine, making them the effective signs of sharing and sacrifice, he committed himself to the looming darkness of the coming night (Jn 13:30). As the Psalmist had foretold, this food mingled with tears would become his bread by day and by night (Ps 41(42): 3). In that simple gesture of table fellowship, Jesus gave to his followers an eloquent sign of what lay ahead of him on the cross. At his Last Supper he issued an invitation to come to the table where we learn what it meant for him to be broken, given and consumed for the life of the world.[14]

E. *Gethsemane: the Mystery of Two Wills Becoming One* (Fig 9)
> When they had sung the hymn, they went out to the Mount of Olives. *(Mt 26:30)*

So Matthew put it in his gospel, repeating the words of Mark (Mk 14:26). In the garden of Gethsemane Jesus stared point blank at what was coming and wrestled with it in great distress. The enormity that loomed on the horizon had now come very close: could this really be the will of the Father? This episode in the garden recalls that first garden in which Adam and Eve, the protoparents of the human race, had so casually disobeyed God's will (Gen 3:1-7). It is a garden that we all inhabit. It recalls too the struggle with Satan in the desert when Jesus had to deal with what kind of Messiah he would become: what would it be, conquering king or suffering servant (Mt 4:1-11; Lk 4:1-13)? Finally it recalls the mountain of the transfiguration, thanks to the presence of the same apostles, Peter, James and John (Lk 9:28-36).

Mark and Matthew typically pulled no punches in describing their weakness, telling us openly that they fell asleep. Only Luke, with characteristic gentleness, softened the blow by claiming that they were sleeping because of grief (Lk 22:45). Some manuscripts of Luke also say that an angel came to comfort him but that most likely reveals the later desire of a scribe to make the agony seem less awful than it really was.

The desolation experienced by Jesus comes across all the more forcefully in Mark's account because while praying Jesus is said to have used the word *Abba* (Mk 14:36), the Aramaic word a child used for addressing its father. That seems to have been a distinctive feature of his relationship with his Father in heaven.[15]

Of all the mysteries of the *kenosis*, the agony in the garden is the most mysterious and impenetrable. How could the eternal Son of God made flesh have experienced an apparent division between his human will and the divine will (both that of God his Father and his own divine will) to the point of having to bring them into alignment? There is no rational answer to that nor can it be 'explained'.[16] All one can do is contemplate the mystery and realise what a deadly struggle was going on between the one thing that generates the evil of the world – the human will, with its frightful capacity to say 'no' to God – and God's will which wishes always and everywhere only the good.

Yet in our own day, reflection on the mystery of the Holy Trinity, by theologians like Hans Urs von Balthasar, can provide some glimmers of light. For him, the distance into which Jesus goes in the garden, on the cross and in the Underworld, expresses in time the intra-trinitarian 'distance' between the Father and the Son in eternity (signifying their hypostatic/personal 'difference') – yet just as that distance is simultaneously 'annulled' through the communion of Father and Son with one another in the Holy Spirit (their being consubstantial in nature), so Christ's increasing journey away from the Father into the isolation of his passion is held and enfolded within the Spirit's embrace. Once again the Trinity casts light on the mystery of the redemption of the world.[17]

Jesus was in himself completely sinless but the human will he had assumed was identical with ours and therefore in need of healing and redemption. In the garden we see the agony he suffered in bringing it into harmony with the will of God – with the Father's will, his own divine but temporarily concealed will, and the will of the Holy Spirit.

The Letter to the Hebrews contains the best interpretation of what it all means and why he did it. The first reason was to cement the solidarity between the Saviour and those whom he saves:

> It was fitting that God, for whom and through whom all things exist, in bringing many children to glory, should make the pioneer of their salvation perfect through sufferings. For the one who sanctifies and those who are sanctified all have one Father. For this reason Jesus is not ashamed to call them brothers and sisters … (Heb 2: 10-11)

The incarnation represented the first stage of that solidarity :

> Since, therefore, the children share flesh and blood, he himself likewise shared the same things, so that through death he might destroy the one who has the power of death, that is, the devil, and free those who all their lives were held in slavery by the fear of death. For it is clear that he did not come to help angels, but the descendants of Abraham.(Heb 2:14-16)

… but it was perfected in the offering of Jesus' life, which the author of Hebrews interpreted using the categories of the Jewish priesthood and temple worship:

> Therefore he had to become like his brothers and sisters in every respect, so that he might be a merciful and faithful high priest in the service of God, to make a sacrifice of atonement for the sins of the people. (Heb 2:17-18)

The struggle with temptation taught Jesus directly, through human experience, what the rest of us have to go through so that nothing human should ever be alien to him. Paradoxical though it may sound, Gethsemane appears as a kind of divine-human 'learning curve' for the incarnate God. However, the fact that he was able not to succumb to temptation underlines the difference between Jesus and us; but it also teaches us that sin as such is in fact inhuman. Authentic human existence does not consist in rebellion against God but in remaining in harmony with God's loving will. Remade in the image of Christ, the saints are therefore the most authentically human beings. It also shows us that freedom is not just a superficial liberty to choose between good and evil but the deeper freedom to sink one's will in God's will, secure in the knowledge that, as Dante put it, 'In his will is our peace', however unclear that may seem at the time. Authentic liberty consists in the freedom to become a servant of love.

The agony in the garden was about compassion, about God's capacity to 'suffer with' creation, made all the more impressive because there was no necessity in it at all: it was the free expression of God's freedom to be such a God, a God of kenotic love. Jesus shows us that rooted within God's very self, deep at the heart of the Trinity, lies some infinitely mysterious transcendent quality, which reflects itself in human compassion. He reveals that God is able to meet us at the lowest level of our lives, for in becoming human he opened himself even to our deepest agonies. Because he himself was tested by what he suffered, he is able to help those who are being tested:

> Since then we have a great high priest who has passed through the heavens, Jesus the Son of God, let us hold fast to our confession. For we do not have a high priest who is unable to sympathise with our weaknesses, but we have one who in every respect has been tempted as we are, yet without sin. (Heb 4:14)

That gives us a new ground for hope in our relationship with God:

> Let us therefore approach the throne of grace with bold-
> ness, so that we may receive mercy and find grace to help in
> time of need. (Heb 4:16)

Finally, Hebrews summarises the mystery by mentioning indirectly the agony in the garden, the memory of which was evidently cherished by the early church precisely because it was such a sign of God's accessibility to us in Christ.

> In the days of his flesh, Jesus offered up prayers and
> supplications, with loud cries and tears, to the one who was
> able to save him from death, and he was heard because of
> his reverent submission. Although he was a Son, he learned
> obedience through what he suffered; and having been
> made perfect, he became the source of eternal salvation for
> all who obey him, having been designated by God a high
> priest according to the order of Melchizedek. (Heb 5:7-10)

One thing is sure in contemplating the mystery played out in the garden of Gethsemane: the *kenosis* of the eternal Son of God was no sacred pantomime, no mere playing at being human. The incarnation was 'for real'.

F. Betrayal (Fig 10)

Eastern Christian Spirituality always shows the deepest respect for the awesome mystery of human suffering and especially the suffering of the incarnate God, but its desire to throw a veil over the mysteries is never so evident as when it comes to depicting the cross of Christ. Sometimes western Christians wrongly imagine that the Orthodox Church underplays or diminishes the human sufferings of Christ, but anyone who is even remotely familiar with that great tradition, particularly as it celebrates Holy Week knows what a caricature that is. Yet in their liturgy and iconography they do refuse to pry into the mystery of redemptive suffering, preferring instead to keep a reverent distance.

There is plenty of emotion in Byzantine icons though it is usually restrained and dignified. But there are no wracked, bleeding, tortured images of Christ and above all no 'Mel Gibson-style' depictions of the passion, where every wound, scar and laceration is excruciatingly exposed to scrutiny. When it comes to the artistic depiction of suffering, less is almost always more. Violating the sacred, penetrating intrusively in a voyeuristic spirit into the privacy of suffering and diminishing the dignity of death, is usually avoided by the Eastern Church (just as it is by classical Roman liturgy) when it contemplates the Saviour's passion. We are never to forget the mystery surrounding every human death, but especially the death of the incarnate God. A magnificent text sung in the Byzantine liturgy on Holy Saturday captures perfectly this ethos of silent reverence:

Let all mortal flesh keep silence
and stand with awe and trembling,
lifted high above all earthly thought:
for behold the King of Kings
and the Lord of Lords is coming forth
to be offered in sacrifice
and given as food to the faithful.
Around him stand the hosts of archangels,
the principalities and dominions
with the many-eyed Cherubim
and the six-winged Seraphim
who chant: alleluia, alleluia, alleluia!

Betrayal is at the heart of the passion of Christ, for he was handed over by his disciple Judas.

Even my bosom friend in whom I trusted,
who ate of my bread, has lifted the
heel against me. (Ps 40(41):9)

But the other apostles all betrayed him too, with the exception of the Beloved Disciple, his mother and the other women. According to the fourth gospel they at least were courageous enough to accompany him even to the cross:

So the Psalmist foretold the painful embrace of Judas who, for whatever motivation, betrayed his master with a kiss (Mk 14:45). But Peter too cursed and swore that he knew nothing of this man

(Mk 14:71). Jesus had taken the cup of sacrifice in the Upper Room; in the garden he had asked that if possible it might be taken away; but betrayal and abandonment by his friends and followers was surely his first real taste of its bitter contents (Jn 16:32):

> The hour is coming, indeed it has come, when you will be scattered, each one to his home, and you will leave me alone. Yet I am not alone because the Father is with me.

Jesus' appearance before Pilate (Mk 15:1-15; Mt 27:1-26; Lk 23:1-25; Jn 18:28-40; 19:1-16) is probably the most remarkable encounter in history viewed from the perspective of Christ's victory at Easter (Fig 11). The Lord and maker of heaven and earth, concealed in the form of an accused criminal, meets the earthly representative of the most powerful political machine the world had ever seen. In a characteristically cruel witticism, Hitler is reputed to have said of the very low-key Spanish Dictator General Franco that he rose to prominence like Pontius Pilate in the Creed. History is so often made by very ordinary and limited people pushed for better or for worse into extraordinary situations yet equipped with unlimited power.

For a brief moment, a typical Governor of a troubled far flung province of the Roman Empire was suddenly thrown on to the stage of world history, though he obviously had no idea of what was actually happening and none at all of the greater consequences to which it would lead. He simply followed judicial procedure as he had most likely done on many occasions before.[18]The gospel of Matthew records that Pilate's wife, one of the most significant dreamers of the New Testament, had a nocturnal warning that Jesus was not a normal malefactor (Mt 27:19). The humiliation of Christ intensifies with the political and religious authorities conspiring together to get rid of a troublesome holy man whilst releasing a genuine criminal (Mt 27:26).

As the hymn for Christ's entry into Jerusalem we have already mentioned puts it, 'A murderer they save, the Prince of life they slay!' In the person of Jesus, incarnate love came face to face with the 'Great Beast' of naked political power and appeared to disappear under its force (Rev 17:1-6). Standing before Pilate, Jesus stood for every man, woman or child who has ever been bound, gagged and dragged before authority on trumped-up charges.

It is hardly possible to hear the accounts of the passion being read each year on Palm Sunday without shivering, not only on account of the brutality the soldiers inflicted on Jesus but because the one who suffered it was God incarnate. The scourging, buffeting, spitting, stripping, clothing in purple, crowning with thorns and imposition of the cross on his sacred shoulders; the stripping and pseudo-investiture with the symbols of royalty: all were a horrible ironic parody of his regal dignity and status as the eternal Son of God, the King and Lord of all creation, who had not clung to his equality with God but voluntarily stripped off his robe of glory, until in his descent he reached the point where he had literally nothing left.

G. The Mystery of the Death of the Son of God (Fig 12)

> ... standing near the cross of Jesus were his mother, and his mother's sister Mary the wife of Clopas, and Mary Magdalene ... (Jn 19:2)

> It is accomplished! (Jn 19:30)

As a text in the Roman liturgy puts it, 'Raised high on the cross Christ gave his life for us, so much did he love us.' As we saw in our earlier discussion of the redeeming death of Christ, theories of penal substitution are to be avoided. However, in re-considering the part played by God the Father in the event of the crucifixion, we need to go much further than just excluding such a cruel notion. The Father's role was an active one. Jesus had predicted at the final supper with his friends:

> The hour is coming, indeed it has already come when you will be scattered, each one to his home, and you will leave me alone. Yet I am not alone for the Father is with me. (Jn 16:32)

One of the themes contemporary theologians like to emphasise is that God the Father was just as personally involved in the passion and death of Christ as he was in his resurrection. It is increasingly evident that if the notion of the Father punishing Christ is false, then equally well the idea of his simply sending the Son, then stepping back to watch the drama unfold is also thoroughly inadequate. It fails to do justice to the New Testament's insistence that God so loved the world that he gave his only Son (Jn 3:16) and that the Son's death is the clearest proof of the Father's love (Rom 5:8, where 'God' clearly refers to the person of the Father). Here is where the question of Jesus' identity, of who he is, becomes really crucial.

When it comes to doing dirty work, love does not send someone else: love chooses to come in person.[19] After the death and resurrection of Christ and the coming of the Holy Spirit, the apostles were led to recognise that in Jesus, God had truly visited and redeemed his people (Lk 1:68). God had not just been acting *through* him but was actually identical with him. But that meant eventually expanding the word 'God' beyond what it had originally designated for the Jews (and the first Christians) – the personal name of the one Father – and reconfiguring the whole notion of 'one God' in the direction of the Trinity.[20]

Judaism had already speculated that God relates to the world though various emanations, but Christian emphasis on the divinity of Christ probably cut that process short. For the Christians, such a development was not just a theological luxury: it was a necessary process forced upon them if they were to succeed in making sense of what had been revealed in the life, death and resurrection of the one whom they acclaimed as Saviour and Messiah. The doctrine of the Trinity was forced into being as the direct consequence of the need to reflect on what had been revealed, render it intelligible and communicate it as Christian teaching: since only God can save, the manifestly human Jesus must have been in some sense divine. The worship of Christ right from the beginning of the church's life forced a redefinition of divinity.[21]

The same imperative was also operative as the church reflected on the work of the Holy Spirit, the Sanctifier. Just as only God can save from sin so only God can purify, illuminate and sanctify believers. The early church's insistence on salvation as divinisation (*theosis*) or deification (*theopoesis*), the doctrine that by sharing in the divine life one shares also in divine qualities like goodness mercy and compassion, assumes the divinity of the agents who grant us access to this life: Christ and the Holy Spirit.[22]

The mystery of the Holy Trinity was unveiled between Good Friday and Easter Sunday in the events of Christ's passion, death and resurrection, but it was perfectly revealed only on the morning of Pentecost: the cross and the upper room in Jerusalem are the original disclosure-zones where God unveiled his inner life to us and invited us to enter in and share its depths. Yet it took centuries before a coherent and systematic articulation of what Christians believed and worshipped could be achieved by the church.

But if Jesus was truly God the Son incarnate, and the cross the manifestation of threefold divine love, we can hardly imagine the Father and the Holy Spirit as having remained largely unaffected by it all. In reading much theology written before the 20th century, one sometimes gets the impression that God the Father was like a kind of ancient Persian potentate watching the drama of Calvary from afar – seated on a high throne at a safe distance and ready to scarper if disaster should strike. A legacy of philosophical theology exalting immobility and changelessness over motion and adaptation, tended to perpetuate such a notion. That, of course, was not necessarily an altogether bad thing. It was an attempt to do justice philosophically to the vivid Hebrew sense of God's stability and fidelity to his promises, a fundamental attribute of the Jewish God (Gen 12:1-3; Ps 24(25)).

But, interpreted through static philosophical categories, it risks minimising the dramatic interventions in history carried out by God as recorded in the Jewish-Christian sacred narratives. It also does less than justice to the fact that in describing God's activities we can only ever use anthropomorphic human language – metaphors, similes, images and analogies. Yet when God revealed himself he did not disdain to take language and press it into his service: consequently, the words of scripture have become more than merely human words. They are vehicles and verbal icons, conveying the mysteries of the divine life to us in a form we can at least partially comprehend.

Given the biblical witness of God's self-revelation, care for his chosen people, all-consuming love of justice and repeated interventions in history one might just as legitimately privilege images of change over those of immobility when speaking about him. Yet the truth is that both change and stability are equally true of God. Both ought, therefore, to be reflected in our theology, our 'God-talk.'[23]

Eastern Christian thinkers following St Gregory Palamas (1296-1359) express that paradox by speaking of God as simultaneously unchanging (in his impenetrable essence which is proper to and known by the three divine Persons alone) and yet capable of movement thanks to the providential actions (God's 'energies') through which the Holy Trinity, emerging from the hidden silence of its innermost sanctuary, creates, sustains and redeems the world. Into that transcendent inner sanctuary of Father, Son and Holy Spirit – as the churches of the east insist – no created intelligence, neither human nor angelic can ever enter; only through God's free and gracious movement out towards us in Christ and the Holy Spirit are we enabled to learn of his capacity to enter into and adapt to time and history through a freely chosen *kenosis* so that he can reach down to us in love.[24]

Right after Christ's death St Mark's gospel records that the curtain of the temple was torn down the middle from top to bottom (Mk 15:38), signifying that God had broken through into the world in a new way and thrown heaven open to us. It was a symbolic summary of the entire mystery of Christ. The dramatic actions of the three divine persons force us to ask: 'If God is like this in his dealings with us, is it not also true that he must be (somehow) like this in and for himself?' One thing is certain: the God revealed in the Jewish-Christian scriptures, the God of the covenant, is a free, acting and loving God. He is anything but static, immobile or detached. Without compromising God's internal stability, it is vital in the light of the New Testament to find our way toward the notion that God the Father (and the Holy Spirit) did somehow share in the suffering of his incarnate Son through love and the intensity of their communion with him.

Historically, art has often dealt more successfully with this issue than theology. Medieval western artists gave us the image of the *Gnadenstuhl* ('the throne of grace') or 'mercy seat', based on the 'propitiatory' or 'expiation,' the place above the Ark of the Covenant in the Holy of Holies of the first Jerusalem temple, where God 'covered' the sins of his people through the High Priest's sacrificial ministrations on the Day of Atonement. That place is described in detail in the Books of Exodus (Ex 25:17-22) and Leviticus (Lev 16:12-15) and mentioned in Paul's letter to the Romans (Rom 3:25) and the letter to the Hebrews (Heb 9:3-12) and the first Letter of John (1 Jn 2:2) where it is used as an image to interpret the atoning death of Christ.[25] The High Priest having taken the blood of a slaughtered bull into the Holy of Holies, remerged to sprinkle (i.e. cover) the sins of the people.

The corresponding medieval image, depicting God the Father cradling his Son's dead body while the Holy Spirit hovers over both (or sometimes in between them), is like a heavenly counterpart to the earthly *pietà* in which Mary holds the body of Christ after he has been taken down from the cross. So Christ comes forth from the Holy of Holies, the transcendent sanctuary of God, sent and supported by the Father and accompanied by the Holy Spirit, to cover the sins of his people.[26]

Iconography may indeed go more confidently where rational reflection can only very softly tread. It is only since the development of kenotic theologies of the Trinity in the 19th and 20th centuries, based on the realisation that God's power includes the capacity to 'self-limit' so as to reach out in love towards the other, that theologians Catholic, Protestant and Orthodox have been able to catch up with art and develop a language to describe how the eternal God is capable of embracing human suffering.[27]

However, talk about the suffering 'in' or 'of' God requires that we also exercise a real theological rigour and self-discipline. We should beware of cutting God down to our size and failing to respect God's radical difference from us. It is theologically sloppy simply to say 'God suffers,' and leave it at that, except perhaps when preaching or singing hymns where a certain amount of emotional rhetoric is acceptable. Making God out to be simply a bigger version of oneself (suffering included) risks reducing the divine to all-too-human proportions and worse, making God a kind of divine 'wimp' marooned in the same boat as suffering human beings. Not only would that be unfaithful to the witness of the Bible but it is hard to grasp how such a one could ever be a God who saves.

We ought, therefore, to handle God's compassionate participation in human suffering carefully, perhaps being content to say tentatively: 'Thanks to the coming of Christ and his death on the cross, thanks to the merciful Father it reveals and thanks to the descent of the Holy Spirit at Pentecost, we have been made aware of something in God corresponding to what we on earth experience as our capacity to suffer with and for others; what precisely that is in God infinitely transcends our limited understanding. It is literally mind-blowing. Yet it is sufficient that thanks to Christ's suffering on the cross we should recognise it and that it should illumine and support both our own capacity to suffer and our ability to sympathise with others in their agony.'

Our task is not to dissect revelation rationally. Rather, standing before God in prayer, having exhausted all normal resources of understanding, we need to prostrate in wonder before the cross and contemplate the staggering truth revealed on its barren wood: God so loved the world that he gave his only Son (Jn 3:16); the eternal Son emptied himself (Phil 2:7-8), becoming like us in suffering and death so to save and transform us; the Holy Spirit was poured out on us through his wounded side (Jn 19:34). By means of this, God has broken through to us but beyond that human reason cannot go. As medieval monastic writers liked to say, love can go in where reason is required to wait at the door.

The deepest meaning of the mystery of the cross lies far beyond reason. It is literally 'meta-rational' and 'meta-logical'. It reveals its logic only to those who have learnt to pray with the liturgy of Good Friday, 'We worship your passion O Christ! Show us also your holy resurrection', those who consent to become themselves passion-bearers, willing to take on their own shoulders the sins and suffering of others according to the model revealed to us by God on Golgotha.

For that reason, the martyrs are always the most authentic interpreters and expositors of the divine pathos revealed through the cross: like the Master whom they followed, what they said was verified by their lives. Such were the saints of Auschwitz – Teresa Benedicta of the Cross (Edith Stein)[28] offering her life for the salvation of her people, and Maximilian Kolbe who exchanged his life for that of the father of a family, surely an icon of the compassionate divine paternity if ever there was one.[29] Such was Mother Maria Skobtsova, an Orthodox nun who like St Maximilian also substituted herself for someone else in a concentration camp.[30] Yet such were also the countless millions who have followed Christ in every age, suffering the 'white martyrdom' of duty bravely borne and loving service of their neighbour.

Each one became a living image of the mystery of Christ's love made know to us by the Holy Trinity in Jerusalem in the time of Pontius Pilate. But we should not limit too narrowly the motivation which leads some to mirror the suffering of the innocent Lamb of God. It is worth considering the medieval Russian church's canonisation of saints Boris and Gleb, sons of Prince Vladimir of Kiev, who were unjustly killed in a dynastic dispute. They died rather than see widespread bloodshed inflicted on others. Russian Orthodoxy recognised them, as we do at Christmas the Jewish children so cruelly murdered by Herod (Mt 2:16-18), as genuine icons of the innocent Christ – bound, gagged and led away for slaughter.[31]

We too should learn to recognise his disfigured face wherever it appears and acknowledge that in the most intense suffering God is always there, whether his presence is explicitly acknowledged or not. All true theology proclaims the mystery of the Holy Trinity disclosed in Christ's passion: it is always the theology of the cross.

H. The Mystery of the Burial of Jesus (Fig 13)

> You descended from on high,
> O merciful Saviour
> and endured the grave for three days
> that you might free us from our anguish!
> Glory to you O Lord,
> our life and resurrection!
>
> *Byzantine hymn*

Mary and John, Mary Magdalene and Joseph of Arimathea, who had been a secret disciple on account of fear yet had shown the courage to claim Christ's body back from Pilate (Jn 19:38; Mt 27:58), are all depicted in this icon laying the dead body of Jesus in the tomb. This kind of image, and indeed the tomb of Christ itself, have long been cherished objects in the devotional life of Christians, especially in the east. In the Orthodox Church's ritual, one of the most moving services of all is the burial procession of Christ held during Matins of Holy Saturday (which is anticipated on Good Friday evening).

After a lengthy service in the church, the *epitaphios*, an embroidered image of the dead Christ laid out for burial, is carried in procession out of the building and taken through the streets of the area as the bells toll their sad lament for the dead incarnate God. Sublimely beautiful Byzantine poems are chanted until the procession returns to the church, at which point the worshippers pass beneath the image on re-entering the building, thereby symbolically evoking the process of being buried with Christ described by Paul in the Letter to the Romans (Rom 6:4).

The archetypal symbols in this service recapitulate many of the mysterious pre-Christian rituals of the ancient world centred on a dying and rising god: the myths of Egypt and Greece which prefigured the death of the Redeemer are thus brought to their fulfilment in reality.[32] At the same time, one of the most painful human experiences – a mother lamenting her dead child – is given an unforgettable outlet in the figure of Mary receiving the dead body of her Son before it is placed in the tomb. Here the power of the liturgy reaches right into the heart, touching emotional chords in the human psyche and triggering affective responses which lie slumbering in the depths of the soul.

It is sufficient to mention only a few of the chants to catch the flavour of the night. They draw out the intense emotion of the mystery: the kenotic descent of the Word made flesh, his saving passion and finally as the Anglican liturgy powerfully puts it in a prayer for Holy Saturday, his entry 'through the grave and gate of death' into the dismal underworld of *Sheol* or *Hades*, the land of the unseen, peopled by the shades of the long dead, a zone of disappearance equally terrifying to Jews and Gentiles alike. The hymns repeatedly record the astonishment of the angels as they behold the saving economy of God being worked out in the burial of Christ:

O my Christ,
O my life!
You were placed in the tomb
while the angels were amazed
and glorified your divine burial!

O Jesus, King and Master of all,
how well we know that you accepted death
for the life of all!
Oh the wonder of such a divine kenosis!

You destroyed the power of Hades
when you were laid in the tomb.

Through your divine death
you destroyed death
and delivered humankind from its decay!

In many of the hymns, Mary the Mother of God, known in Orthodoxy as the *Panagia* or 'All-Holy One', painfully laments the passing of her son. But like the icons at their best these texts are never merely sentimental.

O Jesus, the all-pure one
shed her tears over you.
In agony of heart she gave expression to a mother's love:
'Oh my son, my son,
how shall I bury you in the earth?'

When our most pure Lady saw you laid out for burial,
O Word of God, she wept in agony:
'O my precious Son, my God,
you crushed death by your death
through the power of your divinity;
O my Son I praise you
for your great compassion
which moved you to undergo this death!'

Finally, the all-merciful Holy Trinity is invoked and Mary's prayers besought to obtain for us the vision of Christ's coming resurrection:

O my God, O three-in-one!
Father, Son and Holy Spirit
have mercy on your world!

Most pure Mother of God,
make your children behold
the resurrection of your Son!

At the culmination of the service, special attention is devoted above all to the figure of Joseph of Arimathea, as a fitting reward for his courage. One of the most beautiful texts in the entire Byzantine tradition plays poetically with the theme of Christ as the guest who came to his own but was not received by them:

Seeing that the sun had concealed its rays and that the veil
of the temple had been torn in two when the Saviour died
Joseph went to Pilate. He pleaded with him and exclaimed,

Give me that stranger
who since his youth
had wandered as a stranger.

Give me that stranger
upon whom I look with amazement,
seeing him as a guest of death!

Give me that stranger
whom envious men
estranged from the world.

Give me that stranger
that I may bury him in a tomb
who as a stranger
has no place to lay his head.

Give me that stranger
to whom his mother cried out
as she saw him dead,

'O my son, my senses are wounded
and my heart burns within me
as I see you dead!
Yet with confidence
in your resurrection
I magnify you!'

In such words as these did the ever-memorable Joseph plead with Pilate. Taking the Saviour's body, he wrapped it with spices in a linen shroud. He placed you in a tomb, O you who grant eternal life and great mercy to all humankind!

To recover the dead bodies of our loved ones in order to dispose of them decently is a fundamental human need, regardless of the ways in which a society chooses to deal with its dead. There is perhaps no more moving episode in the whole of pre-Christian literature than the moment in Homer's *Odyssey* when Priam, the aged Trojan king, implores Achilles for the dead body of his son who has been killed and humiliated outside the city walls, carrying it, as the poet Michael Longley wrote, 'wrapped like a present home to Troy at daybreak.'[33]

Some Greek Fathers saw in this epic tragedy a pre-figuration of Christ's passion in pagan culture, or as Simone Weil called it an 'intimation of Christianity among the ancient Greeks.'[34] They read it as a prophecy of a hero greater than Hector, Jesus the Christ, who would also die outside the city and whose body too would be sought by one with great courage.

No funerals are more tragic than those in which the remains are not present because they have been lost at sea or completely wiped out, as in a fire or terrorist attack. A particularly horrible feature of the Holocaust was its obliteration of the victims' remains, literally sending them up in smoke. Yet nearer home, in the Northern Irish 'troubles' one of the worst atrocities was the abduction and murder of a housewife whose 'crime' was to have supported the head of a dying soldier after he had been shot. She was whisked away at night by gunmen and her family never saw her again. For the remainder of their lives they were haunted by the spectre of their abducted mother: but worst of all was the lingering torture inflicted by the killers' refusal to indicate the whereabouts of her remains, so that she could at last be laid to rest. Others too, including at least one prominent British soldier, suffered such a fate in Northern Ireland.

Among the accounts of Christ's resurrection appearances, the one to Mary Magdalene is among the most compelling precisely because it powerfully addresses this theme of the missing remains of a loved one (Jn 20:1-18). Having come to the tomb on Sunday morning, she found that it had disappeared (Jn 20:2). Weeping in great distress she was unable to recognise that Jesus himself actually stood before her. As if his death had not been agony enough she was now reduced to lamenting the even more painful absence of his corpse:

> They have taken away my Lord, and I do not know where they have laid him. (Jn 20:13)

Jesus spoke her name: 'Mary!' (Jn 20:16). The voice awakened vision, her eyes were opened and the terrible void of loss and absence was transformed into a new and wonderful presence. But a deeper paradox followed as Jesus admonished her:

> Do not hold on to me, because I have not yet ascended to the Father, but go to my brothers and say to them, 'I am ascending to my Father and your Father, to my God and your God.' Mary Magdalene went and announced to the disciples, 'I have seen the Lord'; and she told them that he had said these things to her. (Jn 20:17-18)

Mary passed from the pain and confusion of loss and absence to a vibrant new contact with Christ. But even as this happened she was taught that her old way of relating to him had now become a thing of the past. From now on Jesus would be different: he would be a universal person, available not only to her but to all as their Saviour, Lord and friend. In learning this she too was 'universalised.' She received her mission, becoming the Apostle to the Apostles, the first herald of the victory of Christ. Thus Mary passed from the desolation of an empty tomb to the vocation God had planned for her before time began – to proclaim the resurrection of life in the triumph of Christ.

'The mysteries of Christ are our mysteries.' They are given us by God to illumine our path and open our eyes, to bring us new vision. They touch and heal every moment of our existence, every pain we suffer – from the pangs of birth to laying our loved ones in the grave. In this mystery of burial and re-encounter with Christ the Holy Spirit teaches us through Mary Magdalene how to let go if we are to become in our turn effective witnesses to Christ's victory and the heralds of his kingdom. Only by releasing our grip on Christ can we allow God to create the space across which the Holy Spirit comes, for the third person is a Spirit of freedom (Gal 5:1; 2 Cor: 3:17). Had Jesus not promised as much?:

> I will not leave you orphaned; I am coming to you. In a little while the world will no longer see me, but you will see me; because I live you also will live. On that day you will know that I am in my Father, and you in me, and I in you.
>
> I did not say these things to you from the beginning, because I was with you. But now I am going to him who sent me; yet none of you asks me, 'Where are you going?' But because I have said these things to you, sorrow has filled your hearts. Nevertheless I tell you the truth: it is to your advantage that I go away, for if I do not go away, the Advocate will not come to you; but if I go, I will send him to you. (Jn 14:18-21; 16:4b-7)

I. The Mystery of the Exaltation of the Cross (Fig 14)

> Joy to you,
> O life-giving cross,
> shining paradise of the church
> and tree of incorruptibility:
> you have obtained for us
> the joy of everlasting glory!
>
> Through your cross, O Lord
> reveal to us
> the splendour of your beauty!
>   *Byzantine hymn*

As we began with the resurrection it is appropriate to take our leave of the mysteries of the passion with one of the great feasts of the Lord's liturgical year, a feast also featured on this icon. The solemnity of the Exaltation of the Cross is a particularly good example of the poetic imagination of the Christian community reflecting on the great symbols of its faith and bringing them to expression in worship. Yet unlike Good Friday it is not without a certain ambiguity. The development of the feast was intrinsically bound up with the history of the Byzantine Empire, so it might be open to legitimate criticism on that account. Did it just baptise earthly power, making too easy an identification of Caesar's realm with the kingdom of God, an identification Jesus himself had resolutely refused to make (Mk 12:17; Jn 18:36) but which the church in history has sometimes readily embraced (1 Pet 2:17)?[35]

It certainly ran the risk of hijacking the cross for political purposes, transforming it from being a symbol of God's redeeming love, which accomplishes its end through suffering, and using it instead to underpin an imperial ideology identifying Christ with the East-Roman Emperor and the kingdom of God with the Byzantine (or Russian) state. One of the hymns frequently repeated in the Byzantine celebration of the feast might seem to bear this out:

Lord save your people
and bless your inheritance!
Strengthen our Emperor in every good deed
and protect your commonwealth with your cross!

Martin Luther rightly warned of the danger in replacing the 'theology of the cross' set forth in the New Testament with a 'theology of glory' which, attempting to bypass the cross's scandalous nature, would transform it too easily into a cross of light, making it a symbol for worldly power or a programmed ascent to God without suffering or real repentance.[36] Yet his own hitching of the Reformation to the state could arguably be seen as a move in a similar direction, leading eventually to the ultimate scandal: the presence together on the same altars of the cross and the swastika, the last word of betrayal of the Jewish Christ.[37] No church is above criticism in this area, from the time of the Crusades through all the 'most Christian kings' of history who have followed and even worn the cross, up to and including the blessing of tanks for Vietnam. All Christians need to pay careful attention to the hazards involved in hijacking the cross in the interests of political power.

Yet in the New Testament there is also a real theological awareness of the cross as the great sign of Christ's glory. One finds it above all in the four gospels, whose entire structure sweeps onwards towards the passion, but also in the extended reflections of St Paul and the other letters attributed to him. To obtain a genuine understanding of the cross in the New Testament it is important to get behind a merely chronological account of the events between the crucifixion and Easter Sunday. It was not just that first there was the cross with its shame, then the resurrection with its glory. Rather, the cross as the revelatory sign of God's love was already the beginning of Christ's exaltation, as Jesus had openly declared:

'Now is the judgement of this world; now the ruler of this world will be driven out. And I, when I am lifted up from the earth, will draw all people to myself.' He said this to indicate the kind of death he was to die. (Jn 12: 30)

This identification of his agony with his glorification is repeated at the Last Supper, before his death:

But take courage; I have conquered the world! (Jn 16:33)

Christ's exaltation begins therefore with his lifting up in crucifixion, so that the terrible instrument of torture assumes the character of a throne.[38] A profoundly beautiful Latin hymn, *Vexilla Regis Prodeunt*, by Venantius Fortunatus, still sung in the monastic liturgy on Good Friday and on this feast (14 September), captures well this mood of triumph:

The royal banners forward go;
the cross shines forth in mystic glow;

Fulfilled is all that David told
in true prophetic song of old:
Amidst the nations, God,

saith he,
hath reigned and triumphed
from the Tree

O Tree of beauty!
Tree of light
O Tree with royal purple bright!
Elect on whose triumphal breast
those holy limbs
should find their rest ...

The feast of the exaltation of the cross and the mystery it celebrates recalls for us, within the circle of the year, the vision of
God's limitless love, disclosed to us when his incarnate Son
opened his arms on the cross. Therefore the Roman and Anglican
liturgies sing on this feast:

The tree of our defeat became the tree of victory
and where life was lost
there life has been restored.

And at the Eucharist:

Dying you destroyed our death
rising you restored our life.

Drawing on the fourth gospel (Jn 3:14-16) both the Roman and
Byzantine traditions compare Christ lifted high on the cross to the
serpent raised up by Moses in the desert, which became the antidote to the deadly bites the Israelites had received from poisonous
serpents that had afflicted them for their unbelief (Num 21:6-9).
The very scourge which is the cause of death becomes the source
of healing: that is the real mystery but also the true glory of the
cross.

A particularly beautiful Greek text summarises the meaning
of the mystery celebrated on this day:

By its being lifted up the cross is an appeal
to the whole creation to adore
the blessed passion of Christ our God
who was hung upon it!

Christ has destroyed by this cross
the one who had destroyed us.
In his great goodness he brought us back to life
after we had been dead.
In his mercy he has filled us with happiness
and made us worthy of heaven!
Therefore we exalt his name with great rejoicing
and glorify his infinite stooping down to us.

The western tradition too contains many moving texts which view the cross in a similar light. For example, an antiphon in the monastic liturgy addresses it as follows:

O Cross,
surpassing all the stars in splendour!
O world-renowned trophy,
exceedingly beloved by all
and holier than all things!
You alone were counted worthy
to bear the ransom of the world.
How sweet the wood,
how sweet the iron
that bore so sweet a burden.
Give aid to this assembly
who are gathered here
to sing your praises!

In the Orthodox Vigil for this feast the cross is brought into the middle of the church, lowered, elevated and exposed in the direction of the four points of the compass while 'Lord have mercy' (*Kyrie eleison*) is fervently sung. Thus God's mercy is invoked upon the whole universe. What Paul wrote in the Letter to the Ephesians about 'the breadth and length and height and depth' of Christ's love which surpasses all knowledge (Eph 3:18-19) receives a striking symbolic expression in this gesture. It proclaims that God's glory really does fill the earth (Is 6:3) because the redeeming power of Christ's cross radiates to the uttermost parts of the universe. At the same time it ritually re-echoes St Peter's exhortation to believers:

Come to him, a living stone, though rejected by mortals yet
chosen and precious in God's sight … (1 Pet 2:4)

The Roman liturgy celebrates the feast of the exaltation of the
cross because it was imported from Byzantium in the early
Middle Ages, thanks to the presence of Greek-speaking Popes in
the church of Rome. But the most moving and dramatic lifting up
of the cross in the western tradition is that of the liturgy of Good
Friday, one of the most powerful rites of worship ever devised in
any tradition. It is a harmonious blend of early Roman and
Byzantine elements. The former include the stark silent entrance
with prostration of the ministers, long readings (including the
proclamation of the passion according to St John) and ancient
solemn intercessions invoking God's help for all sorts and conditions of people.[39]

But it is the Byzantine elements which really carry the emotional weight of the day. They include the entrance of a veiled
cross, its gradual uncovering and the singing of ancient texts
which unite the pathos of the suffering Servant (Is 53:7-9) with the
triumph of the Son of God who is glorified already in his passion
even before the resurrection. As the faithful approach to venerate
the cross an eastern chant, the *Trisagion* (the 'thrice-holy hymn')
which made its way to Rome from Egypt and Syria via Constantinople, is sung. Although diversely interpreted in the early
church – by the Greeks and the medieval Latins, on account of its
threefold form as a chant in honour of the Holy Trinity, but by
others, especially in Syria, as a song addressed to Christ – in the
Roman liturgy for Good Friday it is clearly directed to him:[40]

O Holy God!
O Holy and Mighty One!
O Holy and Immortal One!
Have mercy on us!

In the entire course of the liturgical cycle, the paradoxical nature
of the Christian mystery is nowhere more apparent than in this
solemn rite when we commemorate the redeeming death of the
incarnate Son of God.

• We sing, 'O Holy God!' to one who died in the most shameful

way possible for a Jew (Deut 21:23), cursed by the Law (Gal 3:
13) dying alone outside the city gates (Heb 13:12-13);

- 'O Holy and Strong One' to a victim whose hands and feet
were fixed and rendered immobile on the cross;

- 'O Holy and Immortal One!' to one who is dying in agony, and
we put our trust in his unfailing mercy: for the salvation of the
world came about when the Saviour could do no more than
hang there, lifted high on the cross.

The rubrics accompanying this service in the Roman Rite provide for two options in carrying out this ceremony. Either one may
bring an uncovered cross through the church and into the sanctuary, or one may unveil a covered cross three times in the sanctuary
itself. In our liturgy at Glenstal, we combine the two in order to obtain the maximum dramatic effect, bringing the cross in procession
from the west door through the church, uncovering it progressively at three staging posts, elevating it three times and at each showing singing in Latin this haunting chant on an ascending note:

Ecce lignum crucis,
in quo salus mundi pependit!
Venite adoremus!

Behold the wood of the cross,
on which hung the salvation of the world!
O come, let us adore!

This progressive unveiling, leading to the manifestation of the
cross and its elevation, always reminds me of the mystical writings of Dame Julian of Norwich which she called her *Shewings*.
They originated in a powerful inner vision of Christ crucified as he
revealed himself to her as the sign of God's limitless love for all
people.[41] But there is also another dimension that speaks to me
year after year as I participate in this moving liturgy. The whole
rite speaks symbolically of how the cross actually arrives in one's
everyday life: 'Behold the wood of the cross!'

At first it appears far away, emerging from the darkness at the
back of the church. We have to turn around to see it because it is
coming at us from behind. It is veiled and therefore not at all clear,

looking rather like a shapeless mass of red material in the murky gloom. Yet, as it passes up and into the body of the church, it is progressively manifested and unveiled until finally it stands in front of us – a hard fact, a reality planted in our midst. We are invited to come forward and to kiss it.

This is so often how the cross enters our lives. I suddenly detect something – at first quite far away, but gradually as it emerges into sight I experience the sickening feeling – nothing can ever be the same again. It can be anything at all which is a harbinger of trouble: a message from a doctor bearing news about an unexpected growth or a dreaded letter of redundancy. It may be a cough that will not go away or a troubling lump on a breast. It may be the sickening realisation of a loved one's infidelity or a telephone call from a casualty ward. It may be a suicide note. It may be an unwanted and unloved sexual orientation or a dreadfully debilitating addiction. Or worst of all it may be simply myself – me, crippled by my sense of meaningless and inadequacy.

In every instance it arrives before me, shattering the silence with the cry: 'Behold the wood of the cross!' It has appeared and will not go away. Instead it advances inexorably up the nave of my life until it is planted permanently in my inner sanctuary. Yet on Good Friday, we sing that on this wood the salvation of the world was hung.

There are three possible ways to react to the cross when it arrives in my life. I may deny its presence totally, although its harsh, unavoidable reality does not permit that reaction to endure for very long. I may fight it, kicking so hard against it that I injure myself all the more in doing so – and still I cannot make it go away. Or I may stumble forward to venerate, embrace and even kiss it – because on this wood I will meet the Saviour of the world. In the end, that option is the only one that will allow me to live with the cross in my life and let it lead me into glory. Then only can the cross be transformed from a dark tree of torture into a radiant tree of light. Then only can it be elevated in my sight: when I learn to see it not just as an instrument of agony but as the glorious tree of life that bore – and bears – the world's redemption.

CHAPTER NINE

The Mysteries of Manifestation

Being the God of peace
and all-merciful Father,
you sent us the great messenger of your will
to bring us knowledge of you
and grant us your peace.
Guided by the light of divine knowledge
and arising from darkness,
we glorify you,
O lover of humankind!

Byzantine hymn for Christmas

The celebration of the mystery of Christ's passage from death to life at Easter was central to Christian consciousness long before the feasts of Christmas and Epiphany first came into being. Yet having experienced God's saving action in history through the death and resurrection of Jesus and the outpouring of the Holy Spirit, it was inevitable that Christ's origins would also begin to be celebrated. Because the early church's theological reflection and spiritual experience was so intimately bound up with its liturgical life, when the 4th century's historicising trend emerged, great feasts developed focused on the manifestations made by Christ from his infancy, to his first public appearance at the Jordan and subsequent ministry. In this way the individual mysteries of Christ (and eventually those of his mother and the other saints) radiated out from the burning centre of Easter, casting new light on the one great mystery of our salvation revealed in Jesus Christ.

A. Christmas: the Mystery of the Word-Made-Flesh (Fig 15)
The Byzantine liturgy for Christmas is of particular interest because this feast, unlike so many others, travelled from west to east.[1] It is an extended poetic meditation on the infancy narratives of Matthew

and Luke and on the church's developed doctrine of the incarnation which owes so much to St John's gospel. It is a Spirit-guided
attempt to make the mystery of the *kenosis* of the Son of God more
intelligible to the eyes of faith. Theology and poetry are carefully
interwoven to proclaim the astounding paradox that the eternal
God began to exist in time and space, self-bound forever to a
human nature. That mystery and miracle is proclaimed as the
liturgical 'Today!' echoes through the celebration of the feast:

Today Christ is born of the Virgin in Bethlehem of Judah!

Today is the origin of the one who has always existed!

Today the Word becomes flesh!

The Magi hastened to Bethlehem ...
and offered him their gifts;
they worshipped him in adoration!
For in the infant lying in a cave
they had seen the God
who is beyond all time!

The western liturgical texts also repeat this 'Today!', as in the
great *Hodie* chant in the Roman Liturgy of the Hours, still sung at
the Second Vespers of Christmas in Benedictine monasteries:
Hodie Christus natus est!

Today Christ is born!
Today the Saviour appeared!
Today the angels sing on the earth
and the archangels are rejoicing!
Today the upright shout for joy:
Glory to God in the highest!

The Byzantine rite carefully spells out the theological implications of the mystery:

... the Word of God entered into the Virgin's womb,
it took flesh and was born of her,
yet left her virginity intact.
He became human
and yet remained what he was ...

Behold the Image of the Father
and his unchanging eternity
has assumed the form of a servant.
He has come down to us from an all-pure mother
while yet remaining unchanged.
Remaining true God as he was before,
he has taken on himself what he was not,
becoming human
out of love for human beings.

Throughout the celebration of Christmas, however, the liturgy is never simply offering us an abstract meditation on dogma or presenting a static account of two natures and two wills (divine and human) united in the one person (divine) of Christ as that had been fought out and dogmatically defined in the teeth of conflicts over heresy in the early church. Christmas is anything but abstract. It is about the mystery of Christ, the work of redemption that the Saviour came to accomplish in his kenotic descent to be with us and to take away our sins by dying and rising again. As the texts assert, echoing Philippians 2 and John 13, the form Christ assumed was that of a servant. Many other texts also underline his humility and how, when the Magi arrived, they encountered not the conventional image of a king but a simple child, apparently ordinary, lying in the poverty of a cave:[2]

What indeed is lower than a cave …
what more humble than swaddling bands?
Yet the splendour of your Godhead
shone forth resplendently in them!
O Lord, glory to you!

Gathering together the key ideas in all these texts, we can see that motifs emphasising the redemption of the human race predominate. Christ's being wrapped in swaddling bands unlooses our chains while Mary's obedience has cancelled the disobedience of Eve; the closed gate of paradise has been reopened to human beings, the advent of the true light has drawn us forth from the shadows of the night; the Angel of Great Counsel has brought us the knowledge of God and lifted us up out of our fallen state.

The fullness of the mystery – the passion, death and resurrection of Christ – are never far away for the gifts of the Magi are given to one who 'will remain three days in the tomb'. This accumulation of images is a helpful reminder that no single metaphor or symbol can ever exhaust the riches of God's redemptive mercy.

The Byzantine liturgy in particular abounds in imagery drawn from the Jewish Temple. Mary is called the throne of the Cherubim on which the great king has taken his seat. This harks back very significantly to the 'mercy-seat' or propitiatory in the Holy of Holies, flanked by two images of the Cherubim. As we have already seen, it was the place into which the high priest went once a year to sprinkle the blood of the sacrifice, thus taking away his own and his peoples' sins (Heb 9:1-28). Mary, who brings the Saviour into the world, is made into that 'place' for Jesus the sinless one: she becomes the throne of the true High Priest who will make purification not only for the sins of his own people but for those of the whole human race (1 Jn 2:2).

> O my soul,
> magnify the one more glorious
> and honourable than the powers of heaven!

> Behold a mystery,
> a strange and mighty mystery:
> the cave has become heaven,
> the Virgin a cherubic throne,
> the manger a noble place
> where Christ our God reposes!

And again,

> Behold the Virgin
> enthroned like the cherubim,
> holding in her arms
> the incarnate Word of God.

There have been various theories about how God accomplished his *kenosis* in the incarnation of Christ, some frankly untenable because in direct contradiction of the testimony of scripture and the best traditions of the church. Paradox ought not to entail total irrationality or unintelligibility, for the mystery was after all revealed for our (at least partial) understanding. Some 19th century German Lutheran theologians suggested that Christ literally abandoned his divinity in becoming flesh. Apart from the metaphysical impossibility of God doing that at all, it is hard to see how it could have benefited the human race since it would have meant that the Redeemer was not truly divine while on earth and was, therefore, incapable of offering us anything more than any other inspired prophet or holy person: such a saviour evacuated of his divinity would not have been able to become the 'Lamb of God who takes away the sins of the world' (Jn 1:29).[3]

Others, such as the Anglican Bishop Charles Gore and the Russian kenotic thinkers of the twentieth century, held that in the earthly ministry of the divine-human Christ, the eternal Son suspended the use of his divine privileges and consented to a certain obscuring of his divine capacity to know everything, in order truly to identify with the human condition. That is broadly the position adopted by Sergius Bulgakov. He suggests, by analogy, the model of ordinary human self-consciousness, making the fascinating (and at that time – the era of Freudian psychoanalysis – very fashionable!) proposal that the self-consciousness of the eternal *Logos* functions as kind of 'sub-(or super)-conscious' in Christ. While that is an undeniably tantalising theory, the truth is that, as Bulgakov well knew, the *kenosis* cannot be fully explained logically or rationally.[4]

There is, however, an image of how Christ participated in our condition which occurred to me many years ago while working with small children. It is essential in such a task that the adult, whether teacher, social worker or pastor, should try to live simultaneously in two dimensions. In any such form of human contact the vital thing is to be able to share in the strange world of the other, in such a way that they do not experience their teacher or carer as distant or detached.

Yet it is also essential to respect boundaries and not to abandon one's own adult reality. Children quickly lose all respect for someone who tries to perform that impossible task – especially if it becomes evident that they are doing it more to satisfy personal

emotional needs than to be of service to others. They need assurance that when it is necessary for the person in charge to be a com-
petent adult, then they really are capable of being that. The most
delicate task in education is knowing when and how to move easily between these two dimensions: identification with the other
and maintaining necessary distance.

To me that offers at least some light, however inadequate, for
making a little more sense of the Christmas mystery, how the Son
of God – as the liturgies of the season tirelessly repeat – without
ceasing to be what he was, became what he was not. The mystery
of the incarnation speaks of God's transcendent liberty and spontaneity. It reveals his freedom to transcend our fixed ideas about
what God 'can' and 'cannot' do. It reveals his eternal decision to
come down and be with us not merely through condescension but
through love, a decision that entailed temporarily abandoning
the blinding glory of his divine privileges so as to share our
human life, and by passing through our death, to grant us admittance to his heavenly kingdom.

B. The Presentation of Jesus in the Temple: the Mystery of Meeting (Fig 16)

Today the gate of heaven is opened!
The Word of the Father who is without beginning
has assumed a beginning in time,
yet without losing his divinity.
As an infant of forty days
he is offered by his Mother in the Temple,
according to the Law.

The old man received him in his arms
and the servant cried out to his Master:
'Let me go, for my eyes have seen your salvation.'

O Lord, who came into the world
to save the human race:
Glory to you!
           Byzantine hymn for the Presentation of the Lord

The feast of the Presentation of Jesus in the temple is based on the account of that event given in St Luke's gospel (Lk 2:22-38). It was the time for the purification of Mary according to the Law of Moses. Luke's rendition of the story is a literary masterpiece, skilfully weaving together themes and motifs from the Jewish scriptures and using them to focus on Jesus, proclaimed to be the glory of Israel and a light of revelation for the Gentiles. It was originally an eastern feast of complex origin, although by the 7th century it had also been established in the west. There it was eventually transformed into a feast of Mary rather than one of Christ.[5]

That emphasis was changed in the reform of the liturgy after the Second Vatican Council which restored the older understanding of it as primarily a feast of the Lord. That was surely a positive development for, in addition to returning to earlier tradition, the feast's association with ancient notions of ritual impurity supposedly contracted by childbearing is unlikely to strike many sympathetic chords with contemporary Christian women. The western church greatly emphasises one of the most beautiful aspects of the feast, namely its stress on Christ as the light of the nations, which it does by equipping the celebration with a blessing of candles and a procession before Mass, thus leading to its western name of Candlemas. On this day the mystery being celebrated is primarily that of Christ as the revelation of God's light, though Mary's own mystery is inextricably interwoven with that of her son (Lk 2:35).

In the Orthodox tradition the feast is known as the *Hypapante*: the meeting or encounter.[6] The texts of the Byzantine rite, some of which passed over into the Roman church and are still used today in the Latin liturgy, are of an incomparable beauty and spiritual depth, playing on the imagery of the temple so characteristic of Jewish mysticism:[7]

> Adorn your bridal chamber, O Sion,
> and receive Christ your King.
>
> Embrace and welcome Mary, heaven's gate,
> who appears as a cherubic throne
> on which the King of glory sits.
> The Virgin has become a cloud of light,
> bearing in her womb a son

who exists before the Morning Star.

Simeon, receiving him in his arms,
proclaimed him to the peoples of the earth
as the Lord of life and death
and the Saviour of the world.

But who is meeting whom in this feast of meetings? Like all the
liturgical mysteries it is characterised by a fullness of symbols and
an excess of meaning. The more one contemplates it the more one
sees how full it really is. There is the most obvious meeting, the encounter of the Messiah with his holy people Israel even though
this Messiah is going to be rejected. There is the meeting of the old
man Simeon with the young child Jesus, but also of Jesus with the
aged prophetess Anna, the daughter of Phanuel of the tribe of
Asher, who lived day and night in the temple serving God with
fasting and prayer. There is also the meeting of the young couple
Mary and Joseph with this old pair.

In the Roman Rite is sung an ancient antiphon *Senex puerum
portabat:*

The old man carried the child
yet the child ruled over the old man,

and in the Byzantine tradition the deepest implications of the
mystery are poetically sketched:

The one who rides on the Cherubim
and is hymned by the Seraphim
is presented today in the temple according to the Law.

He lies in the arms of an old man
yet receives the offerings due to God ...
Simeon when he saw what had been revealed taking place
blessed the Virgin Mother of God,
telling her of the pains she would suffer,
then asked the Lord to be dismissed ...

The divine, holy child, received into the arms of wise old people is a genuine archetypal symbol in the sense put forward by the

psychologist Jung.[8] It speaks directly to a primitive layer of the soul which contains the roots of imagination and is in turn deeply receptive to symbolism. It represents the meeting of the opposites, of the two most fundamental dimensions of life – childhood and old age. There is an added poignancy in it: thanks to the incarnation of God in Christ, this child so young in human years is in his deepest identity one whose origin stretches from everlasting to everlasting – for he is the eternal God whose kingdom will never know an end.

Yet even then the symbolism is not exhausted. There is also the meeting of the righteous ones of the Jewish tradition, represented by Simeon and Anna in the Temple, with the one whom the Roman liturgy for Advent declares had actually given the Law to Moses on Sinai (Ex 19:16-25; 20:1-23), the pre-eternal God made flesh as the child of Mary (Lk 2:7).[9] The Lord of the Temple, the one whose cloud of glory filled the Holy of Holies (2 Chron 7:2-3), who was enthroned over the mercy seat between the wings of the Cherubim (Ps 98(99):1), suddenly comes into his own dwelling place not in majesty and glory, but in the lowliness of human flesh.

It is a bitter-sweet moment in salvation history, for his entry signals both the fulfilment of the religion of Israel and the coming end of the Temple (though not of the Jews as God's chosen people) as a religious institution. Christ himself in his human body is the new temple, just as he is also both priest and sacrifice, fulfilling all previous religious dispensations everywhere. It is a turning point in the history of humankind's relationship with God. For that reason Simeon sings his haunting canticle *Nunc Dimittis* ('Lord, now let your servant depart in peace …') telling God that he is ready to die having seen the salvation prepared for all peoples, the one through whom as Paul declared, the blessing of Abraham might be extended to the Gentiles (Gal 3:14). An early Christian tradition held that Simeon went as a herald into the underworld to announce that the promised Messiah was at last on his way.

Yet if in all the liturgical mysteries one finds always the single great mystery of Christ's saving death and resurrection, then this one is definitely no exception. The shadow of the cross falls menacingly across the light and splendour of both Temples, old and new – the first destined to fall and never rise again, the second to die and rise in glory (cf Jn 2:21-22). Simeon warns that this child, whose sacrifice will replace those of the temple, is the great sign given by God. But he will be a sign of contradiction, a sign that will be rejected so that the secret thoughts of many may be revealed; and he warns his mother that a sword will pierce her own soul too.

The mystery is therefore about offering, the presentation of Christ foreshadowing his own perfect self-offering on the cross. It finds its deepest meaning in the act of letting go. Mary brings the child who is the fruit of her co-operation with the Holy Spirit into the Father's house, the Jerusalem Temple. It is the place of sacrifice and the manifestation of the divine presence *par excellence*.

- Sacrifice: because in the Temple the offerings prescribed by the Law were made, especially the greatest one on the Day of Atonement.
- Manifestation of the divine presence: because there Israel encountered its God. Although dwelling in cloud and majesty and filling the whole universe with glory (Is 6:1-5), the Lord focused the glory in a special place so that his people could pray there, find forgiveness and enter into communion with him (2 Chron 6:1-36). Mary was herself the true 'tent of meeting' bearing the body of the incarnate Son of God into his own house.

Christ's self-oblation is the perfect sacrifice, appointed by the Father since before the foundation of the world (1 Pet 1:19-20; Rev 5:6). In this mystery of his presentation, the momentum of his sacrificial offering, announced at his entry into the world (Heb 10:5-10), and symbolically begun at his circumcision when he first submitted to the Law and shed his blood for our salvation (Lk 2:21), greatly accelerates. The place into which he is carried, the reconstructed second Temple was a highly ambivalent institution for many Jews and would be the place where the final conflict between Jesus and the leaders of Judaism will occur. His later apparent claims to supplant, demolish and rebuild it led directly to his death (Mk 14:57-58).[10]

As Mary carries him in and hands him over a further stage is reached in her abandonment of self to God; as she offers her divinely destined child to the will of the Father, she consents to the coming suffering predicted for her by Simeon. In icons of the Mother of God tenderly embracing her child, one detects the aftermath of the mystery of the Presentation. Mary holds him tenderly but her gentle gaze is not fixed on him. Instead it reaches out into a future focused on Calvary when, having relinquished him into God's hands and the hands of sinful men, she will receive him back as a corpse, torn and bloodied. Like the Baptism of Jesus, the mystery of the Presentation in the temple is a kind of dress rehearsal for what is coming. But what kind of sword was it that pierced Mary's heart and soul?[11]

Roman Catholics and Orthodox are so accustomed to viewing her as perfect, thanks to her having been immaculately conceived and filled with grace (or at least for the Orthodox sanctified from birth), that we are occasionally inclined to imagine her as having been free of all difficulty or uncertainty about her role in God's plan. Yet we see in scripture that even her divine-human Son, though sinless, was not spared the task of struggling to bring his human will into full accord with the will of God (Mk 14:32-41; Heb 2:14-16). If that was so for him, we can hardly deny the fact also for her! Voices like those of Origen and St John Chrysostom, who tentatively examined this issue, tended to get squeezed out in the flow of the great tradition which rightly emphasised her freedom from sin – but as an unfortunate consequence tended to underemphasise her human struggle.[12]

Those two Fathers, for example, suggested that the sword may have been a metaphor for the purification of her faith when, standing at the cross, she witnessed the paradox of life coming through death, healing through suffering and victory through apparent failure. Perhaps we are too inclined to equate uncertainty and insecurity with sin and guilt. Mary, though sinless, was surely not spared the common human experience of anxiety. Were that the case, it would make it difficult indeed for most people to relate to her. In Luke's account of the finding of the child Jesus after he had gone astray (in the Temple) her anxiety is frankly acknowledged:

> … his mother said to him, 'Child, why have you treated us
> like this? Look, your father and I have been searching for

you in great anxiety.' He said to them, 'Why were you searching for me? Did you not know that I must be in my Father's house?' But they did not understand what he said to them. (Lk 2:48-51)

Finally, Yves Congar offers us an excellent summary of the leading themes of this mystery of Christ as presented in the gospel and celebrated in the liturgy:

> Mary is purified, although she is the noblest flower and the purest glory of Israel. She humbly submits to the law of the Temple, empty as it is of the ark of witness, whilst she herself is the temple of the Holy Spirit, the ark of the new covenant. Jesus is redeemed according to the Law of Moses, yet he is himself the redeemer ... not only of Israel, but of the whole world. He is presented in the Temple but he is greater than the Temple (Mt 12:6); it is he who sanctifies the Temple and every offering men can make to God.[13]

C. The Baptism of Jesus: the Mystery of the First Paschal Immersion (Fig 17)[14]

> Once regenerated in him,
> delve into his secrets,
> so that on the banks of the River Jordan
> you may know the Father in the voice,
> the Son in the flesh,
> and the Holy Spirit in the dove;
> and, the heaven of the Trinity being opened to you,
> you may be carried up to God.
>   *St Bonaventure, quoting St Anselm of Canterbury*

> Each blest drop, on each blest limb,
> Is washed itself in washing him.
>   *Richard Crashaw*

In the Orthodox and Oriental Orthodox churches the feast of the Baptism of Jesus on the 6th of January is second only to the Paschal feast itself in importance, being called in Greek the 'Holy Theophany' or manifestation of God.[15] The western churches traditionally include the baptism as one of the 'three great wonders' celebrated on the feast of the Epiphany combining it with the visit of the Magi from the east (Mt 2:1-12) and the changing of water into wine at the wedding feast at Cana (Jn 2:1-11) although the first of those wonders has largely dominated Latin Catholic devotion.[16]

The baptism of Jesus used to be the octave day of the Epiphany in the Roman Rite. However, since the liturgical reforms of the nineteen-sixties in the western churches, both the Roman Catholic and Anglican calendars now include a separate feast of the baptism on the Sunday after the major feast. There is nothing incongruous about the fact that in the Roman Church's liturgy this event is still mentioned during the feast of the Epiphany as well. The mystery of Christ is of such overwhelming plenitude that it is common for several things to be celebrated together: as we have seen the celebration of the passion generally includes references to the resurrection as well.

The Orthodox liturgy is particularly well endowed with rich material for the celebration of this feast, including a powerfully expressive outdoor rite for the blessing of water. I once witnessed this on a freezing cold day in 1989 on a Greek island. At the conclusion of the Divine Liturgy (the Eucharist) the whole congregation went in procession to the harbour where, having blessed the sea, the priest threw a cross attached to a chain into the water. The young men of the village then dived to retrieve it and the winner was the local hero for a week. It was a strong reminder of how rooted Orthodox ritual is in the popular culture of the Greek countryside and a powerful evocation of the baptismal symbol of total immersion.

For Byzantine Christians the Baptism of Jesus is the first great feast which manifests the Holy Trinity. The *Troparion*, a frequently repeated short hymn expressing the principal meaning of each feast, sings of the revelation of the Trinity at the banks of the Jordan:

At your baptism in the Jordan, O Christ our Saviour,
the revelation of the Trinity was made manifest:
for the voice of the Father was heard,

the Son was seen in the form of a servant
and the Holy Spirit descended as a dove!
All Holy Trinity glory to you!

The doctrine of the Trinity is not just a piece of abstract theology. It is an attempt to do justice to what we know of God, thanks to the missions of the Son and Holy Spirit, who have given us 'inside knowledge' of what God is really like. The Trinity is demonstrated to the world when God's only-begotten child is revealed as a servant and the Holy Spirit hovers over the waters in the beautiful form of a dove. Such images remind us that, just as at the dawn of creation God spoke all beings into life through his Word, so his Spirit-breath hovered also over the primal waters (Gen 1:1-5). Just as creation involved the whole Trinity, so too the world's re-creation through the redemptive mission of Christ was a trinitarian action, an active co-operation between the Father, the Son and the Holy Spirit.

Jesus comes as Saviour to rescue a world that, although indestructibly grounded in the goodness of God, has lost its direction and wandered far from the truth. So he lines up at the banks of the Jordan in the throng of repentant sinners, becoming one of the anonymous mob, submitting humbly to the purifying baptism of John the Precursor, although he alone has no need of it (Lk 3:21).[17]

The hymn writers who contributed through their poetry to the splendour of Byzantine worship loved to dwell on the implications of this astonishing event as God-incarnate humbles himself before the hand of a creature. In St Matthew's account (Mt: 3:14-15) the Baptist is unwilling to submit himself to this unprecedented act of divine self-submission but is commanded to do so by Jesus who has come to rewrite all the rules governing the relationship between God and his creatures.

Following the revelation of Christ's divine humility, unveiled at the Jordan and completed in the Underworld, all human ideas about God need to be entirely refashioned according to the model given to us in Christ. For this is the staggering paradox revealed by Jesus: the one who did not need conversion and repentance voluntarily consented to undergo a baptism of repentance, whereas we who really do need it, so often refuse our consent!

John's baptism occasioned the public manifestation of Jesus as the one who came to take away the sins of the world (Jn 1:29-34). It was a further intensification of the kenotic movement in which he stripped away his glory and entered into solidarity with sinful, suffering humanity (Phil 2:7-8). Jesus in his mission was both the archetypal human being and also the eternal Son of God. Perfectly obedient to his Father's will, in the Jordan River he let himself be initiated into the coming struggle to heal human disobedience. Drawing on the Psalms, the author of the Letter to the Hebrews describes what Christ 'said' on first entering into the world in his incarnation:

'Sacrifices and offerings you have not desired,
but a body you have prepared for me;
in burnt offerings and sin offerings
you have taken no pleasure.
    Then I said, "See, God, I have come to do your will, O God"
(in the scroll of the book it is written of me).'
(Heb 10:5-9, freely quoting Ps 39(40):7-8)

His obedient descent into the waters in solidarity with sinners is a mystery in the strictest sense: a symbolic act charged with the grace of spiritual energy, by means of which Christ manifests his passage from death to endless life. But it is also a prophetic act that points ahead to the full and final baptism he will accomplish in going to the cross – his self-abandonment into the hands of sinners, death, burial and descent into the murky 'waters' of the Underworld. Although he begins to manifest the work of redemption, Christ does not publish a manifesto. In humility, he does not cry out or make his voice heard in the street (Is 42:2; Mt 12:19). Instead, making use of a contemporary rite of purification, his public manifestation has an appropriate character of self-effacement as he goes down into the river; but in carrying it out his true identity is clarified and his mission announced by the Father:

'This is (or according to Mk 1: 11 and Luke 3: 22, 'You are!')
my beloved Son!' (Mt 3:17)

The Byzantine liturgy piles up powerful symbolic images to hammer home the point: the coming victory over death is announced as Jesus begins to accomplish the sanctification of the world. He comes as conqueror and victor crushing the head of the ancient dragon in the primal waters. In the Jordan he sanctifies all the waters of the earth, affirming the goodness of the planet, pronouncing a sentence of death on the gloomy subterranean spirits which impede us from living gloriously on the face of God's earth.

The baptism of Jesus is D-Day for the devil. God re-enters his creation and establishes a spiritual beachhead on Jordan's banks. Yet this is not the final victory, for V-E-Day ('Victory for the Earth Day') will come only on the last day. It is the long awaited announcement that since the Liberator is at hand, the long night of sin and death is over. Christ's rising up out of the water and reception of the Holy Spirit (Lk 3:22) point us forward to his future exaltation on Easter morning.

May we go still further and interpret this mystery as telling us something about the psychology of Jesus? Does it shed any light on his inner life, on those stages by which he came to understand his mission and identity? Modern scholars answer such questions negatively, reminding us that the gospels are not biographies in any conventional modern sense but Spirit-inspired testimonies to Christ's saving work, shaped and formed in accordance with the religious needs of those communities where the original oral tradition had passed over into writing.[18] Yet it seems reasonable to allow for something else to be taken into consideration. The basis of the story of Christ is after all grounded in history: it is not simply a myth. What is recounted happened to real people who actually engaged with Christ, eyewitnesses who handed on their testimony through the community of believers.[19]

If we are to take seriously the *kenosis* and incarnation of the Word then we must surely allow for some process of development within the human understanding of Christ, something the gospel of Luke, at least, seems to encourage us to do when it describes him as increasing in wisdom (Lk 2:52). To imagine that an incarnate God, existing kenotically in a freely chosen state of self-limitation never needed to learn anything, risks making an illusion of his self-emptying, or falling into the trap of imagining Jesus as, 'God-pretending-to-be-human', a heresy unfaithful to scripture and condemned by mainstream Christian tradition.

Such a one would not be the Jesus of the gospels nor of the great tradition of the church which solemnly defined (in successive ecumenical councils) and defended the real human nature and will of the Lord, hypostatically (that is really) united to God the Son in the unity of his eternal, divine person. As we have also seen, the Letter to the Hebrews, one of the New Testament books which most emphasises Christ's pre-existence and divine dignity, is also the very one which lays most emphasis on his human fragility and capacity to learn through experience (Heb 5:8-10). All rash speculation ought to be avoided here for we are standing close to the very heart of the Holy of Holies, the mystery of the incarnate God; but while treating it with fitting reverence we should also not evacuate it of meaningful content by reducing Jesus to a demi-god wrapped up in imaginary flesh and lacking the processes of human development that go with a human nature. That would hardly have constituted a real *kenosis*.

Perhaps therefore we may legitimately infer that some intensification of Jesus' unique sense of identity occurred on the banks of the Jordan. Luke shows him immediately after the event, praying to the Father, whom he addresses as *Abba* (Lk 3:21). The intensity of his prayer, reiterated by the third evangelist throughout his gospel, is surely a key helping us unlock, at least to some extent, this awesome mystery. The terrible cry of desolation Jesus uttered on the cross, 'My God, my God, why have you forsaken me?' (Mk 15:34; Mt 27:46), is comprehensible only as the other side of the unimaginably intense communion with God as Father that he enjoyed throughout his life.

Was his baptism by John a major threshold experience through which he attained to the realisation of his unique experience of God as *Abba*? If so, then perhaps there came with it as well the call to mission, to manifest himself as the Lord's messianic suffering servant, anointed by the Holy Spirit (Is 42:1; Mt 12:18). Jesus did not become 'the Christ', the 'Lord's anointed', at his baptism; he was rather revealed as being such already, confirmed by the Holy Spirit for the redemptive work he was to carry out and sent on the mission to which his Father had appointed him.

One may even trace a certain trajectory of progress in the

human self-awareness of Christ, stretching from his finding in the
temple through his baptism (Lk 2:49) and transfiguration (Lk
9:35) to his death and resurrection (Ps 2:4-9). Perhaps it was only
in the final transforming event of his glorification, with the completion of his self-emptying *kenosis* that the full light of self-under-
standing possessed by the eternal Son of God flowed over into the
self-consciousness of his human nature. Yet beyond that, we
ought not to trespass! As we have seen, we should sing with the
Byzantine liturgy, 'Let all mortal flesh keep silence and stand in
fear and trembling.' We ought to prostrate ourselves before the
mystery, adore Christ's unique awareness of his special relationship with the Father as the incarnate Son and give thanks for his
communicating that consciousness to us in the Holy Spirit, making us through our baptism the offspring of Abraham, heirs to the
promise and adopted children of God (Gal 3:25-29: Eph 5:1-2).

The depths of the mystery of the Baptism of Jesus, and why it is
such a major festival in the Christian year, should by now be evident:

- It signifies the revelation of the Trinity, the announcement of
  the coming liberation of the material world, the sanctification
  of the springs of life and the proclamation of the saving mission of Jesus.
- It is his manifestation as the Lord's anointed servant along
  with his growing understanding of his unique divine-human
  identity and messianic mission.
- It is the mystery of his 'first immersion,' a sign of the greater,
  more terrible immersion in death that awaits him in Jerusalem
  (Mk 10:38-39).

Yet since the mysteries of Christ are our mysteries, what light
and life may we draw from this one for our Christian existence?
Two important consequences flowing from the baptism of Jesus
in the Jordan may be identified. Firstly, the life of every Christian
like that of Christ himself is permanently marked with a paschal
character simply by the fact of having been baptised. A Christian
develops by continually reshaping his or her life in accordance
with the pattern of Christ's life from his baptism to his resurrection. Secondly, Christians are initiated through Jesus, the only-

begotten Son, into an intimate adoptive relationship with God as Father through the anointing of the Holy Spirit.

As we have already seen, the importance of baptism cannot be exaggerated: all life, all holiness flows into us through this primal sacramental mystery. Plunged into the image of Christ's kenotic, saving death through the baptismal waters, we are granted entrance to his community the church. It is the gateway to all the other mysteries since it makes Christians into a royal priesthood, ordained to worship God and offer spiritual sacrifices pleasing and acceptable to him (1 Pet 2:1-5). But what does it mean in practice to say that Christian living ought to be shaped according to the pattern provided by baptism, Christ's and our own?

There are two essential aspects to being a Christian, each of which reflects the work of Christ. One is the dimension of descent, stripping and self-abandonment, the other, of ascent and glorification. Having stripped away the garb of divine glory in his incarnation, the vesture which was his by right (Phil 2:7), Jesus stripped himself of his clothing at the banks of the Jordan and went down naked into its water (Mt 3:15). He rose out of it again to receive the gift of the Holy Spirit and a new intensity of relationship with the Father. All this was a potent sign of his coming passage through death to resurrection and transformation by the Holy Spirit.

So too the Christian, stripped of his or her clothing, goes down into the waters of the font and is raised up again into the new life of grace. Anointed with the Spirit s/he is admitted to the community of God's adopted children and called to a life of self-stripping, an active peeling away of all the egoism, pride, arrogance and anger that afflicts us, a laying aside of every weight, and the sin that clings so easily (Heb 12:1-2). S/he is called to rise into intimate communion with God, what the New Testament describes as the freedom of the glory of the children of God (Rom 8:18) and to pray to God as his beloved child (Rom 8:26-27) – and all this in the communion of Christ's people (Jn 17:22-23) which gives its testimony to his resurrection (Acts 4: 32).

Shaping one's life according to the pattern of baptismal grace entails living out these two dimensions of self-emptying (*kenosis*) and communion (*koinonia*) begun in baptism. It means gratefully acknowledging that, having been called away from the isolation of sin and admitted to communion with Christ in his church, one is also called to build just and loving relationships among one's fellow human beings, whether believers or not.

The kenotic renunciation begun in Baptism gives access to a spirituality based on gratitude (Eucharist) and life in community (*koinonia*). There can be no room for what Karl Barth castigated as pious egoism, no exclusive sense of being 'born-again' as if that were simply a matter of one's own personal salvation. Being 'born again' (or 'from above' as the alternative meaning of Jn 3:3 has it) is a birth into a network of relationships, beginning with the three persons of the triune God.[20]

But even more radically, the intimate relationship with God into which baptism grants admittance entails recognising a staggering truth clearly taught in the New Testament and reiterated by Christians throughout the centuries – from the earliest monastic writers through the Greek and Latin fathers, to the medieval mystics, Protestant reformers and a host of others: all that Christ is by nature we are invited to become by grace.[21] Christ is the real, natural, essential child of the Father (Jn 1:18) begotten before all ages yet born of Mary in time (Gal 4:4); all human beings are called to become God's adopted children as brothers and sisters of the Lord (Rom 8:29); through faith and baptism we become that in fact (Gal 3:27-28; 4:5-7; Col 2:11-13). The love Christ receives eternally from the Father is graciously given to us. The great New Testament texts where this privilege is presented associate it especially with the Holy Spirit (Rom 8:15-16), thanks to whose presence in our hearts we are empowered to cry out with Jesus: 'Abba! Father!'

The Christian life is a process of becoming conscious and aware of this tremendous sacred privilege granted us by God in baptism. We are already the children of God (1 Jn 3:2) but we often do not remember it. The spiritual life means appropriating in one's subjective experience what God has already granted through the objective grace of baptism. Monastic spirituality with its various disciplines aims to help believers do just that: to keep alive the constant memory of God (*memoria Dei*) by focusing one's whole existence on his presence in the heart.[22]

To become conscious of one's dignity as an adopted child of God is a life-transforming experience. It means realising that one is eternally and infinitely loved by God – something we often do not wish to believe, perhaps owing to deep-rooted feelings of insecurity or a lack of self worth. Coming to conscious awareness that God has initiated me into such a relationship is a tremendous liberation but it also calls for a response. There has to be inner work on my part – a real attempt at purification of heart and a re-education of the mind away from my own most cherished notions of God in the light of the truth God has revealed about himself.

Out must go God as an angry parent, a pedantic recorder of our failings or a tyrannical potentate who has to be appeased by the accumulation of 'merit' based on religious professionalism. Out must go especially my most cherished ideas of what is sacred or holy, as I find myself confronted by a 'down-and-out God' dying the death of a criminal on the cross, dying to draw me in to his company and out to others in love. As Luther shrewdly observed, a similar dynamic often operates in our relating to God as is at work in our human relationships: as we wishfully imagine God to be, so God effectively becomes to us.[23] Yet in the mystery of Christ's death and resurrection God has punctured our web of projections and dispelled them by the light of his face. Just as in human relationships, there has to be a withdrawing of our projections, allowing God to reveal his face in Jesus Christ.

Thanks to baptism, then, in comes true evangelical freedom granted us by the gospel of grace (Gal 5:13-26; 2 Cor 3:12-18). If we allow the flood of divine presence that was poured into our minds in baptism to inundate our lives, then all our idols totter, fall and are swept clean away; if we let the Spirit's light clarify our hearts then in his presence they recede into ever-murkier twilight. The darkness is passing away and the true light is already shining. (1 Jn 2:8). The image of the true God has been revealed (Rom 8:29; Col 1:15). It is an incarnate (Jn 1:14), crucified (1 Cor 1:22-24) gentle (Mt 11:29) forgiving (Mt 18:23-35; Lk 15:20-32) but for that very reason, demanding God (Lk 10:37); a wounded lover, shining with the light of glory. As he tells us:

Whoever has seen me has seen the Father. (Jn 14:9)

D. *The Transfiguration: the Mystery of the Blinding Light of Love* (Fig 18)

Intending to strengthen the human soul
with the hope of an eternal reward,
Jesus took Peter, James, and his brother John
and led them up a high mountain.
There, he revealed to them the mystery of the Trinity,
foretold the humiliation of his passion,
and showed them through his transfiguration,
the glory of his future resurrection.
The Law and the Prophets bore witness to him
in the apparition of Moses and Elijah;
the Father and the Holy Spirit bore witness too,
manifest as a voice and a cloud.
And truly the soul devoted to him,
solidly established in the truth
and raised to the summit of virtue,
can make its own the words of Peter,
exclaiming with him,
'Lord, it is good for us to be here,
in the peace and joy
of the vision of your face;
where the spirit,
in a state of heavenly and ecstatic rapture,
can hear secret words that no one may repeat.'
St Bonaventure

The important place the transfiguration occupies in the life and work of Christ is abundantly clear in the synoptic gospels (Mt 17:1-13; Mk 9:1-13; Lk 9:28-36). It holds a central position as Jesus moves towards his coming fate at Jerusalem and begins to initiate the disciples into the disturbing news that salvation will come only through suffering and death. Yet its relationship to his baptism is striking as much on account of the differences as the similarities it reveals:

- At the Jordan Jesus descends; on the mountain he ascends.
- In the baptism he is stripped; in the transfiguration he is clothed in the light of heavenly glory (*doxa*).

- At the Jordan he has a single (human) witness in John, the last and the greatest of the prophets (Mt 11:11); at the transfiguration his witnesses are two of the Jewish tradition's most important prophetic figures, Moses and Elijah, along with the apostles, Peter, James and John.

Mark in particular presents the event as part of a triptych in which images of rending and the divine voice witnessing to Christ figure prominently. At the baptism (Mk 1:10) the heavens are torn open and the voice of the Father testifies to the Son; at the transfiguration (Mk 9:7) the voice occurs again; finally at the crucifixion (Mk 15:38) the curtain of the temple is torn down the middle while the pagan centurion attests that this crucified man was a Son of God.

In addition, the presence of the Holy Spirit is indicated at both the baptism and the transfiguration. While at the Jordan God's Spirit is symbolised by a dove, at Mt Tabor the third person appears as a luminous cloud – the hovering, feminine presence later called the *shekinah*, the radiant cloud manifesting the glory of God. On the holy mountain it enveloped the Son's form for in his flesh the glory of God was dwelling. Christ's body was revealed to be the new temple of the renewed covenant.

The 'vision' granted to the disciples, (*horama* to use Matthew's Greek word) was one of mystical and apocalyptic-eschatological fullness. It was mystical because the hidden energy of Christ's divinity, pouring out through the sacrament of his humanity, gave them a glimpse of his most secret, inner nature. It was apocalyptic-eschatological because it revealed to them what will take place at the second coming of Christ: a manifestation or revelation of heavenly light which will transfigure the created cosmos. In the icon of the mystery, the light irradiates not only Christ and the apostles but the very environment in which they stand, including the rocks and earth of the mountain. Jesus is reported to have said beforehand that some of his followers would not taste death until they had seen the kingdom of God coming with power (Mk 9:1). That saying is fulfilled, as the light of the glory of the kingdom appears briefly through him.[24]

Yet not everything is this mystery is luminous. There are also references to Christ's later agony in the garden – in the presence of the three privileged apostles (Peter, James and John) who will eventually witness his extreme dereliction just as they had glimpsed his heavenly glory. In Luke's account the disciples fall asleep, as they will do later in Gethsemane (Lk 22:45) – in contrast to Christ who on both occasions stays awake to pray. For while the revelation of glory in the shining form of Christ scatters the darkness of this world, it also engenders a renewed hatred for the light. The forces of evil regroup around its margins. In Luke's account not long after his descent from the mountain Jesus takes the road to Jerusalem and to the cross.

In addition, according to all three versions, immediately following the vision, having arrived again at the foot of the mountain they are plunged back into the maelstrom of his public ministry (Mt: 17:14-21; Mk 9:14-29; Lk 9:37-43). The episode of the possessed boy and the disciples' inability to exorcise the demon is attributed by Jesus to their lack of faith, thus bringing all of them back down to earth with a bang. Mark has Jesus telling them that this kind of demon can be expelled only by prayer (Mk 9:29), the implication being that their efforts had been inadequate; but Matthew pulls no punches, saying that they were unable to cast it out because they had so little faith (Mt 17:20).

In the liturgical traditions this mystery also occupies a privileged place.[25] In the eastern churches it is one of the greatest feasts of the year but it passed to the west also via the famous Benedictine Abbey of Cluny. It was surprisingly slow in spreading in the wider Latin Church (1457) and even more surprisingly has still not yet acquired the highest festive status, that of a solemnity. Yet from ancient times the Roman liturgy has commemorated it on the second Sunday in Lent so that in the west there are effectively two feasts of the transfiguration, one of which falls on one of the most important Sundays of the year. Associating it in that way with the paschal mystery is very appropriate; yet equally appropriate is the custom some Lutherans have of keeping it during the season of Epiphany on account of how it manifests Christ's glory.

The transfiguration has always held a special appeal for monastic communities both east and west and it is not hard to understand why. It offers an inspiring picture of the spiritual life.

Everything necessary is there. It includes God's call to come apart in order to find a more intense communion with him, ascetical striving symbolised by climbing the mountain, *lectio divina* of the Bible (Moses and Elijah as guides leading us to see the face of Christ shining through the older covenant), contemplative prayer grounded in the vision of the trinitarian glory of God (represented by the overshadowing cloud of the Spirit), the voice of the Father and the luminous form of his beloved Son. It teaches us to wait patiently in prayer until the glory of the Lord is revealed and the kingdom breaks through in power.[26] Yet it is still only a privileged moment on the path to a greater goal, the paschal mystery of death and resurrection. Not the glory of Mt Tabor inaugurates the Lord's final transfiguration, but his suffering on the cross and passage through death: only thus does he enter into his glorification on Easter morning (Lk 24:26).

The glory of Christ on Tabor certainly speaks of vision and enlightenment, yet as we have seen that is not the whole truth. As Peter's behaviour shows (Lk 9:33) the overwhelming splendour of the glory is also disorientating and there is darkness and suffering lurking around the edges. The same ambiguity is characteristic of Christian mystical experience in general. But what is one to do when darkness and disorientation are experienced not just on the periphery but rather right at the centre? What happens when instead of being bathed in luminous radiance, the lights suddenly go out and one is plunged into dark and bitter obscurity? Some clear-headed spiritual thinking is required, guided by the light of revelation, if one wishes to tackle that issue adequately.

It is a mistake to imagine that spiritual experience is always only of one kind (i.e. consoling) and to assume that its absence betokens inadequacy or failure. Yet always singing beautiful liturgical music and contemplating shining icons of the transfiguration may sometimes risk creating that impression. That is why the spiritual traditions of the west, of Latin Catholicism and Protestantism, are also useful for achieving balance in the spiritual life.

All Christian mystics insist that if the life of prayer is ever to progress into deeper levels of experience, purification is essential.[27]

But in order to advance further the necessary purification is more than just moral: it also requires a cleansing of understanding as much as a rectifying of the direction of one's will. Paradoxically, according to such leading representatives of the Byzantine tradition as Macarius the Syrian (4th/5th century?)[28] and Gregory Palamas (14th century),[29] as well as great medieval Dominican and modern Carmelite teachers such as John Tauler (14th century)[30] and John of the Cross (16th century),[31] the thirst for consoling or sensual 'luminous' experiences is one of the main urges which has to be transcended. It actually represents the heart's hidden possessiveness which tries to grasp and cling to reality, to consume, assimilate and make it its own.

But God as revealed in the Jewish-Christian scriptures is never any kind of 'thing', never just another object in the world to be clutched at, consumed and assimilated. Revelation speaks of God's absolute transcendence, his mysterious, irreducible otherness, a dimension referred to in theology as *apophatic* because God's being is beyond all speech, conceptualisation and imagination. The fact that for Jews and Christians God definitely does speak (even, according to Christians, becoming incarnate) does not actually negate God's mysterious otherness: on the contrary, it highlights it to infinity. God enters space and time in order to communicate with us but cannot be contained there. God is more like the ground out of which beings emerge or the backdrop against which they shimmer than an object in the world.

Yet at the beginning of every spiritual search, the yearning for contact with God as another being and for 'divine' experiences is an inevitable and even necessary element. In the first flush of conversion, enthusiasm and energy are focused on achieving spiritual goals. As Denys Turner has perceptively observed, the creation of what he calls an 'ascetic self' represents an unavoidable stage in every spiritual life. One meets it sometimes in monastic novitiates but not only there. In itself it is a good, indeed even essential thing, representing a genuine striving for holiness, spirituality, perfection and union with God. Without it one would never get started on the spiritual path.[32] But it is ambiguous in that it generally conceals an equally strong desire, more or less hidden to the person himself, to gain a reputation as a spiritual expert and be recognised as a guru and a 'mystic'.

St John of the Cross addressed the problem directly, diagnosing it as spiritual infantilism which has to be transcended if one is to get anywhere at all. In the modern context one might also call it spiritual consumerism: God is boiled down, carved up and served to me on a plate through the medium of fast-food-style spiritual fixes. St John is clear. There has to be a radical unmasking of such illusions if real spiritual progress is to occur. It is indeed important to have a well-developed ego and a healthy *persona* (or even a number of them) which furnish us with acquired roles and carefully cultivated self-identities, allowing us to survive and get by in the world: but it is a recipe for disaster permanently to identify oneself with one's *persona*. That is even truer in relating to God, who sees through all masks, than it is in human relationships.

To remain fixated on one's (pseudo) mystical *persona* means imagining that the spiritual life is going to be like an opera by Wagner – full of highs, lows and dramatic episodes. Yet even Wagner's operas have a great many long and tedious recitatives! St John advises that if one wants to make progress then it is most important to accept the darkness and not reach out for the light, to dwell in emptiness and not glut oneself with a false fullness, to live with bitterness rather than dulling one's spiritual senses with artificial sweetness.[33] It is essential to recognise that the preliminary stages of the spiritual life, with their enthusiastic experiences, can become even more of an addictive drug than the ordinary pleasures one has heroically tried to leave behind. Above all, as Turner notes, what has to be pruned away is *possessive* desire.[34]

That is why God takes over, leading the soul into a wilderness where he can wean it from its 'spiritual' dependencies and train it in what really matters. John speaks of the dark night of sense and spirit, in which the mystery of God's presence in all its overwhelming otherness flows directly into the self. It is experienced as aridity, emptiness and deepest darkness. At first this might seem to contradict scripture which asserts that God is light without any darkness at all (1 Jn 1:5) and the express statement of Jesus who promised that those who follow him will not walk in darkness but will have the light of life for their guide (Jn 8:12). But actually, understood properly there is no such contradiction.

St John is reminding us of a truth well understood in eastern Christianity where it is associated especially with three great mystical theologians, St Gregory of Nyssa (4th century), Denys the Areopagite (probably 5th century) and St Maximus the Confessor (6th-7th century): God is a light so absolute, transcendent and intense, that in opening the eyes of the soul to his radiance, the light initially seems to blind us.[35] As T. S. Eliot wrote, it is a light, 'too bright for mortal vision.'[36] Far from providing consoling luminous experiences, it can actually engender a dreadful sense of having been plunged into the most searing darkness.

What then should one do when, having hiked to the top of the spiritual mountain, what follows is anything but luminous and comforting? What is to be done when prayer leaves us suspended in a thick, foggy night? Faced with that kind of experience the spiritual life can seem to be just cold, disappointing and dangerously empty, almost like a kind of mystical atheism. For orientating oneself in the darkness of the mountain top it can be helpful to examine some of the symbols that occur in the mystery of the transfiguration. At the end we shall return to the symbol of light.

1. Solitude

Periods of withdrawal, both from the company of others and from an inner world teeming with thoughts and images, are an essential prerequisite not just for spiritual growth but for maintaining one's psychological equilibrium in the modern world. I was intrigued recently to observe, while passing through an airport, that some enterprising entrepreneur had erected a booth offering an artificially created seclusion into which travellers could escape for some moments of purifying solitude. It was a good reminder of the need to draw apart so as not to fall apart! Although totally abandoning society is never really an option for Christians – since God did not hesitate to embrace it in the incarnation – regular periods of withdrawal can help to secure personal identity, allowing differentiation of one's self from the crowd and encouraging attention to what is really essential in life.[37]

Without allotting oneself focused moments of privileged time dedicated solely to God, it can be extremely difficult to discern the divine presence in the rush of daily life. Yet solitude can initially be panic-inducing, offering only what seems at first an unendurable void. With its lack of immediate stimulants, it demands progressive adjustment to a very different situation. Freed of exterior commitments and responsibilities, the discipline to be learnt is that of patient waiting, in dark, dry, receptive faith for whatever God may (or may not) choose to send.

It is a tremendous learning curve for re-focusing the heart on what is really important. But even more important than external solitude is the search for inner quietude – detachment from the endless flow of thoughts, images, ideas and memories that course through one's conscious awareness like a flood. The real task in cultivating solitude lies not just in shutting out external sounds and images but in clearing a space in the heart for freedom from one's own inner cacophony, and learning to be still. That is a basic condition for any form of serious spiritual life. So whether one's solitude is that of a mountain top, an attic, a park bench or a beach, it is essential to embrace it regularly.

2. Sleep

The drowsiness that overcame the apostles was appealingly human but also indicative of something deeper and less attractive. It was only as the divine light became more dazzling that they finally awoke. Monastic writers have always insisted that sin has a kind of narcotic effect on the soul. The cares and pleasures of this life with their capacity to benumb our senses (Lk 8:14; 12:17-19) either lull us into a sense of false security that denies the tragic or difficult sides of life and locks us into a prison of denial; or they lull us into forgetfulness by ensnaring us in a web of our own and others' 'ultimate' concerns which are frequently no more than exaggerated trivia. Such truncated awareness leads to a kind of sclerosis of the heart (Ps 94(95):8; Mt 13:14-15).

That is why God so often announced his saving interventions in sacred history with a call to get up. Isaiah cried out 'Awake! Awake!' (Is 52:1), John the Baptist roared in peoples' faces (Mt 3:3;

7), St Paul advised the Christians of Rome that it was full time now to wake from sleep as salvation was nearer than they thought (Rom 13:11-12) and St Benedict placed Psalm 94 (95), with its warning that we should listen to God's voice, at the start of his night Office of prayer.[38] For many monastic writers the goal of that life is to throw off the torpor induced by the anaesthetic of sin and be fully awakened to the presence of God. They echo Paul's Letter to the Ephesians (5:14) where he cries:

> Sleeper, awake!
> Rise from the dead,
> and Christ will shine on you.

Orthodox writers note the similarity in Greek between the words *proseuche* (prayer) and *prosoche* (attentiveness) and insist that the two are closely linked.[39] Trying to stay awake, especially in the midst of what feels like sleep-inducing darkness, is one of the most purifying disciplines in the spiritual life which is why vigilance has always been considered a monastic virtue. The goal is to be spiritually awake so as to catch the presence of God as he appears:

> Let the watchmen count on daybreak
> and Israel on the Lord! (Ps 129(130):6-7, *Grail version*)

Yet there are positive aspects to the symbols of sleep and rest in the spiritual life. One is also invited to enter the great Sabbath rest of union with God (Heb 4:1-11) when, having completed one's ascetic striving, with the senses and the mind lulled into inner calm, the outer self can go to sleep and one's heart awaken to divine splendour. The Psalms knew this falling asleep to the world and resting in God:

> As for me, I shall behold your face in
> righteousness;
> when I awake I shall be satisfied,
> beholding your likeness. (Ps 16(17):15)

The Psalmist also used the beautiful image of a weaned child to suggest the repose that fills a soul filled with faith in God:

But I have calmed and quieted my soul,
like a weaned child with its mother;
my soul within me
is like a weaned child. (Ps 130(131):2)

The *Song of Songs*, which employs the image of the bed at night (Song 3:1), also spoke of this repose both physical and spiritual in a line taken up and repeated by mystics, Jewish as well as Christian:

I slept, but my heart was awake. (Song 5: 2)

3. The Mountain

Mountains are among the most primordial and powerful of human symbols. They can be an image of liberation, as for example at the end of the film *The Sound of Music*, where the von Trapp family escape across the Alps into freedom. 'In the mountains, there you feel free,' wrote T. S. Eliot.[40] Rainer Maria Rilke also called one of his poems, 'Exposed on the Cliffs of the Heart' though he conjures up with his imagery a rather less alluring mountain experience.[41] In almost all religious traditions holy mountains, with their associations of solitude, altitude, immensity and wilderness, serve as places of encounter with God.[42] The Bible tells us that the Lord spoke to Moses on Mt Sinai giving him the Law in cloud and darkness (Ex 19:16-25). They are ambiguous places, danger-zones because they are divine disclosure-zones. Gerard Manley Hopkins used them as metaphors for the frightful abysses of the mind:[43]

O the mind, mind has mountains; cliffs of fall
Frightful, sheer, no-man fathomed. Hold them cheap
May who ne'er hung there.

St Gregory of Nyssa in the 4th century also employed the image of standing on a cliff's edge, to capture the spiritual vertigo induced by the dawning awareness of God's infinite, transcendent majesty.[44] Who is capable of negotiating such steep paths of prayer in which glimpses of nothingness – all things as nothing compared to God or God himself as 'no-thing' – crowd into and overwhelm the mind, leaving it paralysed with anxiety and unable to take another step forward for fear of falling? Yet according to St John of the Cross, it is this very state of soul into which God aims to lead us.

One should never underestimate the spiritual short circuit (and inner power-cut) involved in actually experiencing real contact with 'the darkness of God.' It can feel like total loss of faith and seem devastatingly similar to depression. Denys Turner, however, offers helpful criteria for distinguishing between depression and the darkness caused by the purging effect of mystical contact with God. In depression one reacts against the process. One wants to return to 'normality' by restoring the deconstructed self so that in the end no real progress is made and the deadly cycle of highs and lows may begin again.

In purification by God other factors are operative. There is the sense that something more is at work, a flicker of hope induced by what is glimmering obscurely in the gloom. As Turner says,[45]

> The passive nights, on the other hand, are the dawning of a realisation that in this loss of selfhood, nothing is lost; it is the awakening of the capacity to live without the need for it. When the passive nights pass, all is transformed. When depression passes, all is restored, normality is resumed, the emotional life is rehabilitated and so, for all the sufferings of the depressed, which are otherwise indistinguishable from the passive nights, nothing is gained.

By the faint flickering of this inner light, called by St John of the Cross 'no other light except for that which in my heart was burning,'[46] one is enabled to journey on in darkness. Often the most effective prayer is that which is practised in such a mode: in dry, empty fidelity to a God whose presence is felt as absence, in the midst of a 'self' that feels like a crumbling edifice or a carcass pulled apart by hungry beasts. It is God's way of emptying our spiritual faculties.[47]

The appropriate response in such a situation is like the spiritual version of the strategies employed by climbers caught on a foggy mountain: stopping and listening attentively; relaxing the struggle so as to conserve one's strength; putting up with the murky damp in hopeful expectation that the fog will eventually clear; yet keeping one's nerve with the realisation that here is where God means me to be. Faith honed to pure receptivity is learnt in waiting on such spiritual mountaintops. The three traditional monastic vows can be helpful guides in this area.

- *Stability* hangs tenaciously on to God through every fog and every night, hoping to receive all things from him despite appearances to the contrary;
- *Conversion of life* refuses to fill the aching void with vacuous imaginings and vain distractions;
- *Obedience* consents to stay put, simply out of love – because that is what God wants.

It is a matter of suffering God's purifying action, of becoming receptive to his will, for love is not perfect until it pulls us out of ourselves, stretching desire beyond the limits of the self and aligning it gradually with the desire of the beloved. *Kenosis* on the mountain of dark faith is a small experience of Gethsemane.

4. Light

This is where we must return to the symbol of light, which is such a significant factor in the mystery of the transfiguration and in the Christian mystical tradition generally. The illusionary light of spurious fantasies generated by the image-making machinery of the psyche has to be abandoned if one is become a true visionary – to see reality as God wants one to see it. The entire monastic tradition rejects the notion that 'luminous' visions, whether sensory or intellectual can ever be identified as the goal of the spiritual life, for the transcendent God cannot be grasped by the light of human understanding. Faith is a dark knowledge that transcends both reason and imagination. Yet all mystical writers persist in describing experience of God as illumination, speaking of it as a light that dawns in the deepest interiority of the heart, spreads through the soul and shines out through the body into the world.[48]

This light is primarily of two kinds. First, it is a conscious (though obscure) realisation of being 'contacted' by God; second and as a direct consequence of that it is a new type of understanding, a new way of seeing reality through God's light. It brings with it a kind of spiritual x-ray system, implanted by God, that allows one to see into and beyond surface appearances. God brings it into play more and more as the smoke and shadows generated by the fires of passionate attachments are removed – all those illusions to which one is connected and addicted through the image-making projector of the mind. True seeing, like a pair of spiritual spectacles, corrects the distorted view of reality induced by one's own projections, which are the externalisation of prejudice and obsession. The uncreated light, the grace of the divine presence pouring out of God and into the purified self, adjusts and corrects one's inner optic; the light of Christ, God's radiant truth-revealing Image, dispels the shadows of the long night of sin and death and helps us at last to see. Like the man born blind, our damaged eyes are healed by the anointing of the Word (Jn 9:11).

As Christ's light, imparted by the Holy Spirit gradually begins to dawn within, one's entire understanding is reshaped and refined. Emptied of all false supports and pseudo consolations thanks to its long purification in the dark, dry matrix of the night of faith, the soul is granted the new and radiant vision of God's glory and sees the world with eyes illumined by Christ. As the Psalmist put it:

> For with you is the fountain of life:
> in your light we see light. (Ps 35(36):9)

Therefore it is vitally important not to misunderstand or misinterpret this symbol. The light is the mystery of God himself entering into contact with us.

- It is not an object one can handle or trade with, play with or possess.
- It is not some commodity, a 'thing' given as a certificate to prove that, having survived the darkness, one is now a registered genuine 'mystic' duly authorised and commissioned to teach others the path. Were it so, it would simply represent a return to the old, grasping, self-serving ways of the illusionary 'holy self' that God has deconstructed in the purifying night of faith.

The crucial point is this: the darkness is *itself* the irradiating ray that guides one forward for it is God's own presence. It is grace. That is why it is folly to want to escape the darkness, leave it behind or imagine that having 'once' accepted it and 'got over it', one will then be admitted to the titillating rewards of a new sensory or intellectual 'illumination'. That would be a relapse into the old tired grasping ways of spiritual consumerism. What really matters is learning an entirely new language, a new 'God-speak', the language of the dark but illuminating night – it is mystical theology.

It cannot be repeated too often that true mysticism is not about 'leaving the darkness behind' so as to 'obtain' light. Learning that the darkness itself is light means entering deeply into the mystery of Christ and sharing in his transforming passage through death. It is personal experience of the paschal mystery. We have already emphasised the fourth gospel's insistence that Christ's exaltation did not simply follow on after his humiliation: rather his agony on the cross was already the beginning of his exaltation. Christ's glory, concealed in his suffering from the eyes of unbelievers, is the key of knowledge conferring understanding on believers and the authentic model for spiritual enlightenment. Just as the 'failure' of a convicted 'criminal' is in fact revealed to have been the triumph of love, so the experience of living with spiritual darkness and dryness gradually brings to birth a new kind of understanding.

Christ's darkness – aflame with love – was already the beginning of his resurrection light. So too the darkness of faith engenders a new way of 'seeing' God, a new way of understanding reality, a flame of inner resurrection. What does one begin to understand? Certainly it is not new 'things' such as revelations or esoteric doctrines supposedly not granted to 'ordinary believers.' As St Paul observed and as the church has always reminded various gnostics throughout the ages, a false mysticism of special knowledge *puffs up*, whereas love *builds up* (1 Cor 8:1-2).

Nor is this new way of knowing a privileged gateway to spiritual elitism. In this experience one is not granted understanding of extraordinary things: rather one understands the ordinary in an extraordinary manner. It is wisdom (*sophia/sapientia*), the knowledge of God flowing from love. The symbol of light indicates how

God's radiant yet blinding presence also grants true clarity in understanding and expressing the things of God and the self: one is granted perspicacity in spiritual vision and perspicuity in spiritual self-expression.

As one perseveres through dark faith, learning to adjust one's 'spiritual' expectations and bring them into line with God's will, a new type of spiritual sensibility gradually emerges within the self. An inner sensation, that of the eyes and ears of the heart, is born.[49] Deeper than ordinary sense perception, and more penetratingly intuitive than normal intelligence, this inner sensibility gradually awakens under the action of the Holy Spirit. A long line of witnesses, stretching from Origen in the east to St John of the Cross in the west, and including great saints such as Gregory of Nyssa, Benedict, the medieval women mystics, and Ignatius Loyola, speak of these senses of the soul.

There is an inner hearing, seeing, smelling and tasting but above all an inner 'touch', a capacity to 'perceive' through the darkness of the mind the presence of the divine lover dwelling in the depths of the heart. These awakened inner senses convey knowledge as information and transformation. Christ 'in-forms' the heart by coming to dwell in it through the mystery of baptism; and he transforms it through the mystery of the Eucharist, filling it with divine glory by impressing on it the mystery of his saving love.

Certain consequences follow as God communicates this dark, transfiguring wisdom to and through the awakened spiritual senses of the heart. One's understanding of revelation deepens. New insights into holy scripture, tradition and the liturgy are generated. Theology becomes an intuitive mode of understanding, more than simply an accumulation of knowledge about divinely revealed facts. Dogmas, doctrines and the words and rites of worship become like windows of resplendent glass, aflame with divine light; the dazzlingly beautiful interconnectedness of all the truths revealed by God – what theologians call the *analogia fidei* – is keenly realised; the clarity and coherence of the sacramental mysteries (*nexus mysteriorum*) are seen in their underlying unity as shining manifestations of the one great mystery of Christ.

The gift of theology, as that word has traditionally been understood in monasticism, is received. That entails not merely becoming an accomplished scholar or a specialist in religious knowledge but a seer, gifted with eyes purified by the Holy Spirit in prayer.[50] Jewish mystics had already come to know the light that streams from the divine countenance (Ps 4:6; Ps 79(80).[51] Paul later identified this luminous experience with the face of the transfigured Christ, the incarnate Son 'who is the image of God' (2 Cor 4:4-6). It is the same God who created the light in the beginning who shines through Jesus Christ today:

> For it is the God who said, 'Let light shine out of darkness,' who has shone in our hearts to give the light of the knowledge of the glory of God in the face of Jesus Christ.

The full vision of this light will be seen in all its splendour only in the *eschaton*, at the end, when Christ shall come again in glory. Yet the light of grace and that of glory are essentially the same. They are simply different modes of the overflowing radiance of presence which God confers on those who gaze on him in love.

A further consequence of this vision is its slow transformation of the self. Contemplative prayer and the dark enlightenment of faith leads to a new understanding of the self, an experience that is by turns consoling and desolating. God's purifying light is deeply disillusioning in the sense that it gradually purges away all false ideas and images. As Newman wrote about the metaphor of purgatorial fire:

> Learn that the flame of the Everlasting Love
> Doth burn ere it transform ...[52]

One realises the truth expressed by Luther that we are *simul justus et peccator* – simultaneously at rights with God by grace yet also deeply flawed and sinful. However, the proof that one's experience is genuine is that knowledge of this fact is not depressing nor does it cast one into despair: instead it forces the mind continually to implore God's grace and opens the floodgates of compassion for others in their distress.

Gradually, God's purifying light burns away the webs we project and weave around ourselves. It drives out foolish fantasies from the mind replacing the spiritual dainties we confect to gorge our egoism with the hard and dry but more substantial bread of reality.

Finally, this growing enlightenment has practical consequences for living with others. It slowly becomes evident that one has not been seeing clearly at all. Others have been the screens for our projections, which we have played out on them. As the divine light purifies the optic of the heart it helps us recognise the obfuscations we impose on others and, through such recognition, our projections are reduced in quantity and intensity. Others are permitted more space to be. Through contemplative transformation of the self, the light of Christ which dispels the darkness of the mind, allows one to see a little as God does. Whereas human beings tend to see only appearances, God pierces the outer shells of things and sees right through to the heart (1 Sam 16:6-7): through prayer he shares this quality with us. The hidden depths of things begin to shine.

Something of this was once brought home to me when attending an exhibition of paintings by the artist Mark Rothko. I had never been one of his admirers, being unable to overcome my sense that his works confront us simply with great stretches of blackness which ultimately yield nothing. Yet, suspending the analytical suspicions of my critical intelligence, though with little expectation, I determined to stay with the paintings in the hope that simply by holding myself open to the objectivity of the works, a new understanding might emerge.

One day (less out of the blue than out of the black!) I suddenly began to see: the paintings were indeed not just dark at all. The blackness was gradually giving way, revealing the rich underpainting lying beneath. It was shimmering with reds and greens and reflecting also the lights of the room. The colours emerged like an epiphany where before there had been nothing but a blank. Yet the black had not gone away: all was momentarily transfigured. It was like the experience of grace – reality granting us its luminosity, if only it can find an opening to get in. Perhaps in some analogous way, God grants us vision through the light of grace if we consent to stay on the dark mountain top, waiting with hope-filled patience for the radiant vision of Christ's luminous face to appear (2 Pet 1:16-20).

This long discussion of the transfiguration, and especially its symbol of light, may seem to have taken us far from the liturgically inspired vision of Christ's mysteries which is the theme of the book. Yet that is not so. It has been necessary to examine how we share experientially in these mysteries of Christ for as Paul wrote, the mystery is also Christ *in us*, 'the hope of glory' (Col 1:27).[53] The light of the transfiguration breaking through on the dark mountain top is a sign and foretaste of its full and final appearance at the end of time. But it is the same light, concealed in sacramental signs and symbols that we receive in the darkness of faith, every time we celebrate in the liturgy the mysteries of Christ.

CHAPTER TEN

Three Mysteries of Mary

Mary crowned with living light,
temple of the Lord,
place of peace and holiness,
shelter of the word.

Mystery of sinless life
in our fallen race,
free from shadow you reflect
plenitude of grace!

Hymn from the Roman Liturgy of the Hours

Like the Roman Catholic Church, all the Eastern churches emphasise the special place the Mother of the Lord holds in their liturgical and devotional life. Indeed Marian devotion initially began in the east and only gradually established itself in the west, gaining momentum after the definition of Mary as the *Theotokos* (the God-bearer) at the Council of Ephesus in 431 AD. While usually accepting the truth behind this title, Protestants in denying devotion to Mary part company both with their co-religionists and with much of the historic Christian faith, for there is no doubt that devotion to Mary and recourse to her intercession has been a constant feature of the tradition since at least the third century.[1]

Anglicans tend to display mixed reactions to Mary. The High Church tendency contains all shades of contemporary Roman Catholic devotion ranging from Marian minimalism to a degree of veneration that sometimes borders on the excessive. In addition some Anglicans can appear inconsistent in this matter, being at times able to accept more exaggerated levels of eastern Marian devotion than they are prepared to stomach from the Roman Catholic Church. Evangelical Anglicans, for their part, insist that they respect the Lord's Mother but reject the developed doctrines and devotions of Roman Catholics, their fellow Anglicans and Orthodox Christians.[2]

Protestant anxieties regarding this area of traditional Christian faith revolve around three issues. First is the undisputed fact that there seems to be little explicit scriptural justification for much Marian doctrine, second that it seems to overshadow the absolute rights of Christ as sole Mediator between God and humankind (1 Tim 2:5), and third that it seems to have developed in the early church more under the impetus of non-canonical apocryphal literature than under the influence of the Bible.

Catholics and Orthodox will usually answer that in our understanding the New Testament has to be read in the light of tradition. Tradition is not a new revelation but the church's Spirit-guided penetration of the scriptures, often uncovering depths of meaning not usually immediately obvious on the surface of the text. Yet critically intelligent members of both churches will generally acknowledge and deplore the fact that popular devotion can sometimes lose both theological balance and even good taste.

Despite that, both churches are officially committed not only to the definition of Mary as *Theotokos* in 431, but also to honouring her with the highest degree of veneration (*hyperdulia*) accorded to a creature, reserving adoration (*latria*) for the Holy Trinity and the incarnate Lord Jesus Christ.[3] Finally, we do indeed acknowledge the influence on liturgy and iconography of non-canonical books such as the *Protoevangelium* of James which became a fertile source of imagery in both east and west in the medieval period. Their real significance, however, would seem to lie in the testimony they offer us to the development of popular mariology in the early church.[4]

The whole area remains a neuralgic point between Protestants and Christians of a more 'catholic' tendency (whether Eastern, Roman, High Anglican or High Lutheran). Personally I have to admit that I recognise the reasons for Protestant disquiet regarding much Marian piety. I also wonder at times about the wisdom of the Roman Catholic Church having unilaterally defined two extra dogmas about her (her Immaculate Conception [1854] and Assumption into heaven [1950]) which surely created extra stumbling blocks on the path to Christian unity.

Yet as a Roman Catholic I also accept the truths affirmed by these Marian dogmas and acknowledge the importance of the

Lord's Mother not only in the mystery and history of salvation but in my own spiritual life and prayer. Being a Benedictine monk, my approach to Mary is rooted in the celebration of her feasts in the liturgy. The advantage of such a liturgical approach is that while acknowledging her important and even central place in the mystery of Christ (as the living proof of the reality of the incarnation), and her continuing role in the church, the liturgy never fails to highlight the fact that the principal roles in the world's salvation are played by the Lord Jesus Christ and the Holy Spirit.

I am reminded at times of the notorious intervention made once at an international session of the World Council of Churches by the (very ecumenically committed) Fr Sergius Bulgakov. He caused a furore among the Protestant participants by insisting on the important role Mary continues to play in the life of the church.[5] Equally well, however, I do not think that other Christian traditions should be somehow 'de-churched' because they cannot accept these two Roman Catholic dogmas or our Marian devotion. Orthodox, Anglicans and Protestants, who were not in any way involved in the process of the definitions of the dogmas (or even consulted) ought not to have the ecclesial reality of their churches impugned because they are unable to sign up to them. That Mary is the *Theotokos* is of the *esse* (i.e. essentials) of the Christian faith: that she was immaculately conceived and assumed bodily into heaven are surely of the *bene esse* (i.e. added extras).[6]

A little of the liturgical and theological pluralism sanctioned by the Second Vatican Council might perhaps be invoked here: it is after all sufficient for salvation to call on the name of the Lord Jesus and be baptised in his name (Rom 10:13; Acts 2:21). I suspect that if the Catholic Church stopped trying to impose those dogmas on Christians who did not share in their definition, then our co-religionists might be able to hear more easily what we are trying to say about Mary and – more to the point – what we are saying we think the tradition itself means. In such an atmosphere of mutual acceptance, our separated brothers and sisters might find, behind the unappealing façade of Marian theology and devotion, an affirmation of God's saving grace they could eventually make their own. Confessing with us her divine mother-hood and acknowledging that she is a privileged witness to God's grace, they might be able to find their way towards communion with us again – if only we would consent not to impose as a condi-tion of faith this barrier that they currently find impassible.

It is hard to imagine the humble Virgin of Nazareth and Mother of the Church being displeased by that possibility. Communion with God and between human beings – the very goal of the mystery of Christ – only comes about through imaginative, kenotic and creative generosity in the image of the one who did not grasp at his sacred privileges but emptied himself for us.

A. The Presentation of Mary in the Temple (Fig 19)

> Anne the Mother of Mary
> called all her little friends to walk before her,
> carrying flaming torches
> and she said, 'Go then my child,
> go to the one who sent you to me
> for you are vowed
> and dedicated to him!
> You are an incense-offering
> of delicate fragrance.
> Enter in,
> go into the veiled place
> and learn the hidden mysteries of God.
> Prepare yourself
> to become a delightful dwelling-place for Jesus,
> who grants great mercy to the world!'
> *Byzantine hymn for the Presentation of Mary*

Christian artists have for centuries delighted in depicting Mary being presented as a child by her parents Joachim and Anne in the Temple at Jerusalem. Her association with that central institution of the Jewish religion is further highlighted by the leg-end that she was weaving thread for the veil of the Holy of Holies when the Angel of the Annunciation came to her. We owe these

stories to the apocryphal *Protoevangelium* of James which also
supplied the delightful image of the three-year-old child dancing
for joy in the house of the Lord. Legend also says that she was fed
in the temple by the hand of the Archangel Gabriel. Here, let us
frankly acknowledge with Yves Congar that we are indeed in the
realm of legend. In the Jewish religion to which Mary belonged, it
would have been simply unimaginable for a woman to have even
entered, let alone lived in the Holy of Holies.[7]

But in and through the legend and its symbolism, a deeper
truth is waiting to be discerned: it is the relationship between the
Temple and Mary who will become the mother of the incarnate
God. Just as the Jerusalem Temple had once contained within it
the Holy of Holies, with the Ark of the Covenant where the divine
presence was accustomed to dwell and manifest its power (2
Chron 5:7-10), so Mary's own person, body and soul, would become a temple in which the new Holy of Holies the flesh of Jesus
would be given life. The Byzantine liturgy, with its intensive symbolic sense, brings out the many associations of this feast:

> Today the Virgin Mary,
> the most pure temple of the Saviour,
> his most precious bridal chamber,
> the holy treasure house of God's glory
> enters the Lord's house,
> bearing with her the divine grace of the Holy Spirit.
> Therefore the angels of God are chanting:
> 'Behold the coming of the heavenly tabernacle!'

Christ's presence in her body will establish her as the God-
bearer (*Theotokos*), worthy of the highest veneration on account of
her unique role in the mystery of salvation. Showing her entering
the temple compares and contrasts that place with her as the living temple of the incarnation;[8] it also shows how Christ's mysteries are mirrored and reflected in the lives of believers of whom
Mary is the first. At the time of the iconoclastic controversy in the
Byzantine Empire (8-9th centuries), when a section of the Greek
church led by the emperors and army argued for the destruction
of icons and the abolition of the cult of the Mother of God,

Orthodox defenders of both made a number of important points regarding her.

Mary, as they observed, was not simply like a pipe or channel through which the Word of God passed on his way into human existence, or a purse which having once contained gold may be readily discarded when it is empty. No human conception or birth ever happens like that anyway and there would have been no true incarnation at all if such had been the case. As a real mother, Mary gave Jesus his humanity from her own: indeed given the absence of a human father (thanks to her virginal conception of him through the Holy Spirit's power), that is even more true than in the normal situation of childbirth. The 'purse' which contained the gold of the divinity was already beautiful as a human being but was made more so through its adornment with the gifts of the Holy Spirit who dwelt in her as in a temple.[9]

From her, as the Byzantine Rite sings,

> … shone forth the splendid light
> enlightening those who sit
> in the darkness of ignorance.

But after the birth of Jesus, Mary did not cease to be a temple. St Augustine observed that she was more blessed in believing than in conceiving so that her faith was the spiritual womb which had made possible the physical incarnation in her bodily womb.[10] According to the tradition of the Latin church, the whole Trinity dwelt by grace in Mary from the first moment of her existence thanks to her Immaculate Conception, which is better understood as God having filled her with his presence than merely having preserved her from original sin. The Creator-Father chose and prepared her for her mission, the Saviour-Son redeemed her (with only the timing of the application of that gift to her distinguishing her from us) and the Sanctifier-Holy Spirit overshadowed her. Mary was, therefore, from the first moment of her existence the temple of the Trinity, even before receiving the second divine person physically in her womb in his kenotic incarnation.

The Eastern churches, having a different understanding of 'original sin', do not speak of Mary's Immaculate Conception; but they do call her the *Panagia* (all-holy one) and insist that from the start of her life the Most High God made holy the place where he would dwell. They also practise a highly developed Marian devotion which is distinguished by its intrinsic connection with the liturgical life of the church.[11]

Mary as the dwelling place of the *shekinah* becomes an icon pointing in two directions. One is towards Christ as the final true and perfect Temple in which, through the union of human and divine natures in the person of the incarnate Son, God is pleased to dwell forever. In this she is the *hodegetria*, the one who shows the Way (i.e. to Christ: cf Jn 14:6).[12] The other direction is towards the church, as the spiritual temple made up of living stones (1 Pet 2:5-6) where the risen Jesus dwells in the Holy Spirit. The mystery of Mary's relationship to the church is so full of meaning that only a multitude of images and metaphors can do it justice: she is the first member of the church as the model of a believing disciple, but also the mother of all believers who were given to her by the Lord at the cross. She is the icon of what the Christian community is meant to be: the special disclosure-zone for the incarnate God and the grace of the Holy Spirit. She is that in her humanity, redeemed and rendered beautiful by grace through the indwelling of the Holy Trinity.[13]

In the Orthodox Church this mystery of her presentation in the Temple is associated with the making of monastic profession. That is particularly appropriate since monks and nuns aim to live habitually in the presence of God, worshipping the Holy Trinity in the perpetual praise of the church's liturgy and especially in the mystery of the Eucharist. Monastic life entails an offering of self for the ministry of prayer in a particular place, a making-oneself-present to God in response to his call to enter his presence (1 Sam 3:9-10). The monastic person promises to enter into and dwell habitually in the temple of the heart where God dwells permanently, and to burn there the incense of perpetual prayer on the altar of his/her deepest self as an offering of love for God and for the good of all his people:

> Happy are those who live in your house,
> ever singing your praise. (Ps 83(84):4)
> Dwelling in this inner house of God, s/he is fed by the bread of

God's word which calls him / her to become the tabernacle of the Lord and, like Mary, to conceive and give birth through love to the Word-made flesh. The monastic vocation is therefore, in common with that of all Christians, in this profound sense radically Marian.[14] Recognising this Marian dimension is not just a matter of saying prayers to Mary, accepting doctrines about her or making pilgrimages to her shrines. It is possible to do all those things and yet not have grasped the real meaning of Mary. What is that meaning? It is to receive the word of God through humble, receptive obedience to the Holy Spirit and to become, as the Fathers of the church put it, a spiritual *Theotokos* a bearer of God.[15] Whoever does that becomes the image of Mary and offers God the most pleasing gift imaginable:

> Who are my mother and my brothers? And looking at those who sat around him, he said, 'Here are my mother and my brothers! Whoever does the will of God is my brother and sister and mother.' (Mt 12:46-50)

B. The Mystery of the Annunciation (Fig 20)

Two annunciations of the birth of Jesus are recorded in the New Testament, both involving the angel of the Lord, one in Matthew's gospel (Mt 1:18-25), and the other in Luke's (Lk 1:26-38). It was the latter that supplied most of the inspiration for this feast, celebrated on the 25th of March.[16] It is not hard to see why. The encounter between the angel and the woman chosen to become the mother of the Messiah is, despite its serene character, the most dramatic meeting recorded in salvation history. Both the eastern and western liturgical traditions work up the dialogue between Mary and the angel to draw out its full dramatic impact.

The poets of the Byzantine tradition imagined Gabriel mulling the mystery over in his mind as he set out on his mission:

> He came down over Nazareth,
> pondering in his heart
> and bewildered by this marvellous event,
> asked himself,
> 'How could the one whose throne is in heaven

and for whom the earth is a footstool,
ever be contained in a human womb?
How could he have condescended
to be incarnate of her at a single word that only she can say,
he upon whom the six-winged,
many-eyed seraphim
are not permitted to gaze?'

Mary is presented as anything but passive. She engages in a spirited discussion with Gabriel after having been presented with this startling news:

Trying to grasp the meaning of this mystery,
the Virgin asked the holy messenger,
'How is it possible that a son
should be born of a virgin's womb?
Tell me!'

Even allowing for its more sober style, the Roman tradition on the feast of the Annunciation also dramatises the event, expanding a little on scripture as Mary asks the angel,

How may this thing come to pass
O angel of God for I know not man?

Gabriel answers,

Listen, O Mary, Virgin:
The Holy Spirit will come upon you
and the power of the Most High
will cast its shadow over you!

We should be alert to catch the paschal resonances of the event. The resurrection of Jesus is attested to by angelic witnesses, messengers sent by God to appear at the empty tomb (Lk 24:1-7). Here at his origin in the flesh one also finds angelic testimony as the Virgin Mary receives the message that she is to become the mother of Jesus without any (male!) human intervention. What are we today to make of this declaration that Jesus was conceived solely by the agency of his mother and the empowering action of the Holy Spirit – not to mention the traditional Orthodox and Catholic belief that she remained a consecrated celibate after the birth? Before considering that, it is important to clarify that the New Testament speaks only of a virginal conception and not of a 'virginal birth' as such.[17]

However, considerable obstacles face those today who wish to affirm such a virginal conception as being literally true. Two hundred years of critical investigation of the Bible has conditioned us to be immediately sceptical about the miraculous. Such things don't happen to us we are told, therefore they don't happen. Historians of religion remind us that other significant religious founders (such as the Buddha) are said to have been conceived in a similar way: therefore, they say, we should recognise honestly that it is a mythological mode of describing Christ's conception.

In addition, in our post-Freudian world, in which the church's often lamentable record regarding the repression (and abuse) of sexuality and the denial of women's equality is all too apparent, is this not just another bit of ancient mythology that has exercised a baleful influence in relegating ordinary women to the church's margins while exalting one who had all the joys of motherhood yet apparently very few of its woes? In addition, has it not often been used (or abused) to foster a docile, submissive role model for women in both church and society? Might it not be better to jettison it entirely or at least, having nodded in its mythological direction, to deal with it as we have with Mary's presentation in the Temple and pass on quickly to more important and less implausible matters? If we want to get at the deepest meaning of this mystery, we certainly ought to pay heed to such critical caveats.

Yet there are some counter-caveats that might be directed back at the critics. First, as noted above, there are obvious echoes of the resurrection in the story as it stands. It is intrinsically linked to the breaking in of the *eschaton*, God's kingdom which came in the Easter exaltation of Christ. It is not simply describing a natural event but an account of the conception of one whose resurrection had already been experienced as an explosion of divine initiative and energy. Like everything in the gospels, it is a post-paschal story.

Second, it says little about sex at all but a great deal about gender! Feminist friends have observed to me that a major part of the story concerns God's power to bring about the divine purpose in history apart from the will of man – or more specifically the will of men. This mystery takes place between God the Holy Trinity and Mary, and no one else gets a look in. It thus strikes at our obsessions about family and tribal affiliations.

As Sandra Schneiders shrewdly observed regarding the tradition of Christian celibacy in general, while Jewish identity was (and is) held to be transmitted by blood and natural generation, according to the New Testament, Christian identity is different. One becomes a Christian neither by blood, nor by the will of man, but by the action of the Holy Spirit who regenerates us in Christ (Jn 1:12-13). In addition, Jesus struck directly at the root of patriarchy by choosing not to assume the male role in a family. Surely it is not unreasonable to see some intrinsic connection between the way Christians come into being, the way in which Jesus himself originated, and his own celibate commitment?[18]

Nowhere in the New Testament is the doctrine of the absolute primacy of God and his sovereign right to create and liberate – what Lutherans rightly call 'salvation by grace alone' – more evident than in this story of the womb of Mary of Nazareth being filled by the Holy Spirit – except perhaps in the story of the empty tomb at Jerusalem (Jn 20:8). It witnesses to the free act of God who accomplishes his will without the intrusion of man. Mary's conception of Christ through the Holy Spirit alone is, as we sing in the paschal proclamation on Easter night, the humbling of human (here especially *male*) pride.

Mary is the perfect Christian disciple, therefore, not because she provides a paradigm for submissive femininity – a notion unfortunately used at times to devastating effect in the depressing history of discrimination against women in both church and society – but rather because listening, questioning intelligently and responding wholeheartedly with humility to the will of God, she lived by faith alone in total dependence on God's grace alone. That is truly why she is to be called 'Blessed' (Lk 1:46-48):

> My soul magnifies the Lord,
> and my spirit rejoices in God my Saviour,
> for he has looked with favour on the lowliness of his servant.
> Surely, from now on all generations will call me blessed …

In addition, while the ancient tradition of the Syrian, Coptic, Greek and Latin Churches that Mary remained celibate after the birth of Jesus is certainly less theologically important than his virginal conception, it is also surely less implausible than it is sometimes made out to be. We know from the religious context of Palestinian Judaism and early Syrian Christianity, as well as the evidence from the first stirrings of the monastic movement itself, that a strong tradition existed of self-dedication to God through lifelong celibacy. Scholars have uncovered so much material about the kind of Jewish Christianity (in Syria and Palestine) which came immediately after the expansion of the first Christian communities that we should not underestimate the high value accorded to consecrated virginity in the earliest churches.[19]

But that is where context is all important. That high priority is not best explained by what we, post-Freudians living with the pan-sexualism of contemporary society, always identify as 'sexual' motivation. The actual motivation is more likely to have been primarily eschatological, to do with the imminent end-times that were awaited (cf 1 Cor 7:25-31). It was based on the firm belief that in the coming kingdom of heaven people would be like angels, neither given nor taken in matrimony (Mt 22:29-33). It is anachronistic to project our concerns backwards into the ancient world for they are often quite foreign to it. Consecrated virginity in the primitive church was an eschatological phenomenon concerned with the bringing in of the end-times. The choice of such a lifestyle was a sign of God's coming kingdom. That is surely the context in which we ought to locate the notion of Mary dedicating herself in perpetual virginity to the service of the Lord.

The Annunciation icon shows the encounter between Mary and the angel Gabriel. Her amazement at the news he brings is signified by the hand she places on her breast. With her other hand, open and accepting, she places herself at the disposal of God's will, ready to accept the mission entrusted to her. Out of heaven flows a bright beam of light symbolising the Holy Spirit through whose agency the Word, the Second Person of the Holy Trinity, takes the path of *kenosis* and becomes a human being.

The account in St Luke's gospel (Lk 1:26-38) is rich in biblical imagery. The Holy Spirit overshadows Mary, recalling how the Spirit hovered over creation at the beginning of time: in the same way God the creator engenders new life in the womb of Mary (Gen 1:20). Yet this symbol also recalls the cloud of presence, God's feminine *shekinah* which filled the temple in Jerusalem (2 Chron 7:1-3). Mary is a new temple, the dwelling place of God in the Spirit. She is also the throne on which the High King of Heaven, the royal descendant of David's line, seats himself to reign over his creation (Lk 1:32-33). The whole story is rich in mystical symbols from the Jewish tradition as the Virgin Daughter of Sion (Zech 2:10) becomes the bride of the Most High (Rev 21:2). For all these reasons, Mary is designated in the Orthodox liturgy, 'Mother of the Light.'

T. S. Eliot drew movingly on the image of Mary in his poem *The Dry Salvages*, a meditation on life, death and letting go, where the imagery derives from the sea, the gospel of the annunciation and the High Anglican use of the medieval Latin Christian *Angelus* prayer, in which the *Hail Mary* is interwoven with a meditation on her obedient discipleship and the incarnation of the Word. Eliot speaks of,

> the barely
> prayable
> Prayer of the one Annunciation.[20]

That prayer was Mary's *fiat*, 'be it done to me according to your will' – but it is the hardest prayer of all for us to utter. As in her life, such wholehearted consent to God's will has profound consequences and after-effects. What does it mean to welcome God's angelic messenger into one's life and to say yes to his will? What form does that take? The visit of an angel manifests God's presence and declares his will. God's entry is always disturbing: nothing can ever be the same again afterwards. The angel (*angelos* meaning messenger in Greek) may be anyone or anything that awakens me to hear God calling out to me. As the poet Rilke put it, 'Every angel is terrible', a reminder that 'we don't feel very securely at home in this interpreted world.'[21] The angel-messenger may be bearing news of life (love, birth, friendship, joy), or of death (suffering, illness, tragedy or bereavement). But whatever form it takes, it brings me a divine imperative, the revelation of God's disturbing will. It can also come in the form of dreams to which I may respond in various ways.

I may simply try to ignore it and get on with life – at the risk of living in denial or cutting off real contact with a deeper more authentic level of myself. I may laugh in disbelief, like Sarah at the oak of Mamre when she was told that she would conceive in old age (Gen 18:1-15), before it dawns on me that with God the apparently unlikely has a tendency to happen. I may receive it like Zechariah, the priestly husband of Mary's kinswoman Elizabeth. On hearing from Gabriel that his elderly wife would soon conceive John, the future prophet and forerunner of the Messiah, he responded so quizzically that the angel majestically warned him that he would be struck dumb until after the birth (Lk 1:8-20).

Or finally I may receive it like Mary, who entered into dialogue with her messenger (Lk 1:34), gently probing for the meaning of the message and its implications, yet always open to the need to integrate it into the fabric of her daily life. Then like her, obedient to God's voice, I will be enabled by grace to say 'yes', to accept what God wants, even though it appears to me to be not only implausible but humanly speaking impossible. Actually nothing is impossible to God! (Lk 1:37). For anyone who has ever wrestled with an angel of God's presence (Gen 22:22-32), at least initially a dark and apparently menacing messenger, the mystery of the annunciation will resonate powerfully. Its goal is incarnation: flesh-giving and flesh-taking.

The mysteries of Christ are our mysteries: what was accomplished once for Jesus through Mary's Spirit-filled consent, is realised in Christ's followers by the power of the same Holy Spirit. Yet one may also make a similar assertion about the mysteries of Mary. As we have seen, we too are invited to become virgin daughters of Zion and mystical mothers of God. Meister Eckhart and the German Dominican mystics explored what living the mystery of spiritual virginity and motherhood in the likeness of Mary might mean:

- Spiritual virginity signifies an empty, abandoned heart, free of attachments and purified from all illusions, which waits in dark expectant faith for the seed of God's Word to enter and germinate. It finds expression in a way of prayer and of being which is 'actively passive,' a holding open of the self to God in readiness for whatever may be sent.
- Spiritual motherhood entails becoming 'pregnant' with the Word which occurs when the Holy Spirit fills the receptive womb of faith, forming and shaping Christ in it like an embryo. Then like a divine midwife, the Spirit helps us bring to birth in due time the en-fleshed Word through lives of Christian witness and service.[22]

The spiritual mothering-of-God (whether it is done by males or females) means becoming like Mary: a disclosure-zone for divine presence, a living icon of the Mother of God, the Ark of the Covenant and Gate of Heaven. Prayer is the surest path of purification and preparation to become such a vehicle for the Word; and the best of all prayers is always Mary's, 'let it be', her *fiat*, that,

> … hardly, barely prayable
> Prayer of the one Annunciation.

C. The Mystery of Mary's Dormition (Fig 21)

> In her, the first fruits and image of the church,
> you have revealed the fulfilment
> of the mystery of salvation
> and have made a sign of consolation
> and secure hope to shine out in splendour
> for your people:
> for you did not wish that she
> who had given birth to the Lord of life
> would know the corruption of the grave.
> *From the Roman Feast of the Assumption*

Scripture is as silent about the end of Mary's life as it is about her birth – but ancient tradition, long preserved in the eastern churches, teaches that in death as in life she was glorified by God.

The accounts found in various popular non-canonical texts abound in fantastic and mythological details, but the essential truth they convey is one that the Orthodox Church has celebrated in its worship from a very early date: Mary was taken up as a whole person (i.e. body and soul), into the glory of the risen Christ in heaven.[23] Latin Catholicism received this doctrine in the form of a liturgical feast in the early Middle Ages.[24] The churches stemming from the Reformation (with the exception of some Anglicans) do not accept it and are generally sceptical, both about its historical foundations and theological significance.

Yet Catholics ought to acknowledge that in the light of the Second Vatican Council's teaching on the 'hierarchy of truths', it is important to keep it in perspective. The 'hierarchy of truths' does not mean that one truth is somehow 'more true' than another. Rather it asserts that some are more essentially related to the central event of revelation and salvation than others. Obviously, the revelation of the Trinity and its dogmatic formulation is more important than the doctrine that the saints in glory can intercede for us here on earth; the presence of Christ in the Eucharist is more significant than belief in the veneration of relics, and so on.

All defined dogmas and generally received doctrines are held as true, but some are recognised as being more important than others because they lie closer to the heart of the mystery of Christ. The saving death and resurrection of Jesus clearly has a significance infinitely higher than the raising of his mother into glory. The first is the foundation of the faith and its most essential revelatory and saving event. The second is a fruit and consequence of it.[25]

Orthodox and Catholics, however, hold that revelation possesses a depth and fullness often only implicitly indicated in scripture. They believe in the church's Spirit-directed ability to draw out deeper implications from revelation as Christians grow in understanding through the centuries (Jn 14:26; 16:12-14). The Book of Revelation, for example, contains the powerful image of a woman appearing in heavenly glory who turns out to be the mother of the Messiah (Rev 12:1-6). Many diverse levels of meaning can be discerned in such an enigmatic text.

Protestant exegetes, who can sometimes be a bit myopic about recognising so-called 'catholic' elements in biblical texts, tend to see the figure as representative of the people of Israel or the church. Many Catholics and Orthodox, on the other hand, (who at times might with equal justice be accused of reading things into biblical texts) find it surprising that the person of Mary, the actual mother of the Messiah, should be so easily left out of the picture especially since both those traditions tend to see in her the fulfilment of Israel and the embodiment of the church. Trying to embrace the fullness of revelation invites us to plumb its depths in which many levels of meaning are hidden. Both Catholics and Orthodox hold that the ultimate judge in determining the truth-value of what is revealed is neither scientific scholarship nor the tyranny of the universities, but the church as a whole speaking through an ecumenical council – with Roman Catholics ascribing a unique role to the Petrine ministry of the Bishop of Rome.

Yet both agree that the normal 'place' where the hidden depth of revelation's meaning manifests itself in tradition is the assembly of Christian believers as they worship God. In the liturgy, glorifying the Holy Trinity in prayer and praise, the whole church comes to see more deeply into the sacred mysteries set forth explicitly but also contained implicitly in the Bible. Liturgy is essentially a vision. Under the maternal guidance of the Holy Spirit, the church weaves together a rich poetic tapestry of words and gestures in her liturgical rites which bring to expression the depths of the mystery.

Liturgy is like the church's consciousness, floating on the limitless depths of truth contained in revelation. In the liturgy, filled with the vision of the glory of Christ and meditating on the revealed word which is proclaimed there, the church finds her primary source for all theological reflection and dogmatic elaboration. In this sense, the Christian community as whole, like individual believers, is also Marian, formed in the likeness of Mary who treasured all things and pondered them in her heart (Lk 2:19; 51). The church's heart, where tradition is generated, is her communal worship in spirit and in truth (Jn 4:23-24).[26]

A particularly well-know instance of this is the confession of the divinity of Christ, for he was worshipped liturgically as Lord and God long before that truth was ever defined as dogma.[27] As an early Christian axiom put it, *legem credendi lex statuat supplicandi*, in other words, the church's law of worship is what supports her law of faith.[28] That was one of the principles guiding Pope Pius XII when he defined the dogma of Mary's assumption. Yet some Orthodox theologians, without denying the doctrine, were heavily critical of the papal decision to proceed to definition, claiming that it was making public a mystery which is essentially mystical.

Vladimir Lossky, to name just one, suggested that Mary's death and assumption should have remained a hidden, mystical truth cherished at the heart of the church's prayer and worship, rather than being turned into something to be proclaimed before the world. Its truth concerns one who lived a silent, withdrawn life, treasuring the mysteries committed to her and pondering them in her heart. According to Lossky, the Catholic Church should have done the same and not presented Mary as a focal point for public proclamation. It is an alternative point of view that Latin Catholics might do well to ponder.[29]

On the Protestant side, despite the widespread criticism of the papal definition, it is worth mentioning that it was warmly welcomed by the psychologist Carl Jung, free-thinking Swiss Protestant though he was![30] He claimed to see in it a belated gesture of inclusion of the feminine principle in a supposedly male Godhead. That too is a point of view, though Jung's understanding of the Trinity was so idiosyncratic as to be pretty much incompatible with the received orthodox doctrine about the nature of God. Once again, it is perhaps not too unreasonable to suggest that in any future reunion of the divided Christian churches, Orthodox, Anglicans and Protestants might not be expected to assent to this dogma as defined by Rome in an earlier era without any consultation with them.

In the icon and feast depicting this mystery, the appearance of the glory (*doxa*) of the Lord plays a significant part (Ex 24:17; Ez 1 28): Mary was a new temple who had borne the true Temple Jesus Christ, the incarnate God. Her deathbed is therefore illuminated by the presence of Jesus shining with the glory of the resurrection (represented by a *mandorla*, an almond-shaped aureole of light surrounding his body) as he comes to carry home his mother's soul. He radiates risen glory, the energies of his divine nature penetrating his glorified body and coming forth as light. The image of her death recalls that of his transfiguration. In his halo are inscribed as usual the words, 'I am who I am' (*ho on*), the divine name too holy to pronounce, revealed to Moses at Mt Sinai (Ex 3: 15) and conferred on Jesus after his exaltation when he was acclaimed as Lord (*Kyrios*) (Phil 2:11).

At Mary's death her Son appears like a heavenly midwife who has helped his mother give birth to herself into eternity. Her newborn soul is represented as a child wrapped in swaddling clothes, a thought-provoking reversal of his own physical birth when she wrapped him in swaddling bands and laid him in the manger (Lk 2:7). She gave birth to him into time: now he regenerates her into eternity. It is Mary's personal *pascha/transitus*, her journey through death to life: but like that of all other believers it is accomplished not through her own strength but because of the paschal mystery of her Son. As with the resurrection of Christ, Byzantine artists generally did not depict the taking up of Mary's body though the Orthodox Church also confesses that doctrine, but both liturgical traditions stress that in her assumption she is,

> … higher than the Cherubim and incomparably more glorious than the Seraphim.

Indeed one of the most significant features of Orthodox theological anthropology is the idea that in Christ and his Mother, human nature has been exalted to the heights of heaven far above all powers, principalities, thrones and dominations.[31] The Roman liturgy too sings of Mary having been taken up to heaven while the angels rejoiced, stating explicitly that she is 'exalted high above the choirs of angels'. Byzantine worship is filled with splendid poetry announcing her exaltation:

> Behold all the heavenly hierarchies,
> Dominations,
> Thrones,
> Principalities,

Virtues,
Powers,
Cherubim
and Seraphim
sing a hymn of glory to your dormition.
The whole human race rejoices at your glory!
Kings with angels and archangels sing to you:
Hail, O woman full of grace!

Mary's body was the ark of the New Covenant which carried
the incarnate God. So she enters into the highest heavens just as
the ark of the Old Covenant, the locus of divine presence, was
taken up and enshrined in the holy of holies in the first temple:

... let us fill the church with hymns of praise
at the falling asleep of the ark of God!
For today heaven has opened
and received the woman
who gave birth to the One
whom nothing can contain;
today earth gives back to heaven
the woman who became the source of life.

Angels and apostles throng together,
gazing upon the woman
who gave birth to the principle of life
and who now ascends from life to life!

Patristic tradition loved to apply verse 8 of Psalm 131(2) typo-
logically to Mary's assumption, where Christ in his ascension is
the deepest content of the mystical (i.e. hidden) meaning:

Rise up, O Lord, and go your resting place,
you and the ark of your might.

The assumption and Mary's reception into glory are thus symbolically associated with the ascension of her Son into heaven. The
church's liturgical understanding is the authentic matrix of tradition and the theology which both reflects on it and develops it.
The assumption into glory of Mary's body, the body of the second
Eve who made the incarnation possible by her free consent to the

overshadowing of the Holy Spirit in obedience to the Father's will, and helped undo the sin of her proto-parents (Gen 3:15), announces the future destiny of all Christ's disciples.[32] It is a sign of what the church is called to become at the end of time when the Lord will descend again in glory to gather his people to himself. Mary was thus called by Vatican II the image and pattern of the whole church.[33] But as ever, in each of the mysteries celebrated liturgically is always found the presence of the one great mystery of salvation: the passage of Jesus Christ from death to new life.

Among the symbols used in celebrating the feast the most touching is surely the soul of Mary shown as a newborn child. Jesus speaks in the gospel about spiritual childhood, asserting that only those who receive the kingdom with the receptivity of a child will enter it (Mt 18:2-3). Mary's spiritual childhood consisted in just such spiritual receptivity. It was a life of progressive self-abandonment into God's hands, of self-gift so that God's plan of salvation could be accomplished. The supreme realisation of her giving of self was the moment of her death.

One of the most popular and frequently repeated prayers the Latin Church addresses to Mary speaks of that moment: 'Pray for us now and at the hour of our death!' To live one's life in such close union with God as to be able to gather it all up at the end and hand it over to him: that is truly to die in the light of the mystery of Christ. It is to make one's own the passage of Mary into eternity, praying as her Son did on the cross during the agony of his own paschal journey:

Father, into your hands I commend my spirit. (Lk 23:46)

The whole of life can become a preparation for such a rebirth. Death ought to be not just one moment that overpowers us unexpectedly but a passage into eternity for which the whole of life has been a ripening and preparation; then will be fulfilled the words of the psalmist:

Precious in the sight of the Lord
is the death of his faithful ones. (Ps 115(116):15)[34]

CHAPTER ELEVEN

The Mystery of the Celestial Altar: Earth unites with Heaven

In the earthly liturgy we share in a foretaste of that heavenly liturgy which is celebrated in the Holy City of Jerusalem toward which we journey as pilgrims, where Christ is sitting at the right hand of God, minister of the sanctuary and of the true tabernacle. With all the warriors of the heavenly army we sing a hymn of glory to the Lord; venerating the memory of the saints, we hope for some part and fellowship with them; we eagerly await the Saviour, our Lord Jesus Christ, until he, our life, shall appear and we too will appear with him in glory.

Catechism of the Catholic Church

The feast of the passing-over of the *Theotokos*, which focused on Mary's body as a temple filled with divine glory (*doxa*) and translated by her Son into eternal happiness, has brought us with the New Adam and Eve to the very gates of paradise and the celebration of the heavenly liturgy. The church's worship is a mystery of overwhelming plenitude. It embodies and expresses the multitudinous aspects of the overflowing mystery of Christ. In the celebration of the Eucharist that mystery becomes present as the objective memorial of Christ's sacrificial love revealed for us on the cross. The Divine Liturgy, Mass, Lord's Supper, Holy Communion or Eucharist, is the effective symbolic re-presentation of his passion death and resurrection, which allows the whole church and each of her members to share in his sacrificial offering of thanks and praise, thus passing over with him from this old age of sin, death and decay into the new age of the glory of the Father – the very core of Christ's paschal mystery.[1]

As the Lord's Supper it is an invitation from the risen Jesus, who appears among us radiant with divine energy in the power of the Holy Spirit, (though veiled in the symbols of the sacramental mysteries), so that we may share in his sacrificial banquet. Eating and drinking (together) in holy communion the sacred elements of bread and wine transformed into his risen body and blood, we participate in the feast of wisdom (Prov 9:1-11). It is a mystical foretaste of the banquet of the world to come, the sign and means of our communion with the Holy Trinity and with one another in the church, the People of God and Body of Christ. It is the privileged disclosure-zone where we are built into a dwelling place for the Spirit, the New Temple filled with the glory of the risen Christ.

Ancient Christian tradition tried to convey something of that fullness through the image of three liturgies, or to be more precise three distinct but interlocking dimensions of the one sacramental liturgy.[2] In this book, I have concentrated primarily on the church's earthly liturgy in which the Holy Spirit reveals Christ's mystery-presence through signs and symbols, though I have also indicated that personal prayer of the heart is an extended or interiorised form of liturgical worship. But the great traditions, east and west, remind us that all our earthly worship, whether communal or solitary, is but the echo and reflection – the moving image – of the unceasing liturgy of heaven. In our prayer we participate in this third dimension, the supra-mundane, transcendent, celestial act of worship – an eternal liturgy that exists before and beyond us but in which we become concelebrants as we celebrate in time.

Keeping alive this higher consciousness, this priority of the heavenly liturgy, means never losing sight of the celestial background against which we carry out all our earthly celebrations. It is a good reminder that everything in this world is provisional and that all created things are oriented towards an end that transcends them. Above all it ought to teach us ecclesiological humility by reminding us not to *identify* the visible church on earth – which is indeed the sacramental sign of God's kingdom and of communion between human beings – with the reality of that coming kingdom itself, even though the risen Lord does truly manifest it and makes it present in and through the church and her worship.[3]

In considering the heavenly liturgy it is worth turning to the Book of Revelation, a text belonging to the genre of apocalyptic, a literary form which abounded among Jews and Christians before and during the time in which the New Testament was written. Its fascinating but often disturbing imagery and ideas cast much light on this mystery. In the apocalyptic genre, spiritual longing found expression through weird and wonderful symbols, often presenting the celestial visions of a prophet and community who suffer for the will of God yet declaring that the Lord will vindicate his persecuted people.[4]

The historical context of the Book of Revelation is not entirely clear. Revealed on the island of Patmos (Rev 1:9) and traditionally ascribed to the 'John' who supposedly wrote the fourth gospel, the vision seems to presuppose a context of persecution although it may also contain a critique of the second Temple. Its invective may, therefore, be aimed at Jerusalem and the Jewish religious authorities as much as at the Romans.[5]

Much of it, obscure and difficult to interpret, conveys a disturbing impression of violence: certainly as a symbolic book it should not be interpreted literally or manipulated to justify political or ecclesiastical agendas which have nothing to do with its original context. One of the most beautiful aspects of this strange book is its description and evocation of the liturgy of heaven, the unceasing worship carried out by the celestial church of glory in the company of the angels before the throne of God and of the Lamb. Chapter 1, which recounts what happened to the seer on the Lord's Day, sets the scene by speaking of the exalted Lord Jesus Christ, calling him,

> ... the faithful witness, the firstborn of the dead, and the ruler of the kings of the earth. (Rev 1:5)

Christ is the one who has freed us from our sins by his blood, making us a kingdom and priests to serve his God and Father. From the start, therefore, the book evokes the paschal mystery of his transforming passage through death, leading to his creation of a new priestly community.

The two most inspiring visions of the heavenly liturgy are found in chapters 4 to 8 and again in chapter 19, verses 1 to 10. Even though it would be anachronistic to project backwards into the text what Christian communities later adopted in their worship, it is evident that many elements which eventually became typical of the liturgy are present in the worship of heaven: massed choirs (Rev 7:9-13), gestures of adoration such as prostration (Rev 7:11), the offering of incense (Rev 8:3-5), collective silences (Rev 8:1) and the chanting of angelic choruses (Rev 16:4-7; 19:1-8). All is suffused with celestial glory. Although as a latecomer to the canon of scripture in the east, the book is never actually quoted in the Orthodox liturgy, it exemplifies the characteristic ethos of eastern Christian worship.

In the Roman Catholic Church's cycles of worship it appears a number of times. It is read at Mass (Year II) and in the Liturgy of the Hours as the spiral of the liturgical year approaches its end, and again at Eastertide; it supplies several canticles for the renewed Liturgy of the Hours; and it is mined for texts for the Solemnity of All Saints on 1 November, one of the most beautiful feasts in the Roman liturgy. On that day an antiphon drawn directly from Revelation (Rev 7:9) is sung at Vespers (evening prayer):

> I saw a great throng, whom no-one could number; they stood before the throne and before the Lamb, alleluia!

Another antiphon, this time from the Benedictine celebration of this feast, develops its imagery in greater detail, listing in hierarchical fashion the serried ranks of heavenly worshippers and calling on them for assistance:

> O, angels and archangels,
> thrones and dominations,
> principalities and powers,
> virtues of the heavens,
> cherubim and seraphim,
> patriarchs and prophets,
> holy doctors of the Law!
> O all apostles,
> martyrs of Christ,
> holy confessors
> and virgins of the Lord,
> holy hermits
> and all saints:
> pray for us to God!

Modern theologians, particularly Orthodox, alert us to the early church's intense awareness that in our earthly worship this angelic liturgy of heaven has been opened to us by God for our participation. Christians understood themselves as having become the New Temple (especially after the Roman destruction of the second Jerusalem Temple in 70 AD). They believed their liturgical assemblies were now the places in which God dwelt through the Spirit and where Christ disclosed his presence through worship. As the assembly celebrated the liturgy, for a brief period the curtain dividing heaven from earth was drawn aside. The community experienced an ascension into glory to sing the liturgy *in conspectu angelorum*, 'in the presence of the angels' (Ps 137(138): 1, following the Vulgate text), i.e. before God's heavenly throne. In this sense every liturgical celebration is a kind of *Missa de Angelis*, a Mass of the angels.[6]

Byzantine tradition offers various imagistic aids to expand the community's liturgical consciousness beyond its immediate context and to promote awareness of this heavenly dimension. Such things include the regular singing of texts specifically associated with the angelic choirs such as the angels' hymn from the Nativity of Christ, 'Glory to God in the highest', and the two forms of angelic *Trisagion* (the thrice-holy hymn), inspired by the prophet Isaiah's vision in the Temple (Is 6:3): 'O Holy God, O Holy and Strong, O Holy and Immortal One, have mercy on us,' and 'Holy, Holy, Holy …'[7]

The first is used during the liturgy of the word in the Orthodox Church and as we have seen on Good Friday in the western liturgies at the veneration of the cross. The second became a climactic moment in the Eucharistic Prayers of all liturgies east and west, concluding the Preface, the section encapsulating the church's principal act of thanksgiving. According to the Book of Revelation the same threefold acclamation plays a prominent part in the liturgy of heaven (Rev 4:8), but with added depths of meaning in the light of the manifestation of the Trinity through the mystery of Christ and the coming of the Holy Spirit.

In addition, through processional movements, Byzantine worship encourages a sense that one is concelebrating with the angelic choirs. Solemn exits and entrances made by the ministers at various

high points of the celebration are characteristic of Orthodox liturgy.
The symbolic movements of the sacred ministers in the earthly
liturgy both symbolise the movements of the heavenly hosts as
they perform their celestial ballet and communicate with earth in
the service of God's will, and make manifest in the church's worship that the two movements are really one. The ministering deacons are seen as icons of the angels, and many of the prayers in the
Byzantine rite speak of the presence of the hosts of heaven in the
worship of earth. The prayer concluding the 'little entrance', the
procession bearing the gospel book through the doors of the
iconostasis, is an excellent example of this genre of liturgical writing:

> O Lord and Master, our God,
> who in heaven has established the orders and armies
> of Angels and Archangels to minister unto your majesty,
> grant that the Holy Angels may make the entry with us
> and with us serve and glorify your goodness …

Much of the praise justifiably heaped on Easter Christian worship for its resplendent beauty is a reaction to this type of ritual
activity with its hieratic splendour and solemn elegance.

The image of an altar in heaven to which the earthly one refers
is typical of classical liturgical rites, being found also in the
Byzantine prayers for the blessing of incense. But even the archi-
tecture of a traditional Orthodox church, with its division between the nave and the altar (the area called the sanctuary in the
west), enshrines this truth right at the heart of their liturgy: the
concealed altar is a symbol of the heavenly one to which it makes a
permanent reference. A further reference is to be found in the late
Byzantine (and contemporary Orthodox) custom of depicting the
heavenly liturgy and altar with Christ as the celebrant, in the
domes of their churches.[8]

Yet this understanding of worship as the church being taken
up into heaven to concelebrate with the angels is not unique to the
east. It is found also in the Roman Catholic and Anglican liturgical
traditions, particularly at the conclusion of the Preface in the
Eucharist when the presiding priest invites the assembly to join

the hosts of heaven in their triumphant song in praise of God's everlasting glory. In the Roman liturgy, in the second half of the venerable Roman Canon, the presiding priest petitions that our sacrifice may be carried up by the hands of a holy angel to God's altar on high, into the presence of the divine majesty, so that being made partakers of the most holy body and blood of Christ at the earthly altar we may be filled with every heavenly grace and blessing.[9]

Two ideas are helpful for understanding how these two levels of reality are connected. The first is that Christ in his ascension into heaven also exalted human nature with him:

> But God, who is rich in mercy, out of the great love with which he loved us, even when we were dead through our trespasses, made us alive together with Christ – by grace you have been saved – and raised us up with him and seated us with him in the heavenly places in Christ Jesus, so that in the ages to come he might show the immeasurable riches of his grace in kindness toward us in Christ Jesus. (Eph 2:4-7)

The second is that, as the celebrant of heavenly worship, he is the true High Priest who leads the celestial liturgy at the altar on high before God's throne:

> But Jesus has now obtained a more excellent ministry, and to that degree he is the mediator of a better covenant ... (Heb 8:6)

And again:

> When Christ came as a high priest of the good things that have come, then through the greater and perfect tent (not made with hands, that is, not of this creation), he entered once for all into the Holy Place, not with the blood of goats and calves, but with his own blood, thus obtaining eternal redemption ...
>
> For Christ did not enter a sanctuary made by human hands, a mere copy of the true one, but he entered into heaven itself, now to appear in the presence of God on our behalf. (Heb 9:11-12; 24)

In our liturgical assemblies the invisible, heavenly Christ comes again among us through the descent of the Holy Spirit who makes the two dimensions of heaven and earth into one. Christ leads our worship, with its system of sacramental symbols, until that final day when we will pass with him into the unveiled vision of heaven. As the Preface for the Roman feast of the Body and Blood of Christ puts it, earth will then be finally united with heaven in singing the new song of creation and we will praise and worship God's glory for ever. Until that time, in the words of a Byzantine liturgical commentator,[10]

> The church is heaven on earth, and in it, the God who is exalted above the heavens dwells and abides.

The joy and beauty of the liturgy, its music, gestures, smells and communal interaction, its sharing together in the one bread and one cup, ought to be a foretaste of the heavenly glory awaiting us at the end of time.[11] The assembly, as it gathers for worship, becomes an earthly icon of the heavenly liturgy above all through its ordered structure as each one carries out his or her distinctive part in the communal liturgical action. The primary symbols are therefore:

- The community of the baptised faithful who constitute the assembly and manifest the communion of the persons of the Trinity.
- The baptismal font, the tomb/womb of death and rebirth, in which the Holy Spirit regenerates Christians into new life.
- The chair of the President of the assembly, who functions as the icon of Christ and the voice of the community.
- The ambo, the table of God's word, where human words, appropriated by God to mediate the divine message, are both proclaimed and broken for distribution in the homily.
- The altar, Christ's banquet table and throne of glory where his sacrifice of praise and thanks is effectually recalled, our gifts are transformed by the descent of the Holy Spirit and the sacramental mysteries of his body and blood are consecrated and shared by believers.
- The tabernacle (at least in Latin Catholic churches), the place of the Blessed Sacrament, reserved for communion of the sick and contemplative prayer.

All these symbols are disclosure-zones where the invisible but incarnate God makes contact with us through material signs, calling us together in the Spirit to celebrate Christ's presence in the sacramental mysteries and filling us with the glory that is to come. The lesser symbols of the liturgy (such as the gospel book, cross and images) focus and intensify our openness to this presence as it gives itself. The living sign-language of the liturgy, its sounds and silences, its light and darkness, its fire and water, communicate the transforming presence that burns at the heart of the church as it assembles around the chair, ambo and altar: for the liturgy exists to manifest and transmit the glory of God.

Yet, as this book is presenting a Benedictine spiritual vision, it is essential not to forget the importance of the Liturgy of the Hours in this radiation of the grace of worship.[12] Despite the recent worthy reform and renewal of this nerve centre of the church's prayer, it is an unfortunate truism that outside monasteries, some larger cathedrals and assorted religious communities, it has not yet achieved the centrality in Roman Catholic spirituality that it deserves. The case is far different in some other Christian traditions such as a number of the eastern churches and most parts of the Anglican Communion. There the Divine Office, the church's daily round of praise and intercession, remains a vital constituent element in the life of prayer and provides regular contact both with holy scripture and the tradition of the church.[13]

Yet if it also occupies a privileged place at the centre of monastic life, that does not make it distinctively monastic – for it is not! It is the prayer of the whole church. Monastics are not somehow 'deputed' to 'recite' it, nor is it 'delegated' to them by 'authority' as a special duty, as many in the past imagined. Rather, simply because a monastery is a Christian community, composed of baptised members of Christ, this most ordinary form of Christian prayer finds there a natural home. It is ancient monastic tradition that monks and nuns are in some (spiritual) sense 'unemployed'. Tradition calls monastic life *otium sacrum* or 'sacred leisure', seeing the cloister as a special zone where one can devote oneself full-time, as explicitly and consciously as possible, to union with God in prayer. Paradoxically, therefore, the monastic's work for God (*opus Dei*) is also his/her sabbath where s/he rests in God's presence.[14]

What then are we doing when we pray the Liturgy of the Hours at regular intervals throughout the day? It is important to realise that, as with all Christian liturgy – whether the celebration of the Eucharist, the feasts of the church's year of grace or the sacraments – we are always and everywhere celebrating the same thing in different forms: the one mystery of Christ, his passing over in glory from death to everlasting life. That is no less true when we chant the church's daily liturgy of prayer and praise.[15]

Here again the high priestly activity of Christ is central. As the Second Vatican Council reminded us, echoing earlier papal teaching, in his descent into the world to bring about our salvation the Son of God introduced into this land of exile the song which is sung eternally in heaven. After his exaltation to God's right hand as the one Mediator and Saviour, he unites us with himself in singing it forever. We do that especially in the chanting of the Liturgy of the Hours when the voice of the Bridegroom (Christ) and that of the Bride (the church) become one.

- As darkness draws to a close and morning glimmers on the horizon we assemble for Matins, a meditative service of attention to the word of God. The Lord discloses his presence as we recite the Psalms and listen to readings from the Bible and tradition. Following St Benedict's arrangement of the Office, this service opens with Psalm 94(95) which exhorts us not to harden our hearts but to listen for the voice of the Lord.

- At Lauds (morning praise) we celebrate the resurrection of Christ, greeting the rising sun – symbol of Christ's light that triumphs over darkness – in the words of the *Benedictus*, the canticle of Zechariah (Lk 1:68-79), John the Baptist's father.

- At noonday we interrupt our ordinary rhythm of life and work to recall Christ's presence in our midst.

- At Vespers (evening prayer) as the sun sinks, we remember that Christ is risen from the dead and that, in the words of the Byzantine Easter-night service, he is 'the light that never sets'. We sing with Mary her canticle, the *Magnificat* (Lk 1:46-55), as the church's song of thanks to God who is our Saviour.

- Finally, facing into the darkness of the night, we chant Compline (night prayer) commending ourselves through Christ into the hands of the Father, asking for the protection of the angels, invoking the assistance of the Holy Mother of God and looking forward to rising in the morning to celebrate once more the praises of the risen one. We sing the canticle of aged Symeon, the *Nunc Dimittis*, asking God to let us depart in peace into the darkness of sleep, having seen the revelation of Christ, the light that enlightens the Gentiles and the glory of his people Israel.

The ultimate goal of this form of prayer is the continuous awareness that one's life is rooted and grounded in Christ and sustained by the Holy Spirit. It aims to make the whole of life, with all its ups and downs, highs and lows and ordinary quotidian rhythms, into a continuous song of praise, a thanksgiving to and glorification of the Father, the Son and the Holy Spirit for the wonderful gift of creation – and the still more wonderful gift of recreation through the passion, death and resurrection of Jesus Christ the Lord. It is an opening of the heart so that God can impress on it the rhythm of the paschal mystery.

Monastic tradition has always taught that through these times of prayer, privileged moments in which the risen Lord punctures a hole in everyday time and reveals the glory of his kingdom, we are taken up in the Holy Spirit to the very throne of God and made concelebrants with Christ in the liturgy of the angels and saints. We stand at the heavenly altar and glorify together the God of surpassing greatness. Again, nothing here is unique in any sense to monasticism. Monastic communities which celebrate the Divine Office do it with and for the whole people of God, not instead of them or in their place. A monastery is – or at least ought to be – an icon of *koinonia*, a community like the church, formed in the likeness of the triune God. That is never truer than when it is engaged in communal liturgical prayer.[16]

In the celebration of the liturgy, the praying assembly is united around Christ, transfigured by grace and made one with its source in the kingdom. Easter is realised anew: earth is reconciled with heaven and humankind made one again with God. The celebration of the liturgy reveals a vision, the radiant vision of the

Holy Trinity: the Father of all consolation disclosing himself to us, Christ descending in kenotic humility so as to lift us up to the throne of grace, the Spirit leading us, ablaze with glory, into the kingdom of eternal light. The church's earthly celebrations are the reflection and manifestation of the worship of heaven and the foretaste of the glory that is to come.

CONCLUSION

And in the End: the Trinity ... (Fig 22)

Who enlightened you with faith in the holy and adorable Trinity? Who has made known to you the economy in the flesh of one of the persons of the Holy Trinity? Was it not Christ's grace, the pledge of the Holy Spirit, dwelling in you? What could be greater than that grace or what more noble and lofty than that wisdom and knowledge?

St Maximos the Confessor

What is at stake ... is an altogether decisive turn-about in the way of seeing God. God is not, in the first place, 'absolute power', but 'absolute love', and his sovereignty manifests itself not in holding on to what is its own but in its abandonment – all this in such a way that this sovereignty displays itself in transcending the opposition, known to us from the world, between power and impotence. The exteriorisation of God (in the incarnation) has its ... possibility in the eternal exteriorisation of God – that is in his tripersonal self-gift.

Hans Urs von Balthasar

We began with the mystery of the Holy Trinity but have never really stopped speaking about it throughout the course of this book. It should by now be evident that the self-manifestation of the Trinity lies at the very heart of the mystery of Christ.[1]

- The love of the Trinity for creation is the beginning, middle and end of all our knowledge of God. The supreme truth about the divine life as God has revealed it to us in Christ and the Holy Spirit is this: God is able to make room for the created world – to relate to it in love – because his own inner life is an infinitely rich set of interlocking relationships, a circle of self-giving and receiving love that freely moves beyond itself in creating and re-creating the world.

- The presence of the Trinity in Christ and the Holy Spirit, mediated through the signs and symbols offered us in the sacramental mysteries of scripture, baptism, the Eucharist, the icon, mystical prayer and the church's year of mysteries, is the unquenchable source of transforming grace. In the church's celebration of the mysteries of Christ, the three divine persons touch our lives, manifest their presence and guide us by their love. The Trinity is the medium as well as the message that gives us life.]

- The vision of the Trinity will be our eternal fulfilment. We are destined to be taken up by love into the circling whirlpool of divine relationships which is God and to celebrate and consummate with him a mystical marriage begun here below, in the earthly liturgies of the church and of the heart. That is the end towards which our faith, prayer and worship and all our striving tends. It is the transcendent goal of the mystery of Christ which brought him down in kenotic humility to lift us up in love.

Although liturgy, theology and spirituality in the early and medieval church (both east and west) were all distinguished by a vibrant awareness of the Trinity, after the period of the Enlightenment the doctrine was gradually neglected. Even today, therefore, ignorance of its importance in the Christian life is still too frequently encountered. If not directly ignored, it is often seen as peripheral rather than central to Christianity, an obscure sacred mathematics incomprehensible to the average person and with little significance for one's daily life as a Christian: how does three go into one and still remain three?

Indeed up to quite recently theology textbooks and manuals encouraged that notion with their highly recondite (and intellectually hypnotising) enumeration of divine properties and attributes, abstracted from the living message of the God revealed in Christ and recorded in scripture. God had one nature, two processions, three persons, four relations and an infinite number of perfections![2] It is not hard to see that the time was ripe for the astonishing resurgence of trinitarian awareness that marked the 20th century.

Added to that is an idea of God arrived at by rational deduction and philosophical speculation – the 'god' of so-called 'natural theology,' a spectral wisp too readily confused with the true God of Christian revelation and worship. It was against that false 'god' that Barth uttered his resounding 'no!', a negative protest echoed by virtually every Christian theologian, regardless of denominational allegiance, in the succeeding years. The discrediting of this abstract 'god' – 'Dawkins' deity' one might call it – thanks to advances in modern science and philosophy which literally rendered him useless, led simultaneously for many to the debunking of the revealed Christian God.[3]

This abstract, detached 'god', proclaimed dead at the end of the 19th century, was never the God and Father of our Lord Jesus Christ anyway.[4] Christians should rejoice that the radical atheism of the 20th century has finally swept away that idol. We should dance on his grave with the atheists, then get on with proclaiming who God is: the Holy Trinity revealed in Christ's cross and resurrection and the outpouring of the Holy Spirit. For God is no 'unmoved mover' or 'supreme being' but a self-manifesting communion of divine persons, a primordial community of love so intense that he is but one God in his essential nature. [Unmoved movers do not love and are not loveable!]

Christians today ought to proclaim courageously that our God is the Holy Trinity. That is the central revealed reality at the heart of the Christian faith. Our confession of it is entirely dependent on God's own freely-chosen self-disclosure, his self-manifestation to the world in the mystery of Christ. We would know nothing at all about it if it had not been revealed to us through the death and resurrection of Jesus of Nazareth, God's incarnate Word, and the coming of the Spirit of wisdom at Pentecost. It is the distinctively Christian reality.[5]

Neither Jews nor Muslims accept such an idea of God. Many of the threefold images of the divine found in Hinduism are comparable to the Christian idea, yet on close inspection are found to be radically different. They involve only temporary personalised manifestations (*Avatars*) of one underlying divine reality, not the eschatological (that is full, final and perfect) revelation granted us in the real flesh-taking of the incarnate Son. He has made known to us that the three persons of the Trinity are not temporary manifestations but eternal, distinct, divine persons who, because they exist in real, enduring relationships, can receive and bless us as creatures without destroying our (relatively) independent being.[6]

Christians (at least those who are not biblical fundamentalists) do, of course, recognise that God is always speaking to us, right from the beginning of time.[7] Creation is already a partial form of revelation although it only achieves its capacity to manifest God most perfectly when illumined by the light of Christ and the decent of the Holy Spirit. The natural world is a primordial form of the grace of God's free self-communication.

Yet Christians insist that in Jesus Christ the definitive 'exegesis' or unfolding of the hidden God (Jn 1:18) has taken place. Christ's teaching, redeeming death on the cross and glorious resurrection, unveil for us both the hidden mysteries of the divine heart and the enigma of our existence. In his cross the Holy Trinity itself has opened a window into our world and let its light appear. God's self-revelation as the Trinity, made through the manifestation of Christ and the Holy Spirit, has forced a radical redefinition of what 'God' really means.

In the gospels that gracious self-opening to us is conveyed symbolically by the various actions through which God punctured the closed complacency of the world. There is the loud voice heard at Christ's baptism and transfiguration (Mk 1:10-11; Mt 3: 16-17; Lk 9: 35) and just before his lifting up on the cross (Jn 12:28-33); there is the rending of the curtain of the Temple which hung before the Holy of Holies and the opening of Christ's side by a lance (Jn 19:34). That last rending was also a wounding, a sign of how much it cost God to reveal himself.

The Trinity disclosed itself in the pain and passion of suffering, transformed by the light of resurrection. Between Good Friday and Easter the Father gave up his Son to us, the Son gave up himself for us and the Spirit was given to us. The time and space between Golgotha and the finding of the empty tomb is the trinitarian disclosure-zone where God has made himself known in blood, pain and forgiving mercy. Suffering is seen to be the place of divine theophany.

Christ's revelation shines out from an abyss of light so bright that its source can only appear to us as high beyond our reach. Both Jews and Greeks already knew that God far exceeded all that thought could think or tongue could tell (Ps 139(140):6; Is 55:8-9). Mystical writers speak of God as 'darkness' but that darkness is caused neither by any privation in God nor by our human limitations but by the infinitely blinding excess of divine light. God is the supreme mystery beyond all being, knowledge or thought: in the words of Denys the Areopagite, a 'luminous darkness.' As we have seen, that impenetrability has not been annulled by the coming of Christ. On the contrary, it is seen to be even more blindingly impenetrable as we gaze into the abyss of the revealed Trinity.[8] The Anglican metaphysical and mystical poet Henry Vaughan expressed this paradox beautifully:

> There is in God (some say)
> A deep but dazzling darkness; As men here
> Say it is late and dusky, because they
> See not all clear;
> O for that night! where I in him
> Might live invisible and dim.[9]

The manifestation of the Trinity in the darkness of faith, like a wave of light flowing out from the bright ocean of divinity or a drink offered from a fountain we can never drain dry, is a crux for ordinary rationality. Yet just as Christ's cross led him to resurrection, so our surrender in prayer to the mystery of the Trinity leads to a resurrection of the human spirit. Understanding has to take the path mapped out by the Trinity in disclosing itself to us – the way of *kenosis*. It has to undergo an inner crucifixion and descent, entering into depths of darkness previously unimaginable for the mind. Having been baptised with Christ, it has to consent freely to embrace the darkness of his tomb if it is to rise with him into the light of trinitarian truth.

Throughout this book I have repeatedly emphasised that the mystery has been revealed for our understanding even if that can only ever be partial. But God's revelation of himself is not a problem to be solved. True knowledge of God is born of love. It comes when understanding, focused in contemplative adoration of the mysteries of Christ celebrated in worship, opens out through them to their transcendent source and enters into the blinding darkness of God. That experience of luminous darkness is beyond both understanding and precise definition. Yet one can cast some light on what is revealed and experienced, by means of human analogies and imagery as God has given them to us in scripture, liturgy and the church's tradition.[10]

Two important images characteristic of Christ's revelation touch our own experience. They can help us to understand something of God's inner life disclosed to us in the mysteries we celebrate. The images are those of God's self-giving love (the *kenosis* of the cross) and the mutual indwelling (*perichoresis*) of Father, Son and Holy Spirit about which Christ speaks in the fourth gospel, an indwelling which reveals the eternal communion (*koinonia*) at the heart of the Trinity.

Self-Giving Love

God's self-giving love is the centre of the teaching of Christ recorded in the New Testament and handed down to us in the mystery of the Eucharist. His entire life was marked by a kenotic movement (Phil 2:6-8) from his descent into the womb of the Virgin (Lk 1:35) through his baptism, ministry of mercy, betrayal, humiliation, crucifixion and burial. It is summed up in the words of the most important sacramental mystery given us by Jesus to keep his *kenosis* constantly before our eyes: his life (symbolised by blood) is given for us and for 'the many' (a Hebrew idiom for 'all'). Jesus, the humanised God, broken and given to all, pierced and poured out for the life of the world, tells us to do this in memory of him ('This is my body/blood which is for you' [Lk 22:14-20]) so that we may become recipients of divine love.

This Jesus who gives himself to the Father and to us is himself the Father's gift (Rom 8:32; Jn 3:16). God breaks out of his inner circle of life so that, in Jesus, the gift of self-giving love can be poured out into space and time. Through that opening (symbolised by his wounded side) comes also the gift of the Spirit, given to us by Jesus thanks to his re-entry into the circle of divine life following his ascension (Acts 1:6-8; 2:1-4; Jn 15:26). Hence Paul's cry of wonder at the depths of the mystery of God revealed in Christ (1 Tim 3; 16), 'The mystery of our religion is great!'

And elsewhere:

O the depths of the riches and wisdom and knowledge of God! How unsearchable are his judgements and how inscrutable his ways!
For who has known the mind of the Lord?
Or who has been his counsellor?
Or who has given a gift to him,
to receive a gift in return?
For from him, and through him and to him are all things.
To him be the glory forever. Amen. (Rom 11:33-36)

Yet it is much easier to talk about self-giving love than to practise it. Paul says that Christians ought to have the same mind as Christ (Phil 2:5) but in the prose preamble (Phil 2:1-5) to the poem of Christ's *kenosis*, he makes it clear that putting on Christ's 'mind' is not just an automatic process. It is one thing to be baptised into his death, but quite another to let it shape and form one's mind. That happens only in repentance and discipleship, through taking the same kenotic route Jesus took in not grasping at equality with God but emptying himself to assume the form of a slave.

Reflecting on the revelation recorded in the New Testament and celebrated in the Eucharist, we come to see from the events of Christ's life, death and resurrection that God is indeed such a circling flow of self-giving love. The work of salvation carried out by the three divine persons in the mystery of Christ is an icon of the inner life of the Trinity. Love alone is capable of apprehending in Christ that God is love (1 Jn 4:7-12; 16-19).

20th century Russian theologians, especially Bulgakov, asserted that the *kenosis* of Christ on Calvary is a window opened out by God, revealing the *kenosis* going on eternally 'within' the life of the Holy Trinity. Christ's earthly cross points us beyond itself towards the 'cross' of undying love set up eternally within the heart of God. That 'cross' is the self-emptying love of the three divine persons for one another and their love for us, revealed in the eternal decision that the Word would become incarnate and suffer his saving passion.[11]

God is infinitely more than just a monad. The Father gives birth to his Son and Word as his perfect image and self-expression and breathes out his life in the Spirit who 'goes forth' from the Father to the Son, rests on him and is breathed 'back' by the Son to the Father as his eternal response in love. Each divine person goes out of himself towards the others in a self-forgetting movement that paradoxically, in the same 'moment', constitutes each one as who he is. It is the eternal reality underlying the law promulgated by Christ in the gospel: only by losing one's life does one actually gain it (Mt 16:25).

Yet because we exist in space and time we inevitably break reality up into discrete 'moments' which follow one another in strict succession from past to future. In God, all reality is simultaneously present for God 'in himself' is 'outside,' 'beyond' and 'above' time. In the very same 'act' and at the very same 'moment' in which each divine person gives himself away, he becomes who he is in the affirming embrace of the others. God is simultaneously perfect unity and perfect distinction, with each divine person simultaneously differentiated and constituted through his communion with the others.

The life of God is like a circling whirlpool of divinely ecstatic movement. We need to rescue that ancient mystical word 'ecstasy' and return it to its trinitarian context. Divine love is supremely ecstatic because each person of the Trinity becomes himself only by going out of himself to exist in and for the others. Yet it has its echo in created space and time. Trinitarian love is the archetype and source of what (under the limitations of our created state) we experience humanly as self-sacrificial love for a beloved.

Yet once again, as was the case in discussing how God the Father may be held to have shared in Christ's cross, we ought to tread carefully. It would be false simply to project on to God in an unreflective way our usually inadequate notions of sacrifice – a word supremely open to abuse, as the poets of World War I reminded us. We need to recall that all language about God is analogical. We cannot speak about sacrifice in God without remembering that we are using the word metaphorically in a groping attempt to grasp God's staggering self-revelation and its capacity to touch and transform our lives. To forget that would be to risk projecting mythological notions into God rather than drawing out the deeper implications of the truth revealed *by* him. All theological and spiritual language has to undergo a purifying baptism and take the way of the cross before it can be raised to the purity required to lead us into the Holy of Holies.[12]

To speak simplistically, or without qualification, of sacrifice 'inside' God (e.g. 'God died for us on the cross') risks implying that death may somehow exist within the Godhead – the worst kind of Gnosticism.[13] Yet death as such is not actually the essence of sacrifice even as we encounter it in the world of human experience. To make a sacrifice (*sacrum facere*) of something is to make that thing holy to the Lord. Self-sacrifice means dedicating oneself entirely to the service of God: death is but the most radical form of such self-dedication. In the agony of Jesus it was not his physical death or cruel sufferings as such which pleased God but the depth of love and readiness for obedience to God's will that his death signified. Only thus can one echo the words of the Psalmist:

> O precious in the sight of the Lord
> is the death of his faithful. (Ps 115(116):15, *Grail translation*)

To suggest anything else risks turning God into a bloodthirsty monster, more like the Moloch or Baal of the Bible than the compassionate Father of our Lord Jesus Christ (2 Cor 1:3-5). Christ's death was in truth the temporal and spatial translation of his love for the Father who eternally begets him.[14]

The guiding idea of Christian revelation is that what has been revealed allows us to understand to some extent, despite our human limitations, the inscrutable depths of God's inner life. In addition, when the ray of revelation shines on human experience it casts much light on what humanity is all about. It is already our common experience that relationships such as marriages, families, friendships, partnerships, and communities like monasteries, parishes, hospitals, scout groups and schools, only really 'work' when their members live a generous life of self-sacrificial love – even though they may never call it by that name.

Communities not based on generous self-giving are usually dismal places in which to live, or worse tyrannical institutions in which efficiency is guaranteed only through the use of naked power. Totalitarian groups of all kinds thrive not on self-limitation and self-abnegation for the good of the other, but on the annihilation of others for the always abstract 'greater good'. They are the exact opposite of trinitarian communion.

The cross teaches us that our common human experience of community can be a small reflection in this world of the light of the Trinity; but thanks to the cross we also learn that self-giving love, taken up by God can be taken infinitely further. Freely chosen self-sacrifice for the good of others was the medium chosen by God to show us that love – the rhythm of give and take pulsating perpetually at the heart of the Trinity – is the hidden heart of all reality. The cross is the measure given by God to help us transform our human being-together. In God, a perpetual movement out of self allows each divine person to rest eternally in the others: *kenosis* is communion. Each person is so utterly present to and transparent to the others, that the light of each can shine through all.[15]

So too in human relationships, only an ecstatic movement out of self in love enables each person to go beyond their limits, thereby finding meaning and creating communion through, with and in others. Persons in love are already small icons of trinitarian transparency; but Christian communities both local and universal, ought to be shining images of trinitarian love, cities built on hilltops that cannot be concealed, communities held together by the Holy Spirit so that Christ's light might shine before the world and lead all peoples of the earth to glorify the Holy Trinity.[16]

Throughout this book I have reflected on the *kenosis* of the Son and Holy Spirit, but Bulgakov also spoke of the *kenosis* of God the Father. In the case of the second and third persons it has been relatively easy to identify what *kenosis* entails. For Christ it consisted in witnessing to the Father through his incarnation and redeeming death; for the Spirit in witnessing in turn to Christ and mounting the undercover operation necessary to guide creation to its transcendent goal. But what might *kenosis* mean in relation to God the Father?[17]

It may be helpful at this point to recall two models (both based on scripture), traditionally employed by theologians to help us imagine the inner life of the Holy Trinity.[18] Both in the Greek east (the Cappadocian Fathers) and the Latin west (St Augustine), an essentially hierarchical model was generally accepted in trinitarian thought. The Father is the 'source and origin' of all divine life, the originating point in a kind of triangular pattern in which the Son and Spirit proceed from him: to borrow a well-known simile from St Irenaeus of Lyons, they are like his two hands. The Son comes forth (as God's *Logos* or Word) through generation (begetting) and the Spirit (as God's breath or *pneuma*) through spiration (proceeding).

Since there is obviously no time in the eternal life of God, the Father's 'priority' is of course strictly ontological (at the level of being) rather than chronological (occurring in time). Yet the processions of the Son and Spirit are extended into time and space through the incarnation of the Word (who thus has two 'births', an eternal one as God and a temporal one as God-made-human) and the coming of the Spirit (who issues eternally from the Father through the Son and is also sent through the Son in time after Christ's ascension). The Father therefore does have, at least conceptually, a certain priority of being (cf the much debated words of Christ in Jn 14:28) as the uniquely originating divine person.[19]

But Augustine also proposed another, more circular model, destined to have a great future in theology and spirituality, emphasising the mutual give and take within the community of divine life and introducing as well the idea that in giving everything to the Son, the Father also gives him the capacity to breathe forth the Spirit, so that the Holy Spirit proceeds eternally also from the Son. Whereas the 'triangular' model speaks of origins, the 'circular' one reminds us of the mutual equality of the three divine persons united in one nature. 'Hierarchical' and 'communal' models are both limited ways of describing a mystery transcending all attempts to grasp or understand it exhaustively.

Typically, however, eastern Orthodoxy offers us not only conceptual or intellectual models but icons to depict the mystery of the Trinity – or more precisely for symbolising it since God's inner life remains transcendent and inaccessible even in its revelation.

The image known traditionally as 'the hospitality of Abraham' is one such icon (Figs 4 and 22). Abraham and his wife Sarah received a visit from three mysterious messengers from God sent to tell them that the aged Sarah would soon conceive a son (Gen 18:1-15). They prepared a meal for their enigmatic visitors. Sarah laughed in incredulity – always a risky thing to do when confronted with a divine messenger – but did indeed conceive and bear Isaac. Christian writers later saw the three as angels, then as symbols of the three divine persons themselves.

In many forms of the icon Abraham and Sarah were omitted so that the focus could fall fully on the Trinity itself. The most famous is that of St Andrew Rublev (c.1360s-1427 or 1430) a marvel of harmonious proportions and geometric ingenuity. Yet even in less sophisticated examples there is a subtle interplay between the triangle (symbol of the distinction between the persons) and the circle (symbol of their unity of nature). This interweaving of forms reminds us that in God there is the perfect communion of three-in-one and one-in-three.

Interestingly it is clear that no one is absolutely certain which of the angels represents the person of the Father. Opinions vary. Is he symbolised by the central one since according to the triangular model he is the source of divine life and therefore 'entitled' to the higher position? Or is it the angel on the left as one looks at the panel since the other two seem to be deferring in some way to him? In truth no one is sure.[20]

By indicating a certain anonymity surrounding each of the persons, the icon thus enshrines an essential truth of trinitarian theology. It speaks powerfully of the Father's *kenosis* for although he is the source of divine life, he is that in a very different manner from the one we might ascribe to him on the basis of human experience. The Father's primacy is not revealed in self-presentation but in the giving away of self; he gives himself wholly to the eternal process of generating his *Logos*/Son and breathing forth his *Pneuma*/Breath.

Therefore, God the Father is anything but a patriarchal figure or a domineering despot. Rather he exercises his primatial role not in domination but in self-surrender, not in self-assertion but in self-abnegation, not in self-presentation but in 'self-veiling', making himself known in and through the two who reveal him – in other words, he reveals himself kenotically. In this he discloses the divine humility at the root of all that is. The Father gives life by constituting and empowering the other two divine persons, freely giving himself away, pouring himself out and even hiding himself in them.

- In *creation* he does this by withdrawing the overwhelming immensity of divine power and presence, creating 'room' in which to speak the world into being through his Word, and vivify it through his Spirit, allowing it time and space both to be and to become.[21]
- In *redemption* he does it by revealing himself through the Son's incarnation and passion and the outpouring of the Holy Spirit.

In the life of Christ, as we learn from the parable of the Prodigal Son (Lk 15:11-32), the Father's kenotic mercy is the divine prototype supplying the model for Jesus' own ministry of mercy and compassion, for he is the very image of the Father (Heb 1:3).

Divine love, the originating source of trinitarian community, is rooted and grounded in the eternal generosity and humility of the Father, mirrored and reflected in the Son and Holy Spirit. It is directly from the heart of the Father that the two other divine persons receive their capacity for *kenosis*, which has been made known to us in the history of salvation and is proclaimed at the sacrificial banquet of the Eucharist.[22] Jesus bore witness only to what he had learnt from the Father:

> Jesus said to them, 'Very truly, I tell you, the Son can do nothing on his own, but only what he sees the Father doing; for whatever the Father does, the Son does likewise. The Father loves the Son and shows him all that he himself is doing ...' (Jn 5:19-20a)

Mutual Indwelling in Love

A second helpful image for illuminating the mystery of the Trinity is the typically Johannine one of mutual indwelling (summarised in theology by the Greek word *perichoresis* and the Latin word *circumincessio*), (cf Jn 6:56-58; 14:9-11; the whole of 17; also 1 Jn 4:7-

16).[23] It found its way into trinitarian thinking from reflection on the person of the incarnate Word. The expression was originally coined to speak of Christ's two natures (divine and human), which as Bulgakov noted, are not simply juxtaposed in his one divine person but connected, in such a way as to interpenetrate one another. In him, on account of his single divine *hypostasis* ('person') holding both natures in unison, we may say that God was human and a human being divine.[24]

The wonder of the incarnation means that the divinity and humanity of Christ indwell and shine though each other, yet without mixture or confusion. The incarnation, cross and resurrection manifest the freely chosen self-humanising of God which leads to the divinisation of all human beings in and through Christ.[25]

Inspired by Christ's teaching in St John's gospel, this image was taken up in trinitarian theology to illustrate that the three divine persons are also not simply with or 'alongside' one another; being rather of a single nature, they dwell *in* one another. Whereas the image of ecstatic, self-giving love emphasises the out-going character of the divine persons, this one lays stress on how they dwell and rest, each one within the others. At the Last Supper, Jesus told Philip after he had asked Jesus to show him the Father:

> 'Have I been with you all this time, Philip, and you still do not know me? Whoever has seen me has seen the Father. How can you say, 'Show us the Father?' Do you not believe that I am in the Father and the Father is in me? The words that I say to you I do not speak on my own; but the Father who dwells in me does his works.' (Jn 14:9-10)

So important is this message that Jesus hammers it home:

> Believe me that I am in the Father and the Father is in me; but if you do not, then believe me because of the works themselves. (Jn 14: 11)

Paul too, reflecting on the Holy Spirit, emphasises how the Spirit enters by right into the very depths of the Godhead:

> … for the Spirit searches everything, even the depths of God. (1 Cor 2: 10b)

The Father dwells perfectly within the being of the Son and the Spirit; the Son within that of the Father and the Spirit; the Spirit within that of the Father and the Son. In and through this resting-in-one-another, the circulating movement of ecstatic love, each person's 'exodus' from self is completed by their mutual indwelling. It is a perfect fusion of motion and rest accomplished in the stillness of the Godhead, a transcendent paradox so far beyond our capacity to understand that we could never have attained it had it not been revealed, and even still can only grope for metaphors to illustrate it. Within the circle of repose in which the three divine persons dwell, all is perfect harmony and luminous transparency. Each of the three dwells in such perfect, interpenetrating harmony with the others that in God there is but one mind and one will, realising and expressing the unity of the one divine nature.

Some tiny limited grasp of this is granted us in the experience of human love. Carried by the vehemence of desire into the heart of the yearned-for object of my predilection, I am wrenched out of myself; yet I am simultaneously invaded by the presence of the other who moves in and takes possession of my soul, ousting every other affection, controlling every waking moment, dominating every thought. That is why unrequited love is such a torture and the conclusion of a love affair as painful as a bereavement. It is the stuff of poetry and opera.

Human love, no matter how intense the passion or how maddening the desire, is always lived under the conditions of limitation and fragility. After an embrace, no matter how intense, there is always the pain of separation and in the end, death. No human being can ever dwell fully in another or be fully transparent to the other. There is always opacity, limitation and an end. As originated creatures developing in time, we are never fully transparent – even to ourselves.

As I grow and develop I come to see that the finite light of my personal consciousness floats like the peak of an iceberg on the infinite sea of the unconscious – my own and the collective unconscious of my race. In each person and in humanity as a whole lies a dark underbelly, a repository of hidden forces and forgotten factors controlling our behaviour and preventing us from seeing others as they are. But it is also a zone rich in spontaneity and unexpected, unrealised possibilities.[26]

As fallen creatures damaged by sin and desperate for acceptance, we try to love by possessing others. We do not respect their precious otherness: instead of relating to them we want to swallow them up. Human passion for the other can become an all-consuming monster. There is no possibility of truly dwelling in the beloved when one's aim is to devour the other and assimilate him or her into one's own being. The consumptiveness of human desire for intimacy is not unique to romantic love. It is equally true of all intimate relationships whether between spouses, parents or friends.

Thankfully we also know that there are human beings for whom love may be stretched beyond yearning. There are also couples who grow beyond the first passionate urgings of desire into a mutual dwelling together as one; just as there are friends who truly seem to become one soul in two bodies. But that lesson is learnt only gradually, in the painful school of detachment, loss and letting go. It is never learnt without suffering of some kind. Hence the Scottish poet Edwin Muir could write:

Time, teach us the art
That breaks and heals the heart.

Time, teach us the art
That resurrects the heart.[27]

Therefore while the fiery eroticism of bridal mysticism is good for expressing the yearning and self-giving nature of love,[28] such non-grasping, non-possessive relationships perhaps provide better glimpses of that other dimension of the inner life of the God revealed in Christ – the restful, calm, mutual indwelling of the three divine persons in one another.

Since God's inner life transcends time and does not therefore develop, there is strictly speaking no precise equivalent in the Holy Trinity to two distinctively human phenomena: unrequited desire and the unconscious. In us, unrequited desire reflects an insecurity which wants to appropriate and control reality (especially the reality of others), for fear of loss, solitude and loneliness. We are hungry creatures yearning for affirmation; but since in God (to use again an imperfect human analogy) each of the divine persons receives their being fully and perfectly from the others in the same 'moment' in which, going out of self, they confer being on the others, there is no unrequited desire and no concomitant necessity for grasping or clinging.

Since each one relinquishes the self into the embrace of the others, each one is in that very 'moment' self-realised by being affirmed for who they are. The kenotic self-emptying of each divine person grounds the communion of all, being itself simultaneously the expression of that communion. Indwelling and outgoing, outgoing and indwelling constitute the perpetual heartbeat of trinitarian life.

Similarly there can be no zone of unconsciousness in God's inner world, no area of the divine nature not immediately and luminously transparent to each of the divine persons (1 Jn 1:5), who dwell entirely in one another and, being outside time, activate and realise together in one perpetual 'moment' the entirety of their single nature. There is, therefore, no dark heart in God needing to be revealed to Godself, no area of divine life not perpetually and permanently present to the three divine persons.[29] As St John wrote:

> This is the message we have heard from him and proclaim
> to you, that God is light and in him there is no darkness at
> all. (Jn 1:6)

In God, rest and movement, desire and attainment are therefore perfectly at one. As God emerges into our experience through acts of gracious self-disclosure, as God makes himself an object to us, we articulate in paradoxes God's impenetrable mystery, using the human categories God chose to assume when he created the world in his Word and Breath and marvellously re-created it in Christ and the Holy Spirit.

Their missions alone have brought us the knowledge of God's inner life. Through the mysteries of Christ, the Father opened a window into the Godhead that we could never have opened for ourselves and the light of grace and truth are pouring through. But more than that we cannot say: gazing in the bright radiance of revelation into the blinding sun of the inaccessible mysteries of God's inner world, we are simultaneously reduced to silent adoration and exalted to ecstatic prayer. Taken up by the Holy Spirit through Christ into the circling life of the Trinity, we find our rest in a fullness which, because it is infinite, can never exhaust our desire – even as it fulfils it.

The Benedictine monk St Anselm of Canterbury famously asked the question *cur Deus homo*? ('Why did God become human?').[30] The revelation of the Holy Trinity, the divine communion of kenotic, forgiving love made know to us through the mystery of Christ, is the answer to that question. Christ, lifted high on the cross, with the Holy Spirit issuing from his wounded side, holds up before us the true image of God and the goal of human existence: to become through divine adoption a child of God, admitted into the circle of the divine life though his own beloved Son, Jesus Christ, crucified and risen. God's loving kindness, the divine humility (Lk 1:78), *is* the revealed mystery.

- It drew the Lord Jesus Christ down from his Father's side, for he did not cling to his equality with God (Phil 2:6-7):
- It brought him into the womb of the Virgin Mary and into the obscurity of Nazareth (Lk 1:31).
- It led him into the waters of the Jordan and along the roads of Galilee (Mk 1:9, 39).
- It drove him into the desert (Mk 1:12) and into the streets of Jerusalem and its Temple (Mt 21:12).
- It led him from the crib (Lk 2:7) to the cross (Jn 19:18) and beyond – even into the darkness of the underworld (1 Pet 3:19).
- It brings him still in the proclamation of the Word (Mt 28:20), the mysteries of Baptism (Jn 3:5) and the Eucharist (Heb 13:10), the holy icons (Col 1:15), the encounter of prayer (1 Thess 17; Eph 3:14-21) and the liturgical celebrations of his church (Mt 18:20; Rev 6:10).

In all these ways divine humility brings Christ afresh into the midst of his assembled people and into the deepest recesses of their hearts. The persons of the Son and Spirit dwelling eternally within the Father's bosom but revealed in time, descend afresh in every act of worship. Invoked in the prayer (*epiclesis*) of God's people as they recall Christ's saving mysteries (*anamnesis*) in the liturgy, they reach down and draw us up with them, leading us together into the communion (*koinonia*) of God's inner life. The Trinity comes to dwell in the church and in every heart that calls on God, filling his people with glory and making present among us the mystery of Christ. Through all these means and a multitude of others, God's self-disclosure in *kenosis* and the revelation of his life as communion invites our own kenotic response: a response that comes from meeting Christ in his mysteries.

Come all you peoples,
let us worship the tri-hypostatic divinity,
the Son in the Father, with the Holy Spirit!
For the Father begets the Son before all time
co-equal and co-adored;
and the Holy Spirit
is glorified with the Father and the Son,
one power, one essence, one Godhead whom we worship.
Let us all say:
'O Holy God, who made all things through the Son,
with the co-operation of the Holy Spirit!
O Holy and Mighty One,
through whom the Father was made known to us
and the Spirit came down into the world!
O Holy and Immortal One, the Spirit-Paraclete
who proceeds from the Father and rests upon the Son!
O Holy Trinity, glory to you!'

May Christ our true God have mercy on us,
Christ who emptied himself
by leaving the bosom of the Father,
assuming our human nature
and making it divine;
Christ who ascended into heaven from where,
enthroned at the Father's right hand,

he sent down the holy, divine and eternal Spirit –
one in substance with himself and the Father,
co-eternal and co-equal to them in honour and glory –
upon the apostles who were enlightened by him
and through them upon the entire universe!
May this same Christ also save us as well,
through the intercession
of his all-pure Mother
and of all his saints:
for he is good and the lover of humankind.
Amen!

Byzantine texts for Pentecost

Notes

INTRODUCTION

1. The practitioners of the so-called 'mystery theology' in the first half of the last century presented the Christian faith on the basis of St Paul's teaching on the mystery of Christ as that had found expression in the diverse liturgical traditions of the early church – above all, Syrian, Greek and Latin. See, O. Casel OSB, *The Mystery of Christian Worship*, London, 1962. For an excellent overview of the main issues, see E. J. Kilmartin SJ, *Christian Liturgy*, Vol I, *Systematic Theology of the Liturgy*, Kansas City, 1988, 91-108. One of the best one-volume introductions to the history and theology of the liturgy – with particular sensitivity to the issues I will consider in this book – is, K. Senn, *Christian Liturgy*, Minneapolis, 1997. For a classic introduction to liturgical theology, see A. Kavanagh OSB, *On Liturgical Theology*, New York, 1984. Very useful also is the recently published textbook by C. Vincie, *Celebrating Divine Mystery: A Primer in Liturgical Theology*, Collegeville, MN, 2009 – (notwithstanding the omission of both Casel and his theology). The work by J. Corbon, *The Wellspring of Worship*, New York, 1988, is an inspiring introduction to the spirituality of the liturgy and well grounded in the Byzantine tradition. It is also worth mentioning the sections of the *Catechism of the Catholic Church*, New York, 1995 (hereafter *CCC*, cited according to the numeration followed in the text), which deal with the liturgy and the Eucharist. While some of it is uneven, much of it is a distillation of the best modern research in sacramental and liturgical theology with the notion of the mystery of Christ and its liturgical re-presentation at its centre. Among contemporary Orthodox theologians, J. D. Zizioulas' book, *Being as Communion: Studies in Personhood and the Church*, New York, 1985, is certainly the most important representative of a theological vision uniting dogma, liturgy and modern philosophy; but see also the work of A. Golitizin, one of the most interesting writers currently working in this field. See *Et introibo ad altare dei: The Mysticism of Dionysius Areopagita*, Thessalonica, 1994. Golitizin has recovered the biblical basis of Orthodox spirituality and connected it creatively with Jewish apocalyptic and the literature of the Second Temple.

2. I say 'spiritual traditions' because there has always been more than one way of being a Benedictine. For that reason I prefer to speak of 'Benedictine spiritual practices' than of 'Benedictine spirituality' as such.

However, the centrality of the Liturgy of the Hours (*opus Dei*) in St Benedict's Rule has always kept the liturgy at the forefront of spiritual awareness for most Benedictines throughout history.

3. See J. Leclercq OSB, *The Love of Learning and the Desire for God*, London, 1978. Leclercq originally put forward the thesis that 'monastic theology' represented an alternative tradition to scholasticism in Medieval Europe, being the survival of the older patristic model which continued to flourish in the Benedictine and Cistercian monasteries. Today we recognise that medieval spiritual and intellectual divisions were not so simple: there was also the vernacular tradition represented by many of the great women mystics. I am far from imagining that 'monastic theology' is the only method of doing theology or the best way in every circumstance: it has for example little to say about just wars, genetic engineering or the jurisdiction of the Pope. Its main advantage is in keeping the mind and heart focused on the centre of the Christian message as the church celebrates it day after day and year after year in worship, drawing life from the presence of Christ and the Holy Spirit in prayer. One might envisage it as underpinning other forms of theology by helping their practitioners to stay connected to the objective sources of Christian life.

4. There has been something of an explosion of interest in *lectio divina* in recent years. For a clear introduction, see C. Stewart OSB, *Prayer and Community*, London, 1998, 36-41. Stewart's book is the best modern account in English of Benedictine spiritual traditions. It should be read in tandem with T. Kardong OSB, *The Benedictines*, Delaware, 1988, equally the best short account of the institutions and traditions of Benedictine life in general. Both authors reflect and respect the pluralism that has always been typical of this movement in the church.

5. It is erroneous to claim that the reform of the liturgy came only with the Second Vatican Council. That council was actually part of a process stretching from St Pius X to the work of the current Pontiff. One of the most important pre-conciliar reforms was the restoration, in 1951, of the Paschal Vigil to the night of Holy Saturday, followed by the reform of the entire Holy Week liturgy in 1955/6. Among the most beneficial post-conciliar reforms were the provision of a three year cycle of biblical readings after the restricted scriptural diet of the unreformed Roman Rite along with a great infusion of prayers for the coming of the Holy Spirit at the Eucharist – that divine person having previously been relegated to a single invocation in the rite of the preparation of the gifts. Without these three pillars of the church's liturgical tradition – the centrality of Easter, the primacy of God's word and the irreplaceable role of the Holy Spirit – it would be difficult to write a book using the liturgy as a way into the mystery of Christ. Of course, having an excellent liturgical rite does not guarantee that it will always be celebrated well. There are no doubt sloppy, slipshod and unworthy liturgical celebrations at times – as I am reliably

informed was often the case in the unreformed rite.

6. In Glenstal, within the overall idiom of a traditional monastic liturgy, we have evolved what seems to be a generally successful balance between quantity and quality, and tradition and innovation in our worship.

7. See the now classic study of G. Wainwright, *Doxology*, New York, 1980.

8. There is a brief discussion of this vision in I. Ryelandt OSB, *St Benedict the Man*, St Meinrad's Abbey, 1950, 33-34, in which it is located within the wider spiritual life of the great monastic founder.

9. St Gregory Palamas (1296/7-1357), monk of Mt Athos and Archbishop of Thessalonica, referred to the Roman Pope's account of St Benedict's vision in defence of the monks of Athos' claim to have experienced God as light during their mystical contemplation. See, N. Russell, *The Doctrine of Deification in the Greek Patristic Tradition*, Oxford, 2004, 304-309. Surprisingly, Russell mentions neither Pope Gregory's account of Benedict's vision nor the use made of it by St Gregory Palamas. However, his excellent study is now the standard introduction to this topic and essential reading for anyone who wishes to understand the patristic and Byzantine sources of contemporary Orthodox theology.

10. This understanding of the cosmos as permeated by the light of God's energies leads to the spiritual experience of *theoria physike* or the contemplation of nature, in which creation becomes transparent to the inner vision of the heart when it has been purified by prayer and fasting. The world becomes again what God originally meant it to be before the fall: a sacrament of the divine presence. Among modern Orthodox theologians one of the most interesting expositors of this sacramental vision of creation was the Romanian confessor of the faith and theologian, Dumitru Staniloae. See C. Miller's study of Staniloae, *The Gift of the World*, Edinburgh, 2000.

11. The notion of spiritual senses has had a long and complex history in Christian mysticism. See A. Louth, *The Origins of the Christian Mystical Tradition*, Oxford, 1981, 67-70, where he discusses its importance in the writings of Macarius the Syrian.

12. Marmion was a Dublin diocesan priest who entered the Abbey of Maredsous in Belgium in 1886. The monastery was soon to be at the centre of the burgeoning liturgical movement in Europe. For the details of his life, see M. Tierney OSB, *Marmion, A Short Biography*, Dublin, 2000. He was beatified by Pope John Paul II in 2000. Marmion was primarily a holy man, an experienced spiritual guide and an inspiring retreat director. His books, culled from his spiritual conferences, were among the first to reorientate the spiritual life away from an obsession with subjective states of soul and towards the revealed mystery of Christ. He did not live to see Glenstal (Ireland's only male Benedictine Abbey) come into being but its founders, some of whom had been his disciples, were inspired by his memory and teaching. Marmion was fond of emphasising in his spiritual conferences that 'the mysteries of Christ are our mysteries': see, *Christ in his Mysteries*, trs Mother M. St Thomas, London, 1924, 3-18. For a good ac-

count of his life and legacy, see, A. Nichols OP, 'In the Catholic Tradition: Dom Columba Marmion (1858-1923)', in, *Priests and People*, 11, 7 (1997), 282-288.

13. Odo Casel (1886-1948) was a monk of the Abbey of Maria Laach in Germany but spent much of his life as spiritual father to the Benedictine nuns of Herstelle. Casel was much criticised by some in his own day, for supposedly having argued that the ancient pagan mysteries had influenced the Christian liturgy. In fact he argued not for direct influence but for their character as a medium partly inspired by God to serve as a 'preparation for the gospel' when it would be revealed – a perfectly respectable position in mission theology nowadays. In truth his real offence lay in disagreeing with the sacred cow of neo-Thomist theology and in his preferring effective symbolism over instrumental causality. He was a rare example of a scholar monk, mystical theologian and lover of the liturgy combined in one. Casel's works are profoundly theological but written in a beautifully limpid, lyrical style. See, O. Casel OSB, *Mystery*, 56-57. The book was reissued in 1999 with a helpful introduction by A. Kavanagh OSB, locating Casel in historical context. A good account is, A. Nichols OP, 'Odo Casel Revisited', *Antiphon: A Journal for Liturgical Renewal*, 3, 1 (1998), 12-20. For a technical analysis, critical yet sympathetic, see E. J. Kilmartin SJ, *The Eucharist in the West*, ed. R. Daly SJ, Collegeville, MN, 1998, 267-282. Casel tended to underestimate Jewish influences on Christian liturgy, no doubt reflecting the era and ethos within which he lived and probably at times read his own theory too quickly into the patristic sources, but his fundamental intuition remains valid and fruitful.

14. Chapters 1 and 5 of *Sacrosanctum Concilium*, (*SC*), the Second Vatican Council's document on the liturgy, are particularly marked by his influence; while the CCC reflects his thinking at every point in its presentation of the mystery of Christ and its presence in the liturgy.

15. The Rule itself needs to be located within the ongoing stream of the various Benedictine traditions which have lived, adapted and interpreted it throughout the centuries: there ought to be no 'fundamentalism of the Rule'. Important though it is, it is subordinate to holy scripture and the tradition of the church. It is a guide to Christian life according to the gospel rather than a programme of regular observances to be imposed like a straitjacket. For the Rule itself see *The Rule of St Benedict*, trs J. McCann OSB, Stanbrook Abbey, 1937. All references are to the 'Rule', followed by the chapter and page number.

16. The best general introduction remains that of T. Spidlik SJ, *The Spirituality of the Christian East*, Kalamazoo, 1986. Although at times over schematic and rather weak on the importance of the liturgy, it does at least acknowledge the existence of other eastern churches as well as the Orthodox.

17. Quite apart from the fundamental work of the Second Vatican

Council in *Unitatis Redintegratio* (the decree on ecumenism) the life and teaching of the late Pope John Paul II (especially in *Ut Unum Sint*, 1995, his impassioned encyclical on Christian unity) should have made it clear to most Catholics that commitment to ecumenism is a non-negotiable factor in the church's apostolate.

18. See A. Louth, *Origins*, 97; see also the anthology of texts selected from the works of St Gregory, edited and translated by H. Musurillo SJ, *From Glory to Glory*, New York, 1979, 25. J. Daniélou SJ in his introduction (p 25) gives an illuminating commentary on Gregory's experience.

19. I was particularly struck by Newman's sense that rediscovering the teaching of the church fathers might allow the divided churches to find ways to evaluate and eventually resolve the endless debates between Catholics and Protestants regarding issues like grace and the sacraments: in this as in so much else, Newman was a prophet. See, *The Cambridge Companion to Newman*, ed. I. Ker and T. Merrigan, Cambridge, 2009.

20. See G. Collins, *The Glenstal Book of Icons*, Dublin, 2002, 47.

21. The long-awaited translations, whatever their stylistic felicities or failings, should at least provide texts in which the theological substance of the originals will be retained, thus allowing them to be used for scholarly purposes.

22. 'Mysticism' is actually a modern term which has come to mean pretty much anything one wants it to mean. See the entry, 'Mysticism', by D. Turner in, *The Oxford Companion to Christian Thought*, ed. A. Hastings, A. Mason and H. Pyper, Oxford, 2000, 460-462. In the early church people spoke of 'mystical theology' or 'contemplation', meaning a secret, hidden experiential knowledge of God, granted through participation in the church's liturgy and meditation on the holy scriptures. Emphasis fell less on the analysis of one's own subjective spiritual experiences and more on the objective mysteries of Christ: the experiences were of interest only in so far as they exemplified the latter. They were, in the happy phrase of G. Chantraine SJ, 'a lived exegesis of the mysteries of the Lord'. See G. Chantraine SJ, 'Exegesis and Contemplation', in D. L. Schindler, ed, *Hans Urs von Balthasar, His Life and Work*, San Francisco, 1991, 134. In this vast field two essential introductions to the complexities of Christian mysticism can be recommended: the first volume of B. McGinn's magisterial study, *The Presence of God. A History of Western Christian Mysticism: the Foundations of Mysticism*, London, 1992, esp 266-326; and Louth, *Origins*. See also the discussion of 'ecclesial mysticism' by J. Zizioulas in *Communion and Otherness*, London, 2006: his thinking on this topic underpins many of the assumptions in this book. Above all, authentic Christian mystical theology is about being initiated by the Holy Spirit through the celebration of Christ's mysteries, into communion with the Holy Trinity: it is therefore intrinsically pneumatic, ecclesial, christocentric, liturgical and trinitarian; it is authentic only when the one who claims to experience

it is actively trying to live a life of love in the likeness of Christ – the sole criterion for judging any phenomenon in the Christian life (1 Jn 2: 4-6); it is not about esoteric experiences, emotional thrills or introspective navel-gazing.

23. Throughout this book I will be using the notion of *kenosis*, signifying the divine self-emptying voluntarily undertaken by the second person of the Trinity, the Son and Word of God, in his saving mission, out of obedience to the Father's will. In defence of Christ's real divinity and humanity, the church defined (in three ecumenical councils: Nicaea 1 [325], Chalcedon [451] and Constantinople II [680-1]) that a divine person assumed a human nature into unity with himself, so that the incarnate Word Jesus Christ exists in two natures and with two wills. However, apart from stating that the humanity of Christ has its deepest personal ground not in a human personality but in the person (*hypostasis*) of the eternal Son of God, nothing further was defined about how that divine-human person actually operates in those two natures and wills: did he voluntarily limit his divine attributes (such as omniscience and omnipotence) or did he literally abandon them (surely a metaphysical impossibility)? Such questions pertain to the exegesis of scripture and are – providing the basic dogmatic postulates are not denied nor the mystery violated by a spirit of irreverence – legitimate areas for speculation. Two essential introductions are, A. B. Bruce, *The Humiliation of Christ*, Edinburgh, 1881, and the incomparable work by H. Urs Von Balthasar, *Mysterium Paschale*, Edinburgh, 1990. Balthasar's book is a fine example of the theological balancing act required in order not to fall off the tightrope of orthodoxy. His careful use of analogy illuminates the mystery and shows how spiritually relevant it is for the Christian life. He himself acknowledged the influence of a groundbreaking book published in Russian in 1933 by one of the greatest Orthodox theologians of the 20th century, Fr S. Bulgakov: *The Lamb of God*, (now available in English translation, Grand Rapids, Michigan, 2008). *Kenosis* in these writers becomes a guide to understanding God's dealings with the world not only in redemption but in creation as well. The Holy Trinity having revealed itself in Christ's *kenosis* as a self-sacrificing communion of love is also seen as capable of adapting and limiting itself in order to let creation come into existence. Much light is thereby thrown on complex theological problems such as the relationship between the eternal God and a world created in time, and the issue of God's capacity or 'incapacity' to change. It is essential to note that *kenosis* does not mean God somehow temporarily ceasing to be divine, a sublime impossibility indeed. Rather it asserts that his capacity to limit his own power out of love is the greatest possible manifestation of that power. A moving discussion of the practical implications of this theme in Russian spirituality is to be found in N. Gorodetsky, *The Humiliated Christ in Modern Russian Thought*, London, 1938.

24. On the *kenosis* of the Holy Spirit see S. Bulgakov, *The Comforter*, Grand

Rapids, Michigan, 2004, 219-227, the second volume of his epic theological trilogy, 'On God-manhood'. A good synthetic presentation of the theology of the Trinity from an Orthodox perspective, with special stress on the role of the Holy Spirit in the Eucharistic liturgy is, B. Bobrinskoy, *The Mystery of the Trinity*, New York, 1999, 165-196. Since the word 'Spirit' is feminine in Syriac, neuter in Greek and masculine in Latin; and since perfectly respectable theologians such as Matthias Scheeben (1835-1888), Yves Congar OP (1904-1995), Jürgen Moltmann (b 1926) and of course Bulgakov (1871-1944) himself have noted both the feminine characteristics of the Spirit and his/her special relationship with the Virgin Mary and the church, it seems reasonable to use feminine and masculine pronouns (along with s/he) together, to designate this divine person who is not incarnate – and therefore transcends gender. This might go some way towards meeting some of the legitimate aspirations of women, and to acknowledging that since human beings are made in God's image and likeness, it must be possible to speak of a feminine dimension in God. See the thoroughly sensible discussion of this in J. O'Donnell SJ, *The Mystery of the Triune God*, London, 1988, 97-99.

25. See, Bulgakov, *Lamb*, 359-394. For an excellent introduction to Bulgakov's theological method, see, A. Louth, 'Sergii Bulgakov and the Task of Theology', *Irish Theological Quarterly*, 74, 3, 2009, 243-258. A very helpful guide to the complexity of his thought is also available in A. Nichols OP, *Wisdom from Above. A Primer in the Theology of Father Sergei Bulgakov*, Leominster, Herefordshire, 2005.

CHAPTER ONE

1. See Casel, *Worship*, 9-12. One of the most important theologians of the 19th century left us a magisterial treatment of the Christian faith from the perspective of the mystery revealed: M. Scheeben, *The Mysteries of Christianity*, St Louis, 1946. Although somewhat weak on the liturgical dimension (not untypical of the 19th century) this is still one of the most comprehensive investigations of the theme that has ever been made. Three entries in *The New Catholic Encyclopedia*, Washington, 1967, retain their value having been written by scholars each of whom was an outstanding expert in his field: R. Brown SS, 'Mystery (in the Bible)', 148-151; A. Dulles SJ, 'Mystery (in theology)', 151-153; I. H. Dalmais OP, 'Mystery Theology', 164-166. Dulles summarises the various meanings of mystery in the early church: the salvific counsel of God, hidden but partially revealed in the prophets and then unveiled in Jesus Christ; God's mighty acts by means of which he saved us (especially the passion, death and resurrection of Christ); the hidden (typological) meaning of the Hebrew scriptures revealed in Christ; the sacraments and liturgical actions of the church (from the 4th century on); contact with the hidden things of God

through spiritual experience (especially in St Gregory of Nyssa's writings). For a stimulating and synthetic account of the understanding of the mystery in patristic, medieval and modern theology, see L. Bouyer, *The Christian Mystery. From Pagan Myth to Christian Mysticism*, Edinburgh, 1989, esp. 5-18, 72-91 and 95-109.

2. I am aware that not every biblical scholar denies the authorship of Paul in the case of Colossians and Ephesians but there does seem to be a general consensus that those letters (and the Pastoral Epistles) do not come directly from his hand. For a helpful summary of the case for and against, see, A. E. Harvey, *A Companion to the New Testament*, Cambridge, 2004, 610-611, 637-638 and 650-660. Even if they were written by a disciple or group of disciples rather than Paul himself, their inclusion in the biblical canon indicates the church's acknowledgement of their inspiration.

3. Karl Barth's massive *Church Dogmatics*, (CD), is an extended commentary on the theme of God's covenant with humanity in Christ. See E. Busch, *Barth*, Nashville, 2008, 39-57.

4. Busch, *Barth*, 43. For a clear account of traditional Reformed notions of the covenant see R. W. Ward, *God and Adam: Reformed Theology and the Creation Covenant*, Wantirna, Australia, 2003, which summarises the whole tradition from the Reformations of the 16th century to the 20th century. Barth was rightly critical of this tradition for forgetting the absolute predestination of Christ as God the Father's original covenant partner – and the human race in him.

5. See *Nostra Aetate*, (NA) the Second Vatican Council's declaration on non-Christian religions, in *The Documents of Vatican II*, ed A. Flannery OP, Dublin, Dominican Publications, 1975, 740-741; see also, CCC, 62-63.

6. See the opening of *Lumen Gentium* (LG), the council's document on the church, in Flannery, *Documents*, 350: ... the church, in Christ, is in the nature of sacrament – a sign and instrument, that is, of communion with God and of unity among all men ...'

7. Orthodox theologians, with their intense awareness of the resurrection of Christ, particularly emphasise the gift of new life in the Holy Spirit granted by him in Christian faith and baptism. Resurrected life will be the transformation of embodied persons by God's grace, not just the survival of 'immortal souls'. See Zizioulas, *Communion*, 268-269. One of the best Orthodox accounts of how human beings share in the divine life is P. Nellas, *Deification in Christ: The Nature of the Human Person*, New York, 1997. See also C. Yannaras, *Elements of Faith: An Introduction to Christian Theology*, Edinburgh, 1991, 66: 'Faith in *eternal life* (author's emphasis) is not an ideological certainty; it is not defended with arguments. It is a motion of trust, a deposit of our hopes and our thirst for life in the love of God.'

8. See St Ignatius of Antioch's letter to the Magnesians, in *The Faith of the Early Fathers*, trs W. A. Jurgens, Minnesota, 1970, 19.

CHAPTER TWO

1. See Balthasar's profound comments on 'negative theology' (i.e. the progressive denial of all attributes, positive and negative to God, who infinitely surpasses all that can be thought or spoken), quoted by G. Chantraine SJ, in 'Exegesis and Contemplation', in Schlinder, *Hans Urs von Balthasar*, 142-143: 'Here the distinctively Christian twist appears, which is distinguished from all abstract speculation about God ... This turning consists in the fact that the philosophical incomprehensibility of the being of God, expressed in the formulas of "negative theology", is transformed into a "theological" incomprehensibility of the love of God – *for the Christian knows what the philosopher does not, that God is love. It is radically incomprehensible that absolute love, heaped up in the fullness of the Trinitarian view, could, because of the sinner that I am, strip itself of its diverse traits in order to go to death in deepest darkness.* Confronted with this *ridiculous absurdity*, all negative theology is an innocent naïvete ... That Christ, by his completely obedient attitude, *should not present himself* as the supreme source of love; that he should not make of his human existence the revelation of his own eternal love, but the transparent medium of the love of the Father – that makes the paradox at one and the same time *definitively impossible to conceive* and nevertheless susceptible of being existentially understood' (my emphasis added).

2. K. Rahner, 'Mystery', in, *Encyclopedia of Theology*, ed K. Rahner SJ, London, 1975, 1000: 'Because of what God is, it is evident that his incomprehensibility essentially belongs to him and is not something which ceases with the beatific vision.'

3. As the great, much maligned, but recently rehabilitated theologian Origen (c. 185-254) was accused of having taught – justly or unjustly.

4. Orthodox theology in the 20th century has made this idea of God's self-manifestation in his 'energies', while yet remaining impenetrably inscrutable in his innermost essence, a basic principle of the Christian faith. Yet it does not mean that there is some luminous barrier erected between an unknown God and us. God's procession outward towards us entails an existential movement in which he is simultaneously revealed and yet remains unknowable. It is actually no different in human relationships where one truly meets a real person yet never has exhaustive knowledge of him or her: Yannaras, *Elements*, 42-44. At the back of it all is the obscure figure of Denys the Areopagite, a 5th century pseudonymous (probably) Syrian monk whose writings exercised enormous influence on Christianity. His magnificent vision of the world cascading forth in procession from the Trinity and returning thereto moved by desire, is one of the most beautiful cosmic theologies ever devised. See *Pseudo-Dionysius. The Complete Works*, trs C. Luibhéid, with P. Rorem, New York, 1987, 49-58. For two excellent but very different introductions to this important writer, see A. Louth (Orthodox), *Denys the Areopagite*, New York, 1989 and W. Riordan (Roman Catholic), *Divine Light: The Theology of Denys the*

Areopagite, San Francisco, 2008. It is truly remarkable that so shadowy a figure should have generated so much light in Christian history.

5. One of the most creative attempts in modern times to probe the meaning of this primary cosmic revelation was that of the English Benedictine monk Bede Griffiths who, having transferred to India, dedicated his life to building bridges between Hinduism and Christianity. Yet he was no mere syncretist, mixing up various religious elements to produce a faith of his own. Rather he sought to probe the mystery of God's presence in the world through contemplation and dialogue with other spiritual traditions. See W. Teasdale, *Bede Griffiths. An Introduction to his Interspiritual Thought*, Vermont, 2003. See also the work of J. Dupuis SJ, *Toward a Christian Theology of Religious Pluralism*, New York, 1997. It is important to note that this intuitive, contemplative discovery of divine traces in the world, since it presupposes the working of the hidden invisible grace of Christ, is not simply the kind of 'natural theology' constructed by unaided reason (really a tired 18th century preamble to theology, able to be hijacked to suit various ideological projects including National Socialism) against which Karl Barth inveighed so vigorously. See, G. Bromiley, *Historical Theology. An Introduction*, Edinburgh, 1978, 426. Yet the grace is always that of Christ and the Holy Spirit. Barth did not deny that Christ's grace worked beyond the explicit proclamation of the gospel but as a Christian theologian he considered it his responsibility to proclaim where he was certain it was working. See, J. A. di Noia OP, 'Religion and the Religions', in *The Cambridge Companion to Karl Barth*, ed J. Webster, Cambridge, 2000, 253, on Barth's idea of 'words outside the church (Barth says, '*extra muros ecclesiae*') by non-Christians and by Christians exercising their responsibilities in the world. Although these words are not identical with the Word of Christ, they can be neither ignored nor dismissed.' Yet one would not necessarily reach nowadays for the works of Barth in trying to make sense of the world's religious diversity.

6. *The Upanishads*, trs J. Mascaró, London, 1965, 101-102.

7. Krishna is undoubtedly the best-loved of all these avatars. See, *The Bhagavad Gita*, trs J. Macaró, London, 1962, which tells the story of his guiding intervention at a battle symbolising the conflicts which assail the self. It is as much loved by Hindus as the New Testament is by Christians. In his book on the Holy Spirit, Bulgakov reflected on God's self-revelation beyond the frontiers of the Judaeo-Christian traditions and specifically in ancient paganism. Invoking the figure of Melchizedek and employing the notion of 'natural grace' coming through creation, he concluded that although pagan revelation was not on a par with that accorded to Israel, 'It is necessary to recognise and appreciate the full value of pagan piety, expressed in the search for God, in prayer, sacrifice and good works … Pagan piety turns out to be possible and even has a possible religious value … this means that this is not foreign to the Spirit of God.' See

Bulgakov, *Comforter*, 236-239. It is worth noting that he was writing that already in the nineteen-thirties.

8. See, J. J. Castelot, 'The Temple of Jerusalem', in *The New Jerome Biblical Commentary*, ed R. E. Brown SS, J. A. Fitzmeyer SJ, R. E. Murphy O Carm, London, 1989, 1262-1266. On the deeper meaning of the Temple, its place in Jewish religiosity and its influence on Christianity see Y. Congar OP, *The Mystery of the Temple*, London, 1962.

9. Scheeben, *Mysteries*, 331-334; Casel, *Mystery*, 57-58. See M. Barker, *Temple Themes in Christian Worship*, London, 2007.

10. On Eckhart, see the excellent introduction by R. J. Woods OP, *Eckhart's Way*, Dublin, 2009, 80. For St John of the Cross, see *The Ascent of Mt Carmel*, trs K. Kavanaugh OCD and O. Rodriguez OCD, Washington, 1979, 179-180.

11. R. Williams, *Wrestling with Angels. Conversations in Modern Theology*, London, 2007, 101.

12. C. Braaten, *Principles of Lutheran Theology*, Minneapolis, 2007, 146.

13. See, G. Forde, *On Being a Theologian of the Cross,* Grand Rapids, Michigan, 1997, 79-81. See also P. Althaus, *The Theology of Martin Luther*, Philadelphia, 1966, 25-34.

CHAPTER THREE

1. The historical-critical method of biblical interpretation which became the dominant one in the 20th century concerned itself in form-criticism with isolating and interpreting the various fragments which came to-gether to constitute the Bible. Redaction criticism too looked at how the editors achieved their finished products on the assumption that the sacred books are (at least initially) to be interpreted as critically as any other book would be. Unfortunately, using these methods, it can at times be difficult to see how the holy scriptures actually mediate the word of God in and to the Christian community, although they have highlighted the crucial im-portance of the community in the transmission of the texts. Other modern methods such as the canonical approach are more compatible with sys-tematic and liturgical theology in that they deal with the Bible as a whole, i.e. as the book of the church. Traditional patristic methods of interpreta-tion which sought deeper meanings within the texts were out of vogue for much of the last half of the twentieth century but are currently undergo-ing a degree of rehabilitation. Without returning to an exaggerated use of allegory it can hardly be denied that the principle of typology – i.e. within the scheme of revelation and salvation history, persons and events of the old covenant are providentially ordered to their fulfilment in Christ and the church – remains unavoidable. Apart from being used throughout the New Testament, it is actually the church's way of reading scripture, given that in every historic liturgical rite the readings are arranged in a sequence of prophecy and fulfilment and the extra-biblical texts play repeatedly

with the types and figures of the Old Testament and their fulfilment in the new dispensation. On all these issues see the document issued by the Pontifical Biblical Commission, *The Interpretation of the Bible in the Church*, Vatican City, 1993. It is rather weak on the liturgical use of scripture however, saying somewhat disingenuously for example (120), 'By regularly associating a text of the Old Testament with the text of the gospel, the cycle (i.e. of biblical readings) often suggests a scriptural interpretation moving in the direction of typology. But, of course, such is not the only kind of interpretation possible.' Actually that is done without fail on every Sunday and Solemnity of the liturgical year and reinforced by the chants accompanying the liturgical actions.

2. See, C. F. D. Moule, *The Holy Spirit*, Oxford, 1978, 36-37, which explains very well the Johannine concept of the two paracletes.

3. Zizioulas, *Communion*, 190-204 summarises and analyses this development.

4. Among the numerous pronouncements of the Second Vatican Council on the nature of the church, see *Unitatis Redintegratio*, (*UR*), the decree on ecumenism in, Flannery, *Documents*, 453-454: 'After being lifted up on the cross and glorified, the Lord Jesus poured forth the Spirit whom he had promised, and through whom he has called and gathered together the people of the New Covenant, which is the church, into a unity of faith, hope and charity … It is the Holy Spirit, dwelling in those who believe and pervading and ruling over the entire church, who brings about that wonderful communion of the faithful and joins them together so intimately in Christ that he is the principle of the church's unity.'

5. From the vast literature that could be cited, see the entry on christology in 'Aspects of New Testament Thought', in *The New Jerome*, 1354-1359. There had been a tendency in some scholarly circles, influenced by liberal Protestantism in the late 19th century, to view Jesus simply as a Jewish preacher elevated to divine status thanks to the so-called 'Hellenisation of the gospel'. Fascinating revisionist scholarship in the last twenty years has challenged that assumption and through the interpretation of Jewish Second Temple literature and Jewish Christianity has arrived at the more plausible position that a high christology (i.e. Jesus as identified with God) was rooted in Christianity's original Jewish matrix from the beginning. For two interesting though different interpretations, see L. Hurtado, *One God, One Lord*, New York, 1998 and R. Bauckham, *Jesus and the God of Israel*, Milton Keynes, 2008. For a good general historical and theological account of traditional christology, see C. E. Braaten, 'The Person of Jesus Christ', in *Christian Dogmatics I*, ed C. E. Braaten and R. Jenson, Philadelphia, 1984.

6. Hurtado, *One God*, xi-xiii.

7. See the extended discussion in Bulgakov, *Lamb*, 213-261. A slightly more accessible account is to be found in his short work, *Sophia: The*

Wisdom of God, New York, 1993, 88-95. Despite its brevity however, this is not an introduction: rather it is a map for poring over the territory already covered in his larger books. Unnecessary speculation should be avoided: see the occasionally outlandish theories of various German academic theologians of the 19th century in, Bruce, *Humiliation*, 134-163. He wisely concludes (p 191): 'Wisdom dictates that we should clearly and broadly distinguish between the great truths revealed to us in scripture, and the hypotheses which deep thinkers have invented, for the purpose of bringing these truths more fully within the grasp of their understandings.' A good exegesis of the 'hymn of the kenosis' is available in, R. P. Martin, *An Early Christian Confession*, London, 1960, emphasising its character precisely as a liturgical text and not just a statement of doctrine. Had that been remembered more frequently it might have led to better interpretation. Recent attempts to argue that the text does not refer to a pre-existent kenotic decision of Christ but to an intra-mundane *kenosis* reversing the disobedience of Adam leave me frankly unconvinced, quite apart from their being opposed to virtually the entire exegetical tradition of the church – united and divided – until the modern era. See the wise comments of Harvey, *A Companion*, 630: '... Paul speaks in this way of Christ, not as an example of divinely inspired human virtues, but as exhibiting in the broad sweep of his destiny the obedience and self-humiliation of one whose status of equality with God did not prevent him from descending to the depths of human suffering and ignominy, and who only then was awarded his place of supremacy under God in the whole created universe.'

8. Bauckham, *Jesus*, 240-241.

9. For a reliable commentary which clears a path through the thickets of scholarly research around 'John', see, S. Smalley, *John: Evangelist and Interpreter*, Carlisle, 1998.

10. See, G. Bonner, *St Augustine of Hippo*, Norwich, 2000, 81, which both quotes the text and comments on it. The reference is to Augustine, *Confessions*, VII, ix, 13-14.

11. For the history of the development of Trinitarian doctrine, see Bromiley, *Historical Theology*, 81-93 and 148-149.

12. Bauckham, *Jesus*, 57-59; 146-151. Bauckham rightly insist that the worship of Jesus by Jewish-Christians was the surest sign of their certainty of his identity with God.

13. Bouyer, *Christian Mystery*, 111.

14. If it is important not to project back anachronistically the terminology of later theology into the fourth gospel, it is equally important to recognise that the church's developed trinitarian language is firmly rooted there.

15. Smalley, *John*, 128-132.

16. Smalley, *John*, 243-244. Later Jewish tradition called it the divine

shekhinah. See, J. Dan, *Kabbalah: A Very Short Introduction*, Oxford, 2006: 'The term *shekhinah* is not found in the Bible, and it was formulated in talmudic literature from the biblical verb designating the residence (*shkn*) of God in the temple in Jerusalem and among the Jewish people.' See also, L. Jacobs, *Hasidic Prayer*, Washington, 1973.

17. Y. Congar, *Mystery*, 'The link between the glory of God and his presence and dwelling among his people, clearly shown as it already is in the Bible at the stage of the exodus, was stressed by the fact that the same Greek word *doxa* corresponded to both the biblical term *kabod*, glory and to the Aramaic or Mishnaic Hebrew word *shekinah*, presence, indwelling. Moreover, the LXX (i.e. the Septuagint, the translation of the Old Testament into Greek) translated the Hebrew word *shakan*, to dwell, by *kataskenoun*, while the corresponding noun, *skene*, tent, dwelling-place, was used to translate either the Hebrew word for the tent of meeting, or again the Aramaic word, *shekinah*. A further reason for this is that there is a similarity, a resemblance in sound between the two words *skene* and *shekinah* … these ideas of glory and indwelling are found again in the prologue of St John's gospel where they are used of the incarnate Word …'

18. See S. Gilley, 'Life and Writings', in, *Cambridge Companion to Newman*, 4.

19. J. Meyendorff, *Christ in Eastern Christian Thought*, New York, 1975, 134-135. On the progressive embodiment of the *Logos* in the created world, see L. Thunberg, *Man and the Cosmos: The Vision of St Maximus the Confessor*, 74: 'Maximus emphasises very strongly that God wills continually to make himself incarnate …' His theology surely opens a door to dialogue with Indian philosophy regarding the possibility of 'provisional' incarnations, understood from a Christian perspective as stages on the way to Christ.

20. G. Manley Hopkins, 'God's Grandeur', in, *The Major Works*, ed C. Phillips, Oxford, 2002.

21. *Dei Verbum* (on divine revelation), in, Flannery, *Documents*, 758: 'Hence, in Sacred Scripture, without prejudice to God's truth and holiness, the marvellous "condescension" of eternal wisdom is plain to be seen "that we may come to know the ineffable loving-kindness of God and see for ourselves how far he has gone in adapting his language with thoughtful concern for our nature". [St John Chrysostom, In Gen 3, 8, hom 17, 1]. Indeed the words of God, expressed in the words of men, are in every way like human language, just as the Word of the eternal Father, when he took on himself the flesh of human weakness, became like men.'

22. Nichols, *Wisdom*, 37-39 who gives a clear account of Bulgakov's thinking on this difficult matter. P. Florensky, one of the greatest intellectuals and creative thinkers in Russian history and a confessor of the faith who died in a prison camp, was a friend of Bulgakov whom he influenced greatly. In *The Pillar and Ground of the Truth*, trs B. Jakim, New Jersey,

1997, 210, he wrote : 'Divine egoism – that is what would turn God into a demon. By contrast, the Christian idea of God as Essential Love, as Love inside Himself and therefore also outside Himself; the idea of God's humility, of his self-abasement, manifested first in the creation of the world, i.e. in the placing of autonomous being alongside Himself, in the gift to this being of the freedom to develop according to its own laws, and therefore in the voluntary limitation of Himself – this idea for the first time made it possible to recognise creation as autonomous and therefore morally responsible to God.'

23. The notion of 'anonymous Christians', a generous concept proposed by the theologian Karl Rahner in an attempt to vindicate the working of God's grace beyond the visible confines of the church, was opposed by Henri de Lubac and Hans Urs von Balthasar on the grounds that it relativises the specificity of the gospel and undermines evangelisation: why evangelise if all people are already potentially orientated to salvation anyway? Yet both his interlocutors were Catholic theologians and the latter certainly hoped and prayed for the salvation of the whole human race, including those who had not specifically heard the gospel; yet, unfortunately, both seem to have denied that saving grace is actually *mediated* by alternative religious systems such as Buddhism. It seems to me (preserving an apophatic, [i.e. worshipfully ignorant] reverence before the mystery), that we should not speak of 'anonymous Christians' (as being potentially patronising) yet also accept that there is a mediation of grace through other religions precisely *as* religions – yet without denying the absolute nature of the incarnation and saving death and resurrection of Christ and the work of the Holy Spirit. Here St Maximus Confessor's insight into the possibility of partial and progressive 'incarnations' of divine truth and presence on the way to the coming of Christ the Lord, might be helpful. It is absolutely essential not to confuse evangelisation with the exportation of a particular religious culture or to define it solely as a one-way street – one does not bring the gospel (which is in addition not identifiable with the culture of those who bring it) to people simply deprived of truth or of the Holy Spirit, for as the Byzantine liturgy puts it, the Spirit is already, 'everywhere present and filling all things'. God is always and everywhere breaking through the barriers our inner deafness and blindness erect, so as to establish communion with us – but he does that not just through the enlightenment of individual conscience but socially and culturally, making the forms of human interaction and communal being-together the vehicles for his manifestation. For a detailed discussion of these complex issues, see Dupuis, *Religious Pluralism*, 143-149. Newman, as so often, is a helpful guide here. See T. Merrigan, 'Revelation', in *Cambridge Companion to Newman*, 52-53. He was open to God's operation in and through other religions, holding as a Christian that they were at least 'seeds of the Word' scattered abroad in the world by God and reveal-

ing his universal saving will. He derived that notion from some of the early Greek Fathers such as St Justin Martyr. Finally, to return to Barth, as we have already seen his invective against 'religion' (primarily aimed at human self-righteousness and self-justification before God) is by no means as simple as just rejecting 'other' religions. It is opposed to 'Christianity' itself in so far as it functions as a (humanly sustained) religion – and not as receptivity to revelation. Barth could also say positive things about other religions. See, J. Webster, *Karl Barth*, London, 2000, 64.

24. It is probably reasonable to say that although virtually all Christians believe in a primordial 'fall', in general Eastern Christians, Roman Catholics and most Anglicans do not think human beings fell quite as far as some (usually Evangelical) Protestants would suggest. See the good article by I. Mc. Farland, 'The Fall and Sin', in, *The Oxford Handbook of Systematic Theology*, ed J. Webster, K. Tanner, I. Torrance, Oxford, 2007, 140-159. This is not to minimise the seriousness of sin as it is understood in the first three groups but to acknowledge that there are different ways of imagining its effects on the human person. Christ, the Son of God on the cross, is always the standard by which sin is to be judged. Yet as Julian of Norwich said, sin may be everywhere but all shall be well and all manner of thing shall be well, thanks to the revelation of God's forgiveness.

25. Balthasar, *Mysterium Paschale*, 22: '... the incarnation is ordered to the cross as to its goal ... (this gives) the lie to the modern myth ... that Christianity is above all an "incarnationalism": a taking root in the (profane) world, and not a dying to the world ... he who says incarnation, also says cross. And this is so for two reasons. The Son of God took human nature in its fallen condition, and with it therefore, the worm in its entrails – mortality, fallenness, self-estrangement, death – which sin introduced into the world. The second reason has to do not with the man assumed, but with the *Logos* assuming: to become man is for him, in a most hidden yet very real sense, already humiliation – yes, indeed, as many would say, a deeper humiliation than the going to the cross itself.'

CHAPTER FOUR

1. Balthasar, *Mysterium Paschale*, 119-125. This is one of the best modern Roman Catholic works on soteriology (i.e. the doctrine of Christ's saving work). Balthasar insisted that his theology should never be separated from that of his spiritual soul-friend the Swiss mystic, Adrienne von Speyr, who claimed to experience the paschal mystery in her prayer. Without ignoring the at times problematic nature of some of her ideas (e.g. a trinitarian theology sometimes verging on tritheism, an excessive anthropomorphism and a dubiously gender-biased Mariology) it is increasingly likely that she will be recognised as one of the most important Catholic mystical writers of the modern era. See, A. Von Speyr, *The World of Prayer*, San Francisco, 1985; *Light and Images*, San Francisco. 2004; *The*

Boundless God, San Francisco, 2004. Notwithstanding Balthasar's admonition and the manifest importance of the part she played in helping him formulate his thought, there is no individual section dealing with their spiritual relationship in the otherwise excellent *Cambridge Companion to Hans Urs Von Balthasar*, ed E. T. Oakes SJ and D. Moss, Cambridge, 2004.

2. Orthodox theology stresses that salvation is 'deification' but we become like God not by grasping at a divine status far beyond our reach but by following the way of the Son in his descent and humility.

3. The exception as we shall see is the truth that Christ died for all – without exception.

4. For a good overview of the issues surrounding atonement and redemption see, S. Fiddes, 'Salvation', in, *Oxford Handbook of Systematic Theology*, 176-199. A very good popular account is T. Smail, *Once and For All*, London, 1998. Much excellent recent scholarly material is contained in *Stricken by God?*, ed B. Jersak and M. Hardin, Grand Rapids, Michigan, 2007. Three older books are still of immense value: J. McLeod Campbell, *The Nature of the Atonement*, Carberry, Scotland, 1996 (for which teaching he was condemned as a heretic by the Calvinist Church of Scotland which deposed him from the ministry in 1831); V. F. Storr, *The Problem of the Cross*, London 1919; P. T. Forsyth, *The Cruciality of the Cross*, Carlisle, 1997. Notwithstanding Forsyth's occasional swipes at the Catholic Church, no less a one than Balthasar described him as 'outstanding'. See on Barth's approach, Busch, *Barth*, 59-63. The relevant volume in his *magnum opus*, the *Church Dogmatics*, is (*CD*) IV. Many strict Evangelicals today reject Barth's version of redemption as crypto-Catholicism or Arminianism (the teaching of J. Arminius condemned by mainstream Calvinism for denying limited atonement). Being a Roman Catholic I am no 'Barthian' in any simple sense but his doctrine of the redemption seems to me to be one of the purest expositions of why the Christian faith is good news for the world. If one is going to make a mistake, better it is to err in attributing too much generosity to the God who has revealed himself as love (1 Jn 4:7-19) than too little.

5. For an uncommonly balanced assessment of St Anselm see, D. Brown, 'Anselm on Atonement', in *The Cambridge Companion to Anselm*, ed B. Davies and B. Lefttow, Cambridge, 2004, 290: 'He was no cold rationalist imposing purely external criteria on God but a devout monk concerned to explore his faith in a God, the internal logic of whose nature, he believed, entailed his never failing to act beautifully and well.' A classic statement of penal substitution can be seen in L. Berkhof, *Systematic Theology*, Grand Rapids, Michigan, 1949, 373-383.

6. Fiddes, *Oxford Handbook of Systematic Theology*, 187. The 'other theologians' he mentions include W. Pannenberg; the first group contains R. Girard and R. Schwager.

7. A recent book by a reputable scripture scholar puts the case afresh for

penal substitution, and both clearly and exhaustively tries to address the kind of criticism presented here and in the books listed above. See, I. Howard Marshall, *Aspects of the Atonement*, Milton Keynes, 2007. In my opinion it fails. God is presented as though he were ultimately able to be offended in the way a human subject can be. See 33: 'We can now see, incidentally, that the divine response to sin is a condign penalty in that at the heart of sin lies a rejection of God and his will for his creation, expressed in his commandments of love for him and for one another. To disobey God and rebel against him is to break the personal relationship with God, and thus in a sense to cut oneself off from him. *Thus it is appropriate for God to respond to those who cut themselves off from him by excluding them from his kingdom.* Final judgement is the execution of such a penalty after God, in his mercy, has provided a way of salvation that has been persistently refused and rejected' (my emphasis). Barth once said that the trouble with Calvin's God is that he may end up just looking like a bigger and angrier version of Calvin. But is it actually 'appropriate' in the light of God's universal saving will revealed in Christ and recorded in scripture, to imagine God acting like that? Is that not much more how we act – and is the God revealed in Christ not telling us finally that he doesn't act like that? Barth insisted that we ought not to impose our own ideas of what it is appropriate for God to do (or not to do), but instead let revealed truth deconstruct and reconstruct our concepts. It is hard to avoid the impression that some presentations of Christianity make it sound like very bad news indeed. See Smail, *Once*, 97, on how penal substitution theory, '… sometimes undergirds a sin-soaked piety in which the joyful spirituality of new life and resurrection plays an insufficient part.' Howard Marshall does however state that penal substitution need not necessarily be intrinsically connected with a doctrine of limited atonement.

8. See Berkhof, *Systematic Theology*, 394-399, 382: '… the idea of a universal Fatherhood in God, in virtue of which he loves all men with a redemptive love, is entirely foreign to scripture.'; again, 394: 'The Reformed position is that Christ died for the purpose of actually and certainly saving the elect, *and the elect only*' (my emphasis). One may well question how far Calvin himself would have been willing to become a 'Calvinist'! Like all great thinkers, his version of reality was often much more subtle and nuanced than that of his followers. See, 'Calvinism', in *The Westminster Handbook to Reformed Theology*, ed D. McKim, Louisville, Kentucky, 2001, 20: 'Whether Calvin would have accepted the later doctrine of limited atonement may be questioned, as he seems to have believed that Christ's atonement was sufficient for all but efficient only for the elect.' See also, T. F. Torrance, *Scottish Theology*, Edinburgh, 1996, 313, who quotes John McLeod Campbell as having said, 'I hold and teach that Christ died for all men.' Torrance comments in a footnote, 'This was, of course, also the teaching of John Calvin himself, that Christ died for all, for every crea-

ture. He pointed out that the biblical expression "many" sometimes de-
notes "all" – see *Comm. on Isaiah* 53: 12 and *Comm. on Romans* 5: 15.'
Torrance also notes (as we shall see later when dealing with Holy
Saturday) that the doctrine of Christ's effective atoning death for the salvation of all is not the same as 'universalism', which would insist that all
must thereby be saved. There are serious issues about divine and human
freedom and human moral responsibility involved, which cannot be resolved in any merely mechanistic or reductionist fashion. See, Torrance,
Scottish Theology, 288: 'By "universal atonement", however, McLeod
Campbell meant that Christ died for all people, not that all people would
actually be saved.'
9. Part of St Anselm's motivation in rethinking the doctrine of redemption was precisely to avoid ideas such as that God 'paid a ransom' to anyone (e.g. Satan) in rescuing the human race. See Berkhof, *Systematic
Theology*, 384-385. Yet one may suspect that his approach represented a
developing tendency to refuse to let metaphors be metaphors and a loss
of contact with the pictorial/symbolic/liturgical thinking of the early
church. Compare for example the highly concrete imagery employed –
indeed piled up – by St Maximos the Confessor (580-662) in, 'On the
Lord's Prayer', in, *The Philokalia*, London, 1981, 289: 'The *Logos* destroys
the tyranny of the evil one, who dominates us through deceit, by triumphantly using as a weapon against him the flesh defeated in Adam. In
this way he shows that what was once captured and made subject to
death now captures the captor: by a natural death it destroys the captor's
life and becomes a poison to him, making him vomit up all those he was
able to swallow because he had the power of death. But to humankind it
becomes life, like leaven in the dough, impelling the whole of nature to
rise like dough in the resurrection of life (cf 1 Cor 5:6-7). It was to confer
this life that the *Logos* who was God became man – a truly unheard of
thing – and willingly accepted the death of the flesh.' It is scarcely to be
imagined that St Maximos, one of the most subtle thinkers and dialecti-
cians among the church Fathers was incapable of formulating a more intellectual and systematic statement of doctrine. As we know from his
defence of the reality of Christ's human will, he could wield a syllogism
with the best of them. The point is that for describing the excess of divine
love displayed in the work of the Redeemer, iconic language is not only
not second best – it is the best language of all.
10. J. Calvin, *Institutes of the Christian Religion*, trs H. Beveridge, London,
1949, 2:16:11, I, 444. See also Howard Marshall, *Aspects*, 63.
11. On Evagrius (345-399) see the excellent introduction in W. J. Harmless
SJ, *Mystics*, Oxford 2008, 135-157. It would be hard to exaggerate his importance for the development of monastic spirituality, especially as that
was further formulated through his disciple St John Cassian (c.360-c.435)
whose books were among the most read writings of the Middle Ages in

the west. The Orthodox Church officially recognises Cassian's sanctity, calling him 'St John the Roman'.

12. See W. Breuning, 'Analogy', in *Handbook of Catholic Theology*, 5-7.

13. Julian of Norwich, *A Revelation of Divine Love*, ed and mod by E. Dutton, Plymouth, 2008, 79-80.

14. Balthasar, *Mysterium Paschale*, 246-254.

15. Balthasar, *Mysterium Paschale*, 261-262. See also Bulgakov, *Comforter*, 267-298 on Pentecost, the founding of the church and the *kenosis* of the Holy Spirit.

CHAPTER FIVE

1. Senn, *Christian Liturgy*, 30-34; Casel, *Mystery*, 57-61: 'From the mystery of redemption flow the other mysteries as does all grace … All the church's blessings and consecrations are a communication from the cross, or in liturgy, a redemptive grace proceeding from the mystery of the Mass.' See also G. Koch, 'Sacrament,' in *Handbook of Catholic Theology*, 605-609. On the number of the sacraments, see M. A. Fahey SJ, 'Sacraments,' in *The Oxford Handbook of Systematic Theology*, 278-281. Fahey's presentation is a model of accurate scholarship and ecumenical generosity. Listing seven was originally a pedagogical device used in medieval catechesis but having been endorsed by the council of Lyons (1274), it was eventually defined as dogma by the 16th century Roman Catholic Church in opposition to the Reformers. The Byzantine Church had a much less restricted view of what constitutes a sacramental mystery, including at times both monastic profession and the burial of the dead in the number of the sacraments. See J. Meyendorff, *Byzantine Theology. Historical Trends and Doctrinal Themes*, Fordham, 1974, 191-192, who claims that its adoption in later Byzantine theology was based on a fascination with symbolic numbers, but who rightly notes that the 'sacraments' listed were sometimes different from the western seven and that leading theologians like Sts Gregory Palamas and Nicholas Cabasilas acknowledged the primary importance of baptism and the Eucharist. The seven corresponding to the Latin tradition were established in the Orthodox 'Confessions of Faith' in the 16th and 17th centuries. Most significant Orthodox theologians today, like their Catholic and many Protestant counterparts, both emphasise the importance of the two main sacraments ('or mysteries' as they still prefer to call them) and endorse a wider concept of the world as a place of sacramental epiphany.

2. CCC, 1077-1134.

3. Some branches of the Lutheran tradition follow Luther in upholding absolution as a quasi-sacramental action. In addition, Orthodox writers nowadays tend to use the word sacrament itself more frequently, e.g. Zizioulas, *Christian Dogmatics*, 137-138.

4. Vatican II repeatedly emphasises that Christ (with his body the church) is the fundamental sacramental mystery, see e.g. *LG* in, Flannery, *Documents*, 356, '... the church is compared, not without significance, to the mystery of the incarnate Word. As the assumed nature, inseparably united to him, serves the divine Word as a living organ of salvation, so in a somewhat similar way, does the social structure of the church serve the Spirit of Christ who vivifies it, in the building up of the body (Eph 4:15)'; also, *CCC*, 1108, '... the church is the great sacrament of divine communion which gathers God's scattered children together. Communion with the Holy Trinity and fraternal communion are inseparably the fruit of the Spirit in the liturgy.'

5. Hence the truth of Marmion's dictum: 'Christ's mysteries are our mysteries.'

6. The liturgical honours accorded to the Book of the Gospels in all the historic rites testify to this sacramentality of the word.

7. Each of the renewed sacramental rites in the Roman Catholic Church's ritual embodies this fundamental principle of the reform, just as the directive that the homily at the Eucharist is not to be omitted lays stress on the need not only to read scripture but to break and distribute it among the people: the analogy with the bread of the Eucharist is obvious. Sacramental actions are not mechanical. They presuppose the proclamation of the word, faith and conversion. In this area the renewed liturgy is clearly streets ahead of its predecessor.

8. A reduction in the importance of the symbols of incarnation was an unintended and unfortunate consequence of the Protestant Reformations of the 16th century, reinforced by the liberal Protestantism that flourished after the Enlightenment: both Luther and Calvin had very sophisticated theologies of the two principal sacraments even if the latter pruned worship to its most basic constituent elements. See Senn, *Christian Liturgy*, 299-323. But the 20th century has witnessed a great recovery of liturgical and sacramental awareness in many Protestant churches. The Anglican Communion is obviously very different. Having retained many fundamental elements from the traditional liturgy of the Medieval church and progressively and intelligently restored earlier ones which it had lost, it enjoys a rich life of worship and has contributed enormously to the liturgical renewal of all the western churches since the 20th century.

9. See J. Zizioulas, *Christian Dogmatics*, 148-153. The heightened awareness of the role of the Holy Spirit not only in worship but in every other area of the church's life owes a great deal to 20th century Orthodox theology – though some Orthodox tend to exaggerate the so-called 'Christomonism' (exclusive emphasis on Christ) they see as typical of Western Christianity.

10. Casel was unjustly attacked for supposedly claiming that Christ's lit-

eral, historical death was somehow rendered present in the action of the liturgy. He taught rather that between the literal, historically attested facts of Christ's earthly existence, and his full presence in heaven, there is an intermediate presence granted to the church by the Holy Spirit, the unique mode of presence that distinguishes the sacraments *as* sacraments: Christ's mystery presence. That is too delicate and mysterious a thing to be dissected with the blunt instruments of neo-Scholastic theology. See Casel, *Mystery*, 16, and editor's notes, 94-95.

11. The idea of Christ as the perfect worshipper of the Father was often found in the so-called 'French school' of spirituality which considerably influenced Marmion and diocesan priestly spirituality in the 20th century. At best it was a majestic, aristocratic tradition, which emphasised the glory of God and the value of sacrifice. Unfortunately its exponents at times preached so extreme a form of self-abnegation (supposedly clearing the heart so that the indwelling Christ may worship the Father in and through it) that it veered close to self-annihilation and mystical nihilism. However, relocated in the context of a more sound theology of creation, renewed awareness that the Spirit and Christ do pray in and with us as well as through us, and a better understanding of liturgy, it still has some value as a spiritual tradition. See A. Tanquerey, *The Spiritual Life*, trs H. Branderis, Tournai, Belgium, 1930, 78-80.

12. See the prayer of the presiding priest at the preparation of the altar in the Byzantine rite: '… allow these gifts to be offered to you by me, your sinful servant. For it is really you who offer and are offered, you who receive the offering and are given back to us, Christ our God …'

13. 'Ascent to the throne' is a typically Jewish mystical idea taken up into the Christian liturgy. See Bauckham, *Jesus*, 152-181, who argues that the New Testament's insistence on Jesus having been taken up to the throne of God, where he receives worship, indicates his identity with God. Christians are taken up with him through grace. See also, *Jewish Mysticism: An Introduction to the Kabbalah*, London, 1913, an old but still valuable work.

14. For two excellent theological interpretations of this classic theme in Reformed worship, see T. Torrance, *Royal Priesthood: A Theology of Ordained Ministry*, Edinburgh, 1993, and, G. Redding, *Prayer and the Priesthood of Christ in the Reformed Tradition*, Edinburgh, 2003.

15. See R. F. Collins, 'Inspiration', in *The New Jerome*, 1023-1033, for a comprehensive summary of theories of the inspiration of scripture.

16. Bulgakov, *Lamb*, 351-352.

17. Barth, *CD* 1.2, 462-465.

18. Catholic theologians often assert that grace does not destroy nature but perfects it. See J. Alfaro, 'Nature and Grace', in *Encyclopedia of Catholic Theology*, 1033-1038.

19. This notion, associated with Origen, makes communion with Christ

through the words of scripture similar to eucharistic communion.

20. See *Dei Verbum*, in Flannery, *Documents*, 758.

21. The 4th ecumenical council (Chalcedon, 451) taught that Christ is perfect God and perfect man, with these two natures united in his divine personality (*hypostasis*), so that the divinity does not absorb, cancel or destroy the humanity. This 'Chalcedonian principle' has profound implications for the whole of theology, especially the doctrine of creation. The world as a relative being, established by God 'over-against' his own unique being, is yet in union with him otherwise it would simply cease to be. Having established his creation, called it very good and redeemed it through the mystery of Christ, God out of love maintains it permanently in being.

22. Docetism (from the Greek word for 'appearance') is generally held to have reduced the humanity of Christ to an illusion; Monophysitism (from the Greek for 'one nature') was an imperially sponsored heresy in Byzantium, with which the emperors tried (unsuccessfully) to hold the Coptic and Syrian churches in communion with Constantinople during the difficult period of the 6th and 7th centuries. The ancient churches of those regions (the Oriental Orthodox) were not Monophysites and should not be designated as such; the heresy attributed to Nestorius divided Christ into two persons, divine and human, viewing him more as a human being assumed by God than as God incarnate. Whether Nestorius, Patriarch of Constantinople ever actually taught that is a moot point: once again the Ancient Church of the East (and its Catholic offshoots, the Chaldeans and the Indian Syro-Malabars) should never be referred to as 'Nestorian' without serious qualification. On much of this see Chadwick, *East and West*, 40-64. There are also enlightening contributions in the volume, *Heresies and how to Avoid Them*, ed B. Quash and M. Ward, London, 2007.

23. Traditional patristic exegesis spoke of various senses hidden in the Old Testament and made visible in the New.

24. That is equally true for the worship of the synagogue.

25. Luther believed that the gospel of Christ (by which he meant not *just* the four gospels but the proclamation of God's forgiving and justifying grace received by faith alone) is the determining principle which ought to guide all biblical interpretation. In practice he tended virtually to identify it with Paul's theology as presented in Romans, something continued by many later Protestant exegetes. Catholics and Orthodox tend to find that procedure too narrow and insist on the important implications the existence of the canon has for correct interpretation (in addition to the pronouncements of the church's tradition in reading the Bible throughout history): see Althaus, *Martin Luther*, 72-92. Yet it is not at all true that the Protestant Reformers denied the tradition. They certainly did grant it less importance in comparison with scripture, but all the mainstream

Protestant churches accepted the classical creeds of Christendom.

26. *SC*, in Flannery, *Documents*, 762.

27. For an important exposition of this fundamental principle, see K. Irwin, *Context and Text: Method in Liturgical Theology*, Collegeville, Minnesota, 1994.

28. The expression was used by the First Vatican Council. See Scheeben, *Mysteries*, 1-21; 733-761.

29. Eastern monastic tradition also speaks of 'divine reading' but did not develop theories about its 'mechanics' in the way characteristic of western medieval monasticism.

30. St Symeon the New Theologian, *The Practical and Theological Chapters and the Three Theological Discourses*, trs P. McGuckin, Kalamazoo, 1982, 103. 'And when a man knows that he has within him the God who gives men knowledge, he has passed though all the holy scriptures; and because he has picked all the fruit of his reading, he no longer needs to read the books. How is this? Well, if the same One who inspired the scriptural writers abides within this man as his intimate, and initiates him into the secrets of the hidden mysteries, then he himself becomes a divinely inspired book for others. He bears the new and ancient mysteries inscribed in him by the finger of God, for he has fulfilled all things and rests from all his labours in God who is the supreme perfection.'

31. Casel, *Mystery*, 17-19: 'Through the *pneuma* the Christian is made like Christ, the *pneuma* in person and thereby is himself anointed with this *pneuma*.' Other liturgical traditions, e.g. that of the Armenians, stress the gift of the Holy Spirit/Pentecostal aspect of baptism more than that of Christ's passing from death to life. Surprisingly Irwin criticises Casel for neglecting the role of the Spirit, which is strange given that he repeatedly referred to the action of the *pneuma*, keeping the word in Greek so as to highlight its strangeness: see, Irwin, *Context*, 23.

32. Augustine taught this in his commentary on St John's gospel and it was to enter the Latin tradition as a theological commonplace, being repeated often by the Protestant Reformers. See the excerpt contained in *Sacraments and Worship*, ed with comm by P. F. Palmer SJ, London, 1955: 'Take away the word and what is water but water? The word is joined to the element, and the result is a sacrament, itself becoming in a sense, a visible word as well.' Casel insists that Augustine's 'word' (*verbum/logos*) is like the biblical 'word', i.e. not just a statement but an event which effects what it signifies: see Casel, *Mystery*, 42, nt. 1. It is unfortunate that, detached from the context of worship and reduced to mere intellectualism, a misunderstanding of Augustine's notion contributed to the paucity of the traditional (meagre) Latin concept of sacraments popular at the end of the Middle Ages as 'visible signs of invisible grace.' The east, in its understanding of the sacramental mysteries, generally retained a fuller sense of their meaning.

33. In the same section of his commentary, Augustine goes on to mention

infant baptism where this utter passivity is so evident. Luther, directing his teaching on baptism against the Anabaptists who considered infant baptism invalid, highlighted this passivity both to defend his doctrine of justification by grace alone and to insist on the objectivity of the gift given in the gospel sacraments, though later on he even argued, somewhat incoherently, for some form of infant faith. See Althaus, *Martin Luther*, 353-363.

34. Vincie makes this point well in relation to the modern rediscovery of a strong sense of symbol, *Celebrating Divine Mystery*, 120. The archetypal psychology of C. G. Jung has contributed something to the better understanding of symbols and the general importance of symbolism now more prevalent today. See J. Jacobi, *The Psychology of C. G. Jung,* London, 1973, 94-98. Luther remained very close in this area to the previous tradition of the western church. Calvin's sacramental theology, though rich and complex, is rather elusive and hard to define. The Swiss reformer Zwingli (1484-1531) seems to have taught a doctrine of symbolism closer to the more reductionist notion of the symbol often encountered nowadays. See M. G. Reardon, *Religious Thought in the Reformation*, London, 1981, 107-109: 'The function of these rites – the very word 'sacrament', with its pagan origin, he disliked – is simply to serve as tokens or signs of allegiance or profession … The eucharistic rite appeared to him … to be no more than a bare sign, lacking any real relationship between itself and the thing signified, a view therefore which goes to the opposite extreme to the Catholic one, in which the sign itself is to all intents abolished.' One may well question the latter assertion but it is based, as we shall later, on the unfortunate use at times by Catholic theologians of words like 'mere' and 'only' to describe the sacramental symbols.

35. Louth, *Denys*, 108-109.

36. Notwithstanding the Roman Catholic Church's acceptance of the reality of baptism – the one Christian baptism professed in the Creeds and her official commitment to the ecumenical task since the Second Vatican Council – it is surprising that so little emphasis is placed on our shared baptism in evaluating the ecclesial reality of Christian communities stemming from the Reformation. If baptism really does grant entrance to the church as the body of Christ, one might hope that in a spirit of love the natural consequence would be to accept generously that other churches *are* churches.

37. Casel expresses this in the traditional language of Roman Catholic theology, *Mystery*, 14, '… what is necessary is a living, active sharing in the redeeming deed of Christ; passive because the Lord makes it act upon us, active because we share in it by a deed of our own. To the action of God upon us (*opus operatum*) responds our co-operation (*opus operantis*), carried out through grace from him.' Reformed spirituality also places much emphasis on active following of Christ as the response to baptism and re-

ception of the gift of the Holy Spirit.

38. See K. H. Weger, 'Tradition,' in *Encyclopedia*, 1729-1734.

39. Senn, *Christian Liturgy*, 58-61.

40. See M. Barker, *Temple Themes in Christian Worship*, London, 2007, 201-221, who speaks of elements of Temple worship such as the 'bread of the presence' and the 'blood of the covenant' as foundational elements of the Eucharist: 'Jesus took the high priestly rituals of these days – the Bread of the presence and covenant blood – and it is entirely possible that he made them his own, since he was remembered as the Great High Priest.' Barker's work (especially regarding worship) represents some of the most exciting revisionism currently been done in New Testament research even if some of her conclusions are at times a little far-fetched. See also, M. Barker, *The Hidden Tradition of the Kingdom of God*, London, 2007.

41. G. Koch, 'Eucharist, Accounts of Institution', in *Handbook of Catholic Theology*, 230-232, ' ... blood means the living being with blood in it; in the context there is also the connotation of a bloody death. This self-giving of Jesus is interpreted as a confirmation of God's covenant with Israel, or the establishment of a new covenant.'

42. Hence expressions like 'saying Mass' or 'reading the communion service' hardly do justice to the action of carrying out the Lord's command.

43. On all these issues some works remain foundational for later research. See L. Bouyer, *Eucharist: Theology and Spirituality of the Eucharistic Prayer*, Notre Dame, 1968; G. Dix OSB, *The Shape of the Liturgy*, London 1945. An excellent account of *anamnesis*, summarising two generations of liturgical and biblical research is to be found in the document, *Baptism, Eucharist and Ministry*, Faith and Order Paper No. 111, issued by the World Council of Churches, Geneva, 1982 (hereafter cited as *BEM* according to its own numeration system). The document states (*BEM* 5): 'The Eucharist is the memorial of the crucified and risen Christ, i.e. the living and effective sign of his sacrifice, accomplished once and for all on the cross and still operative on behalf of all mankind. The biblical idea of memorial as applied to the Eucharist refers to this present efficacy of God's work when it is celebrated by God's people in the liturgy.'

44. O. Semmelroth, 'Sacrifice' in *Encyclopedia of Theology*, 1494. For another specifically Catholic comment see G. Koch, 'Eucharist', in *Handbook of Catholic Theology*, 229-230: 'The actual sacramental signs of the Eucharist are those of a meal: when bread, the basic food, is distributed it expresses fellowship, as does the wine, which also symbolises joy and a (shared) fullness of life. Admittedly, the Eucharist is a meal of a special kind, a meal of thanksgiving, blessing and sacrifice ... The Lord's Supper is unique. *It is a memorial (anamnesis) of the suffering, death and resurrection of the Lord*, and it also looks forward to the consummation to come; past and future are really and effectively present in the real presence of the Lord himself (emphasis added).' J. Corbon, writing from an eastern Catholic

perspective, mentions the eternal sacrifice of trinitarian love as the underlying source of the event of the liturgical memorial: Corbon, *Wellspring*,
152: 'The body of Christ embodies for us the sacrifice of love that is eternally being accomplished in the communion of the three Persons and that
now sanctifies for God's glory all that human sin had defiled.'
45. *Liturgy of St Basil* (my translation). *God* of course does not *need* to be reminded. The liturgy is for us. It is we who suffer from fatal amnesia. But God,
through his divine-human, saving *kenosis* adapts himself to our situation
which is bounded by space and limited by time. *Anamnesis* heals amnesia
46. A useful recent book on the different eucharistic traditions is, *The
Lord's Supper, Five Views*, ed G. T. Smith, Downers Grove, Illinois, 2008,
though the Lutheran contribution needs to be used with care – it is not
representative of contemporary mainstream Lutheran thinking.
47. Catholics and Orthodox should avoid tired and inaccurate clichés such
as, 'Protestants do not believe in the Eucharist' or, 'Protestants do not believe in the real presence.' One must always reply, 'Which Protestants?'
There is no single Protestant position on these matters, even if one often
encounters a kind of popular 'Zwinglianism' in which the celebration as
viewed largely as an occasion to share a fellowship meal and remember
Jesus (hardly in itself a bad thing though falling far short of the fullness of
the liturgical mystery). Luther himself vigorously defended the 'real presence' of Christ in the Eucharist and Calvin taught a very 'high' doctrine of
communion with the glorified Christ through the coming of the Holy
Spirit. Catholics and Orthodox might remember that despite undoubted
deficiencies in some areas, Protestant liturgical practice kept alive the
reading and preaching of God's word, the vivid awareness that the celebration is a community action and the giving of the cup to the faithful (as
opposed to a spoonful of the consecrated sacrament as in Orthodoxy) – elements emphasised today thanks to 20th century liturgical renewal. In
addition, Catholics (Latin and Eastern), Orthodox and Protestants, could
all learn a great deal from the Anglican tradition: their scholars were (and
are) at the forefront of liturgical renewal while dignified, beautiful and part-
icipatory common prayer remains a central component of Anglican Church
life – at least where it is faithful to the insights of its original tradition.
48. Senn, *Christian Liturgy*, 388.
49. It is important to stress that while the Catholic Church defined dogmatically the sacrificial nature of the Mass, it did not commit its members
to a specific theological explanation of what exactly that entails; hence the
profusion of theologies of the Eucharist in the period after the 16th century.
No group in the church, whether so called 'liberal' or 'conservative', has
the right to claim that a theological theory is itself a binding dogma. There
has to be a legitimate, indeed indispensable plurality in theology if the
fullness of the mystery is to find expression.
50. Unfortunately more people (both Catholic and Protestant) talk about

the Council of Trent (held in three sessions in the 16th century) than actually read its documents. Trent's theology in this area was relatively restrained, although it certainly bore the scars both of deficient knowledge of early liturgical tradition and of polemics with Protestants. That it could have been worse is surely a sign that the Holy Spirit does actually guide the church. On the subsequent, much less fortunate developments in eucharistic theology and piety, see, J. Auer, *Dogmatic Theology 6, A General Doctrine of the Sacraments and the Mystery of the Eucharist*, trs E. Leiva-Merikakis, Washington, 1995, a work made all the more convincing because its author (in collaboration with Joseph Ratzinger) represents a moderately 'conservative' strand of theological reflection. One of the most influential writers positively to influence the council fathers was St Nicholas Cabasilas, a late Byzantine lay theologian whose understanding of the liturgy was a model of balance and good order. (He was later canonised by the Orthodox Church – though not for the use that had been made of him at Trent!). See St Nicholas Cabasilas, *The Life in Christ*, trs C. J. de Catanzaro, New York, 1998; also, *The Divine Liturgy*, trs J. M. Hussey and P. A. McNulty, London, 1960.

51. *BEM*, B.8, 'The Eucharist is the sacrament of the unique sacrifice of Christ, who ever lives to make intercession for us. It is the memorial of all that God has done for the salvation of the world. What it was God's will to accomplish in the incarnation, life, death, resurrection and ascension of Christ, God does not repeat. These events are unique and can neither be repeated nor prolonged. In the memorial of the Eucharist, however, the church offers its intercession in communion with Christ, our great High Priest.' Not surprisingly the so-called, 'Munich Agreement', reached between the Orthodox and Catholic churches, connects the creative recall of the *anamnesis* with the descent of the Holy Spirit in the liturgy: see 'The Mystery of the Church and of the Eucharist in the Light of the Mystery of the Holy Trinity,' Joint International Commission, 1982, in *The Quest for Unity: Orthodox and Catholics in Dialogue*, ed Borelli and J. H. Erikson, New York, 1996. It is hard to see what further precision might be required regarding this matter after so many years of dialogue and discussion.

52. On the descent of the Holy Spirit in the eucharistic liturgy in response to the prayer of the assembly and the direct invocation made by the presiding minister, see Corbon, *Wellspring*, 153, 'But who transforms our offerings into the body and blood of Christ if not the Spirit who acts in the church? It is he who shows his power at the heart of this consecration.' Corbon's study also has the great merit of locating the Spirit's invocation in the Eucharist within the many *epikleses* (invocations) made throughout the liturgy. It should be noted that the invocation is not addressed to the person of the Holy Spirit as such; rather it is directed to God the Father. The liturgy follows the revealed order in which the divine persons accomplished our salvation in the mystery of Christ. There is no abstract or

amorphous 'God' in Christianity – God is always the Holy Trinity who has disclosed himself to us. On the weakness of this dimension in the western Catholic (and by inclusion Protestant) tradition see the comment by Kilmartin in, *Christian Liturgy*, 12: 'As yet the pneumatological dimension of the sacraments has received only marginal attention in Catholic theology.' The relative poverty of the unreformed Roman Rite in relation to the Holy Spirit has at least been corrected by the inclusion of *epicleses* in all the main sacramental actions (two in each of the Eucharistic Prayers composed since the Second Vatican Council's reforms) – but it may take generations for the west to catch up on the east in highlighting this reality in theology and spirituality as a whole. It is one of the terrible wounds the western church undoubtedly received after the disastrous schism with the Byzantine east.

53. One theological inaccuracy associated with the initial stages of the Anglican Oxford movement in the 19th century was the notion that the bread and wine themselves are somehow offered as a sacrifice. The reality is actually more complex. The elements represent both nature and human productivity as we present them to God but they have to become, through the descent of the Holy Spirit and the words of institution, the only sacrifice acceptable to God – that of Christ. One may say that they are 'on the way' to becoming the church's sacrifice but still require the transforming touch of the Spirit. The unreformed Roman liturgy tended to confuse the meaning of the sacrifice by speaking of the bread and wine as if they were already that – at the so-called 'offertory' of the Mass – rather than where the transformation really occurs, i.e., during the (entire) Eucharistic Prayer. By rethinking the Offertory as the preparation of the altar and presentation of the gifts and establishing clearly that the fullness of the sacrifice occurs through the transformation of the gifts within the great prayer of thanksgiving, the liturgical reform has greatly clarified the faith of the church on what constitutes Eucharistic sacrifice. It has also facilitated the removal of an ecumenical stumbling block. The recent opportunity graciously granted by the Holy See to use the unreformed Roman Rite (now known as the 'Extraordinary Form'), a pastoral concession to prevent various groups inclined to schism from damaging the unity of the church, should not be used to encourage the retention of erroneous forms of liturgical theology.

54. *CCC*, 1546-1551, which also clarifies the Catholic understanding of the relationship between the priesthood of the baptised and that of the ordained. In general the common priesthood of the faithful, one of the most important doctrines in the New Testament remains greatly underdeveloped in popular Catholic consciousness due to an exaggerated emphasis on the ministerial priesthood. Perhaps one day some future Pope might designate a year celebrating 'the priesthood of the faithful' to heighten awareness of the dignity of the baptised as the people of Christ. Since all

the baptised, wherever they are, are admitted to that dignity, it should have special ecumenical significance.

55. St Maximus the Confessor, 'Third Century', 7, in, *The Philokalia*, II, trs and ed G. E. H. Palmer, P. Sherard, K. Ware, London, 1981, 211.

56. See R. Saarinen, *God and the Gift. An Ecumenical Theology of Giving*, Collegeville, Minnesota, 2005, an excellent example of how the liturgy in general and the Eucharist in particular can inform the thinking of a Lutheran theologian.

57. For a commentary on this psalm, see S. Terrien, *The Psalms: Strophic Structure and Theological Commentary*, Grand Rapids, Michigan, 2003, 393-399.

58. The recovery of eschatology as the awareness that history is moving towards the glorious final coming of the Lord – anticipated by the church in her liturgical worship – is one of the main fruits of theological renewal in the 20th century. Christ's last great *parousia* (presence) is tasted in the gifts of the kingdom – his real presence in the consecrated elements of the Eucharist. See J. Finkenzeller, 'Eschatology', in *Handbook of Catholic Theology*, 210-219. See the comments of B. Bobrinskoy who laments the loss of the eschatological sense not only in other churches but also in his own Orthodox Church, *Mystery of the Trinity*, 178: 'The *Kyrie eleison* ('Lord have mercy') is certainly a vestige of christological exclamations that have lost their eschatological power. The Pauline and Johannine churches were marked by this sense of expectation, of this unceasing appeal for the imminent coming of the Lord. In the Byzantine liturgy the *anamnesis* certainly expresses this sacramental, and therefore, realised remembrance of the past, celestial, and future Christ ... This sense of urgency and of impatience with the coming of Jesus is infused in us by the presence of the divine Spirit.'

59. Byzantine liturgy for *Pascha*.

60. This translation of the hymn *Adoro Te* is by G. Manley Hopkins, *The Major Works*, 104-105. In addition to emphasising the hidden (i.e. authentically mystical) nature of the eucharistic presence, St Thomas also reminds us of its eschatological reference (the vision of Christ in glory). However, one also detects, in Hopkins' translation, an unfortunate tendency to underestimate the importance of the sacramental signs as symbols – they are not just 'poor shapes' or 'poor shadows' (or 'mere' appearances) but sacramental symbols, the phenomena of bread conveying the genuine Bread of Life.

61. See Auer, *Dogmatic Theology* 6, 206-208.

62. I am speaking here about popular misconceptions but have occasionally heard such opinions expressed in ecumenical discussions. I read a claim recently in a popular Catholic newspaper that heart tissue had been discovered in a monstrance after it had contained the host!

63. Here again one must distinguish between popular presentations of Catholicism and the official teaching and belief of the church as found in her dogmatic tradition and liturgical life.

64. *SC* in Flannery, *Documents*, 4-5. These diverse modes of presence are reiterated in *CCC*, 1088.

65. *Rule*, LIII: 'In the reception of poor men and pilgrims special attention should be shown, because in them is Christ more truly welcomed ...'

66. See K. Rahner, 'Beatific Vision' and R. Schulte, 'Sacraments' in *Encyclopedia of Theology*, 78-80 and 1484-1485.

67. 'Communion theology', developed in the 20th century by Catholic theologians such as Henri de Lubac and by Orthodox such as Nicholas Afanasiev and John Zizioulas established the essential link between the celebration of the Eucharist in each local church and the communion of the churches as the one, holy, catholic and apostolic church. See Zizioulas, *Being*, 143-158; *Lectures*, 120-145. For some critical caveats see also R. Del Colle, 'The Church', in *Oxford Handbook of Systematic Theology*, who warns against the Catholic Church imagining that it 'contains' the mystery of Christ in a manipulative or controlling way – a criticism Catholics ought to heed, especially when our excessively juridical ecclesiastical practice is not in line with our communion-based ecclesial ideals. Still, it would seem fairly indisputable that any ecclesiological vision that wishes to be in continuity with the patristic tradition would have to incorporate some kind of eucharistically based communion ecclesiology.

68. Both images are present in the liturgy – in the case of the Orthodox in the rite of receiving Holy Communion, in that of St Thomas in the antiphon *O Sacrum Convivium*, probably composed by him for the Office of Corpus Christi (since the recent liturgical reforms, now called 'The Solemnity of the Body and Blood of Christ').

69. This is what the Catholic Church intends to affirm by the rather clumsy and quantitative notion of the full presence of Christ by concomitance in each part of the consecrated sacrament. Unfortunately it lends itself to being hijacked by those who would deny the chalice to the laity: if one can receive the total Christ, 'body and blood, soul and divinity' through communion with the host alone – so runs the objection – then why be concerned with receiving the chalice? Apart from the issue of Christ's original intention in instituting the mystery (i.e. 'take this all of you and drink from it'), and the almost universal prevalence of general communion from the chalice in the worship of the early church, such arguments completely miss the theological point. The liturgy is a sign-language made up of symbolic actions through which Christ manifests himself. It is not a matter of 'more' or 'less'. Rather, it is about recognising the symbolic significance attached to the actions of eating and drinking and the richly symbolic meaning of the chalice as set forth in holy scripture.

70. One of the most pressing tasks in the Catholic Church today is to foster a living symbolic imagination in relation to liturgy and sacraments. After centuries of seeing their efficacy as coming about through a kind of mechanical 'cause and effect', we need to understand better that they

actually 'work' through the symbolic media which constitute them: actions, gestures, words, sense perceptions and ritual. These are the basic constituent elements of liturgy. In addition, the transforming power of beauty should not be ignored. In Ireland in particular we may need to ask if the prevailing level of sacramental minimalism and aesthetic barrenness characteristic of much of our worship nowadays, is not in fact depriving the liturgy of its catechetical and transforming power. A sign language deprived of signs – with no communion from the chalice for the congregation, Eucharistic bread that looks like white cardboard, frequently no lay readers, often very poor preaching unrelated to the mysteries being celebrated, no gospel book (with sacred scripture being proclaimed from leaflets), no processions, lights, incense or much of the other sacramental media which constitute the liturgy – is hardly likely to convey the reality of the mystery of Christ effectively.

71. The image of 'sober inebriation' owes much to patristic interpretation of the 'overflowing cup' of Psalm 22(23), verse 5. It was employed by St Gregory of Nyssa in his preaching and turns up in one of the morning hymns attributed to St Ambrose, is still appointed for use in the Latin edition of The Liturgy of the Hours and is currently sung in my own monastery at Lauds (morning praise) on Mondays in Ordinary Time:

> *Christusque nobis sit cibus,*
> *potusque noster sit fides;*
> *laeti bibamus sobriam*
> *ebrietatem Spiritus.*

> Let Christ be our food, and faith our drink,
> joyfully receiving thereby
> the sober inebriation of the Spirit.

A profound and beautiful exposition of this imagery in tradition is to be found in an unexpected place: Dr Pusey's defence of his introduction of material from Roman Catholic devotional books into Anglican circles in the 19th century. See, E. B. Pusey, *A Letter to the Right Hon. and Rev. The Lord Bishop of London, in Explanation of Some Statements Contained in a Letter by the Rev. W. Dodsworth,* London, 1851, 194-221. Pusey's defence has all the more force in that he could hardly have been accused of being a libertine in his personal life. On the use of similar language in Islamic mystical tradition see, Harmless, *Mystics,* 164, who also comments that the imagery of drunkenness is purely spiritual, given that Islam prohibits the drinking of alcohol.

72. Despite so much progress in inter-church dialogue in the last forty years resulting in profound agreed statements, including many on the Eucharist, it is hardly news that the ecumenical ship has been in the doldrums for some time now. The main problem still outstanding between the Catholic and Orthodox churches is undoubtedly the role of the Pope

in the universal church. However, for Anglicans and many Protestants a bigger stumbling block remains: Rome's total inability to acknowledge the reality of ordained ministry and therefore the reality of the Eucharist in their churches. There is unlikely to be any further serious progress before these issues are resolved. See J. Gros, E. Mc Manus and A. Riggs, *Introduction to Ecumenism,* New Jersey, 1998, for a Roman Catholic overview of ecumenism. Three things might move the situation on a little. First the Catholic Church might (seriously) re-evaluate the eucharistic theology of the Protestant churches in a liturgical way, so that e.g. the reality of ordained ministry is not determined solely on the basis of abstract scholastic concepts (such as 'validity') but instead explored in terms of pneumatology and ecclesiology, i.e. Christ manifesting his mystery through the Holy Spirit in the assembly of those baptised in his name. We ought not to ask what the minimum requirements for reality are but rather, 'Is the merciful Trinity really likely to leave Christians who are not responsible for the divisions in which they find themselves today, with only a bare minimum (if even that) of sacramental grace and ecclesial reality?' It is hard to imagine the overwhelmingly generous God who breaks through into the world, becoming present in Christ and the Holy Spirit to call all to salvation, acting like that. Second, Rome might consider designating places in the Roman Catholic Church, (e.g. monasteries) where, for the sake of charity, the current restrictive legislation on eucharistic hospitality could be suspended. The liturgy of these places could be seen as foretastes of the coming kingdom and icons of the New Jerusalem. Third, the most important issue regarding how the papacy operates is not just that of how papal ministry should function juridically. What is needed is not just 'papal ministry' but genuine, creative, imaginative Petrine leadership – the kind shown by Peter after his heaven-sent dream instructing him that food previously designated unclean was now able to be eaten (Acts 10:9-33), thus departing dramatically from 'tradition'. Such imagination, courage, creativity and generosity on the part of the successor of Peter and Vicar (representative) of the one who declares, 'See, I am making all things new!' (Rev 21:5) would surely open up new avenues in the ecumenical journey. One can at least hope and pray.

CHAPTER SIX

1. Senn, *Christian Liturgy,* 305-307 summarises Luther's views on the objectivity of the gift of God's grace conveyed by the words and sacraments of the gospel. Despite his criticism of the mechanical reception of grace associated with the notion of *ex opera operato,* Luther also insisted that the certainty of what is given is not established by faith but merely received by it: it is God who guarantees its objective efficacy. See Althaus, *Martin Luther,* 346: 'The decisive element in the sacrament is accordingly the word of promise ... Since the sacrament is a form in which the word

comes to us, this form has its unique nature and significance beside the oral proclamation. The sacrament gives man a guarantee, a pledge, and a seal of God's promise. This should strengthen faith and help it in its struggle with doubt.'

2. See M. Connell, *Eternity Today: On the Liturgical Year*, I and II, New York, 2006. In these valuable volumes Connell summarises a great deal of very complex historical and liturgical scholarship in a form accessible to non-specialists. See also Senn, *Christian Liturgy*, 156-163; 342-346; 657-661, and J. Baldovin SJ, 'Christian Year,' in *At That Time: Cycle and Season in the Life of a Christian*, ed J. A. Wilde, Chicago, 1989. For a good commentary on the Byzantine liturgical year see A Monk of the Eastern Church (Fr Lev Gillet), *The Year of Grace of the Lord*, London, 1980.

3. See G. Collins OSB, *The Glenstal Book of Icons*, Dublin, 2002, which provides further bibliography. Since then, see also R. Cormack, *Icons*, London, 2007.

4. As I hope should become clear, there ought to be no division or dichotomy between the collective and communal celebration of the mystery of Christ in the church's liturgy, and its celebration in the liturgy of personal prayer: both flow from the same source, are energised by the same Spirit and tend toward the same goal.

5. Connell, *Eternity Today* II, 158-177, summarises the issues surrounding this controversial area.

6. Connell, *Eternity Today* II, 180-181. As an enthusiastic liturgist Connell exaggerates a little the mode of Christ's presence in liturgical celebration, e.g. 'After the Second Vatican Council there was some enthusiasm for an eschatology of "already but not yet", positing that the kingdom of God was "in your midst" during the life of Jesus of Nazareth (the "already") and that it will be so again at the end of time (the "not yet"). The consolation of this errant theology is that it exempts the church today from acknowledging the presence of God in communities of faith and in the world. The teaching of the church would not support such a theology because the gift of God in his Son is not a gift that was taken away.' This seems to confuse the sacramental presence of Christ, for which we invoke the Holy Spirit in the *epiclesis* of the liturgy, with the as yet not fully realised eschatological revelation and manifestation of Christ's glory at the end of time. It also obscures the dialectic involved in the taking away of Christ's visible form at the ascension and his return in the Holy Spirit. His liturgical presence is no less real than his glorified presence in heaven but is precisely a provisional mystery-presence: it is veiled in signs and symbols accommodated to our current state as we await the face-to-face vision of the *eschaton*. See also A. Adam, *The Key to Faith. Meditations on the Liturgical Year*, Collegeville, Minnesota, 1998, which also provides reliable information on the mysteries of Christ in the liturgical year.

7. See Vincie, *Celebrating Divine Mystery*, 113-119.

8. For a profound contemplation of the mysteries of the life of Jesus and

how they reveal God in time and space, see *CCC*, 512-570. This is one of the richest and most carefully constructed sections of the catechism and offers much material for prayer and meditation.

9. *CCC*, 963-975, on the life of Mary and her place in the saving mystery of Christ.

10. Vincie, *Celebrating Divine Mystery*, 118: her short section on the sanctoral is particularly rich.

11. Vincie, *Celebrating Divine Mystery*, 111, offers the interesting comment that 'Ordinary Time' is really 'ordered time'. Opponents of the recent liturgical reforms sometimes bemoan the use of this expression in the renewed liturgy but ordinariness (Nazareth and a tomb?) is precisely the zone in which Christ and the Holy Spirit disclose the mystery of the grace of God's presence. As the poet George Herbert knew, heaven is 'in ordinarie (*sic*)' so we should neither demean it nor bemoan it.

12. Casel, *Mystery*, 63-70.

13. *BEM*: 22-23.

14. Casel, *Mystery*, 67: 'When therefore the church celebrates historical occurrences and developments, it does not do so for its own sake but for that of eternity hidden within it. The great deed of God upon mankind, the redeeming work of Christ which wills to lead mankind out of the narrow bounds of time into the broad spaces of eternity, is its content.'

15. Casel, *Mystery*, 67: 'When the church year fashions and forms a kind of unfolding of the mystery of Christ, that does not mean it seeks to provide historical drama, but that it will aid man in his step-by-step approach to God, an approach first made in God's own revelation. *It is the entire saving mystery which is before the eyes of the church and the Christian, more concretely on each occasion'* (my emphasis).

16. For a critical discussion of these terms and how Luther borrowed them from St Augustine and reshaped them according to his own understanding, see, E. Jüngel, 'The Sacrifice of Jesus Christ as Sacrament and Example,' in *Theological Essays* II, ed J. B. Webster, 163-191.

17. Liturgy can never be separated from ethics: its goal is the transformation of life through grace, a growing in the likeness of Christ.

18. Casel, *Mystery*, 67-68: 'We celebrate Advent, not by putting ourselves back into the state of unredeemed mankind, but in the certainty of the Lord who has already appeared to us, for whom we must prepare our soul ... We do not celebrate Lent as if we had never been redeemed, but as bearing the stamp of the cross upon us, and now only seeking to be better conformed to the death of Christ, so that the resurrection may be always more clearly shown upon us. It is therefore always the glorified *Kyrios* whom we have in our spiritual vision ...' Casel makes the further point that the unity of the mystery is illustrated by the fact that we solemnise every feast in the church's year by celebrating the Eucharist, the one all-inclusive sacramental memorial of the wholeness of the Lord's mystery.

19. I have seen them in use in Lucerne in Switzerland and icons are currently displayed in Christ Church Cathedral, Dublin.

20. See, Collins, *Glenstal Book of Icons*, 6-14, where the 'writing' and 'reading' of the icon is compared to the monastic method of *lectio divina*.

21. Collins, *Glenstal Book of Icons*, 23.

22. M. P. Gallagher SJ, 'Retrieving Imagination in Theology', in *The Critical Spirit: Theology at the Crossroads of Faith and Culture*, A. Pierce and G. Smyth OP, eds, Dublin, 2003, 200-207, here, 204.

23. The famous synagogue excavated at Dura-Europos in Mesopotamia contained figurative art as do Persian miniatures.

24. See the fascinating comments on glory and radiance in temple worship in Barker, *Temple Themes*, 138-139: 'When Isaiah saw the Lord enthroned, he saw that his train filled the temple' (Is 6:1). The Greek text here says that his Glory filled the temple. Isaiah heard the seraphim singing of his Glory filling the whole earth (Is 6:3). Since the great hall of the temple represented the creation, the Glory filling the earth and the Glory filling the temple was a distinction without a difference. How the Lord dwelt in the temple, how the Glory was envisaged, we do not know. Radiance caught by the reflected rays of the sun as it shone through the open door into the holy of holies is but one of several suggestions ... Shining was the sign that the Lord was in the temple.' Barker and A. Golitzin have done a great deal to alert us to the influence of temple theology on later Eastern Christian theology and spirituality.

25. Collins, *Glenstal Book of Icons*, 4; Cormack, *Icons*, 38-41.

26. On the architectural arrangements of Orthodox churches and on church decoration see, H. J. Schulz, *The Byzantine Liturgy. Symbolic Structure and Faith Expression*, trs M. J. O'Connell, New York, 1986, 51-67; 77-103.

27. Zizioulas, *Being*, 99-101: '… the iconological language of the Greek Fathers makes increased sense if seen in the light of primitive apocalyptic theology, such as first developed within the primitive Syro-Palestinian tradition and penetrated throughout the eucharistic liturgies of the East. This tradition presents truth not as a product of the mind, but as a "visit" and a "dwelling" (cf Jn 1:14) of an eschatological reality entering history to open it up in a communion event. This creates a vision of truth not as Platonic or mystical contemplation understands it but as picturing a new set of relationships, a new "world" adopted by the community as its final destiny. So, through its apocalyptic roots, iconological language liberates truth from our "conception", "definition" and "comprehension" of it and protects it from being manipulated and objectified. It also makes it relational, in the sense that the truth of one being is able to be "conceived" only in and through the mirror of another.' See also Meyendorff, *Christ*, 190, who quotes St Theodore of Studios to the effect that making icons is a human creative act that images divine creative action.

28. Schulz, *Byzantine Liturgy*, 111-114.

29. Meyendorff, *Christ*, 190: '… the image of Christ is the visible and necessary witness to the reality and humanity of Christ. If that witness is impossible, the Eucharist itself loses its reality. The theory of the Byzantine iconostasis, manifesting visibly "toward the exterior" the nature of the mystery accomplished within the sanctuary, was certainly conceived in the light of the theology just analysed.'

30. See G. Florovsky, *Creation and Redemption*, Belmont, Massachusetts, 1976, 212, who summarises beautifully the icon's capacity to mediate the mystery-presence and manifest the church's eschatological destiny as the communion of all the redeemed: 'Christ is never alone, St John of Damascus contended. He is always with his saints, who are his friends forever. Christ is the Head, and true believers are the Body. In the old churches the whole state of the church triumphant would be pictorially represented on the walls … this was not just a decoration, nor was it simply a story told in lines and colour for the ignorant and illiterate. It was rather an insight into the invisible reality of the church. The whole company of heaven was represented on the walls because it was present there, though invisibly. We always pray at Divine Liturgy, during the Little Entrance, that "Holy Angels may enter with us to serve with us." And our prayer is no doubt granted. We do not see Angels, indeed. Our sight is weak. But it was said of St Seraphim that he used to see them, for they were there indeed. The elect of the Lord do see them and the church triumphant. Icons are sign of this presence. "When we stay in the temple of thy glory we seem to stand in the heavens".'

31. Gallagher, *Retrieving Imagination*, 204. He also makes the important point that disclosure of truth through the imagination happens not just in 'high creativity' but in the ordinary, everyday experiences of life. The spiritual and aesthetic education the liturgy and the icon offer to the inner and outer senses, teaching us to discern the mystery as it 'presences itself' in worship, should awaken us to its self-presencing also in the world around us. 'Ordinary time' is then revealed to be 'extraordinary time', a time and space filled with divine presence. Observing that much modern imagery, especially that generated by advertising, is in its flight from the definite a denial of incarnation, he says (206): 'In a genuinely "analogical imagination" lies the key to our transformation under grace, through the everyday drama of living with love in the ordinary.'

32. See, M. Magrassi OSB, *Praying the Bible*, trs E. Hagman OFM Cap, Collegeville, Minnesota, 1998. Some modern monastic books on prayer that have acquired the status of classics are worth mentioning: C. Bruyère OSB, *The Spiritual Life and Prayer according to Holy Scripture and Tradition*, London, trs nuns of Stanbrook, London, (no date or year given); A. Bloom, *School for Prayer*, London, 1970 (a Russian Orthodox monk and bishop); Abishiktananda (Henri le Saux OSB), *Prayer*, London, 1974. T.

Merton OCSO, *Contemplative Prayer*, London, 1973, is one of the famous
Trappist's best books, published posthumously. H. Urs von Balthasar,
Prayer, trs G. Harrison, San Francisco, 1986, is full of Ignatian wisdom – a
legacy of the author's days with the Jesuits.
33. Speyr, *World of Prayer*, 19. On *lectio divina*, see M. Casey, *The Art of
Sacred Reading*, Victoria, Australia, 1995.
34. See Spidlik, *Spirituality*, 270-283, who gives a clear exposition of *apatheia* and explains how St Jerome misunderstood it and misrepresented
it to the west.
35. Once again, as with Evagrius and other eastern monastic writers, this
fundamental spiritual virtue should be understood as something positive, an attentive readiness to accomplish God's will by removing all interior obstacles, rather than mere detachment in a negative sense. For an interesting discussion of this core Jesuit concept in the spirituality of Hans
Urs von Balthasar, see W. Löser SJ, 'The Ignatian Exercises in the work of
Hans Urs von Balthasar,' in Schindler, *Hans Urs von Balthasar*, 108-109:
'The correct fundamental disposition of the creature in the face of the
choosing and calling God is abandonment (*Gelassenheit*) or – which is the
same – *indiferencia* or disposability.' However, both Balthasar and Löser
were surely saying too much when they criticised its use in Christian
spirituality before the 16th century: 'While in medieval and late medieval
piety "abandonment" had been understood as an attitude characterised
largely by passivity, it transforms itself in Ignatius into an "active indifference" which remains in an actively open posture of listening and is, at
the same time, ready to let itself be sent into action.' It is not necessary to
generalise so loosely about the earlier tradition – one does not exalt St
Ignatius by downgrading his predecessors.
36. See Woods, *Eckhart's Way*, 102. He rightly observes that just as important for this tradition is the active work of *Abgescheidenheit* (i.e. active detachment). On the Dominican mystical writers in general – one of the
most profound Christian spiritual traditions – see S. Tugwell OP, 'The
Dominicans', in *The Study of Spirituality*, ed C. Jones, G. Wainwright, E.
Yarnold SJ, 296-301. Also, O. Davies, *God Within*, London, 1988.
37. The argument has raged for years about whether Luther was a 'mystic' or not but a lot hangs on what one means by the modern expression
'mysticism'. Certainly he was greatly influenced by the Dominican tradition mediated both through the works of John Tauler OP and the anonymous treatise, the *Theologia Deutsch*. For a good translation of the latter
with a helpful introduction, see *The Book of the Perfect Life*, trs D. Blamires,
Walnut Creek, 2003. In general my impression is that Luther accorded to
faith the part played in Dominican tradition by the 'spark of the soul' or
the 'little castle in the soul'. See, T. Mannermaa, *Christ Present in Faith.
Luther's View of Justification*, Minneapolis, 2005. Mannermaa is the
founder of the Finnish school of Luther interpretation which highlights

forgotten themes like deification and transformation by grace in the great Reformer's works – though some would say he has merely turned an ex-Augustinian 'monk' into an Orthodox one! A good summary of Luther's relationship to the earlier mystical tradition is given in D. H. Tripp, 'Luther', in Jones, Wainwright, Yarnold, *Spirituality*, 343-346.

38. See Tripp's piece on Calvin in the same volume, 354-356: 'Prayer is the acceptance of what God has offered.'

39. St John Climacus, *The Ladder of Divine Ascent* (Step 28, On Prayer), trs C. Luibheid and N. Russell, New York, 1982, 275.

40. See *Rule*, IV, 17; XX, 43-44. Tears as the fruit of *penthos* (compunction of heart) are the normal context for prayer in early monasticism. See, Spidlik, *Spirituality*, 193-205. Yet it was not a gloomy spirituality, suffused as it was with the joy of the resurrection. Repentance and tears opened the heart to the indwelling of the Holy Spirit.

41. On the Jesus Prayer, see Spidlik, *Spirituality*, 315-327. But see, above all, L. Gillet ('A monk of the Eastern Church'), *On the Invocation of the Name of Jesus*, Illinois, 1985. Gillet is one of the unsung spiritual masters of the 20th century. His work is particularly illuminating in relating the Jesus Prayer to the individual dimensions of the one great mystery of Christ. The access the prayer gives to the 'total presence' unifies and syn-thesises the spiritual life, leading it from words to silence: see 91,'This total presence is all. The Name is nothing without the Presence. He who is able constantly to live in the total presence of our Lord does not need the Name. The Name is only an incentive to and a support to the Presence. A time may come, even here on earth, when we have to discard the Name it-self and to become free from everything but the nameless and unutterable living contact with the person of Jesus.'

42. Spiritualities which play down or even ignore the darker sides of human existence and experience are ultimately unsatisfactory.

43. The popularity of climbing imagery in spiritual literature – ladders and mountains especially – should not obscure the central Christian truth of ascent by descent so clearly taught in St Benedict's *Rule*, VII, 23: '… we descend by self-exaltation and ascend by humility.' In other words: pride may blind us into thinking we are going up to God while we are actually getting further and further away from him, whereas by descending to the depths through humility voluntarily embraced for love of Christ, we are in fact being raised up by God. The *Rule* is infused with the *kenotic* spirit of Philippians 2.

44. Almost all the great spiritual traditions of the world use nuptial im-agery to describe the soul's relationship with God. It is not therefore unique to Judaeo-Christianity but Judaism bequeathed to Christianity the Song of Songs as the perfect description of the mystical marriage. In the monastic literature of the Middle Ages, the bride became a polymor-phous symbol: she could at times represent the Virgin Mary, the church

and the individual soul, regardless of gender. See, A. W. Astell, *The Song of Songs in the Middle Ages,* Cornell University, 1995, 73-105; also, D. Turner, *Eros and Allegory. Medieval Exegesis of the Song of Songs,* Kalamazoo, Michigan, 1995.

45. I shall discuss later the liturgy of heaven which is the source, constant context and transcendent goal of the two earthly liturgies, i.e. the church's sacramental worship and personal prayer of the heart. There ought to be no dichotomy between the former and the latter: prayer of the heart is simply communal worship interiorised and offered on the altar of the heart. See Corbon, *Wellspring,* 206-216.

CHAPTER SEVEN

1. Adam, *Meditations,* 68; *CCC,* 651-655.

2. For centuries Catholic theology and spirituality dealt rather poorly with the mystery of the resurrection, tending to view it largely as a confirmation of Christ's divinity. It cannot be said that Protestantism did much better although the Reformers, particularly Luther, did at least preach effectively on it. This weakness surely owed something to the relegation for centuries of the great Easter Vigil to the morning of Holy Saturday and its almost complete disappearance from popular piety. In most places it became an esoteric rite generally performed in an empty, darkened church by the clergy and a devout elite minority. The situation has improved since the vigil was restored by Pope Pius XII but it still cannot be said that for most Latin Catholics Easter has as much spiritual significance as the feast of Christmas. Among Eastern Christians, faith and piety are generally more centred on the paschal celebrations although the level of understanding is often not much more advanced than among western Christians. It ought to be a pastoral priority to reawaken interest and understanding in this mystery of mysteries – it is after all the central mystery of our redemption. See Connell, *Eternity Today* II, 177-181.

3. *CCC,* 631-635. Both Adam and Connell scarcely mention the mystery of Holy Saturday which is surprising given the massive importance it has gained in recent theology and spirituality. Fundamental on all this is Bulgakov, *Lamb,* 315-316 and Balthasar, *Mysterium Paschale,* 148-168. From a Reformed perspective, see, A. E. Lewis, *Between Cross and Resurrection: A Theology of Holy Saturday,* Grand Rapids, Michigan, 2001, a fine piece of academic theology made all the more powerful by its having been written while the author was dying of cancer: it was published posthumously.

4. A good example of this lack of clarity is the textually beautiful and melodically stunning Offertory antiphon of the Requiem Mass in the Roman Rite: '*Domine Jesu Christe* ...' in which *infernus* (hell) is used very loosely in a way that would certainly not meet the precise requirements

of contemporary dogmatic theologians.

5. See for example, the opinion expressed by H. Alfeyev, 'Eschatology', in *The Cambridge Companion to Orthodox Theology*, ed M. B. Cunningham and E. Theokritoff, Cambridge, 2008, 115: '… in the West, under the influence of St Augustine and a number of other Latin Fathers, the doctrine of purgatory was conceived as an interim place between heaven and hell, or rather a special section of hell where sinners are exposed to the fires of purification.' No references are offered to support this assertion. It is not only unsubstantiated by official Catholic doctrine, but actually contrary to it: see *CCC*, 1030-1031: 'All who die in God's grace and friendship, but still imperfectly purified, are indeed assured of their eternal salvation; but after death they undergo purification, so as to achieve the holiness necessary to enter the joy of heaven. The church gives the name purgatory to this final purification of the elect, *which is entirely different from the punishment of the damned* (emphasis added).' Purgatory is not an antechamber of hell – nor indeed can a doctrine be a place.

6. The creation of liturgical symbols is one of the best reminders available that a human being is by nature a *homo symbolicus*, a creature who generates symbols. The Orthodox do not generally use the expression 'Byzantine Rite' but as 'liturgy' in the east is used exclusively to designate the Eucharist, it is convenient here to use 'rite' in the current western sense of 'liturgical worship' to cover all aspects of common prayer.

7. Luther recovered the image of Christ as victor and used it to good effect in his preaching and theology, though as one metaphor among many its importance should not be exaggerated: Althaus, *Martin Luther*, 218-223.

8. For Jung, archetypal ideas and images emerge from the depths of humanity's collective unconscious and find appropriate expression in symbols. Much could be gained by a creative dialogue between liturgists and Jungian analysts since liturgy often employs natural symbols in mediating the mystery. See A. Stevens, 'Archetypes', in *The Handbook of Jungian Psychology*, ed R. K. Papadopoulos, East Sussex, 2006.

9. One of the earliest examples in England is a stone slab in Bristol cathedral.

10. *CCC*, 647: 'Although the resurrection was an historical event that could be verified by the sign of the empty tomb and by the reality of the apostles' encounters with the risen Christ, still it remains at the very heart of the mystery of faith as something that transcends and surpasses history.' In technical theological language it is eschatological: Christ rises both in and out of time and becomes thereby the one who draws all time to its conclusion in his final, glorious coming.

11. See *Mysterium Paschale*, 148-168. The best short account of Balthasar's voluminous writings on this topic and his dense theological vision is that of J. O. Donnell SJ, 'Hans Urs von Balthasar: The Form of his Theology', in Schindler, *Hans Urs von Balthasar*, 207-220.

12. Dupuis, *Religious Pluralism*, 84-126.

13. For a stimulating discussion of this, see G. Wainwright, 'Eschatology', in *Cambridge Companion to Hans Urs Von Balthasar*, 113-127.

14. See Bulgakov, *Sophia*, 147-148, where he links the eventual destruction of evil and the triumph of the good to the kenotic patience of God: 'Evil, like a shadow, possesses but an illusory existence, which sooner or later must disclose the vanity of its illusion. The liberty of the creature cannot stand up to the end against the compelling attraction of Wisdom … This power of persuasion is grounded in the long-suffering of God and wins its victories only by enduring much from the stubbornness of the creature.'

15. D. D. Wallace Jr, 'Descent into Hell', in *Reformed Theology*, 56-57. Berkhof, *Systematic Theology*, 342-343.

16. I am referring to the stimulating and therapeutically enriching work of James Hillman, founder of the archetypal school of Jungian psychology. See Hillman, *The Dream and the Underworld*, New York, 1979, 27-32.

17. Connell, *Eternity Today* II, 167-172; Adam, *Key to Faith*, 88-89.

18. Bulgakov, *Lamb*, 317-318; *Sophia*, 93: 'And the final, conclusive stage of the *kenosis* extends even into the heavens, during those ten days between the ascension and Pentecost, while the Son "prays" the Father to send the Holy Spirit. It is then brought to an end only when the Son is sent the Spirit from the Father. Christ, having left the world, henceforth sits as the God-human at the right hand of the Father in glory, until the time comes for his second and glorious coming, the *Parousia*.'

19. For a comprehensive theology of the ascension (from a Reformed perspective) see D. Farrow, *Ascension and Ecclesia*, Edinburgh, 1999. The connection between Christ's entry into the fullness of divine life and his continuing presence in his extended body the church is well brought out in *CCC*, 669: 'As Lord, Christ is also the head of·the church, which is his Body. Taken up to heaven and glorified after he had thus fully accomplished his mission, Christ dwells on earth in his church.'

20. Connell, *Eternity Today* II,178-185; Adam, *Key to Faith*, 92-95.

21. *CCC*, 1067.

22. Meerson, *Trinity of Love*, 1-21.

23. Theology both east and west uses three forms of discourse in attempting to describe God. *Kataphatic* theology speaks of God using the categories and concepts of revelation (God's partial self-manifestation in nature, perfect revelation in the mystery of Christ and its record in holy scripture and the liturgy); *apophatic* theology negates all predicates, both positive and negative, in order to impel the mind into the unspeakable experience of God who is beyond all ideas and images; yet 're-emerging' from this ineffable experience, *symbolic* theology also speaks in symbols which serve as icons and pointers to the mystery of the divine. All three methods are needed to do justice to God's manifestation and to his transcen-

dence.
24. For a good account of the Holy Spirit in scripture and the life of the
church, see C. F. D. Moule, *The Holy Spirit*, London, 1978.
25. Jesus said that the Spirit would be his witness – as would the disciples
also in their turn (cf Jn 15:26-27 and Acts 1:8).
26. See, Bulgakov, *Sophia*, 98-113 which discusses the relation between
Christ and the Holy Spirit and the kenotic activity of the Spirit.
27. One strand of modern Russian theology, running from Soloviev via
Florensky to Bulgakov, speaks of 'sophiology'. To have a sophiological
vision of the world is to see it as grounded in God's own uncreated wisdom (common to the Father, Son and Holy Spirit), 'reproduced' or reiterated in creation, which is a vast moving image of God's infinite perfections. Although this is not without controversy in Orthodox theological
circles, it is surely a legitimate development of many aspects of patristic
thought and a spiritual antidote to the secularised and mechanised view
of the world so prevalent in Europe today. See Bulgakov, *Bride*, 7-103 and
more accessibly in *Sophia*, 23-82. Sophiology is by no means easy to understand but is in many ways the key to grasping the central intuition of
much modern Orthodox theology. The following is a useful guide: M.
Plekon, 'The Russian Religious Revival and its Theological Legacy,' in
Cunningham and Theokritoff, *Orthodox Christian Theology*, 203-218.
28. It is necessary to stress this essential difference between ancient and
modern paganism if the character of the former is to be understood.
Essential reading on this is M. Eliade, *Patterns in Comparative Religion*,
London, 1958, which carefully documents ancient peoples' awareness of
the divine in its numerous symbolic manifestations. Much of Eliade's
work confirms the belief that God is constantly breaking through into the
world he has created, in an unceasing attempt to establish communion
between himself and his creatures – which is not to deny the oppressive
aspects of paganism, particularly its crushing fatalism.
29. On 'natural grace', see Bulgakov, *Bride*, 247, where he summarises
precisely this sophianic notion of creation as already 'graced' by God's
activity and ordained to its fulfilment in the incarnation of Christ: 'Divine
power ceaselessly flows in the world and sustains the world's being not
only through a single supratemporal and extratemporal creative act of
God, but also through providential action with regard to creation, directed
towards its sophianisation. Creation and providence are inseparable. In
other words, there exists a 'natural' grace of creation, physico-sophianic,
without which and outside of which creation could not exist but would
sink into the abyss of nothing. This grace is communicated directly to creation through the world soul, pre-human or not yet humanised being,
and then through man. Grace in the true sense is precisely the power of
deification, in which creation surpasses itself in man, transcends the

bounds of natural or physico-sophianic being, and acquires the power of new sophianisation by receiving the principles of divine life in Divine-humanity.' Allowing for the difference of idiom and expression Bulgakov is asserting here one of the key ideas of traditional western theology: nature is always sustained by grace, so that when human beings come to fulfilment through life in Christ conveyed by the grace of the Holy Spirit in the sacramental mysteries, they are taken up to a new level of existence, in which their nature is perfected, not destroyed.

30. Hopkins, 'God's Grandeur,' in *The Major Works*, 128.

31. Woods, *Eckhart's Way*, 78-79.

32. Bulgakov, *Sophia*, 111: 'Grace accords with human freedom, it never violates this freedom; it educates and prepares it. This voluntary self-restriction, out of love for the creature and respect for its creaturely freedom, constitutes the *kenosis* of the Third Hypostasis ... It is beyond human comprehension or reason how the almighty and all-holy God can restrict himself in his action. Humankind will never be given to understand how the absolute could restrict himself in the creation of the world. But this *kenosis* of the Spirit, as an aspect of sacrificial love, of necessity springs from the special form of divine ministration in which "all is given by the Holy Spirit", yet only when human freedom is willing to acquiesce and accept.'

33. God's respect for creation's need for time and space is mirrored in his taking time to bring about our salvation. See St Benedict's *Rule*, Prologue, 4.

34. Arianism, which posited a hierarchy of 'gods' with Jesus as a demi-god who was neither consubstantial with the Father nor with us, is probably the most extreme form of subordinationism. See,M. Ward, 'Arianism: Is Jesus Christ divine and eternal or was he created?' in Quash and Ward, *Heresies*, 15-23.

35. It is worth observing that the God of the Hebrew scriptures, whom Christians identify with the Holy Trinity revealed in the mystery of Christ, was anything but a God who refused to dirty his hands with human dealings. In Exodus 3, God expressly tells Moses that he has come down to rescue his people and Psalm 112 (113) sings of him stooping down even to the dung heap to raise the poor and give them a place near his glorious throne. The revelation of the Word in the incarnation and the coming of the Holy Spirit are actually perfectly comprehensible in the context of Jewish faith in a God who saves those whom he loves. The problem for Jews is the assertion that the Word became human (and was crucified in addition) and that the three divine manifestations are 'persons' (even if the notion of person as ascribed to God has to be understood strictly analogically).

36. That was the one of the fundamental beliefs guiding Karl Barth's radical reconstruction of Protestant theology. See K. Barth, *The Holy Spirit and the Christian Life*, trs R. B. Hoyle, London, 1938.

CHAPTER EIGHT

1. For a discussion of the difficult issues surrounding the episode's historicity, see A. J. Torrance, 'The Lazarus Narrative, Theological History and Historical Probability,' in *The Gospel of John and Christian Theology*, ed R. Bauckham and C. Mosser, Grand Rapids, Michigan, 2008, 245-262. It is surely time to question the notion that miracles can't happen because the predominant worldview is that they don't. The 'miracles' recorded in the gospel – and John's signs – indicate the in-breaking of God's reign in Jesus. They are manifestations of eschatological reality – the glory of the world to come – appearing in earthly time. On 'Lazarus Saturday' in the Byzantine Tradition, see A Monk of the Eastern Church, *Year of Grace*, 135: '… Lazarus raised from the dead is shown to us, at the threshold of the Easter feasts, as the precursor of Jesus Christ triumphant over death.' He also connects it with the forgiveness of sins, 137: '… the resurrection of Lazarus allows a sinner to hope that, even though he seems spiritually dead, he could come alive again.'

2. There is a good discussion of this tradition in the Christian East (with a nod at the west as well) in Spidlik, *Spirituality of the Christian East*, 189-193 and 283-287.

3. This debate came to a head in Byzantium with the controversy surrounding the charismatic *Igumenos* (Abbot) of the St Mamas monastery in Constantinople, St Symeon the New Theologian (949-1022). Symeon upheld the ancient monastic tradition of confessing to and receiving absolution from those considered gifted by the Spirit – even if they had not been ordained. However, the later Orthodox Church did not uphold that teaching in its official canonical legislation – whatever about pastoral practice. See H. Alfeyev, *St Symeon the New Theologian and Orthodox Tradition*, Oxford, 2000, 106-108, and 200. Although the Latin Church may appear even more strict on this issue than the Orthodox, its tradition too only codified itself gradually: see H. Ott, *Fundamentals of Catholic Dogma*, trs P. Lynch, Cork, 1954, 439-440, who mentions the medieval western evidence for confession to deacons and laymen.

4. There is always a directly personal element in sin and redemption and we should neither neglect nor underestimate that dimension. However, given the historical difficulties surrounding the celebration of this sacramental mystery – its association for many with guilt, anxiety and scruples – it would seem to me pastorally wise to extend the currently very limited rules on general absolution. Here, as with ecumenical issues, relaxation of rigidity is more likely to encourage people to come to individual confession than enforcing the rules too strictly.

5. See A Monk of the Eastern Church, *Year of Grace*, 140-142.

6. Adam, *Key to Faith*, 64-65.

7. *CCC*, 574-598. Among the unfortunate after-effects of the recent restoration of the unreformed Roman Rite, the resurgence of prayers em-

bodying an anti-Jewish mentality renounced by the church following the Second Vatican Council is among the most serious. Liturgies are not self-standing independent rites: they express a theological understanding of belief. Deficient theologies will tend to generate unacceptable liturgical expressions and in turn be reinforced by ritual celebration.

8. A Monk of the Eastern Church, *Year of Grace*, 142-146.

9. Cullman first alerted us to the sacramental structure of John's gospel but somewhat overstated his case. See O Cullman, *Early Christian Worship*, London, 1953. Foot washing was also viewed in some places as part of the baptismal washing itself.

10. This text comes from the Preface for the feast of the Sacred Heart. Notwithstanding the liturgical imbalance involved in the Sacred Heart having been made a major solemnity (while the Lord's Baptism, Presentation in the Temple and Transfiguration remain only feasts of a lesser rank), the undeniable tastelessness of many artistic depictions of the Heart of Jesus and the frequent association of the devotion with narrow, un-liturgical and neurotic forms of piety, the actual liturgy of the feast expresses very well the essential meaning of the devotion: the heart of Christ as the dwelling place and sacramental sign of the incarnate Word, and its piercing as the source of grace and coming of the Holy Spirit. It is thus more in line with earlier, more liturgically holistic forms of the devotion associated with the great women monastic mystics of the High Middle Ages in Germany. This is well treated in the third volume of B. McGinn, *The Presence of God: The Flowering of Mysticism. Men and Women in the New Mysticism (1200-1350)*, New York, 1998, 266-282. See especially, 270 and 271: 'The nuns of Helfta combine the liturgical basis for Christian mysticism found in monastic traditions with the new visionary mysticism of the thirteenth century ... The union of bride and Bridegroom centres on the uniting of their hearts ... Though earlier Christian theologians and mystics had also seen the heart of Jesus as source of salvation and place of access to God (especially as opened on the cross; cf Jn 7:37-39 and 19:31-37), no one had spoken as insistently, as personally, and as dramatically about the heart of Jesus as the Helfta nuns. Mystical union, for both Gertrude and Mechtilde, is a fusing of the human heart with the heart of Jesus ... As the revelation of the redemptive love of God, the Helfta Cistercians present the heart of Jesus as "the sacrament" of union with God ... This emphasis on the love of God revealed in the heart of Jesus is at the root of the optimism about salvation that is one of the most winning aspects of Helfta mysticism.' In the earlier tradition, Christ's heart was visualised primarily as a locus of divine light and love through whose opening God draws near to us (the original meaning of 'propitiation'). In some later forms of the devotion an all-too-human Jesus complains repeatedly about being wounded and let down by ungrateful followers. Balance has been lost and the vision of the redeeming, glorious Saviour has been re-

placed by a rather touchy God who has to be regularly propitiated himself.
11. Riordan, *Divine Light*, 150-151; Louth, *Denys*, 73-75. For an excellent analysis of this unifying work of eucharistic communion in Denys' continuator, St Maximos the Confessor (who apparently displays a more heightened sensitivity to the mystery of the Trinity than his predecessor), see Thunberg, *Man and the Cosmos*, 168-170. Thunberg is perhaps inclined to exaggerate somewhat the differences between Denys and Maximos.
12. The thesis that the church both 'makes' the Eucharist (being the celebrant of the earthly liturgy) yet is in turn 'made by' the Eucharist (through communion in the body and blood of Christ, as in the reference from 1 Corinthians cited above) derives from the pioneering work of Cardinal H. de Lubac SJ but has also been a major postulate in modern Orthodox ecclesiology and eucharistic theology. See Zizioulas, *Being*, 143-169 and 247-260. It has helped greatly in the brokering of ecumenical agreements as witnessed, for example, in the Catholic-Orthodox 'Munich Statement' on the church and the Eucharist in the light of the mystery of the Holy Trinity. Yet one needs to be careful with the language used to describe this mysterious interchange, taking care not to fall back into the non-liturgical terminology of instrumental causality typical of scholastic reflection on the sacraments. It is not ultimately the church that makes or is made by the Eucharist: Christ and the Holy Spirit as agents of the Father are always the acting subject(s) of liturgical action, who operate in and through the symbols of the liturgy to bring about transforming effects such as ecclesial communion and the deification of believers.
13. From the poem 'Irish,' in, P. Celan, *Selected Poems*, trs M. Hamburger, London, 1995, 287.
14. In reconsidering the issue of the reality of the Eucharist in Protestant churches, the Roman Catholic Church needs to pay more attention to the primary symbols which actually mediate the mystery of Christ in liturgical celebration: the breaking and giving of the sacramental bread and the drinking from the sacramental cup, both of which speak of communion with the crucified and risen *Kyrios*-Lord Jesus in the power of the Holy Spirit. On the other hand, some Protestant churches may need to re-examine their own occasional neglect of the traditional symbols (such as the common cup) and revaluate them in the light of modern liturgical scholarship and a re-reading of the Bible.
15. Harvey, *Companion*, 510-511.
16. Bulgakov, *Lamb*, 233-234, and 243: 'One can say that if obedience to God's commandment was natural for the original Adam and Eve, then for the new Adam, because of his humanity, it required a victory over nature, an agony resulting in a sweat of blood. The union of the natures in the God-man, therefore, does not signify their serene and harmonious coexistence and interpermeation but the intense and unceasing struggle in which this harmony is accomplished ... this harmony and interpenetra-

tion of the two natures in the God-man is *the feat and way of the cross*, which begins in the Bethlehem manger and ends at Golgotha. For the Son, this is the path of obedience to the Father's will, the Son's accomplishment not of his own will but of his Father's will. In this submission to the Father's will the human nature, infirm in its creatureliness and weakened in its sinfulness, is overcome. The union of the two natures in Christ, therefore, cannot at any instant be understood statically as their mere juxtaposition; instead it must be understood dynamically, as an actual interaction of energies' (author's emphasis).

17. H. von Balthasar, 'Spirit and Institution,' in *Explorations in Theology IV*, trs E. T. Oakes SJ, San Francisco, 138: 'For with the *kenosis* of Christ, eternity has put itself in motion and has passed through time with all of its darkness. There is no alienating hiatus between the Father's remaining at home and the Son's going-forth in pilgrimage, for the 'distance' of the *kenosis* is a mode of inner-trinitarian nearness and the circumincession of the divine hypostases.' For an excellent commentary on this, see R. Williams, 'Balthasar and the Trinity,' in *The Cambridge Companion to Hans Urs von Balthasar*, 37-50.

18. See, Harvey, *Companion*, 201: 'Pilate was the governor of Judaea from 26 to 36 CE. He had a bad record of tactless and provocative actions aimed at the Jews, but there is nothing in the following narrative to suggest that he acted irregularly. Under Roman law he was obliged to hold a trial before imposing a severe penalty ...'

19. See Michael Thompson on the Arian heresy in Quash and Ward, *Heresies*, 20: '... God did not send a creature in order to show us how we could bridge the gap between heaven and earth by learning how to follow a wonderful example ... the Son cannot be a bridge between God and humanity if the bridge doesn't fully reach to both ends.' In the Arian understanding of God, 'This God does not give of himself, but sends a lesser, created being to show kindness. God remains an isolated, insular ruler who cannot involve himself intimately with his creation. Orthodoxy is far more radical (and personal) than that!'

20. Bauckham, *Jesus*, 57: '"The Father, the Son and the Holy Spirit" names the newly disclosed identity of God, revealed in the story of Jesus the gospel has told ... we can say that in Christ God both demonstrates his deity to the world as the same unique God his people Israel had always known, and also in doing so, identifies himself afresh. As the God who includes the humiliated and exalted Jesus in his identity, he is the Father, the Son and the Holy Spirit, that is, the Father of Jesus Christ, Jesus Christ the Son and the Spirit of the Father given to the Son.'

21. Bauckham, *Jesus*, 131-132.

22. Russell, *The Doctrine of Deification*, 211, notes that St Basil, like St Athanasius, established the third person's full divinity precisely by the Spirit's power to deify. In the later Byzantine liturgy the Holy Spirit is

praised as the one who deifies and is not deified.

23. See G. F. O'Hanlon SJ, *The Immutability of God in the Theology of Hans Urs von Balthasar*, Cambridge, 1990, for a sympathetic but critical discussion of this area in Balthasar's thought.

24. On St Gregory Palamas, see Russell, *Deification*, 304-311 and Meyendorff, *Byzantine Theology*, 76-78. No more than the theology of the Trinity itself, was the Byzantine distinction between these two dimensions in God simply a speculative luxury. It was an attempt to do justice to what Rowan Williams once called the incurably dialectical nature of discourse about God, especially given the Christian emphasis on divine incarnation and trans-historical events like the resurrection. It has gradually come close to being accepted as a dogma by many Orthodox. See the perceptive comments of F. Sanders in 'The Trinity,' in Webster, Tanner and Torrance, *Oxford Handbook of Systematic Theology*, 50: '... much depends on whether the uncreated energies are thought of in entitative terms, or alternatively as divine actions. The more the energies are described in entitative terms, the more they seem to be buffers between God and the human person. When they are construed more dynamically along the lines of divine actions, it seems clearer that believers are immediately in the hands of God their redeemer.' This interpretation, following the lead of Meyendorff who saw St Gregory as a kind of existentialist theologian, should be acceptable to western Christian thinkers.

25. J. Alison, 'God's Self-Substitution and Sacrificial Inversion,' in Jersak and Hardin, *Stricken by God*, 166-179.

26. Which is not to suggest that all contemporary Christian thinkers have embraced the idea of divine *kenosis*.

27. F. Sanders, 'The Trinity', in *Oxford Handbook of Systematic Theology*, 35-53 gives a helpful and stimulating overview of contemporary reflection on trinitarian theology. The fact that it is the second chapter in the volume also says something about how the doctrine of the Holy Trinity has moved centre-stage in recent reflection.

28. See *Edith Stein. Philosopher. Carmelite. Nun. Martyr,* ed J. Sullivan OCD, Washington, 1987.

29. Consult http://en.wikipedia.org/wiki/maximilian_kolbe.

30. There is a moving and inspiring biography of this spirited and highly unconventional nun who died in Ravensbruck: see S. Hackel, *Pearl of Great Price*, New York, 1982.

31. On Sts Boris and Gleb, sons of Vladimir of Kiev, see H. Iswolsky, *Soul of Russia*, London, 1944, 7: 'In the story of the two brothers, a religious motif which is peculiarly Russian can be discerned. Attacked by their elder brother, who wanted to rule supreme in Kiev, Boris and Gleb ordered their men-at-arms to offer no resistance, preferring death to civil strife. Thus the ideal of non-resistance to evil was articulated ten centuries before Tolstoy. Although they were worshipped by their people

and possessed, it seems, all the attributes of sanctity, the canonisation of Boris and Gleb encountered many obstacles. Their case was difficult to classify. They had been exemplary Christians and had died heroic deaths. Yet, although Boris had said, 'I shall be martyr to my God,' the two brothers could not be considered martyrs for the Christian faith in the accepted sense. They had not preached the gospel or performed miracles; their only extraordinary action had consisted in the meekness and self-abandonment with which they had met brute force. The Greek hierarchy was confused and reluctant to act, but finally the Russian clergy prevailed, and Boris and Gleb were canonised as *strastoterptzy* (i.e., passion-bearers), a term coined by the Russians to define the quality of the young mens' sanctity.' Unfortunately Iswolsky used the word 'worship' rather too loosely: the Orthodox *venerate* their saints, they do not *worship* them.

32. Casel, *Mystery*, 50-62. Casel came under considerable fire by some for supposedly suggesting that the central elements of Christian worship literally owed something to the pagan mysteries (which he hadn't actually claimed) and also by specialists in the field of ancient religion for generalising too loosely about the same mysteries (which he probably had). However, see the sensible remarks of E. J. Kilmartin SJ, *The Eucharist in the West*, 278-279: 'In general, scholars agree on the theoretical possibility of analogies between Hellenistic mysteries and Christian worship … The question of the relation of Christian mysteries to Hellenistic mysteries is a matter about which contemporary scholarship tends to be more cautious than Casel.' It is, however, beyond dispute that some of the Fathers of the 4th and 5th centuries pressed the language of the pagan mysteries into the service of Christian worship. See E. Yarnold SJ, *The Awe-Inspiring Rites of Initiation*, Slough, 1973, 55-62, who suggests very plausibly that the explanation of the Christian rites by the Fathers, rather than the rites themselves, shows the influence of the mystery religions. For an evocative account of the similarities (and differences) between the pagan and Christian mysteries, see V. White OP, 'The Dying God,' in *God and the Unconscious*, London, 1952, 227-245, where he concludes, 'Yes, it is true that the ancient Christian liturgies of Holy Week and Easter closely resemble the old rites of spring. But their significance for those who take part in them is found wholly in what Christ is related to have done "once and for all": they are done in remembrance of him.'

33. M. Longley, 'Ceasefire' in, *Staying Alive: Real Poems for Unreal Times*, ed N. Astley, Tarset, Northumberland, 2002, 350.

34. Simone Weil, *Intimations of Christianity Among the Ancient Greeks*, London, 1957.

35. On the history of this feast, see Adam, *Key to Faith*, 117-120. Byzantium is not the only example that springs to mind: there were also the Holy Roman and Spanish Empires, and Cromwell's godly commonwealth.

36. A good account of Luther's theology of the cross is found in R. Kolb,

Martin Luther. Confessor of the Faith, Oxford, 2009, 55-59.

37. Hence Barth's strident protest in the name of the one Lord whom we are called to serve in life and in death. See E. Busch, *Karl Barth*, trs J. Bowden, Grand Rapids, Michigan, 1994, 222-255. It is worth noting that capitulation to political pressure was not unique to Protestantism. The Catholic response to Nazi Germany was not particularly inspiring either: the Swastika was also found in some Benedictine cloisters and Casel's own Abbot, Ildefons Herwegen was – at least initially – an enthusiastic supporter of the regime. Even allowing for the folly of being wise after the event, and having acknowledged that there were martyrs among both clergy and laity, none of the churches emerged untainted from the Nazi era.

38. It is worth recalling that the Lord, when he appeared to Isaiah in the temple (Is 6:1-6), was high and lifted up and that his suffering servant (whom Christian tradition identifies with the crucified Christ) is also described as exalted (Is 52:13). The cross is the true divine throne.

39. Adam, *Key to Faith*, 73-74; Connell, *Eternity Today* 2, 135-142

40. See A. Louth, *St John Damascene*, Oxford, 2002, 163-4.

41. Julian of Norwich, *Revelations*, 25-27.

CHAPTER NINE

1. Connell, *Eternity Today* I, 88-147; Adam, *Key to Faith*, 20-25.

2. In the Byzantine tradition, the Wise Men from the East are commemorated during the Christmas celebration itself. See A Monk of the Eastern Church, *Year of Grace*, 66-71.

3. Balthasar, *Mysterium Paschale*, 23-34; O. Crisp, 'Incarnation,' in *Oxford Handbook of Systematic Theology*, 171-172.

4. Bulgakov, *Lamb*, 220 and 233-235.

5. Connell, *Eternity Today* I, 199-233, gives a very comprehensive summary of the complicated evolution of the feast. See also Adam, *Key to Faith*, 99-101.

6. A Monk of the Eastern Church, *Year of Grace*, 89-91.

7. Barker, *Temple Themes*, is an essential guide to all aspects of Temple lore in Jewish and early Christian literature; see also her shorter work, M. Barker, *The Hidden Tradition of the Kingdom of God*, London, 2007.

8. In Jungian psychology the appearance in dreams of images of the birth of a divine or holy child embodies the promise of a coming psychological integration called by Jung, 'individuation' (not to be confused with 'individualism'). It is a holistic symbol of healing and harmony, though that is never achieved without great struggle, suffering and sacrifice. See M. Stein, 'Individuation,' in Papadopoulos, *Handbook of Jungian Psychology*, 196-213.

9. One of the 'Great Antiphons' sung during the week before Christmas (the 23nd of December) addresses Christ-Emmanuel as the pre-existent God who spoke with Moses: 'O Emmanuel, our King and law-giver, the

desire of all nations, and their salvation: come and save us, O Lord our God!'

10. See, Barker, *Hidden Tradition*, 4-17, on the suspicion and scepticism with which some Jews of Jesus' time viewed the Temple.

11. Collins, *Glenstal Book of Icons*, 51.

12. Orthodox teaching, having a rather different understanding of 'original sin' from that of western Christianity, denies the Roman Catholic doctrine of the Immaculate Conception of Mary (i.e. her own sinless conception in the womb of her mother, not her virginal conception of Jesus) but insists no less strongly on her absolute freedom from sin. See S. Bulgakov, *The Burning Bush*, trs T. A. Smith, Grand Rapids, Michigan, 2009, on Orthodox mariology, including a critical response to that of the Latin Catholic tradition.

13. Congar, *The Mystery of the Temple*, 119.

14. Christ's baptism was a symbolic mystery prefiguring his future descent into the tomb. For a profound examination of its relationship to his death and resurrection, see H. Urs von Balthasar, 'Descent into Hell,' in *Explorations in Theology IV*, 401-414. Balthasar writes of (406), '… the theme of the connection between the sea's abyss (as the rebellious power of chaos resistant to God, the *tehom*: see also Noah's deluge) and Christ's baptism, where his immersion in the river Jordan bespeaks a first "cultic" anticipation of his definitive baptismal immersion in the abyss of chaos (*abyssos* [Rom 10:7]): the waters of judgement have been "purified" by him and transformed into the waters of salvation.'

15. The definitive work in English on the baptism of Jesus remains that of K. McDonnell OSB, *The Baptism of Jesus in the Jordan*, Collegeville, Minnesota, 1996, which is a masterly survey of the biblical and liturgical material referring to this mystery. See also, A Monk of the Eastern Church, *Year of Grace*, 80-87.

16. Connell, *Eternity Today* I, 151-191; Adam, *Key to Faith*, 32-33 and 36-39.

17. Unlike Western Christians, who have largely lost a living awareness of this last and greatest of the prophets, Eastern Christians generally retain great devotion to St John the Baptist, known to the Greeks as the *Prodromos* or forerunner.

18. See, R. Brown, *An Introduction to New Testament Christology*, London, 1994, 84: '… the hypothesis that the scene tells Jesus who he is has been rejected today by most scholars', which, however, strikes me as being excessively reductionist.

19. McDonnell, *Baptism of Jesus*, 5-6, points out that the gospel accounts, being primarily testimonies to faith by and for believers, probably say more about the early Christian community's belief in Jesus' identity than his own consciousness of who he was; but he still leaves room for some area of growth in vocational awareness on Jesus' part.

20. Barth, *CD* IV.3.1, 481-554, where he discusses Christian vocation and

criticises all forms of pietistic self-absorption and obsession either with one's own salvation or one's personal spiritual experiences', as the antithesis of genuine Christian witness. It is 'spiritual egoism', whereas life in Christ is life in and for community – a Christian community which is not a holy club or a pious ghetto but God's instrument for communicating his salvation to the world.

21. For the New Testament and numerous Greek Fathers, see Russell, *Deification*, 81-82, 196-197 and 267-268; but it is asserted by every serious Christian writer in all traditions. Within modern Roman Catholicism, it is worth remembering that Blessed Columba Marmion in particular laid special emphasis on this key New Testament doctrine, see P. Philipon OP, *The Spiritual Doctrine of Dom Marmion*, trs M. Dillon OSB, London, 1956, 114.

22. For the centrality of this idea in monastic tradition see Spidlik, *Spirituality of the Christian East*, 340-341: 'In a world marked by forgetfulness (*lethe*) of God, contemplation strives to promote an unceasing union with the Lord, to "see" God in everything. The expression *mneme Theou* (memory of God) is Philonian and Stoic, but the idea is biblical. The monks who searched for it saw in it an angelic liturgy.'

23. Althaus, *Luther*, 170, 'Luther ... constantly repeats his basic rule: God is – is for you – the kind of God you think and believe he is.'

24. The transfiguration holds a central place in every area of the theology of the Christian East – liturgy, spirituality, dogma and ethics. The number of works dealing with this theme is vast but the fundamental study in English is J. A. McGuckin, *The Transfiguration of Christ in Scripture and Tradition*, Lewiston, Me., and Queenston, 1986. See also Russell, *Deification*, 304-309; V. Lossky, *The Vision of God*, trs A. Moorhouse, Leighton Buzzard, 1963; Louth, *St John Damascene*, 234-243; G. Mantzarides, *The Deification of Man*, trs L. Sherrard, New York, 1984, 87-115 (on the transfiguration, prayer and the vision of the divine light of Tabor). A fundamental text is the famous *Philokalia* (a massive anthology of [mostly] Byzantine spiritual writings spanning more than a millennium) which teaches the need for purification of the heart and disciplined contemplative prayer if the light of Mt Tabor is to be personally experienced. See *The Philokalia*, trs and ed G. E. H. Palmer, P. Sherrard and K. Ware, (four volumes), last volume London, 1995. In citing it I shall use simply *Philokalia*, followed by the relevant volume number and page. For a creative introduction to the ongoing tradition in modern Orthodoxy, see J. Chryssavagis, *Light Through Darkness: The Orthodox Tradition*, London, 2004.

25. Adam, *Key to Faith*, 116-17 (and for the second Sunday of Lent, 51-53).

26. See Merton, *Contemplative Prayer*, 96-101.

27. See Spidlik, *Spirituality*, 177-193 which deals with praxis (active purification of the heart through spiritual disciplines developed in traditional monasticism such as fasting, watching, confession of thoughts to a spirit-

ual elder, rebuttal of evil images and ideas, *lectio divina*, and incessant prayer). It is the basic spiritual system found in the *Rule* of St Benedict, (especially chapter VII) and throughout the *Philokalia*. As one goes deeper in prayer, however, deeper levels of disconnectedness to God are disclosed, calling for more intensive purification. Western writers tend to speak less of co-operating with grace at this level than of submitting to it and becoming passive under it. This may well be a major difference between the eastern and western spiritual traditions: see Louth, *Origins*, 181-190, where he proposes and defends this thesis.

28. The fundamental work on 'Macarius' (traditionally confused with one of the great monks of the Egyptian desert but almost certainly an anonymous Syrian writer) is C. Stewart OSB, *Working the Earth of the Heart: The Messalian Controversy in History, Texts and Language to AD 431*, Oxford, 1991; see also, K. Ware, 'Prayer in Evagrius of Pontus and the Macarian Homilies,' in *An Introduction to Christian Spirituality*, ed R. Waller and B. Ward, London, 1999, 14-30. 'Macarius' certainly did teach the reality of spiritual experience, using a language so strong that it led to accusations of heresy but, like St Gregory Palamas after him, he rejected spiritual sensuality as a counterfeit version of real experience of God.

29. See Mantzarides, *The Deification of Man*, on St Gregory in general.

30. A good accessible introduction to Tauler is, O. Davies, *The Rhineland Mystics*, London, 1989, 63-88. The Dominican mystic was a disciple of the great (but controversial) Meister Eckhart; his writings in turn had a considerable influence on Luther who referred to him throughout his life.

31. On John's mystical doctrine see the fine study by C. Thompson, *St John of the Cross: Songs in the Night*, London, 2002.

32. D. Turner, *The Darkness of God*, Cambridge, 1995, 237-238, where the paradoxical nature of this ascetical self is carefully analysed according to the insights of St John of the Cross and exposed to the light: 'Now for John, any ascetically acquired selfhood has this character of being more or less a construction of egoism and ... the higher the asceticism the more "spiritual" the egoism ... asceticism can never catch the egoism, for the ascetical "I" must always reaffirm the egoism it seeks to deny precisely in the acts of its denial. And so for John there is an "ascetical self". It is the product of our best efforts, supported by everything there is in us by way of generosity and goodwill, indeed of love of God. But it is a poor, precarious and self-contradictory structure, built up out of the combination of quasi-moral forces, more or less "possessive" desires and wishes, bound together by the countervailing force of an ascetically imposed will.' See also, from an Orthodox perspective, the devastatingly perceptive comments of Fr Alexander Schmemann in his diaries, quoted by V. Larrin in 'Fr Alexander Schmemann and Monasticism', *St Vladimir's Theological Quarterly*, 53, 2-3, New York, 2009, 301-319: 'I keep reflecting on "spirituality". To put it simply, I will say the following: I am amazed by the ego-

centricity of this "spirituality"; the "me" that protrudes from it. It has been my experience for some thirty years that students with tendencies toward "spirituality" are almost always unpleasant – troublemakers. I will write an essay on ascetical theology [they say] – and immediately, automatically, a whiff of pride (look at me!), i.e. the most deadly enemy of spirituality … Sometimes I think that this type of spirituality is a real temptation…'

33. St John of the Cross, chapter 13 of *The Ascent of Mt Carmel*, in *Collected Works*, 147-151.

34. Turner, *Darkness*, 233. John surely bears comparison here with Buddhist writers.

35. Louth, *Origins*, 181-190, who also notes that in general the inflow of the divine light in eastern Christian writers is less marked by painful suffering than in those of the west, though there have been some Orthodox exceptions, including St Symeon the New Theologian who described periods of painful abandonment in his spiritual life which alternated with his luminous experiences: see Alfeyev, *Symeon the New Theologian*, 233. On Gregory of Nyssa, Denys and Maximus, see Louth's three entries in Jones, Wainwright and Yarnold, *Study of Spirituality*, 161-168, 184-190 and 190-195.

36. From, 'Choruses from "The Rock"' in Eliot, *Collected Works*, 173.

37. The classic monastic theme of 'flight from the world' has never been quite as simple as it looks. In general monks and monastic communities (including in Byzantium and in the contemporary Orthodox Church) have been closely involved with the life of church and society: full-scale eremitical withdrawal has always been the exception rather than the rule and even then hermits remain members of the Body of Christ which they serve through prayer. In addition, 'the world' in the best monastic literature is not simply the created order but human society marked by sin and in rebellion against God. Monastic renunciation, ideally, is meant to purify the heart by establishing distance so that one can learn to love in freedom. See, Spidlik, *Spirituality*, 205-231.

38. *Rule*, IX.

39. *Philokalia* (Glossary), 365-366.

40 From 'The Wasteland' in Eliot, *Collected Poems*, 53.

41. R. M. Rilke, 'Exposed on the Cliffs of the Heart,' in *The Selected Poetry of Rainer Maria Rilke*, ed and trs S. Mitchell, New York, 1982, 143.

42. Eliade, *Comparative Religion*, 99-102: 'Mountains are the nearest thing to the sky, and are hence endowed with a twofold holiness … The mountain, because it is the meeting place of heaven and earth, is situated at the centre of the world, and is of course the highest point of the earth.'

43. From the poem, 'No Worst', in Hopkins, *The Major Works*, 167.

44. See the excerpt from St Gregory of Nyssa's commentary on the Book of Ecclesiastes in *From Glory to Glory*, trs and ed J. Musurillo SJ, New York,

1979, 127-128.

45. Turner, *Darkness*, 243.

46. St John of the Cross, 'Upon a Gloomy Night', in *Poems of St John of the Cross*, trs R. Campbell, Glasgow, 1983.

47. In the western tradition these faculties are memory (the ground of personal identity), intellect (understanding) and will (desire and intentionality).

48. St Symeon the New Theologian was among the mystical writers who used this symbol most but it is common to almost all, even if at times the symbolic motif of darkness predominates. Yet the relationship between the metaphors of light and darkness is complex: on Symeon's 'light mysticism,' see B. Krivocheine, *In the Light of Christ*, trs A. P. Gythiel, New York, 1986; see also most of Chrysavaggis, *Light Through Darkness*. Later Byzantine mystics such as St Gregory Palamas carefully distinguished the experience of post-apostolic Christians from that of the apostolic witnesses to Christ's transfiguration. Whereas the latter, being in the actual physical presence of Christ, received the grace of the Taboric light through the transformation of their physical senses, the former normally receive it first in an ineffable interior experience, the immediate context of which is that of ascetical purification and intense contemplative prayer, especially the 'Jesus Prayer'. (However, Symeon the New Theologian *did* sometimes speak of an *external* source for the light but here as in some other instances, it is hard to fit him into the usual categories of Byzantine mystical theology. See Alfeyev, *St Symeon*, 233). Reception of the light is also a direct fruit of having received Christ's transfigured, risen body in the Eucharist. Neither Palamas nor any other Orthodox Byzantine mystical writer claimed that God's light was somehow rendered 'physical' so as to enter the self through the senses – as their opponents claimed. See Meyendorff, *Byzantine Theology*, 76-78: that was actually a heresy called by the Byzantines 'Messalianism'. Orthodox mystical theology (and experience) is an infinitely more subtle thing: see, Mantzarides, *The Deification of Man*, 87-115. Alfeyev, discussing Symeon's experience, offers some conclusions which help to clarify these matters: *St Symeon*, 234-236: the light is not an angel or any created phenomenon; it is identified with God as the Holy Trinity or the Holy Spirit – or as a general luminosity in which Christ is experienced *not* as a form but sometimes as a voice; it is not physical or material (n.b.); it is described primarily in negative, apophatic terms (e.g. as 'immaterial,' or 'ineffable' though he avoids calling it 'darkness'); it is invisible to the bodily eyes but perceived by the 'spiritual senses'. Most importantly, as Alfeyev notes (235), 'Symeon clearly indicates that the term "light" *must not be understood in the sense of material light; the term only symbolises the reality which is far beyond any human word*' (my emphasis added).

49. Louth, *Origins*, 94-95, who observes that while Origen was largely

content to acknowledge the existence of the spiritual senses, St Gregory of Nyssa was more interested in describing how they actually function in relationship with God. Later Byzantine writers such as Sts Symeon the New Theologian and Nicholas Cabasilas strongly emphasised that the spiritual senses are closely linked to the celebration of the liturgy and the grace of the sacramental mysteries.

50. Evagrius identified theology with the vision of God received in a mind purified by ascetical preparation. He thereby launched an entire tradition which understood it in this way: see Harmless, *Mystics*, 153.

51. See Terrien, *The Psalms*: 'A sacramental metaphor of communion that transcends the temple and its official cult, God's "visage" is not the essence of divinity that forever escapes the terrestrial finitude of humans, even Moses (Ex 33:22-23), but the inner luminescence that surges out of previous ignorance and serves as the vehicle of benediction ...'

52. J. H. Newman, *The Dream of Gerontius*, London, 1900, 40. Newman knew that the purgatorial fire of the Latin Christian tradition was a symbol of God's purifying and transforming love.

53. The wider context of this passage – one of the most mysterious and difficult to interpret in the entire New Testament – is important. Paul wrote (Col 1: 24-27): 'I am now rejoicing in my sufferings for your sake, and in my flesh I am completing what is lacking in Christ's afflictions for the sake of his body, that is, the church. I became its servant according to God's commission that was given to me for you, to make the Word of God fully known, the mystery that has been hidden throughout the ages and generations but has now been revealed to his saints. To them God chose to make known how great among the Gentiles are the riches of the glory of this mystery, which is Christ in you, the hope of glory.' It is not easy to explain how anything can have been lacking in Christ's redemptive sufferings, given the emphasis placed elsewhere in the New Testament on their all-sufficiency (cf Jn 17:4; Jn 19:30; Heb 10:14). However, the passage makes more sense if it is seen as referring to what St Augustine called 'the whole Christ, head and members,' that is the Lord Jesus with his mystical body the church. The effective realisation of the mystery in the lives of believers is its final fulfilment– since Christ lived it not for himself but for us and for our salvation: 'the mysteries of Christ are our mysteries.' Having in himself the fullness of grace, he voluntarily – kenotically – chooses to associate the members of his body with himself (by grace alone) so that his salvation may reach to the ends of the earth.

CHAPTER TEN

1. The fundamentals of official Roman Catholic Marian teaching (to be carefully distinguished from popular belief) is found in CCC 484-511 and 963-975. A more liturgical presentation is also available in the following brief section: CCC 721-726. See also F. Courth, 'Mary', 'Mary: Dogmas'

and, 'Salvific Significance of Mary, in *Handbook of Catholic Theology*, 457-459; 464-467; 643-645. On Orthodox Mariology, see Bulgakov, *Burning Bush*. J. Pelikan, *Mary Through the Centuries*, Yale, 1996, 39-67, is a good account of the development of Marian doctrine and devotion by one of the great 20th century historians of Christian doctrine. Pelikan was for most of his life a Lutheran but entered the Orthodox Church shortly before his death. See also, J. Macquarrie, *Mary for all Christians*, London, 1992, for a High Anglican (Scottish Episcopalian) contribution. The Roman Catholic Church and the Anglican Communion recently produced an excellent agreed statement on Marian doctrine, *Mary, Grace and Hope in Christ*, ed. D. Bolen and G. Cameron, London, 2006 – though it remains to be seen how seriously this will be taken by the faithful of the two communions concerned. This document will be cited according to its own internal numeration system.

2. That is why *Mary, Grace and Hope* holds great promise of ecumenical rapprochement: it represents a broad range of Anglican views, including those of moderate Evangelicals.

3. See Ott, *Catholic Dogma*, 215, for an explanation regarding the degrees of worship. It is important to stress that there is an absolute qualitative difference between the highest form of *veneration*, and *adoration* which is given only to God.

4. These texts are well examined in a good article by B. McConvery CSsR, 'Where Do Feasts of Our Lady Come From?' in *Doctrine and Life*, 46, December, 1996, 603-612. See also the recent work by S. J. Shoemaker, *Ancient Traditions of the Virgin Mary's Dormition and Assumption*, Oxford, 2002. An article by I. d'Alton, 'The Assumption of the Blessed Virgin Mary and the Church of Ireland in 1950', in *Search. A Church of Ireland Journal*, 31, 1, Dublin, 2009, 39-53, shows what bewilderment the definition caused in one of the more Protestant parts of the Anglican Communion.

5. See A. Louth, 'Father Sergii Bulgakov on the Mother of God,' in *St Vladimir's Theological Quarterly*, 49, 1-2, 2005, 145-164.

6. I repeat once more my own adherence to these dogmas and the fact of my own personal devotion to Mary the Holy Mother of God – but that is not at issue. What is at issue is the effective realisation of Christ's ardent prayer for the reunion of Christians (Jn 17:20-21). By insisting on imposing these dogmas on others who had no part in their formulation, the work of Christian unity is thereby impeded. See Macquarrie, *Mary*, 76, for a judicious comment: 'While many Christians find profound truth in the dogma of Immaculate Conception, it is surely possible for someone to be a good Christian without explicitly assenting to this dogma. For many centuries, there was no such dogma. The formulation of the dogma had the advantage of making theologians think more deeply about the matters raised, but it would be disastrous if it became an instrument of

exclusion.' Here above all, the Roman Catholic Church has an opportunity to imitate the *kenosis* of her Lord and Teacher (Jn 13:13-14) to bring about communion.

7. Congar, *The Mystery of the Temple*, 254: 'We know that from a historical standpoint, there is no possibility whatever of Mary having spent her childhood in the Temple. There is not the slightest support for any such notion in the fairly extensive documentation we possess on life in the Temple and on Jewish customs at the time when Mary would have been three years of age. We are, therefore, dealing here with a symbolical representation of a profound spiritual reality about which the tradition and the doctrine of the church provide us with valid information.' See also A Monk of the Eastern Church, *Year of Grace*, 52-54.

8. Congar, *The Mystery of the Temple*, 258-259: 'The Virgin Mary is very different from a mere place in which Christ was. As several ancient writers say, she is a living temple, a temple endowed with life … No other creature has been God's temple in a purer, more perfect manner.'

9. See G. Florovsky, 'The Ever-Virgin Mother of God,' in *Creation and Redemption*, Belmont, Massachusetts, 1976, 176.

10. *CCC*, 506.

11. Bulgakov, *Burning Bush*, 47-65.

12. Collins, *Glenstal Book of Icons*, 56-57.

13. *CCC*, 972.

14. Hans Urs von Balthasar and Adrienne von Speyr both stressed this Marian orientation in the life of faith. See A. von Speyr, *Handmaid of the Lord*, San Francisco, 1985.

15. On the centrality of this theme both in the Christian mystical tradition in general and specifically in the mysticism of Meister Eckhart, see Woods, *Eckhart's Way*, 96-97. For an inspired Byzantine use of the idea of the Christian as spiritual 'Mother of God', see St Symeon the New Theologian, *On the Mystical Life: The Ethical Discourses, 1: The Church and the Last Things*, trs A. Golitzin, New York, 1995, 55: 'All of us believe in the same Son of God and Son of the ever-Virgin *Theotokos*, Mary, and, believing, receive the word concerning him faithfully in our hearts. When we confess him with our mouths and repent our former lawlessness, from the depths of our souls, then immediately – just as God, the Word of the Father, entered into the Virgin's womb – even so do we receive the Word in us, as a kind of seed … Be amazed on hearing of this dreadful mystery, and welcome this word, worthy of acceptance, with all assurance and faith.'

16. Adam, *Key to Faith*, 102-105; for the Byzantine Tradition, see A Monk of the Eastern Church, *Year of Grace*, 128-129.

17. It is important not to reduce the mystery merely to issues of biology – even, 'sacred biology'.

18. S. Schneiders IHM, *New Wineskins. Re-Imagining Religious Life Today*,

New York, 1986, 134-135. The current inflexible situation regarding obligatory celibacy for secular clergy prevailing within the Latin Rite of the Catholic Church – unless, somewhat inconsistently, one is a convert clergyman with special dispensation or a member of the new Anglican 'Uniate' body – is hard to justify either historically or theologically, especially when many communities in Europe are in danger of being deprived of the Eucharist due to a shortage of priestly vocations. It has also obscured the distinctively 'monastic' meaning of consecrated celibacy as an intrinsic aspect of Religious Life by assuming that what is actually a gift is always given in accordance with a law. It may be reasonably assumed that if one is called to the dedicated life of the vows, then one is also gifted with the charism of celibacy, however difficult that may prove to be in practice. That is surely not the case for ministerial priesthood where there is no essential or intrinsic connection with celibacy (which is not to deny that some clergy *are* actually gifted with that charism as well). But the lack of *intrinsic* connection between celibacy and ministry (however useful it may often prove to be in practice) is historically indisputable – unless we wish to deny the pastoral effectiveness of hundreds of thousands of married clerics in the eastern churches from the beginning. The church's authorities surely need to do a major re-think on this entire area of ecclesial life.

19. Essential reading on this topic is A. Vööbus, *History of Asceticism in the Syrian Orient: A Contribution to the History of Culture in the Near East* (3 vols), Louvain, 1958-1988; more accessible is S. H. Griffith, 'Asceticism in the Church of Syria: The Hermeneutics of Early Syrian Monasticism,' in *Asceticism*, ed V. Wimbush and R. Valantasis, Oxford and New York, 1995, 220-245.

20. From the poem, 'The Dry Salvages,' in Eliot, *The Collected Works*, 195. The *Angelus* is without specific parallel in Eastern Christian devotion.

21. From the first of R. M. Rilke's, 'Duino Elegies,' in Leishman, *Selected Poems*, 60.

22. See A Monk of the Eastern Church, *Year of Grace*, 128: 'In the life of every Christian there will be divine annunciations, moments when God lets us know his will and his intention concerning us. But all these annunciations must unite to become the one essential annunciation: the annunciation that Jesus can be born in us, can be born through us – not in the same way that he was conceived and brought into the world by the Virgin Mary, for that is a unique miracle that cannot be equalled – but in the sense that the Saviour takes spiritual and, at the same time, very real possession of our being. And then let us remember that every authentic annunciation is immediately followed by a visitation: the divine favour that has been granted to us must straightaway release an impulse in us to let it flow out to our brothers (and sisters: my addition!), which is expressed through some loving word or act.'

23. See F. Courth, 'Assumption of Mary,' in *Handbook of Catholic Theology*, 33-36; for the Orthodox, A Monk of the Eastern Church, *Year of Grace*, 242-244. The definition of the assumption by Pope Pius XII left open the question of whether Mary actually died or not, though the earliest eastern traditions and the title of the feast (*koimesis/dormitio*; 'falling asleep', i.e. death) would seem to indicate that she did. Both Ephesus and Jerusalem lay claim to being the place of her death.

24. For the Latin liturgy, see Adam, *Key to Faith*, 152-155. See also Pelikan, *Mary*, 201-215, and Macquarrie, *Mary for All Christians*, 78-97 for good historical and theological analyses. There are also interesting ecumenical reflections in *Mary. Grace and Hope in Christ*, nos 40 and 58.

25. See the accurate analysis by W. Beinert, 'Hierarchy of Truths,' in *Handbook of Catholic Theology*, 334-336: 'This expression is a formula for the fact that while all dogmas are equally binding and while all expressions of faith are true, their importance varies according to how close their content is to the trinitarian and christological foundation of the Christian faith.' The aim of proposing such a concept was to provide an intelligible structure for understanding how diverse elements of the church's faith are to be interpreted. Tradition ought to be an ocean in which one can swim rather than an ideological straitjacket.

26. See W. Beinert, 'Tradition', in *Handbook of Catholic Theology*, 712-716, though it is rather weak on the importance of the liturgy both as the creative matrix within which the revealed word transmits itself and as a testimony to tradition.

27. See, Bauckham, *Jesus*, 138.

28. Kunzler, *The Church's Liturgy*, 161: 'There is a reciprocity between the church's liturgy and its teaching which is expressed in the formula of Prosper of Aquitaine, *legem credendi lex statuat supplicandi*. On the one hand, liturgical texts influence the formulation of theological statements, on the other hand, liturgical formulas are the concretisation of theological developments.'

29. See K. Ware, 'The Mother of God in Orthodox Theology and Devotion,' in *Mary's Place in Christian Dialogue*, ed A. Stacpoole OSB, London, 1982, 169-181, who quotes Lossky to this effect and adds: '... Orthodox while firmly believing in the bodily sssumption of the Mother of God, have no wish to see it proclaimed as a dogma. It is something that belongs to the inner tradition of the church, to the life of prayer and worship, and not to the public preaching where formal definitions are appropriate and necessary.'

30. See 'Assumption of the Virgin Mary, Proclamation of Dogma,' in A. Samuels, B. Shorter, F. Plaut, *A Critical dictionary of Jungian Analysis*, 29-31. Although Jung's own assumption that Mary's assumption established a fourth (feminine) hypostasis in the Trinity is theologically inadmissible and does not really deal adequately with the necessity to postulate a

feminine dimension in God, it is interesting that he saw it as a 'recognition and acknowledgement of *matter* (authors' emphasis).' See, also Macquarrie, *Mary*, 82.
31. A theme particularly stressed by St Gregory Palamas.
32. Florovsky, 'The Ever-Virgin Mother of God,' in *Collected Works*, 179-180, who mentions Newman's use of this patristic idea and makes it his own: 'The obedience of Mary counterbalances the disobedience of Eve. In this sense the Virgin Mary is the Second Eve, as her Son is the Second Adam. This parallel was drawn quite early ... This conception was traditional, especially in the catechetical teaching, both in the East and in the West.'
33. *LG*, in Flannery, *Documents*, 68.
34. Hence St Benedict's counsel, traditional in monastic spirituality, to keep death daily before one's eyes: *Rule*, IV, 17.

CHAPTER ELEVEN

1.None of the names Christians have used to designate this mystery throughout the ages should be considered exclusive, for each one embodies some aspect of the whole. The Reformed use of 'the Lord's Supper' reminds us of its institution on Holy Thursday night in the context of betrayal and abandonment. It underlines that the table is *Christ's* – he is the one who invites us to sit and eat. 'The Divine Liturgy', as used in Orthodoxy, similarly stresses the divine initiative for it is God's work (liturgy) first and foremost but the Orthodox also use the title, *mystikos deipnos*, 'mystical supper' with reference not only to the meal but to its sacramental, mystical (i.e. hidden) content. 'Holy Communion' as traditionally used by Anglicans (though in their liturgies they also use the term 'holy mysteries') stresses the communal nature of the liturgy, its character of producing *koinonia* (communion) between the congregation and Christ and between believers. 'The Holy Qurbana' of the Syriac tradition (like the Irish word *aifreann*) reminds us that it is a sacrificial offering, the church's gifts being taken up into the one sacrifice of Christ. 'The Mass' as used in Latin Catholicism, and by traditional Lutherans (despite all the heat this word can still generate among fundamentalists, both Catholic and Protestant) is actually the weakest name theologically, being derived from the final words of dismissal in the Latin form of the service. With a certain amount of wishful thinking, one might perhaps see it as hinting at the notion of mission, i.e. being sent out in the power of the accomplished liturgy to witness to the gospel in the world. Most Anglican liturgies do that very well in the text of the liturgy itself. See for example two of the post-communion prayers in the Irish *Book of Common Prayer*, 2004, 220-221:

May we who share Christ's body live his risen life;

we who drink his cup bring life to others;
we whom the Spirit lights give light to the world.

And again:

Almighty God,
we thank you for feeding us
with the spiritual food
of the body and blood of your Son Jesus Christ.
Through him we offer you our souls and bodies
to be a living sacrifice.
Send us out in the power of your Spirit
to live and work to your praise and glory.

In the end, two things seem apparent in contemplating the overwhelming fullness of this sacramental mystery: first, that no single word (as no single doctrine or definition or even liturgical form) is able to encompass its reality; second, that any division between its sacrificial dimensions and the fact of it being a sacred meal is false and artificial – it is a sacramental sacrifice given to us in the form of a sacred banquet and celebrated on an object which is both a table and an altar; third, the best name would seem to be 'the Eucharist' – as expressing thanksgiving, praise, and – in the very root of the word – grace and gift.

2. This theme is found particularly in the Syrian tradition. See *The Syriac Fathers on Prayer and the Spiritual Life*, trs S. Brock, Kalamazoo, Michigan, 1987. Among the fine extracts from these all too little known Syrian Fathers presented by Brock, that from 'The Book of Steps' is particularly beautiful. See Brock, *Syriac Fathers*, 48-49: 'As for the church in heaven, all that is good takes its beginning from there, and from there light has shone out upon us from all directions. After its likeness the church on earth came into being, along with its priest and its altar … This church, with its altar and baptism, gives birth to men and women as children, and they suck her milk until they are weaned. Then they come to growth and to knowledge that belongs both to the body and to the heart, whereupon they make their bodies temples and their hearts altars … then they attain to that church on high which makes them perfect, and there they enter the city of Jesus our King. There they worship in that great and perfect palace which is the mother of all the living and the perfect.' The anonymous author then shows how these three dimensions – that of the heavenly church, that of the sacramental liturgy and that of the inner liturgy of the heart – are indissolubly interwoven: 'Accordingly we should not despise the visible church which brings up everyone as children. Nor should we despise this church of the heart, seeing that she strengthens all who are sick. And we should yearn for the church on high, for she makes perfect all the saints.' A good summary of the interpenetration of the two liturgies is also found in Senn, *Christian Liturgy*, 107-108.

3. On this sacramental nature of the church in relation to the kingdom, see *SC*,1-4, in Flannery, *Documents*, 1-2; also *LG* 1, 350, which says explicitly the the church has the nature of a sacrament – 'a sign and instrument, that is, of communion with God and of unity among all men.' The church's solidarity with the human family in general and its pilgrim nature is stressed repeatedly throughout the conciliar documents. See especially, *GS*, 40, 939-940.

4. On apocalyptic in general and the Book of Revelation in particular, Harvey, *A Companion*, 783-838 offers helpful guidance through its complex imagery.

5. See A. Y. Collins, 'The Apocalypse (Revelation),' in Brown, Fitzmeyer, Murphy, *The New Jerome Biblical Commentary*, 998-999: ' ... there is no compelling reason to doubt the traditional dating of Rev attested by Irenaeus and other early Christian writers, viz. the end of the reign of Domitian (AD 95-96)'; see, however, Barker, *The Hidden Tradition*, 114-123 for a fascinating revisionist reading of Revelation, not itself lacking in visionary elements! Senn, *Christian Liturgy*, 107-108, broadly though carefully accepts M. Sheppard's view that the Book probably reflects early liturgical practice to some extent: 'It is not that the Apocalypse is a liturgy; but the paschal liturgy seems to have served as a basis for the structure of the book, even if it does not provide all the symbolism.' He does, of course, acknowledge that there is no evidence of a paschal vigil as such in the first century.

6. The *Missa de Angelis* is number VIII of the Mass Ordinaries provided in the *Graduale Romanum* for singing the Roman Rite Mass. St Benedict reflected this early Christian eschatological insight when he reminded his monks that they sing the psalms in the presence of the angels: *Rule*, XIX, 43.

7. See S. Brock, 'The Thrice-Holy Hymn in the Liturgy', in *Studies in Syriac Spirituality*, Poona, 1988, 21-29.

8. Schulz, *Byzantine Liturgy*, 77-124, is an indispensable guide to Byzantine liturgical tradition, particularly its employment of allegorical / typological interpretation of the rites of the Eucharist as exemplifying the mysteries of salvation and its teaching on the church building as an effective symbol of heaven. The influential Orthodox liturgical scholar A. Schmemann in *The Eucharist*, New York, 1988, criticised (though perhaps too sharply) the use of 'types' (i.e. that the various processions etc., represent moments in the life and work of Christ) as detracting from the eschatological thrust of the liturgy.

9. Schmemann, *Eucharist*, 60, somewhat exaggerates the difference between east and west in suggesting that western reflection on the Eucharist stresses more the model of Christ 'coming down' on the altar than the church 'going up' to the altar on high: ' ... under the influence of the western understanding of the Eucharist, we usually perceive our liturgy not in the key of *ascent* but of *descent*. The entire western eucharis-

tic mystique is thoroughly imbued with the image of Christ *descending* onto our altars. Meanwhile the original eucharistic experience, to which the very order of the Eucharist witnesses, speaks of our ascent to that place where Christ ascended, of the heavenly nature of the eucharistic celebration (author's emphasis).' Yet he can later assert, 'If we speak of the earthly, of ourselves, of the church in categories of ascent, then we speak of the heavenly, of God, of Christ, of the Holy Spirit in categories of *descent*. But we are saying the same thing: we speak of heaven on earth, of heaven as having transfigured the earth, and of the earth as having accepted heaven as the ultimate truth about itself (author's emphasis).' As we have already seen, the Reformed, Roman and Anglican traditions also considerably emphasise the heavenly dimension of worship as well. Sometimes Fr Schmemann's dogmatism prevented him seeing the values present not only in other traditions but even in his own as well: if it is acceptable for the Orthodox to have their cake and eat it, then presumably that goes for western Christians too! Both *ascent* and *descent* are indeed valid spatial metaphors in their own right, east and west – providing they are not used too exclusively.

10. The commentator was St Germanos the Patriarch of Constantinople (d. 733) who opposed the first outbreak of iconoclasm in the Byzantine Empire: see Schulz, *Byzantine Liturgy*, 71.

11. I am of course describing an ideal situation. The current eucharistic practice of both the Roman Catholic and Orthodox churches can hardly be thought to facilitate a fully catholic (i.e. inclusive) experience of the eucharistic assembly as the image of the new Jerusalem. Zizioulas's inspiring reflections on the church gathered to celebrate the Eucharist take little account of that, apart from stressing that every icon falls short of the reality it represents: see, Zizioulas, *Christian Dogmatics*, 135-139. Yet even if the church is not the 'end times' and, therefore, inevitably falls short of the kingdom of God, that is no excuse for not aiming at writing the best possible icon of the kingdom here below. The goal of the eucharistic liturgy is to manifest the revealed mystery of Christ which is the reconciling and transforming work of the most inclusive community imaginable – the Holy and Undivided Trinity.

12. St Benedict's arrangement of the Divine Office runs from chapter VIII to chapter XIX of his *Rule* though, for understanding its centrality in monastic life and spirituality, it is important to be alert to its presence elsewhere in the text as well, e.g. in the Prologue with its dramatisation of the call to obedience (reflecting the use of the 94(95)th psalm at Matins) and in chapter L, which tells those who are on a journey that they are still required to keep the canonical hours – though, with his customary good sense, Benedict adds, 'as well they can'. It is not a matter of laying a harsh burden on anyone's shoulders but of keeping the goal of unceasing prayer constantly before the monk.

13. The two basic books on the history and spirituality of the Divine Office are still that of P. F. Bradshaw, *Daily Prayer in the Early Church: A Study of the Origin and Early Development of the Divine Office*, London, 1981, and, R. Taft SJ, *The Liturgy of the Hours in East and West*, Collegeville, MN, 1986, (particularly the fourth part, on the theology of the Hours). See also the relevant sections in Senn, *Christian Liturgy*, 156-163; 197-206; 338-342. On the 20th century transition from the Divine Office as a prayerbook for the clergy (the 'Breviary') to a communal prayer service for the whole church ('the Liturgy of the Hours'), see, S. Campbell, *From Breviary to Liturgy of the Hours*, Collegeville, MN, 1995.

14. Taft, *Liturgy of the Hours*, 361-365, in his customarily trenchant way bursts the balloon blown up by some monastics in the past, who claimed that monasteries are somehow 'deputed' to offer a public 'cult' in the name of the church. In the early monastic tradition things were very different, 364: 'The whole of cenobitic life was a communion, and hence also a communion in prayer, but the early cenobites had no notion whatever of participating in an 'official' prayer of the church.' Neither were clerics in the past 'obliged to the Office' as became the case later. Rather the entire church was – and is – called to communal prayer simply because, as the *church*, it is the assembly of Christ's priestly people, 362: 'The novelty is to think that only the clergy is obliged. In the early church it was just as much an obligation of the priest's wife or grandmother as of the priest himself. What is untraditional, therefore, is not the *obligation* of the Office, but its *clericalisation*. As with so much else in the history of the church, what was once the property of the entire People of God has degenerated into a clerical residue, only reminiscent of what it was meant to be' (author's emphasis).

15. Taft, *Liturgy of the Hours*, 346: 'Liturgy, therefore, has the same purpose as the gospel: to present this new reality in *anamnesis* as a continual sign to us not of a past history, but as the present reality of our lives in him … The liturgy of the church presents us with *a multi-dimensional celebration* of this basic reality, but *the reality is always the same*. What we celebrate is the fact that Jesus lived died and rose again for our salvation, and that we have died to sin and risen to new life in him, in expectation of the final fulfilment' (my emphasis added).

16. As Benedict's *Rule* makes clear, the main reason for dedicating oneself to the monastic way is to make the whole of life a single continuous prayer, not merely in the sense of repeating words, but of having the inner state or disposition of the heart, one's deepest spiritual centre, fixed on God. It involves learning to walk constantly before God, since God is always present within our minds: see *Rule* VII, 24 and XIX, 43. For the various ways in which this idea of prayer as a continuous spiritual state has found expression in monastic spirituality, particularly in the Christian East, see Spidlik, *Spirituality*, 315-327. If it is a mistake completely to

identify the Byzantine (and modern Orthodox) doctrine of unceasing prayer with the recitation of the 'Jesus Prayer', important though that is in the tradition, it is equally important not to identify Greek Orthodox spirituality with Eastern Christian spirituality as a whole. On the Syrian doctrine of unceasing prayer, which was for all practical purposes the same as purity of heart, see Brock, 'The Prayer of the Heart in Syriac Tradition,' in *Studies in Syriac Spirituality*, 41-52. He writes profoundly of this phenomenon, 50: '... in modern usage the term "prayer of the heart" is often understood as being synonymous with the Jesus Prayer, the repetition of the Name coupled with a short phrase. In this sense of the term, Syriac spirituality seems to have had nothing quite comparable, although short repeated invocations ... are not uncommon ... What, rather, would seem for them to constitute the characteristic feature of the prayer of the heart is the "remembrance" or "recollection of God", as Br Lawrence calls it. Seen in this light, "the prayer of the heart" once again turns out to be more of a state or disposition, rather than any particular identifiable activity. It is, above all, a loving state of total awareness of God. This is the state where we allow God's presence in our heart to make itself felt, where we allow God to act within us, from the very centre of our innermost being. This divine activity within the human person will invariably have a transfiguring effect, though the nature and intensity of this "transfiguration" will vary enormously.' The Brother to whom Brock refers was Lawrence of the Resurrection (1614-1691), a French Carmelite who was granted an intense awareness of God throughout his daily life.

CONCLUSION

1. Among the many works which have directly inspired this conclusion, see especially Meerson, *The Trinity of Love*, which is an indispensable guide to the complexities but also the glories of modern Russian theology; Bulgakov, *Lamb* 321-410, and *Sophia*, 23-54; Balthasar, *Mysterium Paschale* 49-71, and *Engagement with God*, trs R. J. Halliburton, San Francisco, 2008; R. Williams, 'Balthasar and the Trinity,' in Oakes and Moss, *Cambridge Companion to Hans Urs Von Balthasar*, 37-51; Forsyth, *The Cruciality of the Cross*, Carlisle, 1997; and B. Bobrinskoy, 'God in Trinity,' in *Cambridge Companion to Orthodox Theology*, 49-63. For two excellent summaries of contemporary Trinitarian theology see O'Donnell, *The Mystery of the Triune God*, London, 1988, and Sanders, 'The Trinity,' in *Oxford Handbook of Systematic Theology*, 35-54. Nor is Karl Barth ever far from view: among his voluminous writings see *CD* 1/1, where he performed the revolutionary act of placing the revealed Trinity right at the beginning of systematic theology and *CD* 4/1 where he grappled with its relationship with the mystery of the cross.
2. For a classic example, see Ott, *Fundamentals*, 67-73.
3. Busch, *Karl Barth*, 248-249. Barth vigorously opposed any idea of God

supposedly derived from an inherent natural aptitude for the divine, although he seems to have overlooked the fact that humanity's capacity to respond to God when he speaks is *already* grace, and specifically the grace of Christ. However, his outspoken stand against the bland deistic 'god', blanched, (i.e. 'palliated by misrepresentation' [OED]), put forward in 17th and 18th century philosophy, and the tendency to exaggerate subjective religious feeling in thinkers like Schleiermacher, was of inestimable benefit to Christian theology in pushing it back to its objective sources in the revealed mystery of Christ.

4. This is not to deny that serious philosophical issues do arise regarding how the revealed Christian God is to be understood in the light of other theistic conceptions: it is simply to assert that the fundamental basis for Christian theology has to be the revelation of Christ itself. However, it is important to distinguish between a tired, post-Christian 'natural theology' and the work of great religious prophets, thinkers and mystics beyond the frontiers of Judaeo-Christian tradition.

5. *CCC*, 261: 'The mystery of the Most Holy Trinity is the central mystery of the Christian faith and of Christian life. God alone can make it known to us by revealing himself as Father, Son and Holy Spirit.'

6. Yet 'person' too must be understood theologically and analogically, in such a way that the infinite dissimilarity between divine and human persons is also noted. There are not three independently thinking, feeling and willing 'subjects' in God, otherwise there would indeed be three Gods. Rather personhood is about the inter-relatedness of love. 'Personality' in God is a sublime mystery we cannot fathom but can at least partially adumbrate on the basis of revelation and how it is reflected in our common human experience.

7. Both the author of the deuterocanonical Book of Wisdom (13:1) and St Paul, in the Letter to the Romans (2:19-21) and in the speech attributed to him at the Areopagus in Athens (Acts 17:22-31), speak of God's self-revelation through the world of nature. Fundamentalists tend to see human failure to perceive this as proof of humanity's obduracy in sinning.

8. Turner, *The Darkness of God*, is an extended and illuminating commentary on the understanding of the divine darkness in numerous mystical writers, including Eckhart and St John of the Cross. On Denys the Areopagite, see Bouyer, *Christian Mystery*, 179-186, who rightly connects it to his liturgical theology and also recalls the importance of St Gregory of Nyssa in formulating this language; also Riordan, *Divine Light*, 187: 'This cloud (or "darkness/shadow") is obscure to us precisely because of its overwhelming clarity and brilliance.' According to Barker, *Hidden Traditions*, 18, in the Temple tradition the secret place of the Holy of Holies represented 'the unchanging One at the heart of the creation'.

9. H. Vaughan, 'The Night,' in *George Herbert and the Seventeenth Century Religious Poets*, ed M. A. di Cesare, New York, 1978, 177.

10. Denys the Areopagite held that God is the first theologian in providing us with the names we require (drawn from his revelation in the 'book of nature' and in holy scripture) if we are to speak about him in the first place. Nothing could be more false than to imagine that in the tradition of Dionysian mystical theology we somehow begin with a humanly constructed 'natural theology' before moving on to revelation as such. The cosmos, a moving image of God's inner world of divine ideas, is permeated by his creative energies. It is a sacred cosmos – already the beginning of God's self-disclosure to us. See Riordan, *Divine Light*, 179-195

11. Bulgakov, *Lamb*, 215.

12. See O'Hanlon, *Immutability of God*, Cambridge, 1990; also E. T. Oakes SJ, *Pattern of Redemption: the Theology of Hans Urs von Balthasar*, New York, 1997.

13. But see the unduly sharp comments of Zizioulas, *Christian Dogmatics*, 134: 'The Son is crucified, and the event of the cross and its suffering is *transferred into the eternal life of the triune God*. This theology was advocated by some Lutherans, though *the same sentimentality* can be observed in those Russian theologians who also see the life of the eternal as bound to suffering and the cross' (my emphasis). Although no references are given, this is presumably directed against Jürgen Moltmann (see *The Crucified God*, London, 1974) and Bulgakov and Florensky among the Russian 'kenoticists'. It is true that Balthasar criticised Moltmann for an inadequate use of analogy and for positing a Hegelian interpretation of the cross in which the inner life of God somehow develops because of the incarnation and passion: see, Balthasar, *Mysterium Paschale*, vii. Yet it is worthwhile to locate these three thinkers within the context of their histories. Florensky, one of the greatest scientific geniuses Russia ever produced was separated from his family, imprisoned and eventually executed in the Stalinist terror. His memory was subsequently blackened. Bulgakov fought his way intellectually and spiritually from Marxist Atheism to Christianity, lost two children, was permanently exiled from his homeland and suffered inquisitorial investigations and unfair condemnation. Moltmann was a POW for some years and came to Christian faith in captivity. Since all three were grappling with the problem of horrendous suffering (both personal and national/global – the latter being the Russian Revolution, exile and World War II) it is hard to see how they can be accused of sentimentality. Their theological reflection was an attempt to establish how the God of love revealed in Christ really and actually involves himself with the tragedy of human history. Moltmann, Florensky and Bulgakov did not simply transfer the cross into the inner life of God: rather they read the cross itself as the temporal and spatial exegesis of the unfathomable mystery of trinitarian love.

14. Balthasar, in a magisterial summary of these problematic issues, in some ways says it all. Although long, it is worth quoting. See, Balthasar,

Mysterium Paschale, vii-viii, where he first ruminates, 'No doubt the *kenosis* of the Son will always remain a mystery no less unsoundable than that of the Trinity …', sets out the byways to be avoided (e.g. the notion that Christ suffered in some 'lower zone' of his inner life thus leaving his divinity unaffected) and then indicates the highway to be followed: 'It seems to me that the only way … is that which relates the event of the *kenosis* of the Son of God to what one can, by analogy, designate as the eternal "event" of the divine processions. It is from that supra-temporal yet ever actual event that, as Christians, we must approach the mystery of the divine "essence". That essence is forever "given" in the self-gift of the Father, "rendered" in the thanksgiving of the Son, and represented in its character as absolute love by the Holy Spirit … We shall never know how to express the abyss-like depths of the father's self-giving, that Father who, in an eternal "super-*kenosis*", makes himself "destitute" of all that he is and can be, so as to bring forth a consubstantial divinity, the Son. Everything that can be thought and imagined where God is concerned is, in advance, included and transcended in this self-destitution which constitutes the person of the Father, and at the same time, those of the Son and the Spirit.'

15. Williams, 'Balthasar and the Trinity,' in Oakes and Moss, *Cambridge Companion to Balthasar*, 50, wrestles with both Barth's and Balthasar's trinitarian rhetoric, observing that in the first it can veer close to the ancient heresy of Sabellianism (the persons as simply modes of one divine being) whereas in the latter it sometimes approaches tritheism (the doctrine of three Gods). Tritheism is also a potential hazard in the spirituality of Balthasar's mystical friend, Adrienne von Speyr, whose account of the inner-trinitarian dialogue can be just a little bit too anthropomorphic (cf e.g. Speyr, *World of Prayer*, 61-68). Yet as Williams observes, by holding on to the 'unifying tension' of 'the sheer fact of the narrative of Jesus Christ at the heart of the whole discourse', neither Barth nor Balthasar goes over the precipice. Great theologians should always have something of the quality of tightrope walkers and courageous explorers about them, as indeed Williams does himself.

16. Of course, proposing the Trinity as a model for human community ought not to transgress the bounds set by analogy: no church or community can ever hope to realise perfect communion within the limitations and frailties of earthly existence, any more than any person, however saintly, could ever attain to the model of holiness set before us by the incarnate Son of God. Equally clearly, it would be foolish to imagine that human beings can literally – still less by their own efforts – approximate to the kind of self-giving that constitutes the divine persons. Yet the self-sacrificial, loving communion of the Most Holy Trinity – the revealed heart of the mystery of Christ – is the ideal to which we are asked to aspire and which we have to try to incarnate in our Christian life. That will al-

ways be for us (both individually and as churches and communities) a dialectical process in which 'progress' will be interrupted by sin and failure; yet repentance and forgiveness can return us to the way. A healthy recognition of one's own spiritual (in)capacities – in other words humility – is essential: the kingdom of trinitarian love is not brought in by human effort but by purification, which clears away the obstacles, leaving God space to make it manifest.

17. See the epilogue 'The Father' in Bulgakov, *The Comforter*, 359-395.

18. Karl Rahner, 'On the History of the Theology of the Trinity', in *Encyclopedia of Theology*, 1767-1769. In the light of more recent research, however, it is clear that Rahner's interpretation of Aquinas was not always reliable: see A. Kerr OP, *After Aquinas*, 202-203, and, 237-238. It is not true that 'the Greeks' argued for a pyramidal, triangular model while 'the Latins' favoured a circular one in which the person of the Father as source was somehow relativised or even negated in favour of an underlying unity of substance somehow prior to the persons (a standard Orthodox criticism, [cf Zizioulas, *Christian Dogmatics*, 65-69] which is based on not really engaging with the texts of either Augustine or Aquinas). Latin theology continued to uphold the understanding of the Father as the source of divinity: see Ott, *Fundamentals*, 57, for a strong statement of God's paternity, both absolute (within the Trinity) and relative (in creation), in a standard handbook of scholastic theology. Zizioulas, *Christian Dogmatics*, also makes the sweeping statement that 'medieval dogmatics in the west', 66-67, (no reference given) supposedly followed Augustine in dealing first with the one substance of God, then with his attributes and only then with the Trinity. It is true that St Thomas does speak in the *Summa Theologiae* of the one God, before dealing with the Trinity, but as Kerr observes (*After Aquinas*, 183-185), it is a mistake to understand by this a philosophically deduced God whose existence is established by natural theology: rather it is the one God of the Bible who is in question. It was later neo-Scholasticism which produced the kind of philosophical theology against which Orthodox critics rightly protest. The two greatest medieval scholastics, Thomas and Bonaventure were not to blame. Indeed, the latter began his own systematic theology (cf St Bonaventure, *The Breviloquium*, trs J. de Vinck, New Jersey, 1963,) with the mystery of the Trinity. See W. Breuning, 'Trinity: Doctrine of the,' in *Handbook of Catholic Theology*, 725. Finally, Meerson, in *Trinity of Love*, has successfully demonstrated the important influence exercised by Augustine, the medieval Victorines and Bonaventure on Russian theology in the 19th and 20th centuries.

19. See Alfeyev, *Symeon the New Theologian*, 143-151, for an excellent discussion of different patristic interpretations of these difficult words of Christ (i.e. '… the Father is greater than I') in the context of debates within the 11th and 12th century Byzantine church. Latin Christian tradition

speaks of the Son's eternal involvement in the 'production' of the Spirit, calling him a co-spirator with the Father, and has inserted the word *Filioque* ('and the Son') into the Niceno-Constantinopolitan Creed. This affirms that the Spirit proceeds from the Father and the Son as from 'one principle'. Yet the Latins insist that the Son's eternal breathing of the Spirit does not destroy the delicate *taxis* (order) of trinitarian relationships or deprive the Father of his uniquely originating role since the Son's capacity to spirate the Spirit is entirely dependent on his having received it from the Father. On the whole sorry mess of sacred metaphysics and ecclesiastical politics for which the word *Filioque* is shorthand, see Bulgakov, *Comforter*, 75-95. Less attention to the logistics of exactly where the Spirit comes from and more on what s/he does when s/he gets here might have been a better way for theologians to employ their energies.

20. For a good summary of the issues see J. Baggley, *Festival Icons for the Christian Year*, London, 2000, 156-157: 'The two main schools of interpretation of this icon are agreed that the angel on the right is to be seen as representing the Holy Spirit, but there is deep disagreement over the interpretation of the other two angels. One school of thought sees that central angel as representing the Father, who reveals himself through his two arms, the Son on his right and the Spirit on his left. The other school argues that we should look at the icon in terms of the doxology, 'Glory be to the Father, and to the Son, and to the Holy Spirit', working from left to right.' P. Evdokimov, in *The Art of the Icon: A Theology of Beauty*, trs S. Bigham, 248-249 (a work which should not be read uncritically), opted for the central angel as representing the Father. Baggley rightly insists that the icon does not actually 'depict' the persons of the Trinity anyway but represents them symbolically.

21. Bulgakov drew creatively on the Jewish mystical idea of the *tzim-tzum*, the movement of retraction and withdrawal carried out by the Absolute in allowing relative being to come into existence. Yet he redeemed the idea from imposing any necessity on God to create by seeing it as the expression and outflowing movement of the eternal trinitarian *kenosis* of the divine persons which constitutes the inner life of the Godhead and has been revealed to us through the mystery of Christ. See Bulgakov, *Sophia*, 58-65. This notion of creation as the fruit of divine contraction contrasts strongly with traditional Late Antique pagan and Christian ways of imagining God's creative act as an emanation. For Bulgakov, reading the divine creative activity in the light of Philippians 2, the world begins, and is continually grounded in, an act of divine humility and loving self-limitation, itself rooted in God's own trinitarian being. The ethical and spiritual implications of this 'letting-be' notion of God – and its similarity with many of the ideas of Meister Eckhart – deserves a study on its own.

22. Such a non-paternalistic understanding of the Father's role in the

Trinity badly needs to be brought to bear on how authority is actually exercised in Christian ministry – from the 'Petrine Primacy' to all who exercise authority in communities (abbots and abbesses, bishops, priests and deacons and 'superiors' of every kind). It is indispensable to clarify this matter both for the inner renewal of individual communities and for the wider ecumenical project: in the light of the revelation of how the communion (*koinonia*) of the Trinity is constituted, how can the churches translate that into institutional reality, particularly regarding issues such as primacy?

23. See R. Muller, 'Circumincessio', in *Dictionary of Latin and Greek Theological Terms*, Grand Rapids, Michigan , 1985, 67-68: '*Circumincessio* refers primarily to the coinherence of the persons of the Trinity in the divine essence and in each other, but it can also indicate the coinherence of Christ's divine and human natures in their communion or personal union.'

24. G. L. Prestige, *God in Patristic Thought*, London, 1936: '… it was by origin a christological term, and was only just transferred to the trinitarian field in time for John of Damascus to adopt it. But it afforded an extraordinarily timely and fruitful formula for the idea that the being of the whole three Persons was contained in that of each, and so re-affirmed from a fresh angle, the crucial doctrine of substantial identity.' For a more detailed discussion, see 291-299.

25. 'Divinisation' here indicates obviously not some fusion of divine and human substances but, by the indwelling of the Holy Spirit (and therefore of the whole Trinity) in the heart through grace, a communication of divine life which transforms human beings into God's likeness. Christian spirituality is deeply rooted in this Johannine understanding of God's gracious dwelling in us and us in God, just as the three divine persons dwell in one another; but it is also indebted to Paul's equivalent imagery of the body (both of individual believers and of the church as a whole) as a temple in which the Spirit dwells (cf 1 Cor 3:16-17).

26. See C. Hauke, 'The Unconscious: Personal and Collective', in Papadopolous ed, *Handbook of Jungian Psychology*, 54-74.

27. E. Muir, 'The heart could never speak', in *Selected Poems*, ed T. S. Eliot, London, 1965, 92.

28. See J. Arintero SJ, *The Cantata of Love*, trs N. Marans, San Francisco, 1988.

29. Bulgakov in *Sophia*, 32-53, interprets divine wisdom (*Sophia*), which is common to all three hypostases of the Trinity, as the very content of God's one nature, brimming over with the eternal ideas and images which are realised in time as the created world. This remains today a controversial issue for Orthodox theologians although it is, properly understood, perfectly compatible with traditional Orthodox faith: see Plekon, 'Russian Religious Revival', in *Cambridge Companion to Orthodox Christian Theology*, 204-206.

30. See M. Mc Cord Adams, 'Anselm on Faith and Reason', in B. Davies and B. Lefttow eds, *Cambridge Companion to Anselm*, 39. Contrary to how he is sometimes presented, as a Benedictine monk Anselm knew very well that theological understanding comes not merely from exercising one's reason on the data of revelation but from prayer and contemplation.

Bibliography

A. Abelson, *Jewish Mysticism: An Introduction to the Kabbalah*, London, 1913.

Abishiktananda (Hénri le Saux OSB), *Prayer*, London, 1974.

A. Adam, *The Key to Faith: Meditations on the Liturgical Year*, trs M. J. O'Connell, Collegeville, MN, 1998.

H. Alfeyev, *St Symeon the New Theologian and Orthodox Tradition*, Oxford, 2000.

P. Althaus, *The Theology of Martin Luther*, trs R. C. Schultz, Philadelphia, 1966.

J. Arintero SJ, *The Cantata of Love*, trs N. Marans, San Francisco, 1988.

N. Astley, ed *Staying Alive: Real Poems for Unreal Times*, Tarset, Northumberland, 2002

A. W. Astell, *The Song of Songs in the Middle Ages*, Cornell University, 1995.

J. Auer, *Dogmatic Theology 6, A General Doctrine of the Sacraments and the Mystery of the Eucharist*, trs E. Leiva-Merikakis, Washington, 1995.

J. Baggley, *Festival Icons for the Christian Year*, London, 2000.

H. Urs von Balthasar, *Prayer*, trs G. Harrison, San Francisco, 1986

—, *Mysterium Paschale*, trs A. Nichols OP, Edinburgh, 1990.

—, *Explorations in Theology IV*, trs E. T. Oakes SJ, San Francisco, 1995.

—, *Engagement with God*, trs R. J. Halliburton, San Francisco, 2008.

Baptism, Eucharist and Ministry, Faith and Order Paper No 111, issued by the World Council of Churches, Geneva, 1982.

M. Barker, *Temple Themes in Christian Worship*, London, 2007.

—, *The Hidden Tradition of the Kingdom of God*, London, 2007.

K. Barth, *Church Dogmatics, (CD)*, eds T. F. Torrance and G. W. Bromiley, Edinburgh, 1956-76.

—, *The Holy Spirit and the Christian Life*, trs R. B. Hoyle, London, 1938.

R. Bauckham and C. Mosser, eds *The Gospel of John and Christian Theology*, Grand Rapids, Michigan, 2008.

R. Bauckham, *Jesus and the God of Israel*, Milton Keynes, 2008.

The Bhagavad Gita, trs J. Mascaró, London, 1962

W. Beinert and F. Schüssler Fiorenza, *Handbook of Catholic Theology*, New York, 2000.

St Benedict, *The Rule of St Benedict*, trs J. McCann OSB, Stanbrook Abbey, 1937.

L. Berkhof, *Systematic Theology*, Grand Rapids, Michigan, 1949.

A. Bloom, *School for Prayer*, London, 1970.

B. Bobrinskoy, *The Mystery of the Trinity*, trs A. P. Gythiel, New York, 1999.

St Bonaventure, *The Breviloquium*, trs J. de Vinck, New Jersey, 1963.

G. Bonner, *St Augustine of Hippo*, Norwich, 2000.

J. Borelli and J. H. Erikson, *The Quest for Unity: Orthodox and Catholics in Dialogue*, New York, 1996.

L. Bouyer, *Eucharist: Theology and Spirituality of the Eucharistic Prayer*, trs C. U. Quinn, Notre Dame, 1968.

—, *The Christian Mystery: From Pagan Myth to Christian Mysticism*, trs I. Trethowan OSB, Edinburgh, 1990.

C. E. Braaten and R. Jenson, eds *Christian Dogmatics I*, Philadelphia, 1984.

C. Braaten, *Principles of Lutheran Theology*, Minneapolis, 2007.

P. F. Bradshaw, *Daily Prayer in the Early Church: A Study of the Origin and Early Development of the Divine Office*, London, 1981.

S. Brock, *Studies in Syriac Spirituality*, Poona, 1988.

G. Bromiley, *Historical Theology: An Introduction*, Edinburgh, 1978.

R. E. Brown SS, J. A. Fitzmeyer SJ and R. E. Murphy OCarm, eds *The New Jerome Biblical Commentary*, London, 1989.

R. E. Brown SS, *An Introduction to New Testament Christology*, London, 1994.

A. B. Bruce, *The Humiliation of Christ*, Edinburgh, 1881.

C. Bruyère OSB, *The Spiritual Life and Prayer according to Holy Scripture and Tradition*, trs nuns of Stanbrook Abbey, London, (no date or year given)

S. Bulgakov, *Sophia: The Wisdom of God*, New York, 1993

—, *The Comforter*, trs B. Jakim, Grand Rapids, Michigan, 2004.

—, *The Lamb of God*, trs B. Jakim, Grand Rapids, Michigan, 2008.

—, *The Burning Bush*, trs T. A. Smith, Grand Rapids, Michigan, 2009.

E. Busch, *Barth*, trs R. and U. Burnett, Nashville, 2008.

St Nicholas Cabasilas, *The Divine Liturgy*, trs J. M. Hussey and P. A. Mc Nulty, London, 1960.

—, *The Life in Christ*, trs C. J. de Catanzaro, New York, 1998.

J. Calvin, *Institutes of the Christian Religion*, trs H. Beveridge, London, 1949.

S. Campbell, *From Breviary to Liturgy of the Hours*, Collegeville, MN, 1995.

O. Casel OSB, *The Mystery of Christian Worship*, trs I. T. Hale, London, 1962.

M. Casey, *The Art of Sacred Reading*, Victoria, Australia, 1995.

Catechism of the Catholic Church (*CCC*), New York, 1995.

P. Celan, *Selected Poems*, trs M. Hamburger, London, 1995.

H. Chadwick, *East and West: The Making of a Rift in the Church*, Oxford, 2003.

J. Chryssavagis, *Light Through Darkness: The Orthodox Tradition*, London, 2004.

Church of Ireland, *Book of Common Prayer*, Dublin, 2004.

G. Collins, *The Glenstal Book of Icons*, Dublin, 2002.

M. Connell, *Eternity Today: On the Liturgical Year, I and II,* New York, 2006.

Y. Congar OP, *The Mystery of the Temple*, trs R. F. Trevett, London, 1962.

J. Corbon, *The Wellspring of Worship*, trs M. J. O'Connell, New York, 1988.

R. Cormack, *Icons*, London, 2007.

O. Cullman, *Early Christian Worship*, trs A. S. Todd and J. B. Torrance,

London, 1953.

M. B. Cunningham and E. Theokritoff, eds *The Cambridge Companion to Orthodox Theology*, Cambridge, 2008.

I. d' Alton, 'The Assumption of the Blessed Virgin Mary and the Church of Ireland in 1950', in *Search: A Church of Ireland Journal*, 31, 1, Dublin, 2009, 39-53.

J. Dan, *Kabbalah: A Very Short Introduction*, Oxford, 2006.

B. Davies and B. Lefttow, eds *The Cambridge Companion to Anselm*, Cambridge, 2004.

O. Davies, *God Within*, London, 1988.

—, *The Rhineland Mystics*, London, 1989.

M. A. di Cesare, ed *George Herbert and the Seventeenth Century Religious Poets*, New York, 1978.

G. Dix OSB, *The Shape of the Liturgy*, London 1945.

J. Dupuis SJ, *Toward a Christian Theology of Religious Pluralism*, New York, 1997.

M. Eliade, *Patterns in Comparative Religion*, London, 1958.

T. S. Eliot, *Collected Poems*, London, 2002.

P. Evdokimov, *The Art of the Icon: A Theology of Beauty*, trs S. Bigham, California, 1990.

D. Farrow, *Ascension and Ecclesia*, Edinburgh, 1999.

A. Flannery OP, ed *The Documents of Vatican II*, Dublin, 1975.

P. Florensky, *The Pillar and Ground of the Truth*, trs. B. Jakim, New Jersey, 1997.

G. Florovsky, *Creation and Redemption, Collected Works, Vol III*, Belmont, Massachusetts, 1976.

G. Forde, *On Being a Theologian of the Cross*, Grand Rapids, Michigan, 1997.

P. T. Forsyth, *The Cruciality of the Cross*, Carlisle, 1997.

A. Golitizin, *Et introibo ad altare dei: The Mysticism of Dionysius Areopagita*, Thessalonica, 1994.

N. Gorodetsky, *The Humiliated Christ in Modern Russian Thought*, London, 1938.

J. Gros, E. McManus and A. Riggs, *Introduction to Ecumenism*, New Jersey, 1998.

St Gregory of Nyssa, *From Glory to Glory: Texts from Gregory of Nyssa's Mystical Writings*, trs and ed H. Musurillo SJ, New York, 1979.

S. Hackel, *Pearl of Great Price*, New York, 1982.

W. J. Harmless SJ, *Mystics*, Oxford 2008.

A. E. Harvey, *A Companion to the New Testament*, Cambridge, 2004.

A. Hastings, A. Mason and H. Pyper, eds *The Oxford Companion to Christian Thought*, Oxford, 2000.

G. Hill, *Collected Poems*, London, 1985.

J. Hillman, *The Dream and the Underworld*, New York, 1979.

G. Manley Hopkins SJ, 'God's Grandeur', in, *The Major Works*, ed C. Phillips, Oxford, 2002.

L. Hurtado, *One God, One Lord*, New York, 1998.

St Ignatius of Antioch, 'Letter to the Magnesians', in *The Faith of the Early Fathers*, trs W. A. Jurgens, Minnesota, 1970.

K. Irwin, *Context and Text: Method in Liturgical Theology*, Collegeville, MN, 1994.

H. Iswolsky, *Soul of Russia*, London, 1944.

J. Jacobi, *The Psychology of C. G. Jung*, London, 1973.

L. Jacobs, *Hasidic Prayer*, Washington, 1973.

B. Jersak and M. Hardin, eds *Stricken by God?: Non-Violent Identification and the Victory of Christ*, Grand Rapids, Michigan, 2007.

St John of the Cross, *The Ascent of Mt Carmel*, trs K. Kavanaugh OCD and O. Rodriguez OCD, Washington, 1979.

—, *Poems of St John of the Cross*, trs R. Campbell, Glasgow, 1983.

St John Climacus, *The Ladder of Divine Ascent*, trs C. Luibhéid and N. Russell, New York, 1982.

C. Jones, G. Wainwright and E. Yarnold SJ, eds *The Study of Spirituality*, London, 1986.

Julian of Norwich, *A Revelation of Divine Love*, ed and mod E. Dutton, Plymouth, 2008.

E. Jüngel, 'The Sacrifice of Jesus Christ as Sacrament and Example', in *Theological Essays II*, trs A. Neufeld-Fast and J. B. Webster, ed J. B. Webster, Edinburgh, 1995, 163-191.

T. Kardong OSB, *The Benedictines*, Delaware, 1988.

A. Kavanagh OSB, *On Liturgical Theology*, New York, 1984.

I. Ker and T. Merrigan, eds *The Cambridge Companion to Newman*, Cambridge, 2009.

A. Kerr, *After Aquinas*, Oxford, 2002.

E. J. Kilmartin SJ, *Christian Liturgy, Vol I: Systematic Theology of the Liturgy*, Kansa City, 1988

—, *The Eucharist in the West*, ed R. Daly SJ, Collegeville, MN, 1998.

R. Kolb, *Martin Luther: Confessor of the Faith*, Oxford, 2009.

B. Krivocheine, *In the Light of Christ*, trs A. P. Gythiel, New York, 1986.

M. Kunzler, *The Church's Liturgy*, trs P. Murray OSB, H. O'Shea OSB and Cillian Ó Sé OSB, London / New York, 2001.

V. Larrin, 'Fr Alexander Schmemann and Monasticism', *St Vladimir's Theological Quarterly*, 53, 2-3, New York, 2009, 301-319.

J. Leclercq OSB, *The Love of Learning and the Desire for God*, London, 1978.

A. E. Lewis, *Between Cross and Resurrection: A Theology of Holy Saturday*, Grand Rapids, Michigan, 2001.

V. Lossky, *The Vision of God*, trs A. Moorhouse, Leighton Buzzard, 1963.

A. Louth, *The Origins of the Christian Mystical Tradition*, Oxford, 1981.

—, *Denys the Areopagite*, New York, 1989.

—, *St John Damascene*, Oxford, 2002.

—, 'Father Sergii Bulgakov on the Mother of God', in *St Vladimir's Theological Quarterly*, 49, 1-2, 2005, 145-164.

—, 'Sergii Bulgakov and the Task of Theology', *Irish Theological Quarterly*, 74, 3, 2009, 243-258.

J. Macquarrie, *Mary for all Christians*, London, 1992.

M. Magrassi OSB, *Praying the Bible*, trs E. Hagman OFM Cap, Collegeville, MN, 1998.

T. Mannermaa, *Christ Present in Faith: Luther's View of Justification*, Minneapolis, 2005.

G. Mantzarides, *The Deification of Man*, trs L. Sherrard, New York, 1984.

C. Marmion OSB, *Christ in his Mysteries*, trs Mother M. St Thomas, London, 1924.

I. Howard Marshall, *Aspects of the Atonement*, Milton Keynes, 2007.

R. P. Martin, *An Early Christian Confession*, London, 1960.

B. McConvery CSsR, 'Where Do Feasts of Our Lady Come From?' in *Doctrine and Life*, 46, December, 1996, 603-612.

K. McDonnell OSB, *The Baptism of Jesus in the Jordan*, Collegeville, MN, 1996.

B. McGinn, *The Foundations of Mysticism: Vol. I, The Presence of God. A History of Western Christian Mysticism*, London, 1992.

—, *The Flowering of Mysticism: Men and Women in the New Mysticism (1200-1350): Vol. III, The Presence of God. A History of Western Christian Mysticism*, New York, 1998.

J. A. McGuckin, *The Transfiguration of Christ in Scripture and Tradition*, Lewiston, ME, and Queenston, 1986.

D. McKim, ed *The Westminster Handbook to Reformed Theology*, Louisville, Kentucky, 2001.

J. McLeod Campbell, *The Nature of the Atonement*, Carberry, Scotland, 1996.

M. A. Meerson, *The Trinity of Love in Modern Russian Theology*, Chicago, 1998.

T. Merton OCSO, *Contemplative Prayer*, London, 1973.

J. Meyendorff, *Christ in Eastern Christian Thought*, trs Y. Dubois, New York, 1975.

—, *Byzantine Theology: Historical Trends and Doctrinal Themes*, Fordham, 1974.

C. Miller, *The Gift of the World*, Edinburgh, 2000.

J. Moltmann, *The Crucified God*, London, 1974.

A Monk of the Eastern Church (Fr L. Gillet), *The Year of Grace of the Lord*, London, 1980.

—, *On the Invocation of the Name of Jesus*, Illinois, 1985.

C. F. D. Moule, *The Holy Spirit*, Oxford, 1978.

E. Muir, 'The heart could never speak', in, *Selected Poems*, ed T. S. Eliot,

London, 1965.

R. Muller, 'Circumincessio', in *Dictionary of Latin and Greek Theological Terms*, Grand Rapids, Michigan, 1985.

P. Nellas, *Deification in Christ: The Nature of the Human Person*, trs N. Russell, New York, 1997.

The New Catholic Encyclopedia, Washington, 1967.

J. H. Newman, *The Dream of Gerontius*, London, 1900.

A. Nichols OP, 'In the Catholic Tradition: Dom Columba Marmion (1858-1923)', in *Priests and People*, 11, 7 (1997), 282-288.

—, 'Odo Casel Revisited', in, *Antiphon: A Journal for Liturgical Renewal*, 3, 1 (1998), 12-20.

—, *Wisdom from Above: A Primer in the Theology of Father Sergei Bulgakov*, Leominster, Herefordshire, 2005.

E. T. Oakes SJ, *Pattern of Redemption: the Theology of Hans Urs von Balthasar*, New York, 1997.

E. T. Oakes SJ and D. Moss, eds *The Cambridge Companion to Hans Urs Von Balthasar*, Cambridge, 2004.

H. Ott, *Fundamentals of Catholic Dogma*, trs P. Lynch, Cork, 1954.

J. O'Donnell SJ, *The Mystery of the Triune God*, London, 1988.

G. F. O'Hanlon SJ, *The Immutability of God in the Theology of Hans Urs von Balthasar*, Cambridge, 1990.

P. F. Palmer SJ, ed with comm *Sacraments and Worship*, London, 1955.

R. K. Papadopoulos, ed *The Handbook of Jungian Psychology*, East Sussex, 2006.

J. Pelikan, *Mary Through the Centuries*, Yale, 1996.

P. Philipon OP, *The Spiritual Doctrine of Dom Marmion*, trs M. Dillon OSB, London, 1956.

The Philokalia, II, trs and eds G. E. H. Palmer, P. Sherrard, K. Ware, London, 1981.

A. Pierce and G. Smyth OP, eds *The Critical Spirit: Theology at the Crossroads of Faith and Culture*, Dublin, 2003.

Pontifical Biblical Commission, *The Interpretation of the Bible in the Church*, Vatican City, 1993.

G. L. Prestige, *God in Patristic Thought*, London, 1936.

Pseudo-Dionysius, *The Complete Works*, trs C. Luibhéid with P. Rorem, New York, 1987.

E. B. Pusey, *A Letter to the Right Hon. and Rev. The Lord Bishop of London, in Explanation of Some Statements Contained in a Letter by the Rev. W. Dodsworth*, London, 1851.

B. Quash and M. Ward, eds *Heresies and How to Avoid Them*, London, 2007.

K. Rahner SJ, *Encyclopedia of Theology: The Concise Sacramentum Mundi*, London, 1975.

M. G. Reardon, *Religious Thought in the Reformation*, London, 1981.

G. Redding, *Prayer and the Priesthood of Christ in the Reformed Tradition*,

Edinburgh / New York, 2003.

R. M. Rilke, *The Book of Hours*, trs B. Deutsch, New York, 1975.

—, *Selected Poems*, trs J. B. Leishmann, London, 1983.

—, *The Selected Poetry of Rainer Maria Rilke*, ed and trs S. Mitchell, New York, 1982.

W. Riordan, *Divine Light: The Theology of Denys the Areopagite*, San Francisco, 2008.

N. Russell, *The Doctrine of Deification in the Greek Patristic Tradition*, Oxford, 2004.

I. Ryelandt OSB, *St Benedict the Man*, trs P. Shaughnessy OSB, St Meinrad's Abbey, 1950.

R. Saarinen, *God and the Gift: An Ecumenical Theology of Giving*, Collegeville, MN, 2005.

A. Samuels, B. Shorter, F. Plaut, *A Critical Dictionary of Jungian Analysis*, London, 1986.

M. J. Scheeben, *The Mysteries of Christianity*, trs C. Vollert SJ, St Louis, 1946.

D. L. Schindler, ed *Hans Urs von Balthasar: His Life and Work*, San Francisco, 1991.

A. Schmemann, *Eucharist*, New York, 1988.

S. Schneiders IHM, *New Wineskins: Re-Imagining Religious Life Today*, New York, 1986.

H. J. Schulz, *The Byzantine Liturgy: Symbolic Structure and Faith Expression*, trs M. J. O'Connell, New York, 1986.

K. Senn, *Christian Liturgy*, Minneapolis, 1997.

S. J. Shoemaker, *Ancient Traditions of the Virgin Mary's Dormition and Assumption*, Oxford, 2002.

T. Smail, *Once and For All*, London, 1998.

S. Smalley, *John: Evangelist and Interpreter*, Carlisle, 1998.

G. T. Smith, ed *The Lord's Supper: Five Views*, Downers Grove, Illinois, 2008.

A. von Speyr, *The World of Prayer*, trs G. Harrison, San Francisco, 1985.

—, *Light and Images*, trs D. Schlindler Jr, San Francisco, 2004.

—, *The Boundless God*, trs H. M. Tomko, San Francisco, 2004.

—, *Handmaid of the Lord*, trs E. A. Nelson, San Francisco, 1985.

T. Spidlik SJ, *The Spirituality of the Christian East*, trs A. Gythiel, Kalamazoo, 1986.

A. Stacpoole OSB, ed *Mary's Place in Christian Dialogue*, London, 1982.

C. Stewart OSB, *Prayer and Community*, London, 1998.

—, *Working the Earth of the Heart: The Messalian Controversy in History, Texts and Language to AD 431*, Oxford, 1991.

V. F. Storr, *The Problem of the Cross*, London 1919.

J. Sullivan OCD, ed *Edith Stein: Philosopher, Carmelite, Nun, Martyr*, Washington, 1987.

St Symeon the New Theologian, *The Practical and Theological Chapters and the Three Theological Discourses*, trs P. McGuckin, Kalamazoo, 1982.
—, *On the Mystical Life: The Ethical Discourses, 1: The Church and the Last Things*, trs A. Golitzin, New York, 1995.
The Syriac Fathers on Prayer and the Spiritual Life, trs S. Brock, Kalamazoo, Michigan, 1987.
R. Taft SJ, *The Liturgy of the Hours in East and West*, Collegeville, MN, 1986.
A. Tanquerey, *The Spiritual Life*, trs H. Branderis, Tournai, Belgium, 1930.
W. Teasdale, *Bede Griffiths: An Introduction to his Inter-Spiritual Thought*, Vermont, 2003.
S. Terrien, *The Psalms: Strophic Structure and Theological Commentary*, Grand Rapids, Michigan, 2003.
The Book of the Perfect Life, trs D. Blamires, Walnut Creek, 2003.
C. Thompson, *St John of the Cross: Songs in the Night*, London, 2002.
T. Torrance, *Royal Priesthood: A Theology of Ordained Ministry*, Edinburgh, 1993.
L. Thunberg, *Man and the Cosmos: The Vision of St Maximus the Confessor*, New York, 1985.
M. Tierney OSB, *Marmion: A Short Biography*, Dublin, 2000.
T. F. Torrance, *Scottish Theology*, Edinburgh, 1996.
D. Turner, *The Darkness of God*, Cambridge, 1995.
—, *Eros and Allegory: Medieval Exegesis of the Song of Songs*, Kalamazoo, Michigan, 1995.
The Upanishads, trs J. Mascaró, London, 1965.
C. Vincie, *Celebrating Divine Mystery: A Primer in Liturgical Theology*, Collegeville, MN, 2009.
A. Vööbus, *History of Asceticism in the Syrian Orient: A Contribution to the History of Culture in the Near East* (3 vols.), Louvain, 1958-1988.
G. Wainwright, *Doxology*, New York, 1980.
R. Waller and B. Ward, eds *An Introduction to Christian Spirituality*, London, 1999.
R. W. Ward, *God and Adam: Reformed Theology and the Creation Covenant*, Wantirna, Australia, 2003.
J. Webster, ed *The Cambridge Companion to Karl Barth*, Cambridge, 2000.
—, *Karl Barth*, London, 2000.
J. Webster, K. Tanner and I. Torrance, eds *The Oxford Handbook of Systematic Theology*, Oxford, 2007.
S. Weil, *Intimations of Christianity Among the Ancient Greeks*, London, 1957.
V. White OP, *God and the Unconscious*, London, 1952
J. A. Wilde, ed *At That Time: Cycle and Season in the Life of a Christian*, Chicago, 1989.
R. Williams, *Wrestling with Angels: Conversations in Modern Theology*, London, 2007.

V. Wimbush and R. Valantasis, eds *Asceticism*, Oxford and New York, 1995.

R. J. Woods OP, *Eckhart's Way*, Dublin, 2009.

C. Yannaras, *Elements of Faith: An Introduction to Christian Theology*, trs K. Schram, Edinburgh, 1991.

E. Yarnold SJ, *The Awe-Inspiring Rites of Initiation*, Slough, 1973.

J. D. Zizioulas, *Being as Communion: Studies in Personhood and the Church*, New York, 1985.

—, *Communion and Otherness*, London, 2006.

—, *Lectures in Christian Dogmatics*, London, 2008.